AF608263

# SAMSON'S CORDS

## Imposing Oaths in Milton, Marvell, and Butler

ALEX GARGANIGO

# Samson's Cords

## Imposing Oaths in Milton, Marvell, and Butler

UNIVERSITY OF TORONTO PRESS
Toronto Buffalo London

Toronto Buffalo London
utorontopress.com

ISBN 978-1-4875-0098-6

---

**Library and Archives Canada Cataloguing in Publication**

Garganigo, Alex, 1969–, author
Samson's cords : imposing oaths in Milton, Marvell, and Butler / Alex Garganigo.

Includes bibliographical references and index.
ISBN 978-1-4875-0098-6 (cloth)

1. English literature – 17th century – History and criticism. 2. Milton, John, 1608–1674 – Criticism and interpretation. 3. Marvell, Andrew, 1621–1678 – Criticism and interpretation. 4. Butler, Samuel, 1612–1680 – Criticism and interpretation. 5. Oaths in literature. I. Title.

PR438.O28G37 2018 820.9'353 C2017-906875-X

---

University of Toronto Press acknowledges the financial assistance to its publishing program of the Canada Council for the Arts and the Ontario Arts Council, an agency of the Government of Ontario.

Canada Council for the Arts
Conseil des Arts du Canada

Funded by the Government of Canada
Financé par le gouvernement du Canada
Canada

The seventeenth century was the age of oaths; whatever party was in favour tried to perpetuate that power by solemn affirmations of loyalty to itself or to the religious or political principles it represented.

– Francis Charles Turner, *James II* (1950)

For Oaths the Land doth mourn: and much I fear
That of our Mournings they chief causes are.
LORD, Cautious also make this King to bee
Of wronging Justice and displeasing thee
By his *imposing Oaths*, which may give cause
Of Clashings 'twixt Divine and Humane Laws;
Or which insnare and rarely do produce
Effects equivalent to their abuse:
For to *impose such Oaths* as may insnare,
Which dubious in their acceptations are,
Which Ignorant Deponents may engage
In, or to that whereof they cannot judge,
Or which their Conscience checks at, is an end
To which thou never didst an Oath intend,
And is a wicked and a cursed Gin,
By Tyrants and by tyranny brought in.
Oh! make the King mind and consider it,
That fast and easie his new Crown may sit.

– George Wither, *Speculum Speculativum* (1660)

From *Sampson-Cord Oaths*, snapt asunder with Ease . . . Libera Nos.

– *A New Protestant Litany* (1689)

Now Oaths are so frequent, they should be taken like Pills, swallowed whole; if you chew them, you will find them bitter: if you think what you swear, 'twill hardly go down.

– John Selden, *Table Talk* (1696; wr. before 1655)

. . . as for the matter of Governments, we Women understand them not; yet if we did, we are excluded from intermedling therewith, and almost from being subject thereto; we are not tied, nor bound to State or Crown; we are free, not Sworn to Allegiance, nor do we take the Oath of Supremacy; we are not made citizens of the Commonwealth, we hold no Offices, nor bear we any Authority therein . . . And the truth is, we are no Subjects, unless it be to our Husbands, and not alwayes to them, for sometimes we usurp their Authority . . . but we really govern the world, in that we govern men . . . yet men will not believe this.

– Margaret Cavendish, Duchess of Newcastle,
*Sociable Letters* (1664)

# Contents

# Illustrations

# Preface

Loyalty oaths did not begin with ISIS or Joseph McCarthy, or even with James I. In a sense they began with the biblical Samson. In seventeenth-century England every debate about swearing referred to oaths as ties equivalent to the cords that bound the strongman of the book of Judges. While the analogy to Samson's cords provides one index of oaths' centrality to Stuart culture, a centrality that should occupy a larger place in studies of the period and of Milton and Marvell in particular, something definitely changed at mid-century. This book argues that loyalty oaths became an unprecedentedly pervasive feature of life in Restoration England and that Restoration literature had to respond.

Loyalty oaths and profane swearing were widely understood to be two branches of the same phenomenon and to play a strong role in shaping individual and group identity. At the very time that large numbers of Britons were forced to swear opposition not to communism or Western modernity, but, in effect, to Catholicism, Presbyterianism, and republicanism, writers like Milton, Marvell, and Butler participated in a war over oaths that functioned as proxy for a larger war over religious and political pluralism. Their works not only discussed particular loyalty oaths, debating their morality and effectiveness, but occasionally imitated them, aping their form and function and becoming in effect counter-oaths or anti-oaths themselves. Some, like Butler's *Hudibras*, directly reflect upon oaths and swearing by making them important plot points: characters swear oaths or refuse to swear oaths, and they keep or fail to keep them at great personal cost. Others, like *Samson Agonistes*, ignore official attempts to muzzle arguments against state oaths and succeed at smuggling them in under cover of related speech-acts such as the vow, the obligations of which function as metaphor for all the problems of oath-taking and loyalty under shifting regimes. Still others, like *Paradise Lost*, make a consideration of oaths a launching pad for arguments both against purging dissent with repressive oaths of office and for creating a more inclusive social order in which women, men, and kings are all just citizens. However, as a result of all this clamour over oaths and religion, attempts to decouple the two emerged, increasingly removing religious language from the oath and ultimately redefining this most religious of speech-acts as non-religious. Marvell's satire and panegyric show the way forward to this secularization of the oath.

This study focuses on the first decade-and-a-half of the Restoration and (in comparison with the dramas studied by Susan Staves) the less obviously performative genres of epic, satire, and closet drama, which previous work on literary oaths has neglected. After an introduction that places the Restoration's massive proliferation of oath-swearing of all kinds within a more general history of swearing and within the attempts of performance theory to determine what oaths are and do, the first three chapters establish the book's temporal boundaries by focusing on wildly popular satires about oaths at the head and tail of a single decade. As chapter 1 shows, Butler's *Hudibras* argued for the Clarendon Code's anti-Dissenter oaths in 1662–3. Chapter 2 demonstrates that Marvell's *Rehearsal Transpros'd* (1672–3) argued against both the Clarendon Oaths and the anti-Catholic Test. The final three chapters suggest that in the intervening years Milton used epic poetry in *Paradise Lost* (1667) and *Samson Agonistes* (1670) to oppose state oaths categorically, as well as to reflect more broadly on the problems and benefits of living with, and becoming oneself as a result of many kinds of oaths: not just the Oaths of Allegiance and Supremacy, the Covenant, Engagement, and Clarendon Oaths, but even the king's coronation oath (itself a kind of loyalty oath to the people). One can respond to the call to swear by assenting or refusing, by oath-taking or oath-breaking; and in many ways this book examines the creative powers of perjury. While Butler and Marvell are much more upfront about swearing, mentioning particular state oaths by name multiple times, Milton is more oblique. *Samson Agonistes* discusses vows as a stalking horse for oaths (chapter 4); *Paradise Lost* displays its revised coronation oath proudly (chapter 5) but disguises a consideration of the Oaths of Allegiance and Supremacy and the Clarendon Oaths in the abstention from the fruit (chapter 6).

More particularly, chapter 1 uses the best-selling *Hudibras* to underscore that the Restoration differed from previous periods because it accorded swearing an unprecedented importance. It makes the novel argument that the idea of conjuration as swearing links most of *Hudibras*'s apparently disparate parts. This mock-epic satire proves not as hostile to all oaths as has been claimed, but argues for better enforcement of and additions to the Clarendon Oaths, with the Restoration state allegorized in a hitherto unrecognized way as the Widow imposing oaths on the title character. Moreover, in keeping with its shining light on the performative power of such speech-acts as the oath, *Hudibras* itself has a very powerful performative dimension that functions in a way similar to a loyalty oath. Using a poetics of homeliness to appeal to many audiences, especially provincial officials like JPs, *Hudibras* interpellates a reformed but intolerant Anglican royalism in its readers, displacing the excesses of libertine royalism onto the title character.

Chapter 2, the other temporal bookend, argues that by contrast Marvell's popular prose satire, *The Rehearsal Transpros'd*, simulates the mental processes and coffeehouse banter of a tolerant Anglican in order to undermine the case for any new oath of office that mixes politics and religion. In particular, it attacks the Test Oath of 1673 and recommends that any law designed to ease the lot of religious Dissenters, such as the Ease Bill of the same year, not require them to swear oaths about matters of religion. Along the way, the chapter recounts Marvell's long-neglected grapplings with oaths of all kinds throughout his career, touching upon the *Account of the Growth of Popery and Arbitrary Government*, *Mr. Smirke*, and Marvell's letters. The appendix proposes that in the context of Marvell's struggles with test oaths, a crux in one of his letters, the odd phrase "A new popish Test for Book-Houses," should be emended to "A new popish Test for Both-Houses," i.e., both Houses of Parliament.

Chapter 3 examines what light these pronouncements on oaths in the 1670s can shed on the *Horatian Ode*, which it reads as projecting an Independent viewpoint that counts as secular, if one understands "secular" as religiously tolerant, allowing religion into the public sphere, but not the state into the religious sphere. While familiar with his tolerationist arguments from the Restoration, students of Marvell have been slow to recognize that they appeared as early as 1650.

Chapter 4 argues that "Sampson-Cord Oaths" or the analogy between oaths and Samson's cords was new to seventeenth-century England and that the trope's history, from the Oath of Allegiance debate at one end of the century to the other, provides an important context for Milton's *Samson Agonistes* and *Eikonoklastes*. Since oaths and vows were considered rough equivalents in the early modern period, the chapter demonstrates that in focusing on the hero's Nazarite vow and on many other kinds of vows in a way that the Judges narrative does not, *Samson Agonistes* reproduces the crises of conscience and strategies of evasion familiar to most takers of state-mandated loyalty oaths, from the Oath of Allegiance in 1606 to the Clarendon Code's oaths of office in the 1660s. In Milton's retelling of Judges, Samson's vow is forced upon him – indeed, his mother takes it for him without his consent – and it structures his life. When called upon to perform for the Philistines, to pledge his loyalty and submit to their power, Samson answers with the kind of riddling equivocation and mental reservation employed by many of those who were tendered state oaths like the Solemn League and Covenant, the Engagement, and the Clarendon subscriptions. The poem thus casts vows and oaths as burdens, as cords to be cut and resisted, but at great personal peril. The chapter highlights both Nonconformists asked to take oaths after the Restoration and to a lesser extent Royalists in the same position in the 1640s and 1650s. However, *Samson* casts this burden as simultaneously an identity: the vow makes Samson who he is. Moreover, the poem considers women's identity as participants in the public sphere when it adds to the Judges narrative the idea that Dalila too has been adjured or had an oath imposed upon her; it too structures who she is and what she does.

Chapter 5 opens with the fact that like many contemporary republicans and ancient constitutionalists, Milton regarded the monarch's coronation oath as the exact counterpart of the subject's Oath of Allegiance, as one of a pair of reciprocal obligations binding monarch and subject into a workable polity. This chapter focuses on the former; chapter 6 on the latter. The Miltonic or Whig history of oaths suggested by Milton's controversial prose in the previous twenty years highlights the contractual nature of the coronation oath and ritual, charting the transformation of the monarch from a mystical creature of divine right into something like the first citizen of a monarchical republic. In *Paradise Lost*, thirty-five years before Queen Anne swore coronation oaths containing language taken from subjects' oaths of allegiance, Milton's God swears a kind of truncated coronation oath "by himself" in his coronation of the Son in Book 5: that is, he swears it alone, and he swears it by invoking himself as the highest authority. God's monopolizing of discourse thus problematizes the nature of voice and agency in Heaven and provides Milton with an opportunity to call for reforms in the coronation ritual and constitution that would have led to the more obviously contractual post-1688 polity. He also troubles the reader's notions of the relationship between God and the Son, as well as the utility of promissory oaths in general. It is, after all, this coronation oath that touches off the revolt in Heaven.

However, the coronation also creates the identities of God's subjects and the Son. Chapter 6 examines the fallout from God's self-oath. After pledging allegiance to the Son and God, Satan rebels, taking a third of the angels with him. Abdiel, of course, provides a foil with his unshaken loyalty. But the real interest of *Paradise Lost* lies in God's prohibition of the fruit of the Tree of Knowledge, described as and functioning very much like the Oaths of Allegiance and Supremacy in early modern England. Adam and Eve correctly understand the fruit – or, rather, their abstention from it – as a pledge of allegiance to God. While their initial abjuration of the fruit resembles Restoration oaths that explicitly abjured the Solemn League and Covenant, Adam and Eve soon struggle to stay loyal, and much of the epic concerns various characters' attempts to choose among conflicting loyalties. By eating the fruit first and independent of Adam, Eve breaks her oath of allegiance and supremacy to God and thereby helps Milton distinguish himself from contemporary republicans by making a case for women to be full, oath-taking citizens of a republic. By imitating her, Adam chooses loyalty to Eve over loyalty to God, thereby breaking his oath of allegiance, but in a sense making a new one to her. Although she and Adam are expelled from the Edenic body politic, they have learned something and taken steps towards forming a new polity without hierarchy and the loyalty oaths that underwrite it. Taking its cue from William Blake, the chapter concludes that Milton rejects all state oaths.

# Acknowledgments

Milton would have probably agreed that "a grateful mind / By owing owes not, but still pays, at once / Indebted and discharged" (*Paradise Lost*, 4.55–7). Before expressing my continuing gratitude to individuals, I would like to recognize the Andrew Marvell Society for providing a particularly challenging and nurturing forum for work on the MP from Hull and the seventeenth century more generally. Next I would like to thank those who read all or part of the manuscript: Blaine Greteman, the late Al Labriola, Megan Matchinske, Tim Raylor, Louis Schwartz, and the anonymous readers. Then come those colleagues, students, and friends whose extended conversation and fleeting encounters have helped the project along: Peter Anderson, Matt Augustine, Robert Black, Joan Blythe, Kathleen Campbell, Bob Cape, Scott Cohn, Carol Daeley, Ellie DesPrez, Karánn Durland, Martin Dzelzainis, Joan Faust, Erin Finneran, Jeff Fontana, Stephen Greenblatt, Max Grober, Larry Hass, Derek Hirst, Terry Hoops, Seth Hurwitz, Jim Johnson, Ben LaBreche, Joe Loewenstein, the late Cynthia Manley, Marsha McCoy, Sean McDowell, Elaine McGirr, Bernice Melvin, David Meyer, Larry Pardieu, Shanthi Pardieu, Annabel Patterson, Todd Penner, George Pepe, Roger Platizky, Brendan Prawdzik, the late Stella Revard, John Rogers, Frank Rohmer, Amy Sattler, Norbert Schürer, Regina Schwartz, Nigel Smith, John Spurr, David Stevenson, Rod Stewart, Harriet Stone, Randi Tanglen, Edward Vallance, Nicholas von Maltzahn, Martin Wells, John West, and Steve Zwicker. Any errors that remain are obviously my own.

The library staffs at the following institutions have uncomplainingly provided the necessary materials: Austin College, the University of North Texas, Southern Methodist University, the University of Texas at Dallas, Washington University, and the Huntington Library. Thanks as well both to Duquesne University Press for permission to reprint two articles with additions ("Samson's Cords: Imposing Oaths in *Samson Agonistes*," *Milton Studies* 50 [2009]: 125–49; "God's Swearing by Himself: Milton's Troubling Coronation Oath," in *With Wandering Steps: Generative Ambiguity in Milton's Poetics*, ed. Mary G. Fenton and Louis Schwartz, 3–34 [Pittsburgh: Duquesne University Press, 2016]) and to the Huntington Library, New York Public Library, William Blake Trust, and Early English Books Online for permission to reprint images. Austin College's Academic Affairs Committee and Deans Melvin, Duffey, and Grober have been generous with sabbatical and conference funding, granting a full-year sabbatical early on in the project that allowed me to make significant headway.

Quietly important in a different way have been the relatives who hosted me and my family while I worked on the book: Milena Garganigo and Paul Baudendistel, Mukul Rani Mitra, Punya Priya and Asru Mitra, Alison O'Neill, Deba Prasad and Dipali Nandi, Shyamali and Mrinal Paul, Saumya Nandi and Marta Delgado, Dhurjati and Mita Nandi. Special notice goes to my parents, John and Stephanie Garganigo, for sustaining me through thick and thin. Finally, this study would never have been completed without the love, patience, and common sense of my two girls: Madhu and Rani.

SAMSON'S CORDS

# Introduction: Samson's Cords in Restoration England

We are what we swear, and what we don't swear – or so it seemed in Restoration England. The seventeenth century was "the age of oaths,"[1] and in the revolutionary decades before the Restoration, oaths had defined people. In 1638 a Scottish oath, the National Covenant, had helped trigger the Bishops' War and thus the Civil Wars. During the 1640s and 1650s the king's opponents had whipped up support for themselves in England with a series of nationwide loyalty oaths, among them the Solemn League and Covenant and the Engagement. When Charles II returned to the throne in 1660, he ignored promises he had made in taking the Covenant almost a decade earlier, and his court provided the nation with an object lesson in the excesses of witty, libertine swearing.[2] In order to erase the events of the previous two decades and purge opponents from local government, the Cavalier Parliament promulgated a new series of oaths to the Anglican church-state in the so-called Clarendon Code (1661–5).

The upshot? A fierce and messy debate over swearing of all kinds, accompanied by the purging, jailing, and occasional death of oath-refusers; censorship of anti-oath books; a proliferation of profanity that would become a target of the Campaign for the Reformation of Public Manners in the 1690s; a new definition of the oath; and frequent recourse to the new analogy between oaths and Samson's cords.[3] At one end of a continuum of oath-swearing practices stood the oath-refusing Quaker; at the other, the oath-abusing rake. Contesting the middle ground were Catholics, as well as Protestants of different stripes, Anglican and Dissenting – all of whom alleged the justices and injustices of particular state oaths. In such a culture, then, swearing and its implications were unavoidable, and it should come as no surprise that Restoration literature, in currently underappreciated and sometimes disguised ways, frequently addresses this central fact of life in seventeenth-century England. I will argue that it participated energetically in this war of culture and religion. This study will concentrate on the radically different contributions to that struggle by Milton, Marvell, and Butler.

Before considering the ways in which the epic and satire of our three authors engaged with loyalty oaths, we must step back to define terms and then consider the work done on swearing by performance theorists and historians. Early modern Britons by and large hewed to the ancient definition of the oath as an appeal to God to strengthen one's word. As Hebrews 6:16 had established, "men verily swear by the greater"; and what could be greater than God? The appeal could be spoken or written, explicit or implicit, voluntary or involuntary, in all or in part of the utterance. The swearer's word could be an assertion about the past or present (I swear that Charles II is king of England) or a promise of future action (I swear to defend him and his heirs).[4] Oft stressed was the sacred nature of the oath as an act of worship that recognized God as the highest authority and called upon him to witness the swearer's truth and punish with damnation any departure from it – any lie or failure to perform an obligation. Oaths thus implied a conditional self-curse.

For many early modern writers, the division between assertory and promissory oaths provided a loophole in Christ's apparent prohibition of all swearing in the Sermon on the Mount (Matthew 5:34–7; James 5:12). According to the Church of England's Thirty-Ninth Article, echoing the Homily against Swearing and Perjury, Christ had thus forbidden only "vayne and rashe swearing" (largely assertory), not the largely promissory state oaths required by "the Magistrate . . . in a cause of faith and charitie," and to be performed "accordyng to the prophetes teaching [Jeremiah 4:2], in iustice, iudgement, and trueth."[5] Profane oaths and judicial oaths were assertory, but only the former were illicit. Oaths of office and allegiance, as well as oaths sealing commercial transactions, were both promissory and licit. As in the present day, the verb "swear" more often referred to the assertory variety; the noun "oath" to the promissory. However, the assertory-promissory distinction itself, like J.L. Austin's one between constative and performative, could easily break down.[6] Judicial oaths, for example, clearly promise to perform the future act of asserting the truth, while speech-act theory demonstrates that assertions often have the force of promises, and vice versa.[7]

The oaths of allegiance and office that provide the context for my examination of Milton, Marvell, and Butler effectively promised by asserting loyalty to king and church – and by implication to the state and the office itself. But following the lead of Milton and company's contemporaries, I treat them as promissory, since whatever element technically predominated, their illocutionary force was clearly that.[8]

According to early modern ways of thinking, the damnable crime of perjury could thus be either assertory or promissory: telling a lie under oath or breaking a sworn promise. Antijurists opposed oaths; projurists favoured them. Jurors swore them; nonjurors didn't. Corporal oaths were spoken oaths accompanied by a bodily gesture such as raising fingers or hands, stretching out arms, placing hands or lips on the Bible. The subject of an oath designated the proposition sworn to (I will fight you at dawn tomorrow), while the object of an oath meant the thing or person sworn by, on, or to (By God, I swear that I will fight you at dawn tomorrow) – sometimes a physical object touched or gestured to by the swearer. Swearing by the creatures, which Christ had outlawed in Matthew 5:34–6, thus referred to making a person or thing other than the Creator the object of one's oath (By this light, I swear that I will fight you at dawn tomorrow).

Despite a steady drumbeat of homilies against profane swearing,[9] the history of oaths in early modern Britain is in a crucial sense a history of imposed oaths: loyalty oaths imposed by the state rather than the church; loyalty oaths that competed with but ultimately failed to crowd out people's profanities. In the Tudor period, Henry VIII had confirmed the break with Rome by imposing Oaths of Succession (1534) and Supremacy (1535) acknowledging him as "Supreme Head" of state and church. Refusal of them cost Thomas More his head.[10] Elizabeth revived and revised the Oath of Supremacy (1559) by changing "head" to "governor."[11] Further state oaths emerged under the Stuarts, along with a new analogy between oaths and Samson's cords. As chapter 4 shows, in the wake of each major loyalty oath in the seventeenth century there appeared an attack or defence that alluded to his cords, the breaking of which merited praise or blame as occasion demanded. In 1667, for example, a poem by the Anglican John Tabor placed the blame for the God-sent punishments of plague, fire, and war on, among others, oath-breaking Samsons:

> But beside Slanders, Errors, Heresies,
> False Oaths, Equivocations, Perjuries,

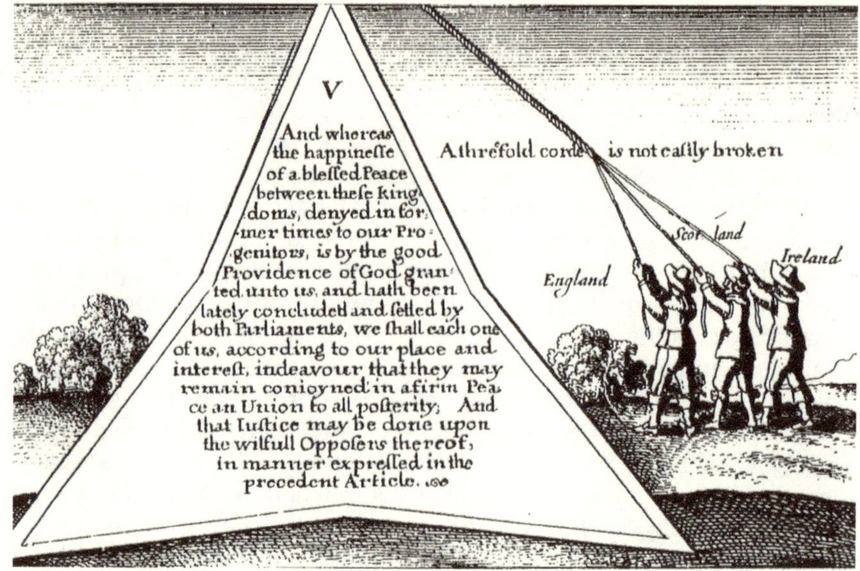


Figure 1 Wenceslaus Hollar, illustration from *A Solemn League and Covenant* (1643), RB 124654, The Huntington Library, San Marino, California. Image produced by ProQuest as part of *Early English Books Online* (www.proquest.com) and published with permission of ProQuest. Further reproduction is prohibited without permission.

> Are in these sinful dayes among us found,
> To grow, and thrive, and spread in *English* ground:
> Oaths of Allegiance, some like *Sampsons* cords
> Can snap asunder, while a pack of words
> They call a Covenant, contrived by
> A pack of Knaves, must hold inviolably.[12]

Political and religious dissenters, according to Tabor, hypocritically broke their Oaths of Allegiance to the king as easily as Samson broke the Philistines' cords – even as they refused to break the Solemn League and Covenant by abjuring its provisions in the Corporation, Uniformity, and Vestry Oaths promulgated in the early years of the Restoration. Tabor drew on a tradition of representing the Covenant as a set of cords (Figure 1), itself indebted to the novel seventeenth-century trope of oaths as Samson's cords.

As demonstrated by historians such as Christopher Hill, Caroline Robbins, John Spurr, Edward Vallance, D.M. Jones, Conal Condren, Stefania Tutino, and Jonathan Gray, the many oaths of obedience required by the state after the Reformation, and especially during the Civil Wars and Restoration, threw members of the political nation into considerable difficulties, forcing them to respond with tactics of equivocation and mental reservation hitherto associated with Jesuits.[13] In the half-century between the Scottish National Covenant and the Glorious Revolution (1638–88), some adult males were asked to swear perhaps a dozen oaths of loyalty to the state, many of them conflicting.[14] In addition to the Tudor Oaths of Allegiance and Supremacy, renewed and revised by James I, the list includes the Protestation (1641), the Vow and Covenant (1643), the Solemn League and Covenant (1643), the Engagement (1649), the Clarendon Code's many oaths of office at the Restoration, and the new Oaths of Allegiance and Supremacy required by William and Mary (see the list below).

**State-Mandated Loyalty Oaths in Britain (1534–1702)**

Henrician Oath to the Succession (1534)
Henrician Oath to the Supremacy (1535)
Elizabethan Oath of Supremacy (1559)
Jacobean Oath of Supremacy (1603)*
Jacobean Oath of Allegiance (1606)*
Scottish National Covenant (1638)*
Etcetera Oath (1640)
Protestation (1641)*
Vow and Covenant (June 1643)*
Oath of Abjuration (August 1643)
Solemn League and Covenant (September 1643)*
Negative Oath (1645)
Engagement (1649)*
The Clarendon Code's Loyalty Oaths (1661–5)
  Corporation Oath (1661)
  Militia Oath (1662)
  Uniformity Oath (1662)
  Schoolmaster's Oath (1662)
  Vestryman's Oath (1663)
  Oxford Oath (1665)

First Test Oath (1673)
Second Test Oath (1678)
William and Mary's Oath of Allegiance (1689)
William and Mary's Oath of Supremacy (1689)
Oath of Abjuration (1701)

As the asterisks indicate, adult women seem to have sworn some of them too, especially the Jacobean Oath of Allegiance, National Covenant, Protestation, Vow and Covenant, Solemn League and Covenant, and Engagement – but significantly not the Restoration oaths of office (our main concern here).[15]

The number of oaths grew so fast that books were printed simply to keep track of them all, presumably for local officials such as the constables and Justices of the Peace who would tender them to the king's subjects (see chapter 1). Listing over 200 oaths of office for everyone from monarchs to midwives, aldermen to aletasters and trash collectors, a *Book of Oaths* appeared just after the Civil War (1649) and the Glorious Revolution (1689, with updates into the eighteenth century). The reason these "imposing oaths" exercised so many casuists and polemicists[16] was that the penalties for refusal were harsh, including one or more of the following: imprisonment; fines; loss of land and property; transportation; denial of the law's protection; exclusion from living or preaching within a five-mile radius around corporate towns, as well as from public office.[17] As we have noted, the unhealthy conditions of English jails sometimes spelled death for oath-refusing Quakers and Baptists.[18] But this is no mere story of doom and gloom. I hope to show that some historians of oaths have fixated on their downsides and that literary historians have joined them in neglecting the relationship between oaths and gender, as well as the literature of oaths' active participation in, rather than mere reflection of, the Restoration struggle over swearing.

## What Oaths Do

To ask what oaths are and what oaths do, to offer preliminary answers about how their saying is a kind of doing – these are Austinian moves; and we now turn to the contributions of speech-act and performance theory to the study of swearing. However, despite Hebrews 6:16's characterization of swearing as "an end of all strife," it seems almost invariably to have done the opposite. This most troublesome of speech-acts has posed problems for theorists from the start, resisting easy classification and raising troubling questions of intention and affect. Oaths would seem to fall within the purview of speech-act theory, yet Austin and his followers have had surprisingly little to say about them. Because of its dual aspects, assertory and promissory, "swearing" or "oath" denotes two separate speech-acts in Austin's and Searle's taxonomies: the promissory variety designated as "commissive" by both of them; the assertory as "expositive" by the former and "assertive" by the latter.[19]

Austin's lectures at Harvard in 1955 (collected as *How To Do Things With Words* in 1962) famously introduced the distinction between language that describes the world (constative) and language that changes it (performative), a distinction he deconstructs by book's end with the result that all language becomes a performative speech-act in one way or another.[20] And justly so. He also distinguished usefully between an utterance's locution, illocution, and perlocution: what one says (locution), what one tries to accomplish by saying it (illocution or illocutionary force), and whether one actually accomplishes it by changing the mind or behaviour of someone else (perlocution).[21] However, Austin hardly knew what to do with oaths, which refused to fit neatly into his taxonomy of speech-acts and remained among the "loose ends" and "exceptions" he identified in the final lecture.[22] The few times he mentions them, oaths are usually synonymous with the promise, his paradigmatic commissive and performative.[23] Austin does admit that words like "Damn" and "Bloody" are not exactly constative, but he fails to specify what or how they perform. At one point he doubts that they do at all.[24] As a result, he lumps swearing together with other "non-serious" speech-acts such as literature (including the speech-acts of literary characters) in a category of unsolved problems labelled "expositives" – yet now absent literature.[25]

Austin's followers issued corrections. Derrida questioned Austin's segregation of speech-acts in literary texts from speech-acts in the "real world." Surely the former were not so distinct from the latter, not so "etiolated" or "parasitic" upon it as to have no effect on those reading or hearing the literary text?[26] John Searle tidied up the taxonomy of speech-acts by focusing on illocutionary acts rather than locutionary verbs:

Assertives (tell people how things are)
Directives (try to get them to do things)
Commissives (commit the speaker to doing things)

Expressives (express the speaker's feelings and attitudes)
Declarations (bring about change in the world by means of the utterance).[27]

Searle dubs promises and (promissory) oaths paradigmatic "commissives" and in a later book admits that swearing can also be "assertive."[28] Pushed to its logical conclusion, his scheme would also place profane oaths under the rubric of "expressives," in that they express speakers' emotions, but often in a most imprecise, non-propositional manner. As Keith Allan and Kate Burridge have put it, profane oaths' illocutionary force overshadows and occasionally eclipses their locutionary form. In other words, one can express anger (or surprise or irritation) by using widely divergent terms like "fuck," "damn," or "shit," without intending any reference at all to sex, damnation, or excrement.[29] Thus swearing belongs in at least three of Searle's categories, and a case might be made for the remaining two as well. Yet I will stick to "assertory" and "promissory" as rough equivalents of Searle's "assertive" and "commissive" because these were the terms used by the early modern writers I study. Apart from their scant treatment by Austin and Searle, oaths hardly figure at all in classic speech-act theory.[30]

### Further Extensions of Speech-Act Theory: Derrida, Agamben, and Schmitt

Before Giorgio Agamben's 2008 book on oaths, the only writer in the realm of speech-act and cultural theory to pay sustained attention to swearing was Derrida. The Levinasian turn to ethics and politics in Derrida's later career entailed a clearer engagement with the real world than before,[31] and he could be said to have compensated somewhat for Austin and Searle's neglect of the oath, rather than the promise, as the true paradigm for all speech-acts. The later Derrida accords oaths much more social constructionist power than Austin and Searle, drawing on the French tradition of social contract that includes Rousseau, the Tennis Court Oath, and French Revolution but only reluctantly admits its Anglo-Saxon forbears – a tradition stretching from the Magna Carta through Hobbes and Locke to the American Revolution and Declaration of Independence.[32] Oaths, on this view, are absolutely inaugural: they inaugurate brotherhood and thus society as democracy. But along with civil society comes the frenemy problem, somewhat reminiscent of Carl Schmitt's decisionist creations of friend and enemy.[33] Derrida regards all human relations as founded on contract and thus oath, with the word "yes" as the ur-oath.[34] This contract/promise/oath creates almost everything: law, ethics, politics, even God and religion – at the very least, community. Extending Levinas, Derrida stresses again and again that the oath consists of addressing, responding to, taking responsibility for, bearing witness to, for, and before the other.[35]

Yet Derrida's deconstructionist impulse to distrust the apparently overrated first term in the binary *speech/writing* leads him to doubt the effectiveness of the spoken oath.[36] If speaking requires the bodily presence of the speaker and audience, as well as the self-presence of the speaker, can the speaker ever really tell or witness to the truth, especially when swearing to do so? Are we not all fundamentally perjured from the start?[37] For these and other reasons the later Derrida only partially assumed Levinas's mantle, refusing to shed his own deconstructive misgivings about intentions and signification. In the end, his most important contributions to oath-theory lie in the constructivist notions that oaths perform various forms of community, though with great complications and setbacks along the way, and that all speech-acts are iterable and citational, which, *pace* Austin and Searle, levels oaths in life and art to a roughly similar status.[38] For Derrida, speech-acts often lie outside their speakers' control. Embedded in numerous, ramifying contexts, they have effects unconfined to the immediate one. Hence, an oath in a literary text is, as we have intimated, not as etiolated, parasitic, and ineffective as Austin guessed in the 1950s and Searle confirmed in the 1970s. Literary oaths can affect people "outside" the text – if indeed it has any outside – and literary texts can perform by offering readers ideas and psychic structures to be imitated.[39] No other speech-act makes such a strong appeal for identity and loyalty to people outside the text.

A fuller account of oaths as speech-acts has arrived in the latest instalment of Giorgio Agamben's *Homo Sacer* project: *The Sacrament of Language: An Archeology of the Oath* (2008; English translation, 2011), which emphasizes the power of language to create subjectivity, law, and society through a kind of performative decision à la Schmitt.[40] For Agamben the oath is not an appeal outside the self to God but a self-enclosed appeal to and reconfirmation of the magical powers of language itself, specifically the subject's experience of such power. In this respect he follows the lead of nineteenth-century ethnologists such as Edward Westermarck and Edward Tylor, who stressed the importance of the self-curse in the oath, the curse constituting an act of language distinct from any being that might enact or enforce it.[41] Salutary is Agamben's emphasis on the creative potential of swearing, as performing subjectivity, law, and society itself. But he seriously underestimates the bodily and ritual dimensions of oaths, which draw the swearer out of the closed circle of language. In this respect he falls into the same trap as classic speech-act theorists, who frequently occlude all kinds of context, decontextualizing speech-acts by focusing on illocutionary verbs in the first person present active indicative in isolated sentences, in something approaching what one linguist called "null context."[42] Over all, *The Sacrament of Language* fails to pursue in any depth what is suggested by its placement within the *Homo Sacer* series and its dependence on the Roman concept of the *sacramentum*. The oath is something placed outside the profane normal world: not just a series of words but a physical object or bodily gesture. Agamben appears to have forgotten that as Schmitt and his disciple Ernst Friesenhahn showed in the 1920s, the oath is a decision that excludes and includes, that creates even as it separates friend from foe, rule from exception, one religion from another. One could call a loyalty oath the subject's act of consent to the sovereign's decision. Yet even Friesenhahn, when pressed for a definition, only defined the oath as a "solemn or ceremonial promise" (*feierliches Versprechen*), in contradistinction to its traditional definition as an "appeal to God" (*Anrufung Gottes*).[43] As we shall see, the Restoration's redefinition of the oath anticipated the potential Schmittian (and Derridean) argument about oaths and externality.[44]

## Performance Theory

In contrast to Agamben and the political theologians, performance theory has proved more open to the importance of the body and its movements in time. It has opened the door of the prisonhouse of language a crack with respect to oaths – arguably one of the strongest, most complex commissives, equally or more powerful than Austin's classic performatives (marriages, bets, christenings, adjournments), and most clearly instrumental to the dissemination and reproduction of social norms. What little work there is has followed the lead of both Austin and Judith Butler, whose social constructionism in the context of gender and sexuality offered an influential paradigm for investigations in a number of disciplines of the performative construction of reality and identity. As we shall see, my argument depends upon a less totalizing version of Butler's ideas that grants more agency to the individual, as she begins to do in *Undoing Gender*,[45] and agrees with ritual theorists such as Catherine Bell and Roy Rappaport that performed ideology is not entirely constitutive of identity. There are limits to what ritualized behaviour can do.[46] On my account subjects possess considerably more coherence and self-presence than Butler or Derrida would allow, and speech-acts function as relays that help but do not bear entire responsibility for creating and maintaining subjectivity.[47]

Standing on the shoulders of Arnold van Gennep and Victor Turner, a few performance theorists focusing on ritual have recognized oaths, especially oaths of office, as rites of passage from one social status or role to another.[48] Rituals such as coronations of monarchs, swearings-in of presidents, and the American Pledge of Allegiance have merited passing attention in their work.[49] Ritual theorists and other performance theorists thus articulate what seems obvious to Derrida, Butler, Agamben, historians of British oaths, and psycholinguists investigating profane swearing: that oaths perform identity within community. As Elizabeth Bell puts it, the Pledge of Allegiance and thus all loyalty oaths exemplify performance's capacity to "create, maintain, and transform" identity within groups defined by "race, ethnicity, gender, desire, class, age, abilities, and geopolitical region." All performances do so because they "make implicit and explicit claims about what is valued in and by the group and how members ought to act."[50] Paying more attention to the human body, Rappaport stresses that among the Maring of New Guinea a dance can be just as effective and performative a pledge of allegiance as a spoken oath and that merely showing up to participate in a ritual of allegiance "renders . . . impotent" any private reservations these participants might have about the object of their allegiance.[51] However, he adds, spoken oaths are "sanctified expressions" that relay "Ultimate Sacred Postulates" (group values) and thus help create and maintain community. Swearing them as part of larger, public rituals makes the commitments they entail more explicit and harder to break. Coronation rituals with oaths alluding to supernatural beings reinforce those beings' existence and thus fold together all these functions.[52]

My account of oaths moves beyond Derrida, Butler, and Agamben's insistence that all humans are necessarily defined by others because they use language and live in communities. The wealth of research done by anthropologists and ethnologists in the nineteenth and early twentieth centuries on swearing rituals from the Bantu to the Babylonians emphasizes that in oral cultures especially, oaths take place in ritual spaces, in tandem with ritual objects, ritual sacrifices, and other kinds of verbal and physical ritual.[53] Agamben's work is one sign of the return of this approach in a veritable Renaissance of oath-studies among students of Western antiquity, especially Hellenists and Hebraists.[54] I supplement modern performance theory by treating many of this early work's universalizing claims with caution and applying a later paradigm that emphasizes the ways swearing, oral and written, performs self-in-community by means of exclusion and inclusion. Oaths are rituals and objects that involve the voice and body's reaching out towards other things and people, even as they remain separate from them. They adjust the boundaries between self and world. In the pages that follow, we will savour the accuracy of George Wither's observation that "imposing Oaths . . . give cause / Of Clashings, 'twixt Divine and Humane Laws."[55] The imposition of imposing oaths after the Restoration laid down boundaries that excluded Presbyterians, Independents, Catholics, republicans, monarchists, the Devil, and women.

## The Restoration and the History of Swearing

Historians of both promissory and assertory oaths have largely presented narratives of decline. In the wake of anti-Communist loyalty tests in the United States, Christopher Hill's foundational essay "From Oaths to Interest" (1958) traced a more or less linear decrease in the number and efficacy of state oaths and promissory oaths in general during the transition from feudalism to capitalism.[56] Under capitalism self-interest apparently replaced oaths as the tie binding people to good behaviour. Megan Matchinske has dubbed this process a "desacralization" of oaths.[57] Recent work has joined John Spurr in questioning the smooth linearity of the decline and posited shifts of emphasis within the content of state oaths.[58] D.M. Jones, Edward Vallance, and Jonathan Gray have demonstrated that they increased in number and strength after the Reformation and that any decline took much longer than Hill allowed, especially for the governing classes.[59] According to Spurr and Jones, the Restoration marked oaths' resurgence; according to the latter, the rot of oath-deflation set in after 1700.[60] That deflation had, however, been prefigured by de factoist justifications of oaths like the Engagement and the Williamite Oath of Allegiance.[61] By contrast, Vallance has shown that oaths of office and association, at least, remained of great importance well into the eighteenth century – a case made even more strongly by Spurr.[62]

They have also shown that during the many centuries of promissory oaths' ascendancy – even into the nineteenth century, when an elected MP, the atheist Charles Bradlaugh, was initially denied his seat for scruples about oaths' religious content – there were actually shifts of emphasis within that content itself: shifts from conduct to belief, from person to community, and from England to empire. Instead of swearing personal loyalty to an English suzerain or monarch, oath-takers in Britain and the colonies began to swear loyalty to specific religious and political beliefs, as well as to the community itself, expanding beyond the bounds of England.[63] This resulted in a net expansion of the political nation.[64] The fact that religion gained rather than lost prominence in post-Reformation oaths complicates the thesis of Schmitt and other political theologians that oaths were one of a number of cultural phenomena that involved a secularization of previously religious content.[65]

Conal Condren disputes Jones's and others' de factoist reading of the Williamite and Engagement controversies, but he usefully underlines the centrality of oaths to early modern England, where their main function was essentially to create identity, which he describes as the "persona" of an officeholder. On his view almost every social role or function was conceived of as an "office" in the Ciceronian sense of a set of privileges and duties to others; and oaths of entry were the keys to these offices. The person who occupied the office had been "fashioned through words" into a new persona with an altered identity.[66] This insight, shared in principle by Derrida, Agamben, and performance theorists, informs my analyses of Milton, Marvell, and Butler.

Historians of assertory oaths (profanity or cussing) have noted a parallel set of shifts. Geoffrey Hughes has traced a general secularization of the oath's content as it moved from being dominated by religious concerns in the Middle Ages, to bodily concerns thereafter, and finally to racial/ethnic concerns in the modern era.[67] More recent work in literature, linguistics, and psychology has not challenged this thesis of a shift from religious to bodily to racial/ethnic swearing.[68] While no one regards these shifts within assertory swearing as a decline, historians do tag them to the idea of promissory swearing being replaced by assertory swearing in the modern age.[69] Thus, from a holistic perspective that takes stock of both varieties (promissory and assertory), religious and promissory swearing have been elbowed out over the *longue durée* by profane and assertory swearing; as have loyalty oaths by cussing – even as another variety of the assertory – judicial oaths – rose to prominence in courts of law.[70]

There have been comparatively few studies of oaths in early modern and especially Restoration literature – John Kerrigan's recent study of Shakespeare's "binding language" providing a welcome exception.[71]

J. Douglas Canfield's 1989 book on oaths and vows from Chaucer to Rochester mostly accepted Hill's Marxist framework, reading a number of Restoration texts other than mine from a perspective that emphasized oaths as a prop of class: that is, of the nobility's honour code. Hence, his various treatments of oaths and vows in Restoration drama and poetry argued that they merely reflect this inexorable decline of aristocratic oaths to middle-class interest.[72] In the 1970s Susan Staves's seminal chapter on oaths and vows in various Restoration texts – including Butler but excluding Milton and Marvell, and focusing more on drama – offered a more nuanced account of oath history, but more or less shared the idea of decline, even if she posited its happening later (in the eighteenth century). Like Hill and Canfield, she accepted the notion of literature's merely reflecting rather than intervening in the history of oaths.[73] Megan Matchinske's chapter on Mary Carleton and Restoration swearing has offered several correctives, taking it for granted that oaths in literature function as concrete interventions in political debates and that, as David Cressy's work on women and the Protestation has shown, the historiography of oaths has largely neglected gender.[74]

Combining the existing work on oaths and religion with approaches to performance and gender will allow us to place Milton's *Paradise Lost* and *Samson Agonistes*, Marvell's *Rehearsal Transpros'd*, and Butler's *Hudibras* within specifically Restoration crises over oaths, religious tolerance, and the role of women in politics. The existing literature on Miltonic epic and Marvellian satire has basically ignored swearing, and I overturn the most recent argument about Butler's treatment of the issue.

## The Restoration of Oaths

A number of factors made the Restoration distinctive as an episode in the history of English swearing, chief among them its proliferation of both kinds of oath: promissory and profane. While John Gauden faulted Parliament for needlessly multiplying oaths in the 1640s, in what he called "Superfoetations" of oaths (over-production of oaths like abortive fetuses), Andrew Marvell suggested in *The Rehearsal Transpros'd* that the Cavalier Parliament had produced even more: a "Superfoetation" of laws designed to purge Dissenters after the Restoration via loyalty oaths.[75] To our ears promissory and profane oaths might sound like entirely different speech-acts. Yet contemporaries saw them as points on a continuum of appeals to God and linked all kinds of oath-infraction. The same John Tabor who castigated Nonconformist breakers of loyalty oaths as Samsons soon turned his ire against "the swinish Drunkard" who, with "Oaths, and Curses in his mouth," "Gods Service . . . contemns" and "his Sundays spends / At some good fellowship of drunken friends: / He little Honour, or Obedience shows / To whom he Honour, and Obedience ows; / Be they Parents or Preists, Prelates, or Prince."[76] Jeremy Collier was hardly the only critic of oaths on stage and street.[77] For every rake who peppered his discourse with "Shit," "Fuck," "Cunt," and "Pox" like Lord Rochester, there was a John Bunyan who opposed both profanities and oaths of allegiance. Tellingly, it is the Devil and his representatives who seek to impose loyalty oaths on Bunyan's Pilgrim and town of Mansoul, and who have "Damn-me blades" for followers, with names like Mr Swearing.[78]

Keeping in mind the primal energies that oaths harness, another pairing of Restoration writers reinforces the nexus between the two types of swearing and introduces the variable of gender. In Sir Robert Howard's comedy *The Committee* (1662), which Samuel Pepys liked enough to see four times in the 1660s, the true-blue royalists outwit the dull Puritan members of the local Committee for Sequestrations in order to regain their rightful property.[79] In their way lies the obstacle of the Solemn League and Covenant, an oath employed by the victorious Parliamentarians after 1643 as both test of loyalty and requirement for royalists to regain their confiscated lands. While the Cavaliers, Colonel Careless and Colonel Blunt, punctuate their discourse with trivial assertory oaths such as "'Slife," "What the Devil!" "Pox on't!" "Plague on her!" and the like, they adamantly refuse to swear promissory oaths such as the Covenant. The only way to win back their estates is to blackmail the Puritan chairman of the Committee into waiving the requirement.[80]

The play is notable, however, for laying bare Puritan hypocrisy towards swearing. On the one hand, Puritans demand oaths of loyalty from everyone, especially Cavaliers. On the other, they forbid all profane oaths like the ones that become tags for the Cavaliers. Lest we protest that this merely constitutes heavy-handed regulation of oaths rather than true hypocrisy, Howard shows us that most of the Puritans themselves break their own rules, supplementing statements with "I dare swear," "By my honour," and even "damned."[81] So when the Committee requires the Cavaliers to take the Covenant merely to gain an audience with them (let alone regain their lands), even the most innocuous of the Cavaliers' oaths, "Faith" (short for "In faith") sets the Puritans off:

> COLONEL CARELESS: Faith, would I might ask one question?
> NEHEMIAH CATCH: Swear not, then.[82]

Howard's joke is that Careless and Blunt are being told to swear one moment and not to swear the next; surely the mild "Faith" is nowhere near as important as a lengthy loyalty oath? Yet for Puritans it is; and Howard indicates just how connected both kinds of swearing were in the minds of most people after 1660. Both this fact, and the struggle over having to swear a Covenant so ambiguous in parts that many did not know what it meant, adumbrate the comedy of swearing in the subject of chapter 1: Butler's mock-epic *Hudibras* (1662), an almost exact contemporary of *The Committee.*

Moreover, the fact that the play's spirited women Cavaliers also swear oaths of both kinds anticipates a concern of Margaret Cavendish's *Sociable Letters* (1664).[83] In a passage from the sixteenth letter quoted among the epigraphs for my book, a fictional female correspondent decries women's exclusion from political life, emblematized by their not taking the Oaths of Allegiance and Supremacy to the king. She then consoles herself with the thought that women actually rule men unofficially in the domestic sphere, and through them in the public sphere itself.[84] A better solution to this problem arrives in a play Cavendish published in the same year as *Hudibras* and *The Committee*. Her utopian closet drama *Bell in Campo* (1662) stages a scene in which a group of women secede in order to create a new army and polity of their own by swearing allegiance to a woman general. This Fifteen Commandments scene looks back to Moses at Sinai and Moab and forward to the signing of the U.S. Constitution, taking in everything in-between, including Hobbesian and proto-Lockean contract theory on the one hand and the attempts at drafting an English constitution in the Levellers' Agreement of the People, Cromwell's Instrument of Government, and Harrington's *Oceana* on the other. The laws that comprise Cavendish's social contract include requirements to wear armour continuously, participate in "masculine" physical exercises, hear other women preaching sermons on war, worship Mars, Athena, and other goddesses, and, above all, to obey their Generalless. They also contain prohibitions against drinking, plundering, and fraternizing with men. Outdoing Moses with half again as many commandments, Cavendish's Generalissima imitates his actions at Moab by asking each woman to swear consent to the new polity by voice and in writing, with right of refusal guaranteed.[85] These women warriors go on to win battles their men have lost. But after the war, they retreat with a few token modifications to the domestic sphere and the status quo ante. No utopia can last. Yet *Bell in Campo* does reveal that it was possible for early modern Englishwomen to conceive of oaths of allegiance as privileges rather than obligations, as empowering rather than burdensome, as invitations to participate in rather than become casualties of, the political process.[86] In this light we should consider the political activism of women in Butler and Milton: the nameless Widow and the oyster women *Hudibras* castigates for crying "No Bishop!" in the 1640s; the biblical women who deserve both praise and blame for their activism in *Samson Agonistes* and *Paradise Lost*.

Besides the linking of the different types of swearing and the attention to the political significance of women's oaths, other factors made Restoration swearing distinctive. First, as Susan Staves has shown, the Restoration featured the first state oaths in England that explicitly invalidated other state oaths like the Solemn League and Covenant.[87] Second, both Staves and Vallance point out that they included unprecedented claims about the application of oaths to people other than the swearer. Subscribers had to deny the Covenant by name, specifying that they spoke not just for themselves but for every person who had taken it, even if some of them regarded it as still in force: "there lies no Obligation upon me or upon any other person from the Oath commonly called *The Solemn League and Covenant*."[88] Third, they explicitly denied subjects the right of taking up arms to resist the king and his government under any circumstances, however dire – thereby enshrining a Hobbesian view of resistance.[89] Fourth, in addition to non-resistance, clergymen had to swear a non-alteration clause, promising not to try to change the church or state in any way, which ruled out even positive reformation: "there lies no Obligation on me, or any other person, from the *Oath* commonly called the *Solemn League and Covenant*, to endeavour any Change or Alteration of Government, either in Church, or State."[90]

Fifth, the Restoration oaths expanded from England into Scotland and Ireland, reversing the vector of oath-promulgation that had begun in Scotland with the National Covenant in 1638 (a watershed for the three kingdoms in that it included most Scottish women) and continued with the Scottish-inspired Solemn League and Covenant in 1643.[91] Sixth, unlike other oath controversies in the century, such as that over the Engagement oath in 1650 and the new Oaths of Allegiance and

Supremacy in 1689, the intense debate in the early years of the Restoration focused less on forms of government (though these concerns were not absent) than on how subjects should live within the existing form. Seventh, oath-refusal had never been so prominent, both in person and in print, or so illegal. Quakers were hardly alone in turning their backs on both the unprecedented number of state loyalty oaths and the outrageous profanities of Rochester and Mr Swearing, but the Quaker Act of 1662 explicitly outlawed the printing of arguments against state oaths. Finally, as if in response to these developments, a new, more secular definition of swearing arose during the Restoration: the oath as an appeal to externality (something external to, outside the swearer and the subject of the oath), rather than to God. In 1675 the Quaker Gervase Benson insisted that the oath is an "Addition [to a statement or promise] of somewhat more, as an *outward* Sign or Pledge" – which might include physical objects in a ritual setting.[92]

The 1670s also saw increasingly stringent oaths of office aimed at weeding out Catholics: the Tests of 1673 and 1678, the first of which Marvell arguably attacked in *The Rehearsal Transpros'd*, despite his later fear-mongering about French-Catholic absolutism in the *Account of the Growth of Popery and Arbitrary Government*. As we shall see in chapter 2, the Tests grew increasingly specific in their rejection of Catholic doctrines. The Exclusion Crisis (1678–81) featured several kinds of oath that became the focus of controversy. *Hudibras* decries the "knights of the post" plaguing law courts: professional perjurers selling testimony to the highest bidder. However, judicial oaths became a firebrand during the Popish Plot and Exclusion Crisis because of the mostly false testimony given in court against imagined Catholic plotters. Much printed and staged satire dealt with this issue.[93] Also during the Exclusion Crisis, oaths of office continued to be relevant in the flap over whether Protestant Dissenters such as Slingsby Bethel and Henry Cornish could swallow the Anglican sacrament along with the Supremacy Oath in order to assume civic office in London under the Test Act.[94] Moreover, the proto-Whig Exclusionists floated the idea of creating a sworn Association of subjects to safeguard England in the case of a tyrannical Catholic successor to Charles II. During the Tory Revenge that followed the defeat of the Exclusionists, the Earl of Shaftesbury was imprisoned for possessing a draft of this Oath of Association.[95]

After the Catholic James actually became king, he did his best to hamper enforcement of the Test oaths and other anti-Catholic oaths of office in the late 1680s, and the Glorious Revolution was sealed by

Parliament's drastic revisions of both the monarch's coronation oath and the subjects' Oaths of Allegiance and Supremacy, now including the anti-Catholic language of the Tests.[96] In 1702 a clause denying the authority of the Pretender was added to the subject's oaths.[97] The better-known controversy engendered by the revised Oaths of Allegiance and Supremacy in the immediate aftermath of the Revolution issued in a class of Nonjurors, clergymen who refused to swear allegiance to and hold office in the service of the new monarchs because they had already taken similar oaths to the previous king.[98]

A context for all of our authors, the early Restoration argument over oaths proved more intense in a short period than the one over the Jacobean Oath of Allegiance of 1606, and was at least as intense as the better-studied ones over the Solemn League and Covenant (1643), Engagement (1649), and Williamite Oath of Allegiance (1689).[99] Not only were state oaths unprecedentedly numerous and potent in the early Restoration, but there was a concomitantly large number of new books on oaths of all kinds: almost ninety in the first five years alone.[100] This war of oaths deserves attention in its own right since, among other reasons, it featured questions of agency, subjectivity, and religious toleration.

The Restoration had been preceded by attempts to prevent it by tendering various versions of the Engagement to MPs. In the first half-decade of the Restoration, Presbyterians pushed for and failed to obtain a Presbyterian ecclesiastical settlement in accord with the Solemn League and Covenant's pledge to reform the Church "according to the example of the best reformed churches."[101] Not only did the hangman burn the Covenant, but the Cavalier Parliament's Corporation, Uniformity, and Vestry Acts (1661–3) forced, as we have seen, virtually all public officeholders, including ministers, town councilmen, and schoolmasters, explicitly to repudiate the Covenant as part of new oaths of office that included an additional oath of non-resistance. The Quaker and Five-Mile Acts (1662 and 1665 respectively) extended these provisions by adding penalties for non-officeholders refusing oaths; and their refusal of judicial oaths and the Oaths of Allegiance and Supremacy sent Quakers to jail in droves, along with some Baptists,[102] where they wrote loud protests.[103] In late 1662, the king entered the debate by ordering the general distribution and teaching to students of Richard Mocket's pre-Civil War defence of the Oath of Allegiance.[104] Catholics protested their loyalty while expressing discomfort about the Oath of Supremacy's repudiation of papal authority,[105] and

Anglicans roundly condemned everyone else as disloyal for refusing to stay within the body politic by mouthing the requisite words.[106] As chapter 4 reveals, the Samson's cords metaphor featured prominently in the debate, and chapter 1 demonstrates that *Hudibras* played a particularly important role in 1662 and 1663. The controversy also proved formative to *Paradise Lost*, probably written between 1658 and 1665. Chapter 2 provides more detail about its revival in 1667, around the time of the epic's publication.

# 1 Conjuring Oaths and Identities in *Hudibras*

The single best introduction to Restoration oaths remains Samuel Butler's *Hudibras* (Part I, 1662; Part II, 1663; Part III, 1677). In octosyllabics with wacky rhymes and wackier subject matter, this mock-epic casts the previous twenty years of British history as the quixotic attempts of the title's (oxy)moronic Presbyterian knight, accompanied by his fiercely Independent squire, Ralpho, to woo a nameless but rich widow, who stands for, among other things, England herself, especially after the execution of her "husband," Charles I.[1] In recasting the Civil Wars and Interregnum as a series of disagreements between Presbyterians and Independents, as a series of comic failures to court the noncommittal Widow and thus a populace unwilling to give up traditional carnivalesque sports – such as bonfires, bear-baitings, Skimmington Rides and that other cruel spectacle, the pillory – Butler's satire celebrates the triumph of "merrie old England" and the Restoration of king and Church.

As recent work has begun to show, however, this most popular of Restoration poems looks forward as well as backward.[2] I will argue that the first two parts of *Hudibras* (1662–3) focus on the swearing of oaths in order to intervene directly in the Restoration's politics of religion, recommending the passage of the Clarendon Code and its oaths, as well as those laws' strict enforcement.[3] In this early version of a country strategy, anticipating by several years that of the proto-Whiggish country party, *Hudibras* targets as a main audience local officials in the counties – officials who both took oaths themselves and tendered them to others. By swearing together or conjúring, they conjure up in order to conjure away the ghosts of Dissent, past and present. The poem paradoxically disempowers women by making the Widow a giver of private oaths rather than a taker of public ones.

Central to Butler's narrative, such as it is, are commentary on and breaking of oaths.[4] In the second canto of Part II, Ralpho ticks off a list of virtually all the loyalty oaths imposed on the people by the king's enemies in the so-called Good Old Cause:

Was not the *Cause* at first begun
With *Perjury*, and carry'd on?
Was there an *Oath* the *Godly* took,
But, in due time and place, they broke? . . .
Did not our *Worthies* of the *House*,
Before they broke the *Peace*, break *Vows*?
For having free'd us, first from both
Th'*Allegeance*, and *Supremacy-Oath*;
Did they not, next, compel the *Nation*,
To take, and break the *Protestation*?
To *swear*, and after to *recant*
The *Solemn League and Covenant*?
To take th'*Engagement*, and disclaim it,
Enforc'd by those, who first did frame it? (2.2.141–58)[5]

With form pressed into the service of ideology, these forced, broken, double and triple rhymes (*House/vows; recant/Covenant; disclaim it/did frame it*) present a prosodic equivalent to what Butler sees as the duplicitous Parliament's forced and broken oaths. He charges that by requiring the populace to swear in the Protestation of 1641 to protect king and Church against the enemies of Reformation, Parliament forced subjects to break their former Oaths of Allegiance and Supremacy to the king. Moreover, in swearing a Solemn League and Covenant (1643) that promised to Presbyterianize the English Church in exchange for the Scots' cooperation in the war against Charles I, Parliament again broke its oaths to obey the king as head of the bodies politic and ecclesiastic, and again forced subjects to collude by subscribing the Covenant as condition for preserving their estates, rights, and liberties. Some of the same Parliamentarians – crucially without the support of most Presbyterians, though Butler scarcely acknowledges it – then proceeded to execute the king and widow the nation, sealing the deal by imposing yet another loyalty oath, this time to a republic without king or House of Lords. The Engagement of 1649 thus rescinded all previous oaths.

Epitomized by the catalogue from *Hudibras* are both the Scots-Presbyterian obsession with oaths, vows, and covenants and their apparently slippery, hypocritical enforcement of such commissive speech-acts. Perfectly willing (like Howard's Committeemen) to scold others for so much as taking the Lord's name in vain, the Presbyterian Hudibras defends the rights of his fellow saints to break their own oaths when the spirit so moves. After all,

> *Oaths* are but *words*, and *words* but *wind*,
> Too feeble implements to *bind*. . . .
> W' are not commanded to forbear,
> Indefinitely, at all to *swear*,
> But to *swear* idly, and in vain,
> Without self-interest, or gain.
> For, breaking of an *Oath* and *Lying*,
> Is but a kind of *Self-denying*,
> A *Saint-like virtue*, and from hence,
> Some have broke *Oaths*, by *Providence*,
> Some to the *Glory of the Lord*,
> *Perjur'd* themselves, and broke their word. (2.2.107–8, 129–38)

Although his squire Ralpho speaks these words, they very accurately reflect Hudibras's own attitude and actions. Unheeded go the injunctions against swearing by the Lord's name in the Third Commandment and Sermon on the Mount, the Quakers' core proof-texts. Unheeded goes the apparently contradictory and equally controversial injunction in Hebrews to "swear by the Greater" so as to "end . . . all strife" – not to mention God's severe punishment of oath- and covenant-breakers throughout the Old Testament.[6]

Hudibras blithely exemplifies such hypocritical perjury in his oath to the Widow: he promises to endure a whipping before asking for her hand in marriage (2.1.896–8, 835–40). Yet, as she later sums it up, his performance comes up short:

> When being free, you strove t' evade
> The Oaths you had in Prison made:
> Forswore your self, and first deny'd it,
> But after own'd, and justify'd it.
> (Part III, "The Ladies Answer to the Knight," 21–4)

When he fails to persuade Ralpho to become his literal whipping boy so that he can propose to the Lady, Hudibras argues himself into avoiding the whipping altogether, lies to her about this breach of oath, and then exhibits no shame when she discovers the sin. Blithely breaking his oaths, the Presbyterian knight becomes little more than a knight of the Post, a professional perjurer.[7]

Previous criticism of the poem has turned on the issues of intention, genre, form, intertextuality, period, politics, and allegory.[8] Over all, it has concentrated too much on who Butler was and thought, and not enough on what his published writings did and do. This chapter sheds new light on *Hudibras*'s politics, form, and allegory by arguing the following. First, that the idea of conjuration as swearing (both swearing together and practising word magic) links most sections of the first two parts of *Hudibras*. Second, that the poem is not as hostile to all oaths as has been claimed, but in the context of the early Restoration debate over swearing of all kinds argues for the better enforcement of the Clarendon Code's oaths. *Hudibras*'s nameless Widow becomes an allegory for the Restoration church-state demanding oaths of allegiance from its subjects and officeholders. Third, if oaths are a kind of performance, the poem itself mimics loyalty oaths by engaging in its own powerful counter-performance, striving to create a loyal Anglican reader with a homely consciousness like that of its narrator and implied author. This poetics of homeliness especially appeals to an audience of provincial officials, interpellating a royalism purged not just of Dissent but of everything objectionable about Cavaliers. All of these faults are then displaced onto Hudibras himself, who becomes a scapegoat for the Great Rebellion. Hudibras is truly Cavalier in making and breaking so many oaths.

## Conjuring Oaths

At the heart of *Hudibras* lies the idea of conjuring, and an important pun on the word, which highlights the idea of swearing oaths, has apparently eluded critics. While they have long recognized the astrologer Sidrophel as a figure who combines anxieties about bad science, bad medicine, bad religion and metaphysics, they have largely ignored the significance of his various kinds of pseudo-magic, or conjuring – specifically word-magic. At root, "to conjure" means to swear with or together with someone else (*OED*, I.1a). The Latin word for conspiracy is thus *coniuratio* because conspirators often swore oaths of secrecy and oaths of resolve to carry out a rebellion; and that meaning of "conjure" and "conjuration" was available in the early modern period (*OED*, I.1–2).[9] However, a more common use of the verb concerned the use of magic-working words (*OED*, III). Witches conjured up spirits or the Devil, for example. This sense of the word usually involved stressing it on the first syllable: cónjure. As magic incantation, cónjuring could denote two separate but connected kinds of word-work: uttering a higher authority's name in order to raise a spirit or bind a sentient being to perform some action or forcing other beings to perform actions by making them swear a promise to that effect. In other words, the issue was who swears the oath in magical conjuring: the conjurer or the conjuree, as it were. If the former, the conjurer swore an oath for or about someone else.[10] If the latter, the conjurer essentially imposed an oath on someone else, forced someone else to swear.[11] As we shall see, *Hudibras* consistently condemns conjuring as the act of imposing oaths on others, especially when performed by rebels.

Alternatively, the word could be stressed on the second syllable, conjúre, and refer to the act of exhorting other people to action by making them swear an oath, literally or figuratively. It could thus mean "To constrain (a person to some action) by putting him upon his oath, or by appealing to something sacred; to charge or call upon in the name of some divine or sacred being; to adjure" (*OED*, II.3): for example, "I conjure you in the name of God to leave us." The direct invocation of an external authority could also drop out so that the word meant "to appeal solemnly or earnestly to; to beseech, implore" without the overt use of an oath (*OED*, II.4a): for example, "She conjured them to leave."

So in a sense these were two separate words with a common origin but marked by different stress patterns. Yet this distinction was never hard and fast. People might, for example, stress the first syllable, cónjure, when referring to the more abstract, less magical, and more oathy senses of the term normally indicated by the rival pronunciation. The *OED* acknowledges this bleeding together of meanings back towards the Latin etymology by placing all of them in a single entry.[12]

For Butler the very ambiguity of the verb, with its magical and non-magical senses, its ties to and distance from oaths, is a strength, allowing a convergence between apparently separate attacks on the genres of romance and epic, the excesses of Presbyterians and sectaries, and the flimflams of astrology and the Royal Society's brand of science. Butler attacks these different genres' penchant for magical and supernatural events taking place against the backdrop of knightly quests, now unmasked as mere lies and illusions, often self-delusions. Hudibras frequently describes the literally bad shit that happens to him in magical events or places. The stocks in which he is imprisoned become an "enchanted mansion," for instance (2.2.627–32, 821–8; 1.3.1006). We will hear later of the dung thrown at him. So it comes as no surprise that the hero, like his predecessor, Don Quixote, would view ordinary people like jailers or Justices of the Peace as conjurers. But more important, Butler argues that Hudibras and his ilk are conjurers in the root sense of the word. They swear oaths to conspire against the king; they force others to take oaths to help them do so; and when that fails, they swear oaths for others, in others' names, to force them to collude or comply with rebellion. In expending so much animus on the many kinds of rebel conjuring (conspiracy, astrological prophecy, oath-taking), Butler acknowledges, if scornfully, the performative nature of language and oaths – a point to which we will return.

Butler's Sir Sidrophel has long been recognized as based in part on the Parliament-friendly astrologer and almanac-writer William Lilly, whom opponents derided as a conjurer and whose conjuring they connected to the swearing of oaths.[13] Sidrophel is certainly related to Butler's prose character of An Hermetic Philosopher (ca. 1667–9), who really is a "conjurer," despite his taking "Pains to prove, that Magic is not conjuring." The Hermetic Philosopher makes "solemn Vows to Almighty God, never to discover *the great secret*" of his art "to any Person living . . . and yet presently will undertake to teach it; but conjure every Scholar to keep it to himself."[14] He thus cónjures in working magic and conjúres in forcing students to share his own vows of secrecy.[15] Moreover, the oathiness of his art features in two other passages where an implicit comparison emerges between the Philosopher and the English Commonwealth with its oath of Engagement. The Hermetic Philosopher believes that "Spirits have a strange natural Allegiance to hard Words," such as his hocus-pocus, hictius-doctius incantations, even "though they mean nothing"; and he has encouraged a revolution of demons in Hell that suspiciously resembles the recent one in England: "By [his] Advice the Fiends lately attempted a *Reformation* of their Government, that is, to bring all Things into Confusion, which among them is the greatest Order." Among other things, he has given Hell's few honest lawyers, "the Pettifogging Devils, that were thrown over the Bar for their Honesty," permission "to practise again, having first taken an *Engagement to be true and faithful to the Government*."[16] As suggested, this paraphrases the Commonwealth's compulsory oath of allegiance, the Engagement of 1649, which engaged the swearer to "be *true and faithful* to the Commonwealth of England, as it is now established, without a King or House of Lords."[17] The Philosopher regards himself as akin to the Commonwealth in demanding that spirits obey his own "hard Words" and that demons mouth an oath of loyalty to a government he has inspired in Hell.[18]

*Hudibras,* of course, identifies "hard words" as one of its themes from the outset (1.1.3) and often associates Sir Sidrophel's faux-conjuring with oath-taking and oaths like the Engagement. When the hero decides to break his oath to the Lady, he hits upon going to Sidrophel to prognosticate the consequences of such an action, for, as Ralpho says,

> Do not our great *Reformers* use
> This *Sidrophel* to foreboad *News*? . . .
> And has not he point-blanck foretold
> Whats'ere the close *Committee* would? (2.3.171–2, 179–80)

Just as Parliament and Commonwealth used an astrologer like Lilly to broadcast ideology in the form of prophecy, so Hudibras can turn to a caricature of him to predict and thus produce the object of his desire: marriage to the Widow. Sidrophel's so-called predictions have thus encouraged the populace to take the rebels' oaths. He has made "The *Scorpion* take the *Protestation,* / And *Bear* engage for *Reformation*"; he has made "all the *Royall Stars* recant, / Compound, and take the *Covenant*" (2.3.185–8). Metonymies make it sound as if the constellations that Sidrophel/Lilly claims predicted the swearing of these state oaths (the Protestation, the Solemn League and Covenant, the Engagement, and possibly the Negative Oath) have taken the place of the human oath-takers and sworn the oaths themselves. Such confusion of alleged cause and effect (future events are thought to cause an omen of themselves that can be read, but here the omens take the place of the events they predict, becoming both cause and effect) is symptomatic of the underhanded double-dealing and lies of the king's enemies and their lackeys.[19] More important, though, is that the passage immediately gives way to Hudibras, the man who has decided to break his own oaths, calling Sidrophel a conjurer. "The case is cleer," says the hero, "The *Saints* may 'mploy a *Conjurer*" (2.3.189–90; cf. 202). That is, at the behest of the Parliamentarian "Saints," Sidrophel/Lilly cónjures oaths into being with his prognostication, oaths that are themselves a kind of conjuration. In effect, he conjúres people to take oaths.

This pun on cónjure/conjúre helps us appreciate the full force of a later remark in *Hudibras*. In a slightly digressive dialogue between a nameless Presbyterian and a nameless Independent that recapitulates some of the animus between Hudibras and Ralpho, the Independent accuses the Presbyterians of having used "all your Charms" in the 1640s "To conjure *Legion up*, in Arms, / And raise more Devils in the Rout, / Then e're y'were able to cast out" (3.2.1137–40). On the face of it, he states that the Presbyterians stupidly tried to use the rabble, the common people, to further their ends but soon lost control of them. But the pun on "conjure" suggests that the lines refer more specifically to the Presbyterian-dominated Parliament's use of state oaths such as the Covenant, which they inflicted on the populace as a whole. Should they have been surprised when a populace called into action by state oaths gained a mind of its own and suggested further reforms? Should they have been surprised that people who regarded these oaths as drafts of written constitutions for a reformed polity, and even wore them in their hats as proof of their commitment to such reform, would speak up in documents like the Agreement of the People, in fora like the Putney Debates, and more generally, in the refusal of the radicalized Army to obey Parliament in the late 1640s? In any case, a hundred lines later, the Independent calls the Devil the "*Author / O'th' Covenant*" (3.2.1245–6), cementing the point that "conjur[ing] Legion up in Arms" refers specifically to using an oath like the Covenant as a means of recruiting people for the war against the king.[20]

Now, although this reference to conjuring legion appears in Part III of *Hudibras*, published in 1677, it nevertheless picks up on this important pun in the first two parts (1662–3). First, Hudibras defeats Crowdero, gives him quarter, and then conjures him into the stocks, described as a "magic circle" (1.2.1111–12, 1130–70, esp. 1142–3). In other words, he forces Crowdero to take an oath not to take arms against him again – the joke being that the "arms" Crowdero has just used against Hudibras are, in fact, his wooden prosthetic leg. But the larger quarry here is that a forced oath precedes a forced appearance in the magic circle of the stocks. Later, a version of the same thing happens to Hudibras himself. On two occasions in the initial instalments of *Hudibras*, women's oaths are tied to conjuration and have a great impact on the hero. Most closely related to Sidrophel and to Presbyterians as oath-swearing and oath-requiring conjurers is the Widow's first appearance to Hudibras in the stocks:

> She came upon him in his wooden
> *Magicians* Circle, on the sudden,
> As *Spirits* do t'a Conjurer,
> When in their dreadful shapes th' appear. (2.1.111–14)

The metaphor is apt. Since Hudibras thinks of himself as a knight on a quest and perceives of the stocks as an enchanted mansion (1.3.1006; 2.1.94), he may also entertain the illusion that as conjuring oath-taker himself, he can speak magic words to summon tutelary spirits to free him. Butler's works abound with references to magicians conjuring within their magic circles,[21] and the joke here is that the circle has narrowed to the size of his neck (or hands) and rotated into a position perpendicular to the ground. It is nothing other than the stocks, and to think otherwise is to delay the clear thinking that might help free him from them.

However, he cannot rescue himself. It is the Widow who learns of his punishment and "vows" to free him (2.1.87–94). Butler uses the terms "oath" and "vow" interchangeably in the poem to denote solemn commissive speech-acts; and what at one moment is referred to as an oath – for example, Hudibras's promise to be whipped – can at another be called a vow.[22] So in the poem's terminology an oath can be vowed as well as sworn – for example, when the Widow refers in Book 3 to men's false promises to women as "all the Oaths to us they vow'd" (3.1.966). No sooner has the Widow "vow'd" to free him from the stocks than she appears before him "As *Spirits* do t'a Conjurer." It is almost as if Hudibras has used magic to make the Widow swear an oath to appear to him and do his bidding; he has seemingly conjured in the root sense of the word. The fact that this has not taken place at all and that her vowing merely coincides with his wish to be freed is beside the point: in the romance fiction he uses to console himself about his miserable life, he has conjured her.

It seems fitting that a woman should free him since a woman helped put him there in the first place, and with a vow. After Hudibras is literally beaten by the Amazonian Trulla, she takes mercy on him ("gives him quarter") and then prevents the rest of the mob from drubbing him by vowing that they will not: she "vow'd they should not break her word: / Sh' had given him quarter, and her bloud / Or theirs should make that quarter good" (1.3.940–2). She then convinces her cohorts to put Hudibras in prison. Significantly, the Narrator describes the whole process as a conjuration:

> . . . *Trulla* straight brought on her charge,
> And in the self-same *Limbo* [the stocks] put
> The *Knight* and *Squire* . . .
> Where leaving them i'th' wretched hole,

Their bangs and durance to condole,
Confin'd and *conjur'd* into narrow
Enchanted mansion, to know sorrow. (1.3.10008)

Somewhat later, the Narrator reiterates that Hudibras has been "conjur'd into safe Custody" (2.1.34). Again, "conjur'd" speaks both to Hudibras's delusions about living out a life of romance frequented by magical and supernatural events – delusions that help him make sense of the apparently arbitrary and mysterious elements in it, such as imprisonment – and to the fact that for Presbyterians and other oath-makers, vows and oaths should work like magic, should bring about measurable changes in the world. That those changes should be consistently brought about not by the Presbyterian knight but by the poem's women reflects badly on the eponymous knight, who, in Sidrophel's words, merely "vapour[s]" in his "huffing" braggardry (2.3.1003, 1034). Also significant here is that the boundaries between conjurer and conjuree shift or disappear altogether. The only certainty is that some act of conjuring has put Hudibras in jail as well as rescued him from it. Strictly speaking, the women have done both acts of swearing and moving him in or out of jail. Yet his romance-addled brain would like to take credit for it as a conjurer, or perhaps to imagine that both he and the women are victims of some other magician. But as we shall see, once Hudibras is in jail, the only way he can get out is by reluctantly swearing an oath the Widow imposes on him – an oath with many resonances for an early Restoration audience.

## Conjuring Self and Nation

At one point Sir Sidrophel declares, "I can, what I affirm, make appear" (2.3.1004), which sounds very much like J.L. Austin's description of a performative. As a charlatan, Sidrophel is clearly lying or self-deceived, but what he says about conjuring words certainly applies to the many state oaths Presbyterians like Hudibras employed to shape the polity in the 1640s. Butler's satire insinuates that during the nightmare of the Civil War and Interregnum, words were too performative. *Hudibras* reflects this problem by endowing oaths with simultaneously too much and too little power.[23] On the one hand, oaths fail to bind the title character's future behaviour. On the other, oaths in the poem create and reflect religious, political, class, and gender divisions. Butler uses both oaths and the poem to perform an Anglican royalist self and advocate for a set of oaths of office that would create and sustain an Anglican royalist nation. One has first to admit the utter failure of oaths and language to perform much of anything within the narrative of *Hudibras*. Sworn promises are repeatedly broken. We have heard Ralpho say that "*Oaths* are but *words*, and *words* but *wind*, / Too feeble implements to *bind*" (2.2.107–8); and this couplet, with its failed rhyme, aptly describes his and his master's attitude towards oaths, which they regard as failing to bind unless convenient. Yet despite the fact that Butler often lumps all Dissenters together as non-Anglicans, it expresses very accurately one of the fissures among Dissenters: Independents' and other sectaries' scepticism towards Presbyterian-produced oaths.

However, one should also admit that another difference in the poem, this time between oath-keeping and oath-breaking, is determined by gender. The examples of "conjuration" that imprisons and releases Hudibras from the stocks demonstrate that the poem's women keep their vows.[24] Trulla vows to show him mercy and put him in the stocks; and she does, forcing other men to go along with her. The Widow vows to release him from the stocks; and she does. The fact that neither character has the purest of motives is beside the point. They do what they swear. Not surprisingly, in Part III Hudibras accuses the Widow and women more generally of being conjurers or enticers of men via words and gestures ("An Heroical Epistle of Hudibras to his Lady," 184). In this respect the poem uses different swearing practices to construct gender differences.

*Hudibras* also constructs class, ethnic, and religious differences via oaths. In the early modern language of "sorts" and "ranks," *Hudibras* distinguishes between "the rabble" and the peerage on the basis of swearing. According to the poem, the political ferment of the 1640s inappropriately involved large numbers of people from the lower ranks in the political process, in part via oaths (1.2.505–56, esp. 521–6 and nn. 545–6). Peers, on the other hand, did not have to swear, or if they did, only by their own honour (2.2.202–4). In terms of nation and ethnicity, *Hudibras* hardly stands alone in its Scotophobia, attacking England's Presbyterian neighbours in the north for swearing countless covenants and then imposing them on England in 1643.[25] Here as elsewhere in the poem, faith apparently cannot be kept with unreliable outgroups. As for religio-political divisions within England, both before and after the Restoration, the poem paints a general picture of non-Anglicans treating oaths cavalierly – manufacturing, imposing, and breaking them with great frequency – and of Anglican royalists keeping their oaths and refusing new ones that would force them to perjure themselves. This is implicit in Parts I–II in the sections that condemn the Parliamentarian Presbyterian rebels for breaking the Oaths of Allegiance and Supremacy, the implication being that royalists have not. Part III makes the point explicitly (2.2.151–2; cf. 1.2.651–2n.; 3.2.163–76, 276). But mostly what is performed in and by *Hudibras* is a less tangible but infinitely more powerful Anglican royalist consciousness or sensibility – a self characterized by a humble humour with no tolerance for balderdash.

## *Hudibras* as Response to the Clarendon Oaths

As we saw in the introduction, the controversy over oaths in the early years of the Restoration was fierce, even poisonous. Into such an atmosphere enter *Hudibras*. Susan Staves argued thirty years ago that Butler is himself guilty of a kind of hypocrisy in, on the one hand, faulting Nonconformists for their obsession with oaths and, on the other, insisting that they snap to and take all of the new oaths required by the rabidly Anglican Cavalier Parliament.[26] By these lights Butler's mock-epic argues for – or at least not against – the newest raft of state oaths.[27] Alvin Snider, however, has claimed that *Hudibras*'s attack on oaths is consistent and total, extending even to the new oaths promulgated by Butler's ideological compatriots. According to this argument, oaths simply will not work. Human nature being what it is, there is no way an oath could ever extract loyalty from anyone.[28] This was certainly an argument that some contemporaries made, but usually from a Quaker or occasionally Catholic, rather than Anglican, perspective. Yet Ashley Marshall's recent work would suggest that Staves's reading of Butler's position on oaths in *Hudibras* makes more sense.[29]

Despite critical myopia about this fact, the poem's first two parts do tackle the oaths of office imposed by the Clarendon Code. The Widow, after all, imposes oaths on the hero. The Cavalier Parliament had created at least four new oaths before Part II of *Hudibras* was published in late 1663, and a more detailed discussion of them is now in order. The Militia Acts of 1661–2 required all soldiers and officers in the trained bands to swear allegiance to the king in the Oaths of Allegiance and Supremacy and to reinforce that allegiance by reiterating in a separate oath their rejection of taking arms against him or his officials.[30] The Corporation Act (1661) required these same oaths from members of city and town corporations, adding an abjuration of the Solemn League and Covenant in an effort to purge them of Dissenters.[31] In order to bar Dissenters from the Church of England, the Act of Uniformity (1662) demanded from Anglican ministers the same non-resistance and anti-Covenant oaths, plus their "assent and consent" to the Book of Common Prayer and episcopacy, along with a promise to conform to the Anglican liturgy. It also required all schoolmasters to take the same oaths, minus the "assent and consent."[32] The Vestry Act (1663) applied to vestrymen the same oaths required of schoolmasters.[33] The Quaker Act (1662) made it a crime for Quakers or anyone else to refuse, or even to criticize in speech or writing, any oath mandated by law, including judicial oaths, the Oaths of Allegiance and Supremacy, and the Clarendon subscriptions – punishments to range from fines to imprisonment to transportation.[34] Passed after Part II of *Hudibras* had appeared, the Conventicles Act (1664) stiffened the penalties for oath-refusal and required officials to tender Quakers and other oath-refusers the following oath about oaths: "I doe sweare that I doe not hold the takeing of an Oath to be unlawfull nor refuse to take an Oath on that account."[35] The Five Mile Act of 1665 required Nonconforming ministers living or preaching within five miles of corporate towns to swear a stronger non-resistance oath that promised "not at any time [to] endeavour any Alteration of Government either in Church or State."[36] Susan Staves has argued persuasively that the anti-Covenant provision in the laws passed before 1664 was unprecedented in requiring swearers to make commitments binding people other than themselves – or in *Hudibras*'s terms, to conjure others.[37]

Butler's poem arguably addresses the first four of these oath-imposing laws not only in Trulla's swearing an oath that binds other characters but in the Widow's requiring oaths from Hudibras. After demanding that he whip himself as a condition for escaping the stocks and marrying her, she requires two oaths: a promise that he *will be* whipped ("This *swear* you will perform"); and once that has happened, an assertion that he *has been* whipped ("Bring me on *Oath*, a fair account, / And *honor* too, when you have don't") (1.3.937–42; 2.1.825–40, 893, 835–6).[38] Without hesitation he complies with the first: "I do *profess* and *swear*, / And will perform what you enjoyn, / Or may I never see you *mine*" (2.1.896–8). But second thoughts follow, and he spends much of the next canto in the famous dialogue of oaths with Ralpho, arguing himself casuistically out of his sworn promise (2.2.37–500). In terms of performing it, however, that is where the story ends in 1663. We must wait until 1677 for Part III's spectacle of Hudibras's swearing falsely that he has been whipped (the second oath) and being immediately exposed as a liar (3.1.163–522, esp. 163–8, 200–4, 408, 485–96, 497–510). He never gains the Widow's hand. But in the story as it stands at the end of Part II, the Widow has imposed two oaths on Hudibras. He has performed the first, which promises harm to himself, and he has in effect promised to perform the second in the future, which will assert that the harm has been done.

The whole plotline of oaths imposed and evaded is allegorical. The Widow functions as allegory not just for England and the English people, as critics have long recognized, but for the episcopal church-state. The Widow, or "Dame Religion" as she is called in the opening lines (1.1.1–8), has demanded that a Dissenter, Hudibras, swear an oath. For contemporary readers this would have recalled two different oath-dilemmas confronting Dissenters in the early 1660s: that of Quakers and Baptists asked to take judicial and loyalty oaths or go to jail and that of all Dissenters required to take new oaths in order to enter public office.[39] In the first instance, the Quaker Act of 1662 made it possible for Quakers and those Baptists who were also nonjurors to be imprisoned for refusing any state oath, and local officials often tendered them oaths solely to jail them when they refused. As we have seen, many died from the poor conditions in prison because of this law. Hudibras's situation most obviously resembles that of nonjuring Quakers and Baptists already in prison and repeatedly asked by the local magistrate to swear oaths, often the Oaths of Allegiance and Supremacy, and thereby to free themselves from prison. The "conjuring" astrologer William Lilly, for example, did just that in January 1662.[40] Moreover, Ralpho is also in the stocks with his Hudibras, and with his recourse to the "inner light" most resembles a Quaker. Although not asked to take an oath, Ralpho finds his fate resting on Hudibras's doing so. Paramount here is the demand for an oath, not the actual swearing of it. Tempted to swear an oath he regards as harmful (the promise to whip himself), Hudibras swallows his pride and does so. He is immediately released from prison, like the few Quakers and Baptists who chose to deny a core tenet of their faith to escape indefinite confinement and possible death. From Butler's anti-Dissenting point of view, Hudibras as representative of quaking and baptizing Dissenters has just displayed his and their hypocrisy. Quakers and nonjuring Baptists claimed to ground their identity in oath-refusal, and yet some of them were willing to swear when push came to shove. They cannot have been real nonjurors in the first place.

In addition to functioning like oaths of release, as it were, the Widow's imposed oaths resemble oaths of office. She herself has decided "To do the office of a Neighbour" and release her neighbour Hudibras from jail (2.1.89). Tellingly, she does so by arming herself like a knight and sallying forth with her lady-in-waiting as squire in order

To do the office of a Neighbour . . .
And from his wooden Jayl the Stocks
To set at large his Fetter-Locks,
And by Exchange, Parole, or Ransome,
To free him from th'Inchanted Mansion.
This b'ing resolv'd, she call'd for hood
And Usher, Implements abroad,
Which *Ladies* wear, beside a slender
Young waiting *Damsel* to attend her. (2.1.89–98)[41]

The description obviously parodies scenes in which attendants help epic heroes arm for battle, with a lady's hood replacing a man's helmet. As for the rest of her battle "implements," she turns a male servant into something like a sword – a gentleman usher whose job it is to hold her arm and accompany her outside the home for propriety's sake.[42] In the spirit of satiric inversion, it also seems fitting that her lady-in-waiting, instead of acting as a passive damsel, becomes her squire. Thus, it is a measure of her world's topsy-turviness that one woman has to do all this for two men because of their inability to rescue themselves and save her as a damsel in distress (2.1.777–88). Her status as an upstart woman, termagant, or scold is also hinted at by the actions of her double, the embarrassingly martial Trulla, and by the Skimmington that punishes women for henpecking their husbands (1.2.769–950; 2.2.565–712; cf. 1.2.961–4). Hudibras characteristically fails to see the Spenserian irony: that the Skimmington really emblematizes his own unmanning by two successive women.[43] Indeed, his very blindness to their powers is what allows him to be unmanned in the first place.

Yet we must ignore these "flaws" to understand the full force of the allegory. While a woman has taken the office of both neighbour and knight, she has also imposed what amounts to an oath of office on Hudibras – an oath to enter the office of husband.[44] He may think he has conjured her up as tutelary spirit, but she has really conjured him in both senses. "This *swear* you will perform," she declares, "and then / I'll set you from th'inchanted *Den*, / And the *Magician*'s Circle clear" (2.1.893–5). In asking the hero to swear to be whipped, and even to swear later that he has kept this promise, the Widow as the English church-state (or even the Cavalier Parliament) forces Presbyterians and non-Anglicans to swear to something that would similarly hurt: denying key aspects of their objections to Anglican doctrine and discipline. The fact that the Widow makes this whipping, and the oaths surrounding it, conditions for marrying her, parallels the English church-state's requirements that dubious religious radicals do something painful to marry themselves to it and its offices, to make a firm commitment to king and bishops. Only then can she make a firm commitment to him. For Presbyterians in particular, renouncing their own core-text, the Solemn League and Covenant, and with it any chance of a Presbyterian-friendly church settlement, would feel like self-flagellation. Although the Corporation, Uniformity, and Vestry Acts were often spottily enforced – as Ashley Marshall shows[45] – they did require lay and clerical Presbyterians to deny a fundamental part of their religion, if not their religion itself, in order to become or remain corporation members, schoolmasters, vestrymen, and ministers in the Church of England. Hudibras's prevarication, in trying at first to avoid the whipping by finding justifications to break the oath and eventually swearing a false oath that he has been whipped, parallels what Butler saw as the unreliability and hypocrisy of Presbyterians and Dissenters more broadly, who either refused the Uniformity and Corporation oaths or took them in bad faith – mentally reserving, for example, a continuing resolve to push for a more Presbyterian state church. The next section of this chapter heads off an important objection to the rest of my argument.

**Butler's Antijurism?**

The crucial question, then, is whether this bit of topical as opposed to historical allegory – about the 1660s rather than the 1640s and 1650s – has an antijurist slant. In other words, does Butler oppose all oaths on principle? Although no recent critic has really acknowledged the presence of such detailed and polemically topical allegory about oaths in the poem, Alvin Snider has claimed that *Hudibras* is antijurist, and Susan Staves would probably claim that it is not. Marshall suggests but does not specify agreement with Staves on the issue.[46] However, the evidence indicates that Snider's argument only has some purchase on Butler's work after the first two parts of *Hudibras*.

Before the Test Act of 1673 – a crucial moment for Marvell as well – Butler was certainly not opposed to all oaths, just to the Parliamentarian and Presbyterian ones of the 1640s and 1650s. After 1673, perhaps under the influence of the Duke of Buckingham,[47] Butler seems to have changed his mind and become more disillusioned about the efficacy of state oaths. His writings from the years 1667–9, principally the *Characters* and related MS poetry, support the Uniformity oaths and condemn ejected ministers.[48] Butler's *Transproser Rehears'd* (1673), an attack on Marvell's *Rehearsal Transpros'd* of the previous year, speaks approvingly of the Oath of Allegiance.[49] Most tellingly, the third part of *Hudibras* (1677) praises royalists who "to their faith . . . firmly cleav'd" by keeping their Oaths of Allegiance and Supremacy at great personal cost during the Civil War and Interregnum.[50] Moreover, Parts II and III refuse to reward Hudibras for his bad oath-behaviour, denying him the Widow's hand and punishing him with a sound beating. It is only Butler's remarks about and after the Test oath of 1673 that indicate any change of position. The Test required officeholders to prove they were not Catholic by denying transubstantiation. Butler expressed opposition to this Test and test oaths in general in prose and verse only published after his death, as well as in a passage in the final part of *Hudibras*, published in 1677.[51] Since the word "test" did not enjoy wide circulation as a synonym for oath of office before 1673,[52] all of these passages almost certainly postdate Parts I–II of *Hudibras* (1662–3).[53]

I would submit, therefore, that after the Test Act Butler changed his mind about some state oaths such as the Test. This may have been due to his patron Buckingham, who may, after initial support for an Ease Bill that included something like the Test, have eventually decided to oppose the Test Act on the grounds that it failed to eliminate the other oaths that discriminated against Protestant Dissenters and that it forced them to take Anglican communion and acknowledge the king as head of the Church.[54] Buckingham seems not to have voted for the Test Act; he was apparently absent when it came to a final vote on 20 March 1673.[55] Butler worked for Buckingham from sometime in 1670 to at least June 1673,[56] and it would not be surprising if the anti-Test passages we have discussed so far represent Butler's adoption of Buckingham's views on the Test. Since the third instalment of *Hudibras* (1677) praises Cavaliers and their oaths and condemns various Dissenters for opposition to the Oaths of Allegiance and Supremacy,[57] his antijurism would seem to be more limited than Snider allows and to postdate the parts of the poem contemporary with the Clarendon Code.

## Conjuring Homely Officials by Displacement and Substitution

To make the case that for Butler swearing is integral to the construction of identity, we now focus on *Hudibras*'s larger project of reformation and interpellation. Butler creates a poetics of homeliness that displaces perjury and other kinds of bad swearing from royalists onto Nonconformists, thereby whitewashing contemporary jailings of Dissenters for oath-refusal and other crimes in the early 1660s. Another price of this construction of a "homely" Anglican identity based on persecuting Dissenters with oaths is the exclusion of women from politics.

In order to understand *Hudibras*'s homeliness and thus its appeal to local officials in the provinces, we first consider its genre. As a mock-epic or burlesque satire, *Hudibras* creates a dissonance both within and between form and content. The discrepancies within content and form have seemed less obvious to Butler's critics than those between them. They have for the most part argued that the poem mismatches high form with low content.[58] But this mischaracterizes its content, which is in a sense divided within itself. What subject matter could be grander than the history of a nation and its wars? And yet Butler has deliberately selected from this rich canvas nothing but material traditionally considered low: bear-baitings, brawls, beatings, Skimmingtons, pillories, food, the body, animals, bogus astrology, the courting of widows.[59] But what is left after such a reductive culling functions as a giant synecdoche for the missing whole of national history over the previous two decades, a synecdoche that never allows the reader to lose sight of that loftier whole. Thus, both high whole (the subject of national history) and low part (the subject of local bear-baitings, pilloryings, and so on) are visible from the vantage point of the poem, resulting in a gap within its content. The gap within form, on the other hand, results from pitting two different aspects of it – genre and style – against each other: high genre and low style. The trappings of classical epic and Renaissance romance (invocations, epithets, similes, catalogues, arming scenes, ekphrases, allegory, cantos, synoptic prefatory "arguments") clash with the apparent failures of prosody (the short lines and comic rhymes) and narrative (the vaguely discernible story line that constantly disappears in the minutiae of dialogue and digression). These inner faultlines only widen the gap between form and content frequently remarked by students of Butler: the now low subject matter clothed in the only partially high form of epic-romance.

Through both form and content *Hudibras* projects what I call a poetics of homeliness that attempts to purify royalism of the taint of courtly, Cavalier libertinism. Out of the varieties of royalism available to him[60] Butler created one that largely excluded both Cavalier and king. *Hudibras*'s royalism lacks the "roaring" Cavaliers: the wine, women, and song; the violence of war; the martyrs and mourners; the fetishism of honour and king.[61] He accomplishes this repackaging of royalism by displacing some of these characteristics onto another knight, the poem's protagonist. It is neither damn-me Cavaliers nor courtiers but Sir Hudibras who displays bodily disorder in the form of drinking and whoring, and civil disorder in the form of excessive swearing and perjury.

Butler left a poem in manuscript that his eighteenth-century editor Robert Thyer labelled a "Satyr upon the licentious age of Charles the 2d, contrasted with the puritanical one that preceded it." Internal evidence suggests that it dates from the late 1660s, after the plague and Fire of London.[62] According to A.D. Cousins, the poem "argues that the new cavalier court masks the same habit of mind as informed the recent puritan regime" and "elaborate[s] the puritans' worst traits."[63] "The mock religious sensibility the cavaliers have evolved," Cousins asserts, "paradoxically identifies them with the puritans." Moreover, they "go far beyond the deceit and folly of the puritans" "in experiencing and seeking disorder" and "pervert[ing] language."[64] I would stress the idea of "identify[ing] them with the puritans." If this poem says that courtly rakes turn themselves into a new version of Puritan vice, *Hudibras* does something like the opposite, identifying Puritan vice with Cavalier vice and then excusing the Cavaliers altogether. It projects royalist vices onto Hudibras and turns him into a scapegoat for the vices of both Nonconformists and royalists, before and after the Restoration.[65]

If royalists had been accused of engaging in excessive violence, physical or verbal, on or off the battlefield, all these qualities appear in Sir Hudibras, but in attenuated, bumbling form. If Cavaliers had been faulted for excess corporeality in their drinking and whoring, these drives reappear in Hudibras's desire for food and drink and in his failed pursuit of the Widow using terms from the Cavalier love lyric. If Cavaliers had sworn too many profane oaths,[66] Hudibras swears too many state oaths. In this sense the Solemn League and Covenant truly is just another "*God-dam-me* rant" (1.2.509–10). If Cavaliers had been imprisoned, so is Hudibras; if they are released on parole or by compounding, so is he. If compounding Cavaliers had been accused of being changeable, disloyal, and trimming in the wake of the Parliamentarian victory, then it is Hudibras who has few if any loyalties, with opinions that change at the drop of a hat, and who compounds for sins and release from prison (1.1.213–14; 2.1.871–2). If critics had pummelled the greatest of Cavaliers, Charles I, for being henpecked by his wife, what are we to make of Hudibras's dealings with the Widow and Trulla, who have their way on almost every issue and conjure him in and out of prison with imposing oaths? If Charles and other royalists had suffered martyrdom, the "Saints" consider themselves martyrs here – wrongly, of course (1.1.260; 1.2.523; 2.1.769).

But most telling of the items on the list of displacements above is, once again, what corresponds to the conjuration/adjuration scene in prison. During the Civil War and Interregnum, imprisoned royalists had often been released on condition that they swear oaths. To be released "on parole" originally meant to be released after taking an oath, either to behave well thereafter or to return to custody at some future time.[67] Jailed royalists were often tendered oaths: the Negative Oath (a promise not to continue fighting for the king against Parliament) and/or the Solemn League and Covenant.[68] In broader terms, the process of being released from prison in this way and then "compounding" or negotiating to keep one's real and personal estate by handing some of it over to the authorities, often in the form of a heavy fine, genuinely harmed royalists and provided an important analogue for Hudibras's reluctantly swearing an oath to harm himself at the Widow's sadistic behest. Obviously this kind of collusion in harming oneself was something royalists wanted to forget once the king was restored. But they could not, in part because not all of the lands and property confiscated by the compounding process ever returned to their original owners. Such collusion, as opposed to steadfast opposition to the rebels' governments, was a fault worthy of psychological suppression or repression.

As a substitute for royalist misbehaviour in the 1640s Butler creates a narrator with a homely mindset whose literary performance, with its deliberate lack of polish and affectation, can only be described the same way: as homely. When Hudibras winds up in the stocks after a scrap with some bear-baiters, he refers to his plight as a "homely case" (2.1.164),[69] a phrase that also describes the stocks (a case or frame that contains his body), as well as his body itself, crowned by dirty face and torn beard. Later, almost no irony enters the knight's own characterization of the dung thrown at him during the Skimmingtons as "homely treats" (2.2.877, 857–8, 821–7). However, even before this, the Widow has crudely alluded to animals' tails (men's phalluses) as "comely," despite the fact that the "*Vulgar* count them homely" (2.1.745). Butler's prose character of A Tedious Man is so because he inflicts dull and long-winded stories on everyone else, stories with subjects as familiar to himself as his home, because, as far as he is concerned, "though *home be homely*, it is more delightful than finer Things abroad."[70] Furthermore, the character of A Bumpkin or Country-Squire has acquired a "homely education." Since *Hudibras*'s Narrator also calls its eponymous knight a "*Bumkin*," that knight's flawed learning, as displayed in the first canto and elsewhere, counts as homely too.[71] Marvell's riposte to Butler in *Last Instructions to a Painter* registers this poetics of homeliness when it describes the Dutch navy's Skimmingron Rides up the Thames as a "homely sight."[72]

"Homely" in many senses, positive and negative (and mostly non-Freudian), would describe Butler's mock-epic itself.[73] The *OED* defines the word variously as "Of or belonging to the home or household . . . esp. a humble home . . . unsophisticated, simple; plain, unadorned, not fine; everyday, commonplace; unpolished, rough, rude. (Sometimes approbative, as connoting the absence of artificial embellishment; but often apologetic, depreciative, or even as a euphemism for 'wanting refinement, polish, or grace.')" In contrast to Butler's character of The Tedious Man, "to speak homely" can also mean to speak "Without reserve or circumlocution; directly 'home'; straight to the point; plainly."[74]

*Hudibras*'s subject and style seem homely in the sense of ugly, mediocre, incomplete, careless (like scatterbrained and capricious Puritans at their worst, as Butler saw them), but also in more positive senses, straightforward and direct, devoid of affectation, familiar, everyday, earthy, energetic, insouciant (like Anglican royalists at their best).[75] Every aspect of the poem, from its subject matter to its prosody to its muddled attempts at allegory, is homely, and deliberately so. While Hudibras can do nothing other than bumble, Butler's digressive narrator, if not quite a bumbler on his protagonist's scale, comes across as a genial and carefree country gentleman – no great shakes, but full of good common sense that sees through Nonconformist hypocrisy and pretension.[76] The aphoristic atomism and episodicality he lends the poem are virtues rather than vices. Above all, the poem broadcasts the message that Nonconformists are not our sort and must be kept in check, even though many of them figure as basically harmless bumblers like Hudibras. In place of Nonconformist enthusiasm the Narrator offers that homely good sense.[77]

His is a world of food, animals, the town stocks, and not much else – a homely and humble world where little happens and all pretensions go unrewarded, eventually to be stripped away entirely. The first two books of *Hudibras* are set in a georgic landscape of towns and villages where plants and beasts are cultivated, and life goes on serenely, in and out of the households that consume them.[78] Fish are caught, foxes hunted, animals of many kinds domesticated and protected from disease, crops sown and reaped.[79] The cuckoo's tone can be heard, and larks caught at night, at the same time that barn owls catch mice.[80] Cider is made to be drunk in taverns and homes.[81] Inside these modest country dwellings other work goes on: the spinning of wool and laundering of clothes.[82] No prodigy houses, they range in size from small farmhouses to squires' halls.

*Hudibras* may have won great popularity precisely by making such an appeal to a homely readership: not, or not just, denizens of the capital of all ranks, but a rural audience of country gentlemen and parsons – the gentry and the middle sort whom he needed to convince both to avoid and to prosecute Nonconformity wherever found. As Michael Braddick and others have shown, these men acted as relays for the regime's policies, serving in such offices as constable, JP, sheriff, and militia officer.[83] *Hudibras* is thus a poem about local officials and for local officials,[84] and as such forms part of an incipient country strategy on the part of the Cavaliers, a strategy designed to counter the incipient country opposition that would eventually form the core of the Whig party. Hudibras himself holds the office of Justice of the Peace with a commission from Parliament rather than king, but, as Susan Staves so memorably puts it, "his activities produce neither justice nor peace."[85] This fact is most glaringly obvious in the first book of the poem, where Hudibras takes it upon himself to break up and hold someone responsible for the traditional pastime of bear-baiting. The fact that he ends up in the stocks himself provides some redress for what Butler sees as the injustice the knight has thereby caused. Butler himself knew provincial officialdom well, having occupied several secretarial posts to provincial worthies such as the Countess of Kent and "Mr. *Jefferys* of *Earls-Croom*," Worcestershire, a magistrate. He was, in fact, serving as a minor official himself, as steward to the Earl of Carberry at Ludlow Castle (the setting of Milton's *A Maske*) in the marches of Wales, while writing *Hudibras*.[86] But his poem's focus on local officials in the provinces – the Dogberries and Justice Shallows who both gave and took oaths of office and whom Butler elsewhere dubbed "small Officers" – has eluded most recent critics.[87] The relative absence of justice and competent Justices of the Peace in Part I is intensified by the the spurious Part II of *Hudibras*, a continuation of the poem written by someone other than Butler and published within six months of the first.[88]

As a JP with a commission from the Parliament during the 1640s and 1650s, Hudibras is a precursor of those tasked after 1660 with helping to enforce the Militia, Uniformity, and Corporation Oaths. The second Militia Act (1662) commissioned JPs to tender militia members both the Oaths of Allegiance and Supremacy and the following non-resistance oath: "I. A. B. doe declare and beleive that it is not lawfull upon any pretence whatsoever to take Armes against the King[,] And . . . I doe abhor that traiterous Position that Armes may be taken by His Authority against His Person or against those that are commissioned by Him in pursuance of such military Commissions. So help me God."[89] The Act of Uniformity empowered JPs and other local officials to jail preachers who failed to take the oaths it prescribed, as well as to help convict incumbent ministers who failed to read the Book of Common Prayer and administer the Anglican sacraments. For the latter purpose JPs were to administer judicial oaths to two witnesses.[90] The Corporation Act asked specially appointed Commissioners and JPs to tender its oaths to Corporation members and fellow JPs.[91] In all three instances, then, JPs acted as relays between national and local government, helping in the last two cases to smoke out, as much as possible, Dissenters seeking civil and religious posts and to force them into a dilemma: either convert to the state religion and secure the post or stay a Dissenter and give it up. Either way, the argument went, dangerous people would be identified and removed from the Church. And even if they were not, they would be forced to damn themselves to hell by perjury (swearing a false oath). Certainly, former Dissenters who swallowed the new oaths could be monitored as suspicious. Since a local official such as a JP would be instrumental in enforcing both of these laws and rooting out malignants, one of *Hudibras*'s arguments is that even true blue Anglican JPs, entirely above suspicion, should not succumb to compassion for Dissenting neighbours and fellow officials and thus neglect the enforcement of these laws. Hudibras's mistaken crackdown on harmless traditional sports such as bear-baitings and Skimmingtons thus emblematizes both Anglican JPs and constables who concentrate on the wrong "crimes" and the few Dissenting JPs and constables who remain uncommitted to the Anglican Church (as identified with traditional folk culture) and refuse to purge it of their fellow Dissenters.[92]

Hudibras also represents the other side of the enforcement coin: Presbyterians and other Dissenters asked to take the Corporation and Uniformity Oaths. Some swallowed them and denied their Dissent in order to acquire the post of JP or minister. Others refused and were cashiered.

## Samson's Cuffs, Cords, and Women

We can conclude by noting that Butler also represses and displaces women's involvement in oaths and politics. On the one hand, the poem shows women and women's oaths to be more powerful than men and their oaths. There are women in the offices of knight and neighbour (the Widow and Trulla); and women more often impose oaths on men, and with greater success. On the other hand, *Hudibras* encourages us to see all this as threatening. The Widow's proto-feminist rants against marital subjection and the inequalities of courting mostly function as signs of her rebelliousness and of a social order turned on its head. Yet in these rants we may also detect the voices of disempowered women speaking through and in spite of Butler: the very oyster women Butler scorns and Milton celebrates for swelling crowds and presenting petitions. Seen through the eyes of Dissenters and unreconstructed radicals after the Restoration, the Widow's and Trulla's assertiveness can provide models for women to follow rather than avoid. It certainly anticipates the actions of Milton's Eve and Dalila. Hence, it could be argued that there is yet another displacement at work. Butler acknowledges women's yearnings for involvement in oaths and politics, but displaces them onto an allegory of the English church-state (the Widow) actively imposing oaths on men like Hudibras.

If the Widow is something like a Dalilan coercer of oaths (see chapter 4 below), Hudibras is the poem's Samson. The opening canto compares his long beard to Samson's alluringly long hair:

> Like *Sampson*'s Heart-breakers, it grew
> In time to make a nation rue . . .
> It was monastick, and did grow
> In holy Orders by strict vow;
> Of Rule as sullen and severe,
> As that of rigid *Cordeliere* . . .
> . . . 'twas to stand fast,
> As long as Monarchy should last.

But when the State should hap to reel,
'Twas to submit to fatal steel,
And fall, as it was consecrate,
A Sacrifice to fall of State. (1.1.251–72)

As several critics have pointed out, this vow to grow the beard until victory is attained, even though anticipated by Rabelais and Cervantes, also recalls the similar oaths of various Independents and Presbyterians, including one of Hudibras's models, the Presbyterian Sir Samuel Luke, who allegedly swore not to cut his beard until the king was defeated.[93]

This likening of Hudibras to a vow-taking Presbyterian Samson prepares us for another instance of the trope of Samson's cords. When Hudibras threatens in Book I to execute the fiddler Crowdero, Ralpho quickly reminds his master of his promise to adhere to the justice outlined in the military code of conduct:

For Words and promises that yoke
The Conqueror, are quickly broke,
Like *Sampson*'s Cuffs, though by his own
Direction and advice put on. (1.2.1091–4)[94]

"Cuffs" must be a fanciful way of referring to Samson's withes or ropes in Judges 16:7–12, which he clearly directs Delilah and the Philistines to put on him, and secondarily to the bands and cords of Judges 15:13–14, which he allows the men of Judah to put on his hands and arms.[95] Butler probably uses "Cuffs" rather than "cords," which as a monosyllable would not change the metre, because it helps establish the context of local legal processes in which Crowdero will be put in the village stocks (1.2.1150–2). Appropriately enough, Hudibras then orders Ralpho to give Crowdero (actually Crowdero's prosthetic leg!) a non-resistance oath akin to the Negative Oath Parliamentarians put to royalists, and once Ralpho has done so, he ties Crowdero up in cords and allows Hudibras to lead him to jail (1.2.1111–17). The connection between oaths and cords has been seeded by the previous reference to Hudibras's beard as kept unshorn by a "strict vow" like that of the "Cordeliers," an order of Franciscans who "wore a *Cord* full of knots" around their waists (1.1.258).[96] Only now it is Crowdero rather than Hudibras who has been bound by oaths and cords, almost literally oaths as cords. Butler here literalizes the metaphor of oaths-as-cords in order to poke fun at the Dissenters who so often employed it. As we will see, his account of oaths, cords, and women differs from Milton's in *Samson Agonistes* and *Paradise Lost*, which, in response to *Hudibras*, present a more thoroughgoing consideration of state oaths and women's political speech-acts. But before that, we examine *The Rehearsal Transpros'd* to see what Marvell learned from Butler's use of an Anglican persona in a polemic about state oaths.

# 2 Testing the Tests in *The Rehearsal Transpros'd*

Bishops even there rebel . . .
New Oaths 'tis necessary to invent.

– Marvell, *The Loyal Scot*

[I desire] that, during this King's reign, we may apply ourselves to preserve the people in the Protestant Religion, not only in the profession of it, but that men may live up to it, in morality and virtue of Religion, and then you establish men against the temptation of Popery, and a Prince that may be popishly affected. If we do not practise upon ourselves, all these Oaths and Tests are of no use; they are but Phantoms.

– Marvell, Speech to the House of Commons, 27 March 1677[1]

In *The Rehearsal Transpros'd* Marvell translated the verse and ethos of the Duke of Buckingham's farce *The Rehearsal* into prose, satirizing the persecutory clergyman Samuel Parker as the counterpart to Buckingham's Mr Bayes, himself a parody of Dryden. *The Rehearsal Transpros'd* competed with *Hudibras* for the prize of most popular Restoration text – so popular that the king himself deigned to read and champion both. In this satire Marvell characterized Butler's "Performance" in the poem as that of a "copious" wit applied to a "barren" theme – presumably persecution of Dissenters.[2] Yet in a response to *The Rehearsal Transpros'd*, the rabidly Anglican clergyman Edmund Hickeringill called Butler Marvell's friend.[3] There is truth to both of these statements. Even if Marvell was no actual friend of Butler, his printed work certainly owed a lot to him; and although Marvell would hardly have considered his own theme in *The Rehearsal* barren, it nevertheless exhibits a similarly drolling copiousness in ringing changes on one's theme.[4] By the 1650s Marvell already knew how to create personae via ventriloquism and parody, as the private lyrics and Fairfax poems demonstrate, and could venture further into the public sphere with anonymous Cromwellian panegyric. From Butler he learned how powerful these devices could become in widely printed, if still nominally anonymous, satire on religio-political subjects. Both men were probably clients of the Dissenter-friendly Buckingham at some point in their careers, and the advice-to-a-painter satires Marvell may have written at his behest display characteristics akin to those of *Hudibras*: the multi-genre Menippean humour that mocks the heroic and pastoral and seems open-ended, informal, breezily conversational;[5] the prosody that at times approaches the Hudibrastic, with its broken rhymes and crude diction; the sense of dirt and degradation; the misogyny.

But most of all, Marvell noticed how devastating a humorous Anglican persona could be. Somewhat visible in the painter poems, this device becomes the central strategy of *The Rehearsal Transpros'd*, where he employs a similar persona in a non-poetic medium and for entirely different purposes: to advocate toleration of Dissenters and to caution against the use of state oaths as instruments of intolerance. Where Butler employs a rustic Anglican gentleman as his animating persona or consciousness, Marvell makes his Anglican an urbane, tolerant coffeehouse wit. It was this cosmopolitan gentleman's banter that caught the public's attention and allowed a genial tolerance, as opposed to *Hudibras*'s genial intolerance, to work on its readers.[6] Lodged chronologically between these diametrically opposed uses of an Anglican persona for purposes of religious satire and interpellation lie Milton's reflections on state oaths in *Paradise Lost* and *Samson Agonistes*.

Marvell's experience with promissory oaths began early, and they provide concrete instances of his committing himself publicly to some proposition or doctrine, without the distancing of a masklike persona. A month before his eighteenth birthday in 1639, he subscribed support for the Book of Common Prayer, the Thirty-Nine Articles, and the royal supremacy in order to receive his Cambridge BA[7] Marvell had probably sworn support for the royal supremacy and the episcopal hierarchy at least once before – almost a year earlier, on 13 April 1638, when he took an oath for a scholarship at Trinity College.[8] If he harboured scruples about such oaths of allegiance and obedience, they emerged only later: perhaps in his flirtation with Catholicism in late 1639; perhaps in his falling afoul of the Trinity authorities and losing his MA scholarship in 1641; and perhaps most tellingly in his apparently false claim in

*The Rehearsal Transpros'd* that at Oxford in the early 1660s Samuel Parker had "shifted Colledges to Trinity [College, Oxford], and, when there, [gone] away without his Degree, *scrupling forsooth the subscription then required.*"[9] Since Parker actually did proceed to the MA at Trinity in July 1663, for which he must have taken the oaths, Marvell is likely projecting his own erstwhile qualms onto a younger alter-ego at another Trinity College.[10] As we shall see, something similar happens in his *Mr. Smirke* (1676), this time with the king as alter-ego.

Marvell took the Protestation in 1642 but was on the Continent at the time of the Solemn League and Covenant in 1643.[11] However much the *Horatian Ode* reflects upon the controversy surrounding the Commonwealth's oath of Engagement in 1650, we do not know whether he swore it, though it seems increasingly likely that he did, given his later service to Cromwell and his clients.[12] We do know, however, that he took oaths as an MP: the Oaths of Allegiance and Supremacy as well as the Test of 1673, to which he alludes in *The Rehearsal Transpros'd*.[13] In June 1678 he took a much lesser oath of office as Warden of the Deptford Trinity House.[14] By contrast, two of Marvell's relations, his nephew-by-marriage, Thomas More, and his brother-in-law, Edmond Popple, refused state oaths at some point in their careers (the Uniformity oaths in the first case and the Corporation Oath's abjuration of the Solemn League and Covenant in the second). His paternal grandfather had apparently moved to Yorkshire to avoid the Forced Loan of 1626–7, which, as *The Rehearsal Transpros'd* reminds us, sometimes involved resisters being forced to swear ex officio oaths to interrogators.[15]

This chapter will focus on the oaths that constitute an important but still neglected theme in that satire. Both instalments of *The Rehearsal Transpros'd* abound with apparently whimsical references to oaths big and small, promissory and assertory, which I only list here. Consider, for example, the pageboy's unpunished cussing; the wilfully misinterpreted phrase "Jernie Dieu"; the imagined oath by "God's Moral Accomplishments"; the "Dutch" oath of "Sacraments, Sacraments"; and the description of Parker's "conjúring" Marvell as friend – that is, appealing to him with an oath by their supposed friendship. Then there are the more consequential discussions of priests swearing curses and committing perjury; the forced renunciations of Christianity under Julian the Apostate; the surprisingly controversial subscriptions to the Thirty-Nine Articles under Elizabeth; the parody of the Engagement; the comparison of Parker's mock-Declaration of Indulgence to the Etcetera Oath of 1640; and, of course, the already mentioned ex officio oaths accompanying the Forced Loan.[16] These odd and seemingly tangential references to swearing increase almost fivefold in Part II and add cumulative weight to an argument that oaths are unreliable and invasive and that the king's Declaration of Indulgence should be superseded by a parliamentary toleration requiring as few of them as possible. Marvell did not wish to abolish all oaths, as Quakers wanted, just oaths that did not assume a separation of church and state. The only oaths he seems to have endorsed without reservation are the ones Independents such as John Owen supported: the Oaths of Allegiance and Supremacy, and at most a subscription to the doctrine in the Thirty-Nine Articles.[17]

Part I of *The Rehearsal Transpros'd* (late 1672) defended the Declaration. But in the previous six months fears had been expressed about its possible abuse of the royal prerogative: if Charles had granted indulgence to Catholics and Dissenters without Parliament's consent, could he not take it away again?[18] As a result Marvell had begun to consider or reconsider parliamentary alternatives. As a specimen of the advice-to-parliament genre, Part I supported the Declaration against parliamentary pressure to rescind it, but it also anticipated that any replacement legislation would have to involve existing oaths of office in some way, by revision or abolition. Part I's largely sceptical attitude towards test oaths that confound religion and politics, religious and civil loyalties, thus functioned as a suggestion that any new law should scale them back to a bare minimum: not much more than the Oaths of Allegiance and Supremacy. When Parliament finally convened in February 1673, one of its first actions was indeed to force Charles to cancel the Declaration. Two laws were proposed to supplant it – the Bill for Ease of Protestant Dissenters and the Test Bill – and both included loyalty oaths as requirements for holding public office. In the event only the latter passed, not only preserving the old oaths but adding a new one with more explicit anti-Catholic statements. Part II of *The Rehearsal*, composed after Parliament passed the Test, calls, among other things, for a second Ease Bill to replace the one that had come so close to passing – an Ease Bill that would make religious toleration less vulnerable to royal whim. While he admits to taking the required Test himself, Marvell seems to regard it as little more than an expression of civil loyalty to the king, like the Allegiance and Supremacy oaths, rather than a declaration of religious belief. Future legislation, he suggests, should steer clear of such "Oaths and Renunciations," such "tests and picklocks" of tender consciences.[19]

My argument will place *The Rehearsal Transpros'd* within the context of Marvell's final decade, approaching the text from two chronological directions. The first section moves backwards towards the text through his last five years and is followed by another that approaches the text through the previous decade: from the Restoration to the renewal of the toleration debate in 1667 to the Declaration of Indulgence in 1672. Both tracks then converge in a third section that reads *The Rehearsal Transpros'd* as a response to the politics of oaths in 1672–3. In the final section and subsequent chapter, the lessons learned there lead to speculations on the enigma of Marvell's religious views and a new reading of the *Horatian Ode* as promoting a tolerant "secularism" like that of the Engagement oath. The appendix suggests an emendation to a puzzling phrase in one of his letters from 1675: the odd reference to "A new popish Test for Book-Houses."[20]

**Oaths in Marvell's Final Years**

We examine Marvell's final works first because they directly address the fundamental issues in Restoration oath debates. Then, working backwards through the last half-decade of Marvell's life towards *The Rehearsal Transpros'd*, we highlight a consistent bias against state oaths, with the exception of those that assume a separation of church and state and prescribe nothing specific about religious doctrine and discipline. To begin with, his final work, the *Remarks upon a Late Ingenious Discourse* by Thomas Danson (1678), concurs with the Church of England's Thirty-Ninth Article in refusing the Anabaptist/Quaker argument that all oaths are forbidden by Matthew 5:34. Marvell contends that in this part of the Sermon on the Mount Christ only forbids "Prophane Cursing and Swearing."[21] In doing so, he employs the first part of a common Restoration defence of oaths: that Christ had only prohibited the assertory kind. Since state oaths were almost universally regarded as promissory – despite containing some assertory elements – this constitutes an oblique endorsement of at least the idea of state loyalty oaths and oaths of office, if not particular specimens of them. It says nothing, however, about the relationship between church and state.

For that we consult the previous year's *Account of the Growth of Popery and Arbitrary Government*, which provides the clearest evidence of opposition to the test oaths mentioned above. The *Account* concentrates on three oaths from the 1670s: the Earl of Danby's proposed non-resistance Test in 1675; the bishops' proposed anti-Catholic oath in 1677; and the only one of the three that actually became law – the anti-Catholic Test of 1673.[22] The latter required all holders of public office, from schoolmasters to MPs, to reject transubstantiation and thus Catholicism. The bishops' proposal in 1677 would have imposed a version of the 1673 Test on both themselves and any future monarch, most immediately the king's Catholic brother and heir, James, Duke of York. Danby's 1675 Test would have required all officeholders, including MPs, to abjure armed resistance to the king and his officials, as well as any attempt to alter "the Government either in Church or State," even in the smallest way.[23] Marvell's *Account* offers all three Tests as proof of a conspiracy to impose French-style absolutism on England.

In his scathing account of Danby's attempt to secure a more compliant parliament by means of this non-alteration and -resistance Test, Marvell compares oaths to ominous comets: "there is nothing more portentous, and of worse *Omen*, then when such an Oath hangs over a Nation, like a New *Comet* foreboding the Alteration of Religion, or Government."[24] Both this passage and the one on the Bishops' Bill attempt to dissuade Parliament from creating still more Tests, such as the one for MPs that passed a few months after Marvell's death (to be discussed shortly). Recent commentary on the Bishops' Bill passage has stressed its anticlerical nature; and anticlericalism and its complexities have of late become a potent tool for explaining away some of the seeming inconsistencies in Marvell's life and works.[25] But I would like to suggest that the bare transcription of the Bishops' Test Bill, as opposed to the extensive commentary on Danby's, speaks as much to the failure of oaths to do their job of prevention as it does to prelatical ambition and self-aggrandizement – a formidable power manifest in the clergy's censorship of books and in an atmosphere of repression that made speaking out against the bishops and their tests dangerous. In the absence of critical commentary from the *Account*'s author, the text of the bill must speak for itself.

Although the bill prescribed pro-Protestant, anti-Catholic test oaths for both bishops and monarch, one MP, William Sacheverell, described it as giving the king a Test oath – presumably in addition to or modification of the coronation oath – which he found anathema.[26] Marvell seemed to feel the same way in his notorious outburst against the bill in the House of Commons – the outburst that won him a metaphorical box on the ear from Speaker Seymour. In the speech that provides an epigraph for this chapter, he vents the fear that despite both king and bishops taking anti-Catholic oaths, the great loadstone (a newly crowned

Catholic James) will exert more power over the iron objects (the Protestant bishops) than vice versa and pursue his absolutist designs unchecked: "let these [the Bishops] come to the King to administer the Oath, 'Tis a pretty experiment, Just a tryal, whether the Loadstone will attract the Iron, or the Iron the Loadstone. Who can think that any body of men, that must depend upon the King, *&c*? Which way, think you, it draws?" In other words, to what extent could officeholders dependent, like the bishops, on the future king's favour hold him to account and force him to renounce his Catholicism? "All these Oaths and Tests are of no use," Marvell exclaimed, "they are but Phantoms."[27]

The original Test (1673) had confounded matters temporal and ecclesiastic just as much as the Bishops' Test. Hence, as part of a defence of civil and religious liberties, Marvell's *Account* charges that the Test Act of 1673 was a ruse on Parliament's part, designed to divert attention from its shameful capitulation to Charles II's sham need for money for a shameful and unnecessary war against the Dutch.[28] It was agreed to by Charles, under the influence of the unnamed but seemingly ubiquitous conspirators who form the ostensible target of the book, only because the king needed the money. The conspirators themselves only allowed it to pass because they hoped to reverse its anti-Catholic provisions at a later time.[29] As history, this makes little sense, but as propaganda it scores a number of hits.[30] For Marvell, not only was the Test conceived of and enacted for the wrong (i.e., mercenary) reasons; it was a failure on pragmatic grounds as well: it simply did not accomplish its stated goal of weeding out the popish and corrupt. As he points out, some Catholics, like the Irish Major General John Fitzgerald, perjured themselves by taking the Test and denying their Catholicism. Others continued to exercise their duties through puppet deputies who nominally held the offices.[31] But more important, Marvell claimed to find the Test distasteful because it forced many able and principled men out of office, many of them, paradoxically, Catholics whom, like the Duke of York, he now lauds for their refusal to lie under oath.[32] This praise of Catholics, seemingly counterintuitive in an attack on popery,[33] is part of a larger paean to those of principle and honesty, Protestant and Catholic, in Parliament and out, who refuse to become "men of *Arbitrary Principles*, that will *Bow the Knee to Baal*, in order to their Promotion to all Publick Commissions and Imployments" – in other words, to those who "honourably forsook their Places rather than their Consciences."[34]

Marvell's other writings from these years display a clear hostility to the unnecessary multiplication of oaths. *Mr. Smirke* and *A Short*

*Historical Essay Concerning General Councils, Creeds, and Impositions in Matters of Religion* (published together in 1676) provide evidence of anticlericalism that issues in opposition to oaths. According to these texts, clerics such as bishops often convene to formulate creeds they will soon impose on others, thereby using persecution as a tool for self-advancement. To impose extra-scriptural creeds is to require laypeople to subscribe or swear belief in such creeds on pain of excommunication or loss of office and preferment. So wide-ranging is his attack on creeds that it even strikes at the Thirty-Nine Articles, at first cast as more objectionable than the much simpler Apostles' Creed, to which people or priests could swear. But even that creed comes under suspicion eventually, especially in the *Essay*, and one begins to doubt whether Marvell would allow any oaths as conditions of membership in a mandatory state church, indeed any compulsory oaths about religion, period.

*Mr. Smirke* and the *Essay* on councils especially oppose the Uniformity Act and its oaths. Marvell attacks what the law allegedly caused: uninformed and at times equivocal "assent and consent" by an ignorant clergy to the Book of Common Prayer and the Thirty-Nine Articles. In *Mr. Smirke*, Marvell defends the moderate Anglican Herbert Croft's call for some measure of toleration against the animadversions of the high-flying Francis Turner. Marvell asserts that "all sober men cannot but give their Assent and Consent to" Bishop Croft's book "unasked" – in other words, without a law forcing them to do so, as the Act of Uniformity had ministers to subscribe (or "Assent and Consent" in the Act's own words) to the Book of Common Prayer and Thirty-Nine Articles.[35] Some pages later he casts doubt on Turner's contention that the Act was "glorious" by saying that it was "all of a piece" with the Licensing and Conventicles Acts, both of which Marvell opposed in the Miltonic discussion of censorship that opens *The Rehearsal Transpros'd*.[36]

In the *Essay* Marvell draws an explicit connection between modern Test oaths and the creeds that self-aggrandizing bishops use as "meer Instruments of Equivocation or Persecution":

> By this means every Creed was grown up to a Test, and under that pretence, the dextrous Bishops step by step hooked within their Verge all the business and Power that could be catched in those Turbulences, where they mudled the water and fished after. By this means they stalked on first to a spiritual kind of Dominion, and from that incroached upon and into the Civil Jurisdiction.[37]

While ostensibly discussing early Christian councils and bishops, Marvell intends the remarks to apply to Restoration Tests, specifically those of 1673 and 1675. Only the bishops, he claims, benefit from persecuting Dissenters. Creeds are "Instruments of Equivocation" as well as persecution because ministers often swear approval of them either in ignorance of their meaning (they are often worded ambiguously) or with a kind of mental reservation that alters it. In the peroration of the *Essay*, after advising the bishops to "inspect the Morals of the Clergy" because "the Moral Hereticks [among them] do the Church more harm, than all the Non-conformists can do, or can wish it," Marvell requests that "before [the bishops] admit men to subscribe the Thirty Nine Articles for a Benefice, they try whether they know the meaning."[38] "They" probably refers to both the candidates and the bishops themselves. Likewise, the bishops should not ask ministers to swear their "Assent and Consent" to an edition of the Prayer Book they have not seen, as they did in 1662.[39]

All of this helps explain the odd passage in *Mr. Smirke* where Marvell pretends that Charles II took a university degree without subscribing any oaths.[40] Charles had clearly never earned a university degree and thus never taken the Uniformity oaths and the Oaths of Allegiance and Supremacy that it entailed – which, in any case, would have been oaths to himself, perhaps not unlike God's oath to himself in *Paradise Lost*.[41] Why, then, does Marvell make such an absurd claim? First, as hinted earlier, it may allow him to express a wish that he himself had taken his own degree from Cambridge without swearing oaths. Second, it is part of an attack on Danby's proposed Test oath, which figures prominently in the *Account of the Growth of Popery and Arbitrary Government*, as we have seen. Third, it contributes to an attack on the existing Uniformity oaths. *Mr. Smirke* extols Croft for being "a true Subscriber" to the Thirty-Nine Articles "without that Latitude of Equivocation which some others use." Marvell thereby casts suspicion on this swearing by returning to the charge that ministers equivocate when they approve of the Articles.[42]

Even more to the point, Marvell burlesques Turner's claim that the Church of England "*admits the many* [or laypeople] *in thousands and hundred thousands, without any Subscription*, ad Communionem Laicam,"[43] which implies that lay Nonconformists should not be concerned about test oaths because they are only imposed on clergy. On the contrary, Marvell suggests, many laypeople do take such oaths, including all university graduates and schoolteachers.[44] To the list of subscriptions he might have added the very similar religious oaths of office demanded of the laity by the Vestry Act, as well as the civil oaths under the Corporation and Militia Acts.[45] To include the king within the number of those who supposedly do not have to take religious oaths, but really do, merely extends the absurdity of Turner's claim. While the king had not graduated from the university, he had taken a set of coronation oaths, a kind of oath of office that promised, like the university oaths, to uphold the Church's episcopal hierarchy.[46]

To call attention to the fact that the king did not have to undergo the same oaths of office his government was forcing on others in 1676 may be an oblique way of asking the following questions: how true has Charles been to his own oaths of office as king? how well has he preserved the Church, as well as the religious and civil liberties of his subjects? does persecution of religious and political minorities accomplish any of these goals? Whatever the case, Marvell's own patently false claim about Charles taking a university degree without oath is itself a kind of untrustworthy oath, just as false as the claims that equivocating ministers make about church doctrine and discipline and that ignorant ministers make about books they have not seen and articles they do not understand.[47]

Doubt about religious tests also informs Marvell's last half-decade of letters. They assiduously note the various proposals for new Tests in the mid-1670s, of which there were at least six, including the bill that would become law soon after his death in 1678. See the appendix below, which argues for emending a passage about test oaths in one of Marvell's letters to William Popple in summer 1675, where the phrase "Both-houses" (as in both Houses of Parliament) has probably been mistranscribed in modern editions as "Book-houses." As the appendix demonstrates, that letter's summary of the first session of Parliament in 1675 has nothing good to say about test oaths – or rather religious test oaths. The proposed anti-bribery test mentioned in a letter of 18 June 1678[48] seems to chime with his interest in bills to rid Parliament, or curb the influence, of bribed placemen, which this test would seem to do; and it does not concern religion at all. Just about the only oaths Marvell seems to support are the Oaths of Allegiance and Supremacy, which, as we have seen, were integral to the naturalization process. There is nothing in the Oath of Allegiance strictly about religious doctrine; it only asks the subscriber to acknowledge the king's temporal supremacy and reject the pope's power to depose him, directly or indirectly.[49] The Oath of Supremacy likewise says little about religious doctrine, ritual, or church organization, other than to note that the king sits atop the religious hierarchy.[50] Both of these oaths, then, while glancing at the pope and at the king's religious supremacy, could be considered essentially civil oaths, designed to prevent disturbances of the peace and rebellion. As Sir Thomas Meres put it in a report to the Commons on the 1673 Ease Bill, "the Oaths of Allegiance and Supremacy . . . are the *civil* Obligations of the Subjects of England to their King."[51]

I will argue shortly that *The Rehearsal Transpros'd* provides evidence that Marvell only accepted the 1673 Test insofar as it underlines this civil allegiance to state and king. Here it is important to emphasize that the Oaths of Allegiance and Supremacy seem to be just about the only ones about which Marvell has nothing bad to say. As we have noted, he took them several times himself as student and MP. After the Great Fire of London, when he sat on a committee to inquire into its causes in late 1666, he wrote to the Hull Corporation that these oaths should be tendered to all officers, including military ones, in order to protect against the Catholics many suspected of setting the Fire. Because, according to Marvell, "Many informations are daily brought in to the two Committees about the Fire of London and the insolence of Papists," "all officers civill or military not taking the oaths of allegeance & supremacy within 20 days [are to] be displaced" and "all Papists or suspected papists, who refuse to take those oaths [are to] be disarmd."[52] Moreover, his work on a committee for naturalization of foreigners suggests that he did not object to the Oaths of Allegiance and Supremacy as minimum qualifications for becoming a British subject.[53] As we shall see, the discussion of the 1673 Test in *The Rehearsal Transpros'd* essentially renders it equivalent to the Oaths of Allegiance and Supremacy. The next section establishes the urgency of oaths as an issue before 1673.

## The Decade Before: Oaths, the Restoration, and the Toleration Debate

In the runup to *The Rehearsal Transpros'd*, the debate about toleration, both early and late, included a debate about oaths. As we noted in the introduction and chapter 1, in the early years of the Restoration there was fierce controversy over the shape of the restored Church of England – a battle the Presbyterians lost, thereby failing to implement the provisions of their beloved Solemn League and Covenant. It was the Clarendon Code that drew Marvell's charge that the Restoration had given birth to a "Superfoetation of Acts" against Nonconformists.[54] Oaths had become penal: no longer means of ensuring loyalty, but instruments of persecution, as Marvell would argue in the *Essay* on councils.

Various letters indicate that Marvell may have sympathized with his brother-in-law Edmond Popple's principled refusal of the Corporation Oath's renunciation of the Covenant, and with his nephew Thomas More's refusal of the Uniformity oaths. Scattered remarks in his letters on both of these laws anticipate his views on the subject in *The Rehearsal Transpros'd*. We do not know whether Marvell voted for the Corporation Act, although that seems doubtful. A letter of June 1661 contains his report that one version of the Corporation Bill would have allowed the king to "place & displace whatsoever magistrates in Corporations for these three years next insuing." Given Marvell's reservations about royal absolutism from at least 1670 onwards, this provision of the law is unlikely to have been welcome ten years earlier.[55] In another letter from the same month (27 June 1661), Marvell described the process of selecting commissioners to carry out the Corporation Act's provisions in Hull as "an unpleasing businesse. I would we were well over it or of it" – which strongly suggests opposition to the Act as a whole.[56] Moreover, December 1669 saw Marvell as teller for a vote to allow the election of the friend of Dissent, Sir Francis Rolle, as MP for Bridgewater, despite the fact that, as Nicholas von Maltzahn puts it, "too many of his voters proved to have been disqualified under the Corporation Act."[57] Marvell does not seem to have felt that failure or refusal to take the required oaths in this case should prevent people from sitting on the corporate bench and voting for an MP. The cumulative evidence of all these incidents suggests animus towards the Corporation oaths.[58]

A letter from 1677 also indicates antagonism towards the Act of Uniformity and its oaths. In November of that year he wrote Sir Edward Harley with apparent regret that the Nonconformist hotbed of "Taunton is forced to be a corporation," with "Bishop [Peter] Mew[s] and [the] Earle of Rochester [as] two of the Aldermen."[59] In other words, the Crown had restored government by corporation in Taunton so as to remove Dissenters from positions of influence, Dissenters being barred from corporations by the eponymous Act. Bishop Mews, notes Marvell's letter, immediately set about examining an ejected minister, George Newton, as to why he had refused his oath of "Assent and Consent" to the Book of Common Prayer in 1662 under the Act of Uniformity, which required additional oaths similar to those of the Corporation Act. "Why could he not conforme [to the Church of England] now [after

1662] as well as then [before the Civil War]?" asked the bishop. An insolently punning answer from Newton apparently failed to satisfy.[60] Spoken to here and in the Popple incident is a hostility on Marvell's part to the Centre's interfering with the localities and thus to religious oaths as instruments of that interference.

The struggle over oaths was, as hinted above, really a struggle over religious toleration. In effect, to persecute is to require oaths; to tolerate is to do without them. So when the pressure of continuing conventicles and the disasters of plague, fire, and war brought the toleration issue to the fore once again in 1667, oaths played a prominent role. Marvell's letters to the Hull Corporation in 1668 and 1670 provide just one index of the fact that advocates of both comprehension of Dissenters within the state church and toleration of them outside it pleaded for the abrogation or revision of the existing oaths of office for ministers and laypeople: either abolish them entirely and simply require the Oaths of Allegiance and Supremacy or revise them by omitting the Declaration against the Covenant, the oath "assenting and consenting" to the Book of Common Prayer and episcopacy, the non-alteration and -resistance clauses, or some combination of the three.[61] High-flying opponents of toleration, such as Marvell's nemesis, Samuel Parker, resisted these calls for reform and defended the existing oaths. They insisted that Nonconformists produce evidence of their unwillingness to pull the nation back into Civil War: a clear and public sign of their loyalty to monarch, monarchy, and Church; a public recantation of their past crimes in the 1640s and 1650s; and a promise of future good behaviour. All of these lay ready to hand in the non-resistance and anti-Covenant provisions of the oaths of office already required by the Clarendon Code, especially the Uniformity and Corporation Acts.

While unsuccessful toleration proposals were an almost perennial feature of Parliament's meetings from 1660 until the passage of the Toleration Act of 1689 (with its considerably relaxed oath requirements),[62] something changed in 1667. Samuel Parker argued that the catalyst was the burning of the Royal Navy by the Dutch at Chatham in June of that year.[63] Whatever the case, the number of books and parliamentary bills in support of religious toleration shot up in the wake of the Chatham debacle, and Marvell began writing his most famous poetic satires, the *Last Instructions to a Painter* chief among them.[64] People wanted to blame someone for the blows dealt to England by plague, fire, and war; and one frequent answer to the question of why God was punishing the nation for these things was that it had persecuted religious minorities.[65]

Not surprisingly, Marvell wrote in one of his letters from this year that this was the best time to press for religious reforms.[66]

The Presbyterian John Humfrey initiated the latest round of the toleration debate[67] within days of Chatham, advising Parliament to pass legislation to comprehend sober, peaceable Nonconformists, mostly Presbyterian, within a broader Church of England by removing some of the ceremonies and aspects of church government to which they objected, including test oaths, which he likened to Samson's cords.[68] He was soon opposed by Thomas Tomkins, Richard Perrinchief, and Simon Patrick – all associated, like Parker, with Gilbert Sheldon, Archbishop of Canterbury. Sheldon's group of hired pens pressed the case to retain all the existing hierarchy and ceremonies, however indifferent in themselves, including the ceremony of oath-taking.[69] The Independents John Owen and Sir Charles Wolseley joined Presbyterians like John Corbet, John Norton, Samuel Rolls, and Richard Baxter in defending both toleration and Humfrey, who spoke up again in 1669.[70] They claimed that ceremonies such as kneeling at communion, making the cross in baptism, and wearing the surplice were not things indifferent under the control of the magistrate but in fact things unnecessary because not commanded by God and thus should be abolished as repugnant to tender consciences. They also opposed the Clarendon Oaths – the most recent of which had arrived in the Five Mile Act of 1665 – which the toleration proposals of 1667–8 sought to repeal or revise.[71] In fact, a number of people on both sides of the toleration debate argued that oaths were the sticking point for most of the Nonconformist ministers ejected in 1662 for failing to subscribe Uniformity. These oaths, they claimed, loomed larger in their minds than the other ceremonies, and removing them would remove much of the barrier to their conforming. They found the Uniformity Oath's renunciation of the Covenant especially repugnant.[72]

All these books, along with Milton's *Paradise Lost* (1667) and Parker's *Ecclesiastical Politie* (1670), were likely timed to influence legislative efforts to ease the lot of Dissenters by comprehension or indulgence.[73] In 1668, Marvell's letters to Hull noted the Commons' short-lived inclination to repeal two of the Uniformity oaths: the "assent and consent" clause and the abjuration of the Covenant.[74] If the *Essay* on councils, with its hostility to creeds imposed through oaths, was written around this time, 1668–9, as von Maltzahn has suggested, Marvell may have also envisaged its contributing to the legislative push for toleration.[75] At the time of the debate over the Second Conventicles Act in 1670,

Marvell reported "a strong motion" in the Commons "for an Act to take away oaths imposd since his Ma$^{tys}$ coming in," a motion that initially "seemd to gaine good footing." But when another MP "inlarg[ed] the motion toward a generall toleration[,] after an houres debate it fell of[f] & the house went to their other businesse."[76] In the event the Conventicles Act passed, and in its wake the debate over toleration and oaths continued.

When the various proposals for comprehension and toleration emanating from Charles II's Cabal ministers and elsewhere failed, the king's Declaration of Indulgence for Dissenters in March 1672 attempted to accomplish what Parliament could not. Frank Bate's work on the Declaration reminds us that it circumvented the issue of oaths altogether by licensing Nonconformist preaching without the Uniformity subscriptions,[77] in effect enacting a solution more radical than those envisioned by many Nonconformists, who might have accepted oaths that did not include a renunciation of the Covenant. When an uneasy Parliament tried to place the Indulgence on a more solid constitutional footing that would confine it to Protestant Dissenters alone,[78] the two proposals, first the Ease Bill and then the Test Bill, featured oaths prominently. The former would have reduced the Uniformity oaths to a mere repetition of the Oaths of Allegiance and Supremacy accompanied by a subscription to the Thirty-Nine Articles, without further reference to the Book of Common Prayer and the episcopal hierarchy. Only those who had actually sworn the Covenant would have to abjure it.[79] The Test Bill's oath against transubstantiation (and thus Catholicism), which emerged as a stand-alone item distinctly after the Ease Bill, was probably conceived as the second part of a single initiative to replace the royal indulgence with a parliamentary one that excluded Catholics.[80] In the end, while the Test Bill passed fairly quickly, the Ease Bill failed, in large part because Charles adjourned Parliament just as the two Houses were ironing out their differences over the bill.[81] Among the sticking points were the three sets of oaths mentioned above: the Oaths of Allegiance and Supremacy; the abjuration of the Covenant; and the subscription to the Thirty-Nine Articles.[82] The result was a return to the intolerant status quo, enforced by the unrevised – in fact, strengthened – Clarendon Oaths.

Samuel Parker's tediously bullying responses to the demands for toleration denied the authority of the individual conscience in not complying with oaths and other ceremonies the Church of England deemed indifferent, despite what he regarded as Nonconformists' feeble protestation that these things were not indifferent but unnecessary and unlawful.[83] In the last three of his contributions to the debate, from 1671 to 1673, Parker tirelessly repeated his call for Nonconformists to confess publicly that they had sinned during the Civil War and Interregnum, to renounce their past crimes, and to promise better behaviour in the future.[84] In his answer to Marvell's *Rehearsal*, the *Reproof to the Rehearsal Transprosed* (1673), Parker insisted that Nonconformists "ask forgiveness" and "give . . . Assurance of their future Allegiance," presumably in (renewed) Oaths of Allegiance and Supremacy that would cancel out their subscription to the Solemn League and Covenant.[85] Indeed, the *Defence and Continuation of the Ecclesiastical Politie* (1671) demanded that Dissenters "give us some competent Tokens of your Repentance" for regicide and rebellion "*before* you presume to tender us any Security of your Allegiance." Otherwise, "what signs have you given us of your having renounced this Principle of Rebellion? And till you have, what assurance can you give us of your Return to Loyalty; seeing 'tis not possible for any Oaths to bind you to your Duty."[86] In other words, the Oaths of Allegiance and Supremacy were not enough: Dissenters must also take the Clarendon subscriptions, with their abjurations of the Covenant. Moreover, since Parker did not specify a context of being sworn into public office, he seemed to call for the Clarendon Oaths to be made universal, for all adult males at least, as the parliamentary oaths of the 1640s had been.[87] Yet even this seemed insufficient, since Parker's *Defence* included a draft of a two-page confession of contrition and loyalty for all Dissenters to make to the king.[88]

I will discuss Marvell's response to such bullying below, but for now suffice it to say that many of the hostile replies to the first part of *The Rehearsal Transpros'd* shared and magnified Parker's support for loyalty oaths.[89] Parker had used the *Reproof*'s discussion of Nonconformists' so-called disloyalty in refusing to swear allegiance to the king and to renounce past crimes like the Solemn League and Covenant as a way of hitting at Marvell's own supposed disloyalty.[90] After all, Marvell had an embarrassing past as Secretary for Foreign Tongues to Cromwell. Parker's fellow critics, whom Marvell dubbed his "posse Archidiaconatus" to emphasize the similarity of their arguments to Parker's and thus to allege that Parker had authored, co-authored, or directed all six of them,[91] also questioned Marvell's loyalty. The anonymous *Common-Place-Book out of The Rehearsal Transpros'd* attacked Marvell's "want of due Loyal[t]y" and suggested that he was "sure to be excluded from many places...of imployment in the Commonwealth ... for refusing to" swear the clause common to all the Clarendon Oaths: *"that it is not lawful upon any cause whatsoever . . . to take up Arms against the King."*[92] Edmund Hickeringill attacked both Marvell and Nonconformists for disloyalty in taking the Covenant and refusing to forswear it to assume civil or religious office. The only matter on which "we will believe him without swearing," Hickeringill added, is that he continues to support Nonconformists and the Good Old Cause.[93] Likewise, responding to the Nonconformist plea that their tender consciences would not allow them to participate in unlawful and imposed ceremonies, including the ceremony of oath-taking – a plea Marvell supported – Samuel Butler charged in *The Transproser Rehears'd* that according to *The Rehearsal Transpros'd*, subjects owe allegiance only to King Conscience rather than King Charles: "To this, all must swear Allegiance and Supremacy, and those that are Loyal to Conscience, may lawfully be Traytors to their Soveraign."[94]

## Opposition to the Uniformity Oaths in Part I of *The Rehearsal Transpros'd*

Recent criticism has failed to acknowledge just how important oaths are to the mission of *The Rehearsal Transpros'd*. Pierre Legouis and others have misread Marvell's one explicit remark on the Test Act in Part II (that he has "come not long since from swearing religiously to own that Supremacy") and thus missed the force of his many other, apparently whimsical allusions to oaths,[95] a force certainly visible to his first critics. It is not the case that when he published Part I "In the autumn of 1672," Marvell "probably could not foresee the Test Act," as John Wallace argued.[96] Oaths were likely to have been very much on Marvell's mind in late 1672, given the many discussions of them in the toleration debate, in which the responses to Part I participated. While Wallace is right to say that Marvell "may have had in mind something like the Bill of Ease for the dissenters that made headway in Parliament before prorogation cut it short" in March 1673,[97] he ignores the fact that any attempt to ease the lot of Protestant Dissenters – by toleration, comprehension, or both – would necessarily have involved the revision or abrogation of test oaths. To "ease" almost certainly meant to revise or relax oaths, and a new Test had been proposed as recently as the previous session of Parliament in 1671, which had considered it as part of "An Act to prevent the Growth of Popery."[98] During the session of spring 1673 both Humfrey and Baxter made revision and abolition of oaths central to their proposals for easing the lot of Protestant Dissenters.[99]

When Parker attacked the Declaration of Indulgence in his preface to Bishop Bramhall's writings in 1672, Marvell rose to defend it, and, I would suggest, to argue against any reimposition of oaths as tests for office. Why else would he complain in *The Loyal Scot* about the bishops inventing new oaths to exclude Dissenters from public office, oaths they wanted Parliament to pass? Probably written between 1667 and 1673, this poem shares *The Rehearsal Transpros'd*'s concerns about clergy imposing new forms of persecution on Nonconformists and provides an epigraph for this chapter: "Bishops even there [in Hell] rebel . . . New Oaths 'tis necessary to invent."[100] I will claim, in fact, that in the first part of *The Rehearsal Transpros'd* (1672) Marvell anticipated the upcoming bills for a Test and for the Ease of Protestant Dissenters, appealing to a broad audience to stop the former and support a version of the latter containing as few oaths as possible. Part II, written within months of the Test's passage and the Ease Bill's failure, responds to both the Test Act of 1673 and his critics' discussion of loyalty oaths and his own loyalty, performing the tightrope act of opposing the Test by innuendo, even as it admits that Marvell took the Test himself.

Given the politics of oaths in 1672–3, we turn to four episodes from Part I of *The Rehearsal Transpros'd* (late 1672) that attack the Uniformity Act and its subscriptions. Marvell opposes both the Act's provisions (including the oaths of office) and its effects (principally the "outing" or resignation of many ministers in August 1662). According to Marvell, these Nonconformist ministers were and continued to be loyal to king and kingdom, even if they could not swallow oaths approving the new Book of Common Prayer in its entirety and abjuring the Solemn League and Covenant, to which many of them, especially Presbyterians, remained committed, if only in spirit.

The nub of Parker's attack on Nonconformity in the *Discourse of Ecclesiastical Politie* had been that the plea of tender conscience does not exempt Dissenters from participating in indifferent ceremonies, among which he numbered oaths. It was possible, he claimed, to object to a rite in the privacy of one's mind but to comply externally. Parker's oxymoron "public conscience" nicely encapsulates his argument's contradictions.[101] On the one hand, Dissenters can think what they want about a ceremony, regarding it as necessary or indifferent as they wish, but they must comply with it in body if not in mind. On the other hand, they must agree that the ceremony is a thing indifferent and thus subject to the state's control, and still they must comply. Hence, in the matter of religious discipline, if not doctrine, Nonconformists had to make their normally private consciences a "public conscience," or, differently put, make their private consciences conform to the single "public conscience," and an Anglican conscience at that.[102]

In the first of our episodes from *The Rehearsal*, Marvell responds that this position does not, as Parker/Bayes claims, leave subjects free to think their own thoughts while complying with external rites and ceremonies:

> if the freedom of thoughts be in not lying open to discovery, there have been wayes of compelling men to discover them; or, if the freedom consist in retaining their judgments when so manifested, that also hath been made penal. And I doubt not but besides *Oaths* and *Renunciations*, and *Assents* and *Consents*, Mr. Bayes, if *he* were searched, hath twenty other tests and picklocks in his pocket.[103]

There are many astute points here. First, oaths invade subjects' privacy by compelling them both to admit their thoughts, which could be subject to penal legislation, and to change their thoughts if found wanting by the examiner. Parker had finessed this distinction, and Marvell calls him on it. Second, if oaths try to coerce people into changing their minds, they may fail, and if subjects are still forced to swear them, they are being coerced into perjury, attesting to one thing under oath while thinking another; and perjury could send them to Hell. Third, the italicized phrases "*Oaths* and *Renunciations* . . . *Assents* and *Consents*" make it clear that Marvell quotes from the Uniformity Act in particular, even though his point applies to nearly all state oaths, especially those involving religion. The Act required ministers to swear the following: "I A.B. do hereby declare my unfeigned Assent and Consent to all and every thing Contained and prescribed in and by the Book, Intituled, The Book of Common Prayer and Administration of the Sacraments and other rights [i.e., rites] and Ceremonies of the Church" – with "A.B." functioning as a blank space for the specific oath-taker's name. Ministers also had to promise to "conform to the Liturgy of the Church of *England* as it is now by Law Established" and renounce both resistance to the king and his officers, on the one hand, and the Solemn League and Covenant and its obligations on the other.[104]

Marvell's genius lies in casting the subject's thoughts, opinions, and conscience as personal property, not subject in an ideal world to theft or to what amounts to the same thing: search-and-seizure. He places Parker in several radically different positions: that of thief caught in the act and examined by the authorities; that of the examining authorities themselves, cast as little different from the thief; and finally, that of propertied subject being examined by the authorities. By implication, Parker would resist such search-and-seizure as much as the ministers forced to subscribe these oaths or leave the Church. While they have committed no crime in Marvell's eyes, Parker has, and his property, his tools for picking the locks of men's consciences (their right to remain silent and keep thoughts to themselves), consist of "test" oaths. The authorities would be more than justified in seizing these tools and clapping him in jail. If they were not thieves of conscience themselves, the authorities would confiscate the "twenty other tests and picklocks in [Parker's] pocket" – that is, new oaths, above and beyond the Clarendon subscriptions. We shall return to Marvell's choice of the word "test."

A less oblique attack on the Act of Uniformity comes after Marvell's famous discussion of the Civil War, whose causes he identifies as, among other things, persecuting clergymen and their allies in Parliament. These same men have continued to persecute Dissenters after the Restoration. Why?

> To show that they were Men like others, even cunning Men, revengeful Men, they drill'd things on, till they might procure a Law, wherein besides all the Conformity that had been of former-times enacted, there might be some new Conditions imposed on those that should have, or hold any Church-Livings, such as they assur'd themselves, that rather than swallow, the Nonconformists would disgorge all their Benefices. And accordingly it succeeded; several thousands of those Ministers being upon one memorable day outed of their subsistence.[105]

The law is, of course, the Act of Uniformity, which, on St Bartholomew's Day, 24 August 1662 (soon dubbed Black Bartholomew), "outed" almost 2000 ministers who refused to "swallow" the newly imposed oaths to keep their benefices. Marvell adverts to these deprived or silenced ministers in *The Rehearsal Transpros'd*'s discussion of "Persecution recommended": Parker's fifth argument. There Marvell accuses him of keeping "a List of the Fanatick Ministers, whom he reckons to be but about an hundred *Systematical Divines*: though I believe the Bartlemew-Register or the March-Licenses would make them about a hundred and three or a hundred and four or so."[106] The quibble over numbers is, in fact, a kind of meiosis, for Marvell means to imply that the numbers were much higher than "an hundred and four or so," despite the many attempts of Parker and his fellow opponents of toleration to drive a wedge between Nonconformist clergy and laity by downplaying the numbers to make it look as if a very small cadre of Nonconformist ministers were using conventicles to entrap the unsuspecting masses into rebellion.[107] Nevertheless, the larger point in this passage is that any such listing and numbering of Nonconformist ministers constitutes yet another instrument of persecution under the Uniformity Act.

In the third episode from Part I, Marvell's suspicions about the Uniformity oaths morph into a defence of his own and Nonconformists' loyalty against the nasty charges of Parker and his posse.[108] Written sometime between June and November 1672 – and thus before Parliament resumed in February – the first part of *The Rehearsal* nicely summarizes the charge of disloyalty levelled against Nonconformists and himself in Parker's last three books: "Bayes . . . summons-in all the World, and *preacheth* up only this *Repentance*: and so frequently in his Books he calls for *Testimonies, Signal Marks, Public Acknowledgements, Satisfaction, Recantantion*, and I know not what."[109] In a kind of contrapasso, Marvell turns Parker into the Nonconformist minister exacting confessions and signs of godliness from his followers, thereby making "the *process of Loyalty* more difficult than that of *Salvation*." "What *Signal Marks*," Marvell asks, "what *Testimonies* would he have of this Conversion?"[110] In order to convert to Anglican loyalism, not only must one publicly renounce such "sins" as Nonconformity and supporting Parliament in the Civil War, but one must present a compelling spiritual autobiography, replete with evidence of conversion and justification at every step – which sounds suspiciously Puritan.

However, Marvell takes the analogy with Puritan practice a step further by leaving the meeting house and comparing Parker to a conventicling preacher. When he later exposes the absurdity of Parker's implicit claim that the king's authority trumps Christ's, Marvell warns that "no man that is sober" should accept it, "lest som Justice of Peace should make him pay his five shillings."[111] Five shillings was both the price to buy Parker's *Reproof* and, as Marvell himself noted in a letter to the mayor of Hull of 8 December 1670, the penalty under the Second Conventicles Act (February 1670) for laypeople caught for the first time at a conventicle.[112] In other words, Parker entices readers into his brand of persecution in the same way Dissenting preachers lure people to conventicles. By contrast, Marvell considers it "highly penal for any man [such as Parker] to impose other conditions upon his Majesties good Subjects than the King expects, or the Law requires" – conditions such as public recantation of one's supposedly disloyal past as Commonwealthsman or Dissenter. He continues, "When you have done all" that the king and law require – such as swearing the oaths of Allegiance and Supremacy, for example, and perhaps even the Uniformity oaths – "you must yet appear before Mr. Bayes his Tribunal, and he hath a new Test yet to put you to."[113] For those reading the sentence in late 1672 – early 1673, "new Test" would not only have recalled Parker's demand for what Marvell called *"Testimonies . . . Public Acknowledgements . . . Recantantion*, and I know not what" but have anticipated the new oaths sure to be considered in the parliamentary session only weeks away.[114] The message would have been clear: do not pick the locks of Dissenting consciences with yet another Test.

A way of trying to prevent the anticipated Test or Tests was to suggest alternatives, to demonstrate that loyalty could be expressed in ways other than oaths and that Nonconformists had already done so. In the earlier round of the toleration debate all sides had suggested alternatives to existing oaths. Some had argued for the replacement of the Clarendon Oaths by the Oaths of Allegiance and Supremacy, with one Catholic writer essentially asking to omit the latter's rejection of the pope's authority.[115] Others had advocated keeping the Clarendon Oaths but omitting the abjuration of the Covenant.[116] Some proposals involved cutting down the Uniformity oaths even further, leaving just the subscription to the Thirty-Nine Articles.[117] Others urged oaths that merely approved of doctrine (left unspecified) that other Reformed churches considered necessary, rather than of discipline in things indifferent.[118] Still others called for individual ministers to be allowed to reword the oaths as needed to make them palatable.[119] It was also possible to substitute a poem for formal oaths of loyalty and obedience. The Presbyterian Robert Wild, for example, responded to the Five Mile Act of 1665's new oath for Nonconformist ministers (which included a non-alteration clause that provided a model for Danby's Test, as Marvell points out in the *Account*) by writing a broadside that reads roughly like an oath in verse form: *The Loyal Nonconformist* (1666).[120] Trumping all of the above were proposals to do away with not just these state oaths but all oaths.[121] Parker's proposed confession of sin for Nonconformists clearly aimed to supplement, not replace, all existing oaths, especially the Uniformity Act's abjuration of the Covenant.[122]

We must view Marvell's discussions of alternate ways of expressing loyalty in light of these proposals. If a poem will do, why not a loan? In our fourth episode from Part I of *The Rehearsal Transpros'd*, he clearly rejects the notion that the best way to display loyalty to king and Church is to persecute Nonconformists, especially with oaths and with books like Parker's that advocate additional forms of persecution.[123] If there must be "evident & unquestionable tokens of Loyalty from the Nonconformists," they do not have to be oaths.[124] As the Yale editors note, the larger statement from which this quotation comes – "I believe Mr. Bayes knows that his Majesty hath received such evident & unquestionable tokens of Loyalty from the Nonconformists" – probably refers to the London Nonconformists' loan of £40,000 to Charles II in 1670.[125] As a later section shows, this voluntary loan involved no oaths of any kind. In that section Marvell attempts to refute Parker's argument that clergymen should play a role in politics, especially as royal spokesmen and advisers, by placing the Forced Loan of 1626–7 within the context of what he regards as the bad clerical advice that led to the Civil War. Not only were the Forced Loan and the imprisonment of the Five Knights who refused it unconstitutional, but the clergymen, such as Robert Sibthorpe and Roger Mainwaring, who preached that subjects should display loyalty to the king by lending him money against their wills, seemed almost as harmful.[126]

As indicated earlier, Marvell's grandfather had refused the Forced Loan, perhaps because of its oaths; and it is telling that Marvell's account of the Loan makes sure to mention both clergy and oaths. Archbishop Abbot, one of the few exceptions to his animus against clergy in this episode, and soon to be replaced by Laud, had refused to license Sibthorpe's sermon in favour of the Loan after he had read the instructions for collecting the Loan's money:

> Then the Arch-Bishop takes notice of the *instructions for that Loan*. "Those that refused, to be sent for Souldiers to the King of Denmark. Oaths to be administered with whom they had conference; and who disswaded them, such persons to be sent to prison &c."[127]

Refusers of the Loan were to be imprisoned or impressed, and ex officio oaths, essentially forced confessions under forced oaths – the object of much Puritan obloquy at that point and into the next decade – were the instruments by which other refusers and agitators were to be discovered. Marvell's summary of the instructions for the Loan slightly downplays details of it other than the oaths. His choice to quote what is, in fact, Abbot's own account in Rushworth of the instructions allows Marvell both to detail the cruelty of the measures designed to enforce it, which anticipates his later statement that "the whole kingdom was turned into a Prison, upon occasion of this Ecclesiastical Loan," and to reproduce the crises of conscience undergone by those receiving tyrannical orders.[128] Moreover, Marvell's somewhat selective quotation makes the issue of oaths more prominent than in the original, where scriptural and geographical analogies dwell more prominently on the issue of the punishments rather than the means of discovering those to be punished.[129] Obviously, judicial oaths like those *ex officio* (essentially promises to tell authorities the truth) are not loyalty oaths. Yet they are close enough. Place this passage next to the earlier one on the Voluntary Loan of 1670, and you have a coherent statement against showing loyalty by any kind of required gesture, including oaths. The latest loan provides a model for the display of loyalty, Marvell seems to say. However, he may also suggest that even this loan was more or less forced from Nonconformists, just less violently this time, and without oaths.

## Opposition to Tests in the Second Part of *The Rehearsal Transpros'd*

When Marvell sat down to write the second part of *The Rehearsal Transpros'd* sometime after March 1673, the spring session of Parliament was over and one of the oaths in question had become law. Yet while Marvell admits to taking the Test, we need not conclude that he approved of it. For his only reference to it – and an oblique and passing one at that – immediately restricts the oath's meaning to support for the king's supremacy in matters spiritual, as reasserted in the previous year's Declaration of Indulgence. Analysing Parker's citation of the Declaration in his *Reproof* to Part I of *The Rehearsal Transpros'd*, Marvell states:

> He [Parker] quotes his Majesties Declaration to make good his – *making use of that Supream Power in Ecclesiastical matters, which is not only inherent in the Crown, but has been declared and recognized to be so by several Statutes and Acts of Parliament*. I honour the Quotation, and am come not long since from swearing religiously to own that Supremacy.[130]

"Swearing religiously to own that Supremacy": this is an odd way to announce one's compliance with the Test. To begin with, it is extremely selective: swearing the Oaths of Allegiance and Supremacy was only one part of the process that led to an officeholder's taking the Test. First, one had to take Anglican communion and receive a certificate of confirmation from the minister. Then one had to swear the Oaths of Allegiance and Supremacy and present both the certificate and two witnesses to a JP or assize court judge in order to prove one's having received the Sacrament. Only then could one swear the Test oath against transubstantiation. So to say that one has sworn "*religiously* to own that Supremacy" is to refer only to the Oaths of Allegiance and Supremacy, and possibly just to the latter; it does not admit to taking the Test itself. Moreover, "religiously" is a squinting modifier: does it refer to "swearing" or to "own[ing] that Supremacy"? Does it mean "swearing religiously": that Marvell has sworn the Oaths of Allegiance and Supremacy repeatedly and thus "religiously" – this last time being the latest in a long series? Or "religiously to own that Supremacy": that in the process leading to the Test he has "religiously owned" or "testified in a religious manner" to the king's supremacy? And even the kind of supremacy seems in question. While the context of the previous sentences would seem to make it clear that Marvell is responding to Parker's remarks about the king's religious primacy, the subject of the Oath of Supremacy, Marvell cheekily avoids saying that in no uncertain terms. If "religiously" just refers to an act of repeated swearing to some unspecified kind of supremacy, perhaps Marvell only claims that he swore to the king's civil supremacy.[131]

He may, in fact, indicate disapproval of both the Oath of Supremacy and the Test itself, leaving only the Oath of Allegiance intact. He may, in fact, imply that as far as he was concerned, going through the motions of compliance with the Test Act's requirements simply constituted an acknowledgment of the king as executive, nothing more. Marvell may, then, insinuate that he exercised mental reservation in swearing the Test oaths, outwardly denying transubstantiation but inwardly restricting it to an endorsement of the king's ecclesiastical supremacy, and perhaps not even that. Returning to the Declaration of Indulgence, an extension of the royal supremacy in matters spiritual, might have seemed a lesser evil in comparison to a new loyalty oath. Even if Marvell did personally agree with the Test's rejection of transubstantiation – as the satire on Richard Flecknoe suggests he had thirty years before – he may not have wished to force others to do the same.[132] Whatever the case, he has slighted the Test by in effect replacing it with one or two other oaths.

This limiting of the Test to a comparatively small matter of church organization or discipline, while ignoring its doctrinal implications, helps explain the implications of two other episodes in Part II. In the passage about the attacks on Part I of *The Rehearsal Transpros'd*, both by volunteers and by Parker's hired "posse," Marvell argues that what they all have in common is a desire for ecclesiastical preferment:

> since the day of St. Bartholomew, there has not appear'd so great an expectation of an universal Donative . . . the more hungry starvelings generally look'd upon it as an immediate Call to a Benefice, and he that could but write an Answer, whatsoever it were, took it for the most dexterous, cheap, and legal way of Simony.[133]

In doing so, these "starvelings" emulate Parker himself, who allegedly wrote the *Discourse* for Sheldon as an obsequious bid for promotion. One of them, we should recall, had opined that Marvell was "sure to be excluded from many places . . . of imployment in the Commonwealth . . . for refusing to declare *that it is not lawful upon any cause whatsoever . . . to take up Arms against the King*" – the clause contained in all the Clarendon Code's oaths, including that of the Uniformity Act.[134] Marvell's reference to the day of St Bartholomew's Feast on 24 August immediately calls up the ejection in 1662 of ministers who refused to conform to the Church of England by swearing the Uniformity oaths. In underlining the point that some of his attackers expect to be rewarded with church livings, Marvell in effect follows the suggestion and casts himself as the counterpart to the ministers silenced on Black Bartholomew. This corollary or subsidiary part of the comparison has wide implications. It suggests that Marvell himself, despite his father's being a minister in the Church of England and despite what may have been his own continuing attendance in that church, is nevertheless in something like the position of those ministers silenced by and ejected from the Church in 1662.

What could this mean exactly? I think it implies that the newest Test oath has caused a more recent round of Black Bartholomew silencings and ejections. This is not to say that Marvell was pro-Catholic; only that both sets of test oaths, in 1662 and 1673, are instruments of the high-flying bishops' persecution of even the most moderate of Dissenters and that they are the first step on a slippery slope towards more repression and more repressive oaths. Such an oath would soon appear in Danby's 1675 Test. Although Marvell admits to taking the 1673 Test, he suggests, as I have claimed, that he has done so reluctantly and in a severely limited sense. The remarks actually indicate that Marvell is like the ministers who complied very reluctantly with the oaths in 1662, and only with great pangs of conscience that caused him to resort to the underhanded tactic of mental reservation, usually associated with Jesuits swearing forced oaths. If he had had his druthers, he would never have taken the Test. Moreover, to represent himself as the reluctant complier with the latest round of Black Bartholomew oaths is to claim that his opponents in the argument over the Declaration of Indulgence and the Test have not beaten him, have not scored enough points to replace him in the sphere of public opinion. Even if they have won some kind of preferment from Parker and Sheldon, they have not earned the benefice of public approval for their intolerant policies. Whatever Marvell's or the Nonconformists' faults were, they have atoned for them and sworn loyalty in the Oaths of Allegiance and Supremacy. Those ministers who complied with the Uniformity oaths have atoned even more expressly and shown their allegiance in their abjuration of the Covenant. So the bishops dominating the Church "cannot of right, as you would have it, demand another Allegiance," whether something as ridiculous as Parker's suggested recantation or something as repressive as the Test oath.[135]

In our final episode from Part II, Marvell asks Parker to place himself more fully in the shoes of Nonconforming ministers and undergo the humiliating confessions he demands of them – in short, to undergo a test. Parker had recently licensed a slanderously false account of Baptists flaying an Anglican minister in New England, entitled *Mr. Baxter Baptized in Blood* (1673). Building on his earlier claim that in a print culture regulated by censors, authorship sometimes becomes collective, Marvell implies that just as Parker's authorial imprint can be discerned in the work of his fawning "posse Archidiaconatus," the stable of writers he allegedly hired to attack *The Rehearsal*, so can it be felt in the imprimatur he gave to this other bit of slander. In both cases Parker is "the same person that Licensed the falsehood."[136] Since he gave approval for this anonymous book to be printed, Parker is at best partially responsible for its claims and at worst its secret author; after all, he did not append his name to any of the four books Marvell answers in *The Rehearsal Transpros'd*. But the way Marvell makes this argument is even more interesting. He begins by almost swearing a judicial oath: "I dare not swear," he says, "but it was *the Author of the Ecclesiastical Polities* own handy-work."[137] The italics allude to the fact that Parker's *Reproof to The Rehearsal Transprosed* had not confessed to his own authorship.

In the next few pages Marvell imagines what would happen if Parliament passed a law holding censors accountable for the accuracy of books they license:

> . . . had we but an Act of Parliament to abridge Licensers from publishing falsehoods . . . and to command and enable them to authorize truth, there would be a sensible amendment in our modern History, Polity, and Theology. I know he will take it unkindly that this should be revived after, he will say, he hath given so ample satisfaction for it in his testimonial to the contrary. But he may please to consider that this [licensing of a criminally false book] was [or has occurred] since the late Act of General Pardon [the Act of Oblivion and Indemnity (1660) and thus not excusable under its terms]; that it all happen'd since the writing of the Reproof; that he hath only given a Masterly Certificate as it were from a Justice of Peace, instead of making an humble Recantation as an Offender; that it is but the same Law which he every where would exact of the Non-conformists.[138]

As things stand, Parker's "testimonial to the contrary," to his not having licensed a false book, is no more trustworthy than a certificate from a JP stating that he [Parker] gave such sworn testimony, or that he admitted licensing a false book. By now admitting to the public and not just to a JP that the slanderous book actually is false,[139] Parker has essentially proved the worthlessness of any "Masterly Certificate" presented by or to a JP. In this context it would be hard not to think of the Test certificates as worthless too. The passage may allude to the already mentioned requirement of the Test Act that a certificate and two witnesses be produced before a JP or other official to prove a potential officeholder's claim to have taken Anglican communion. Marvell thus fancies this gruelling humiliation being visited upon Parker – but with a twist: as a test of the truth not of his Protestant beliefs but of the books he writes and licenses. This is a test Parker cannot pass.

Marvell then turns the knife in the wound by imagining Parker as committing a kind of idolatry in licensing the slanderous book: "I dare undertake that when he came to the Licensing of that Pamphlet, he felt such an expansion of heart, such an adlubescence of mind, and such an exaltation of spirit, that betwixt Joy and Love he could scarce restrain from kissing it."[140] A part of the ceremony of taking courtroom oaths and probably state oaths was putting one's hand on the Bible and kissing it so as to help prove the swearer's statement to be as true as the Bible. Marvell thus compares licensing someone else's argument in a book to swearing the truth of one's own words. The jab here is that Parker has made the slanderous book about New England Baptists into something as worthy of veneration as the Bible. Since it is clearly not the Bible, it deserves no worship of any kind. The fact that it is a false book makes things much more idolatrous: worshipping a false book approaches the idolatry of worshipping a false God. In comparing this whole imagined process to a judicial oath on the Holy Book – Parker's licensing the book and then disclaiming authorship, giving sworn testimony and producing a certificate – Marvell may also imply that Parker idolizes (false) oaths, such as those demanded by the Clarendon Code and Test Act. At the very least, he has tried to show Parker what it feels like to undergo a Test oneself.

So if Marvell tests the tests and finds them wanting in both parts of *The Rehearsal,* surely he calls for the repeal of the latest one as well for some fix to the larger problem of Nonconformity, either by parliamentary comprehension in a second and improved Ease Bill or, if absolutely necessary, by royal toleration in a second and better-defended Declaration of Indulgence. A residual interest in the latter in the months before Danby welded Court and Cavaliers into a seemingly invincible coalition may be indicated by Marvell's admitting to having sworn the royal supremacy. Marvell's *The Loyal Scot* implies that it is unnecessary to invent new oaths – and *The Rehearsal Transpros'd* seems to agree.[141]

But how far did Marvell want to cut oaths back? He may have considered doing away with them altogether or at least granting significant exemptions from them. Near the end of his life, Marvell seems to have tried to accommodate Quakers who wished to express loyalty to the king without swearing oaths. His letter to the Hull Corporation of 23 March 1678 speaks of Quakers and other Dissenters who, under the Quaker and Conventicles Acts, risked losing much of their property, presumably if they refused to swear oaths like the Oaths of Allegiance and Supremacy. In order to avoid such seizure, they were willing to "subscribe" that loyalty in writing or speech according to a formula in a document presented to the House of Commons that Marvell encloses for the Corporation's perusal (now lost): "the Quakers deliuerd this inclosed as a thing which their whole party are ready to subscribe."[142] It is highly unlikely that Quakers, whose core religious identity consisted of, among other things, an opposition to swearing of all kinds, would have included in such a document any language smacking of oaths. It was probably a language of "promising" or "affirming" rather than swearing – like the language the Toleration Act of 1689 would allow Quakers to use in a revised, technically non-oath version of the Oath of Allegiance after the Glorious Revolution.[143] Yet if Quakers finally got what they wanted, one irony of the Revolution year was that Samuel Parker did not. After promoting test oaths in the books Marvell had attacked, he had curried favour with James II by opposing the 1678 Test for MPs. But that test would survive Parker, James, and the Revolution.[144]

In any case, the Oaths of Allegiance and Supremacy are the only ones about which Marvell never had anything bad to say. In his mind they might have been preferable to other ones as requirements for public office, in that they did not confound civil and religious loyalties.[145] We have already considered Sir Thomas Meres's claim that "the Oaths of Allegiance and Supremacy . . . are the civil Obligations of the Subjects of *England* to their King."[146] In the last five years of Marvell's life, the only other oaths of office that would have kept religious and civil loyalties separate were those proposed for MPs in the Place Bills.[147] But in the end these proved as much a phantom as the others, never making it into law. We now step back in time to see how Marvell dealt with an earlier oath in "what may be the greatest political poem in English": *An Horatian Ode upon Cromwell's Return from Ireland.*[148]

# 3 An Horatian Oath: The *Horatian Ode*, Secularism, and Toleration

Attending to Marvell's oaths allows us to see not just that he desired some separation of church and state in the 1660s and 1670s but that a similar idea already animates the *Horatian Ode* in 1650. Does this mean that the *Horatian Ode* is secular, though? In 1927 H.M. Margoliouth pronounced it "free . . . from any bias of religious politics."[1] In the following year, Pierre Legouis proclaimed that there is "nothing Christian in this ode," adding almost four decades later that the work has a "pagan character." By 1971 Legouis had dropped the idea of paganism and concluded that "religion is conspicuously absent" from the *Ode*.[2] In 1962 Joseph Mazzeo equated the poem's "predominantly secular conception of Cromwell" with Machiavellianism.[3] For Warren Chernaik, however, the classical more generally appears to *be* the secular, and the "perspective of the 'Horatian Ode' is essentially secular."[4]

But in light of current debates about secularism, this whole line of inquiry needs an overhaul.[5] In a way, Margoliouth came closest to the mark by not foreclosing the possibility of religion or Christianity. Instead of arguing for the *Ode*'s complete and impartial avoidance of religion, then, I will retrofit John Wallace's seminal argument[6] and suggest that the poem follows the cue of the Commonwealth's oath of Engagement by leaving religion largely out of a civil matter. Thus, if "secular" means definitively non-religious or atheist, the *Horatian Ode* is probably not secular.[7] But if it means tolerationist and interested in separating church and state, the poem probably is. While Nicholas McDowell has suggested that Marvell's anti-Presbyterianism and anti-clericalism inform the *Horatian Ode*, he does not go so far as to say, as I do, that the almost complete lack of religion in the poem is itself an argument not just for liberty of conscience but for a more thoroughgoing and non-Erastian separation of church and state, as well as of the religious and the political more generally.[8] The *Ode* does not stand above the fray but occupies a recognizable position on the religious spectrum: Independency.

## A Secular Ode?

The word "secular" derives from the Latin *saeculum* (age, period, generation, century),[9] and early moderns often applied the word to actions on earth in present or future times, long and short, as opposed to the different place and different time (or non-time) of Heaven. By extension "secular" could denote the earthly rather than the heavenly, the human rather than the divine, the profane rather than the sacred, the temporary rather than the eternal, the governmental or lay rather than the ecclesiastical – even "*in* the world" among laypeople rather than in a religious order, as in secular vs. regular clergy.[10] Rarely did it imply the non-existence of God and Heaven, or an absolute division between church and state. Only in the modern era has the word shifted to meaning definitively non-religious or atheist.[11]

Since "secular" at root means "of the age," "of the saeculum," John Dryden's *Secular Masque* (1700) provides an analogue of sorts for Marvell's ode, which is certainly secular in this root sense. Dryden explicitly describes the end of an age, the seventeenth century (especially the Restoration), and it is evident that both he and Marvell draw on Horace's *Secular Ode* (*Carmen Saeculare*), commissioned by Augustus to cap the Secular Games (Ludi Saeculares) in 17 BCE, as well as a period of about a century (110 years).[12] A number of Horace's odes (4.6, 4.2) paint the poet as a bard of festivals, especially festivals that mark the end of a *saeculum*'s cycle.[13] The much-discussed Actium Ode (1.37) marks transitions between time periods by speaking of Cleopatra's noble death, a model for Marvell's account of Charles I's execution, while Odes 4.2 and 4.5 do the same thing by looking forward to Augustus's triumphant return to Rome, a model for Cromwell's return from Ireland.[14] A "secular ode" in this sense celebrates the end of one age and the beginning of another. In Dryden's words, "'Tis well an old age is out / . . . And time to begin a new."[15] It may also remind the leader of the culture's central values: in Horace's case, agrarian citizen-soldiership. Marvell's *Horatian Ode* is secular in marking the end of the English monarchy and acknowledging the beginning of the English Republic, which may soon become a dictatorship under Cromwell, the new Augustus and a potential patron. It is also like the *Carmen Saeculare* in being antiphonal, with its duelling couplets of iambic tetrameter and trimeter. The *Carmen Saeculare* consists of alternating stanzas that Marvell's contemporaries thought had been sung first by a chorus of boys and then by a chorus of girls,[16] which reinforces the antiphony of sorts in the metre of the poem's Sapphic stanza (with its shorter fourth line), as well as the antiphony in the alternation of subject matters throughout all four books of Horace's odes (serious vs. trivial; politics/war vs. love/drinking).

In Marvell's time, Hobbes's *Leviathan* (1651) is fairly typical in using the word "secular" to refer to different branches of the Church: priests rather than Jesuits; lay deacons rather than preaching pastors.[17] While "secular" does not appear in his first draft of the system of ideas that became *Leviathan – The Elements of Law* (1640) – it does rear its head in his second version, *De Cive* (1642, translated in 1651 as *Philosophicall Rudiments Concerning Government and Society*), as part of an Erastian argument that the civil sovereign does and should rule both the "secular" and the "sacred" realms. On this occasion Hobbes feels the need to define the word, using it to designate humans' relations with each other, rather than God: "as for the *Secular Lawes*, I mean those which concern justice, and the carriage of men towards men."[18] By this definition *Leviathan*'s "war of all against all" is purely secular. While *Leviathan* and the English translation of *De Cive* appeared after the *Horatian Ode*, *The Elements of Law* was in print in the months before Marvell wrote the poem (February and May 1650). Despite the many huntings and tamings of *Leviathan* that followed, all three texts are decidedly not atheist.[19] *De Cive* deems atheism a foolish and imprudent sin punishable by the supreme civil magistrate, and Hobbes anticipates criticism by proclaiming himself "an enemy to Atheists."[20] We shall consider the ingredients for religious toleration in Hobbes's work in due course.

For the non-Erastian Marvell, however, the word "secular" designates the non-clerical and non-ecclesiastical, and almost always accompanies an argument for the separation of church and state (an argument that students of Marvell have not sufficiently appreciated).[21] In *The Rehearsal Transpros'd* he maintains that "God never intended the Clergy for Political and Secular Imployments," which equates the secular and the political and regards any priestly actions in that realm as "intanglements" and "intermeddlings."[22] In Marvell's *Account of the Growth of Popery and Arbitrary Government* the argument grows shriller. He finds it "unconceivable" and "destructive to all Government" that princes should allow the clergy to be "exempt from the power of all Secular

Jurisdiction" (or outside the monarch's control) and that clergymen, "being all bound, by strict Oaths and Vows of Obedience to the *Pope*, should evacuate the Fealty due to the Sovereign."[23] Given that fealty to suzerains was understood to be sworn, Marvell has sussed out the conflict between oaths (oaths to a religious superior vs. to a civil superior) and thus between the jurisdictions they represent. In general, the passage highlights the close association, in his mind at least, between oaths, secularity in several of its senses, and church-state separation.

In this light *The Rehearsal Transpros'd*'s parody of the Commonwealth's oath of Engagement (1649) seems all the more telling. If the Engagement asked all adults, possibly even women, to swear the following:

> I do declare and promise, that I will be true and faithful to the Commonwealth of England, as it is now established, without a King or House of Lords,

Marvell's parody asks,

> Will you be true and faithful to the Government establish'd, without Christ, &c?[24]

His local point is that Parker has arrogated to the civil magistrate a power greater than Christ's because preceding him: there were human magistrates long before Christ was born. Thus, someone swearing allegiance to the civil magistrate must swear to obey a government established without Christ because established before Christ. Yet Marvell's parody strikes so close to the bone precisely because its original is conspicuously non-religious: the Engagement makes no reference to Christ or religion. In effect, the parody comments on the absence of religion in the oath – though not necessarily in the minds of the people who took it.

## The Varieties of Religious and Secular Experience

In a sense, modern secularization theory has only just caught up with Marvell, Hobbes, and their contemporaries. In *A Secular Age* (2007), the philosopher Charles Taylor notes the early modern variations on the idea of "secular" as timebound and worldly, and then identifies three kinds of modern secularism that can be placed on a sliding scale from unbelief to belief.[25] Secularism 1 consists of a decline and possible extinction of religious belief and practice.[26] Under Secularism 2, religion survives but is removed from public spaces to the private realm.[27] With Secularism 3, religion remains in public spaces, which might include the government, but a variety of religious viewpoints jostle elbows with each other, and any religious belief is just one among many, including non-belief.[28] What Taylor calls "mainstream secularization theory" tends to conflate Secularisms 1 and 2 and ignore Secularism 3, his own contribution to the debate.

Taylor identifies essentially two paradigms for understanding the process of secularization from 1500 to the present: a subtraction theory and an addition theory. The subtraction model has it that after something is subtracted, secularism is what is left. The addition model sees secularism as the result of an addition of something newly invented in order to take the place of the old. Broadly speaking, mainstream secularization theory has hewed to the former, attributing the growth of Western secularism to various phenomena: chief among them, empiricist science, but also the rise of urbanization, industrialization, rapid communication and transportation, mass education, and democracy – in other words, modernity. Once religion and other forms of superstition have been dispelled by rational modernity, what remains is the secular, the unvarnished truth about ourselves and the world. We might add that political theology in the wake of Carl Schmitt belongs in this camp since it accepts (even as it complicates) Schmitt's view that many of the ideas and institutions of modern society consist of old religious forms drained of their religious content.[29] Although Schmitt's recent followers seem uninterested in oaths, his acolyte Ernst Friesenhahn pointed in 1928 to the loyalty oath as a signal instance of the process of secularization,[30] in that oaths had been understood as religious acts in the early modern period, as appeals to the divine to confirm one's word, but had since lost their religious associations.

By contrast, Taylor offers what could be called an "additive" account of secularization, in which secularism consists of a presence rather than an absence. Instead of revealing truth by lifting the veil of religious distortion, we moderns have instead constructed a new lens or "social imaginary" through which to perceive the world. Rather than using reason to remove all barriers between ourselves and the truth, secularism constitutes an addition or substitution of a newly constructed immanentist liberal ideology, hostile to religion as well as to anything that transcends the atomistic individual self.[31] Taylor asks us to admit that far from banishing religion from society or driving it into asymptotic decline, modernity has in fact multiplied the varieties of religious experience. Instead of a single process of secularization that began in the West and spread to less enlightened parts, we see secularisms (plural) today – various accommodations between religion and the state.

In a larger sense, then, secularization has added a toleration of different viewpoints, religious and non-religious: Secularism 3. Many forms of secularity today, especially outside Europe, involve not just the presence but the saturation of the public sphere with religious discourse. And some modern governments are not secular in any sense, instead requiring religious belief and practice in private and public. Even countries that try to separate church and state, such as the United States, have hardly removed religion from public space. Taylor wants us to face these facts squarely and make the public sphere even more open to a variety of viewpoints, religious and non-religious.[32] In the end, though, his greatest insight is the simple notion that religion can coexist peacefully with secularism and modernity over the long term.

### Additions and Subtractions in the *Horatian Ode*

Turning to Marvell's *Horatian Ode*, we find something useful in both the addition and subtraction stories, as well as in Taylor's taxonomy of secularisms. While his account of secularization does not map precisely onto the *Ode*, it does suggest that we pay more attention to what things seem conspicuously absent and present in the poem. The *Horatian Ode* arguably displays versions of both Secularism 2 (religion outside public spaces – part of the subtraction story) and Secularism 3 (some plurality of religious and non-religious beliefs – part of the addition story), but no conclusive evidence of Secularism 1 (the subtraction account's claim of an absolute decline of religion).

The subtraction account explains a lot about the *Ode*, which presents change as loss and absence. In the line about "Nature's . . . hat[ing] emptiness" (41), the final word ("emptiness") advertises clear subtractions in progress: of king, kingship, possibly of divine right. Justice "plead[s] the ancient rights *in vain*" (37–8, my emphasis). If monarchy is "The great work of time," it has been "ruined" (34) – although, as I have argued elsewhere, the poem cannot quite let go of the old monarchical trope of the king's two bodies.[33] The three kingdoms may still be kingdoms, but they await "another mould" (35–6) that has yet fully to arrive. On the scaffold, Charles pointedly does not call on the "Gods," let alone

God, for help (61–2). Do gods or God exist? Is "angry heaven's flame" (26) really evidence of Providence, of divine endorsement or at least toleration of Cromwell? Or do we, like the *Ode*'s speaker, just project the divine onto nature because that is what we did before the Regicide and the abolition of monarchy? After all, "much to the man is due" (28), rather than to some transcendent force, whatever it is. Cromwell can do "so much" by himself, without help, because he "does both act and know" (75–6). But the corollary may be that he will also have no help in keeping himself in power: "The same arts that did gain / A pow'r must it maintain" (119–20). And there is another kind of emptiness present in the cold, almost scientific account of a universe of impersonal, Hobbesian forces in which Cromwell is a force of nature using the sword's force to attain his ends (13–16, 21, 116–17) – although, yet again, such a conclusion may result from the speaker's letting a simile get out of control.[34] If Cromwell is "*like* the three-forked lightning . . . Breaking [through] the clouds where it was nursed," does this really mean that he *is* "angry heaven's flame" (13–16, 26, my emphasis)? Is this not to mistake metaphor for reality? The receding of the larger world view, of which divine right forms but one part, makes it hard to tell. If the poem chronicles the rise of an individual, which sounds like Taylor's additive account, it comes across more as a loss than as something new and positive. Marvell does not offer an account of a whole society turning individualistic. The relative absence of religion is thus not definitive evidence of Secularism 1: the decline of religious belief. Religion may just be in abeyance at the moment, or it may inhabit private rather than public spaces (Secularism 2).

On the additive side, the poem features some presences. It depicts Cromwell as something genuinely new, something that fills the void left by the Regicide. He may be sui generis, or he may be the vanguard of a new individualism, setting his own ambitious goals and bringing them to fruition through his own knowledge and action. Likewise, one might see in the poem a newly impersonal, objective, non-evaluative, and thus scientific world view – "Hobbesian" only to the extent that one ignores Hobbes's remarks on religion in *Leviathan* and elsewhere. Cromwell is an unavoidable reality, and the poem simply describes him, with a minimum of value judgment. Whatever one thinks of him, he is a man on the rise and likely to do to the Scots what he did to the Irish. Praise or blame comes in a distant second. In the context of the Engagement debate this constellation of additions sounds like a version of Secularism 3.

## "Secularism" in the Engagement and Engagement Controversy

John Wallace long ago identified the debate over the Commonwealth's new loyalty oath, the Engagement, as a defining context for the *Horatian Ode* in June–July 1650.[35] As we have seen, the Engagement oath committed its takers to being "true and faithful to the Commonwealth of England, as it is now established, without a King or House of Lords." The fierce argument over the oath, an argument that ran to more than seventy printed tracts pro and con,[36] sheds light on many aspects of the poem – especially, I shall argue, its stance towards religion. What has received short shrift in accounts of the Engagement controversy is the notion of some separation of church and state. Back in 1607, James I had defended his new Oath of Allegiance in something like these terms, maintaining that it was temporal rather than religious. But this argument became an important force in the Engagement debate forty years later[37] because the Engagement differed from previous oaths by design. It was shorter and contained no religious references; it technically was not even an oath, lacking the word "swear" or any overt invocation of God as witness, even though it may have been sworn in churches or in the presence of ministers. Perhaps its most important defender, John Dury, author of nine pro-Engagement tracts, asserted tirelessly from one book to the next that the Engagement was a civil oath, not a religious one.[38] Agreement came from *The Engagement Vindicated*, the pamphlet of 7 January 1650 that anticipated the *Horatian Ode* with the words "climacterick" and "mould" and the argument that Providence sometimes permits things without approving of them.[39] Later that spring, Marchamont Nedham chose his words carefully when referring to the allegiance secured by oaths of allegiance (and thus by the Engagement) as a "political tie"; and Henry Parker extended the whole point in 1651 by saying that the Engagement's civil, non-religious nature was precisely what distinguished it from previous oaths. Comparing it to the Bishops' Canonical Oath and the Solemn League and Covenant of 1643, Parker explained that "those were Religious, so is not this."[40] The anti-Engager Henry Hall accused the Rump of deliberately framing it so as to conceal the fact of its being an oath in the first place: "As for this Engagement[,] indeed[,] it is politiquely gilded like a poysoned Pill, with as much subtilty and craft to induce people to take it as may be, for they call it *An Engagement*, not an Oath, for then they supposed people would scruple it, but it is only subscribing to two or three words, and there's an end."[41] And he was right. Its name suggested not an oath but a commitment to the Commonwealth. Previous oaths of allegiance had pledged loyalty to a person rather than the community and had mentioned God or religion in some way.

Wallace, as well as Perez Zagorin before and Quentin Skinner after him, emphasized the de facto nature of most arguments for the Engagement.[42] In this context "de facto" meant accepting the "is" of the current political reality, rather than the "ought" of an imagined better situation. Whatever one thought about them, ran this line of argument, the Rump and Council of State did in fact control England, and the Engagement simply recognized that fact, committing swearers not to disturb the peace by rebelling against the government – no more, no less. By contrast, de jure arguments, for or against the Engagement and Republic, turned on the notion that the form and leadership of government ought to be determined by some higher morality or law, whether of God, nature, or nations. For anti-Engagers employing a de jure argument, monarchy was the right form of government and Charles II the true king of England, even if he was not currently in control; and the Engagement should be avoided. For Engagers making a de jure argument, a republic was the right form of government in that it respected the people's wishes and liberties; and the Engagement was to be taken since it harmonized with the presuppositions of all previous loyalty oaths, including the Protestation and Solemn League and Covenant.

In his recent accounts of the Engagement controversy and the *Horatian Ode* Conal Condren has proved that the Engagers employed both modes and that the *Ode* follows suit, arguing both de jure and de facto for Cromwell and the Republic: both "morality and prudence should lead us to accept the powers that be." For Condren, though, the former predominates as the poem celebrates "a providentially blessed evangelical republic, threatened but energetic in the processes of reformation and imperial consolidation."[43] But Condren also questions the utility of the de jure/de facto distinction itself, extending the point made by historians such as Glen Burgess and Edward Vallance, who supplied a needful corrective to Wallace's and Skinner's earlier accounts of the Engagement debate as proceeding solely along a de facto/de jure axis. There were other arrows in the Engagers' rhetorical quiver. They appealed, for example, to the idea of Providence as either permitting or causing the abolition of the old monarchical order; and they countered charges of perjury against previous oaths such as the Oaths of Allegiance and Supremacy and the Solemn League and Covenant by claiming that the Engagement was not inconsistent with them, in that all were at heart oaths to the community at large, to the English polity, rather than to its monarch, and that they were all means to a larger end: preserving peace, property, and liberty.[44] Yet it remains the case that both sides did argue de jure and de facto,[45] the Engagers stressing the latter and their opponents the former.[46] Why did the Engagers depend upon de facto arguments? Probably because the Engagement itself came close to making no value judgment at all, merely recognizing the status quo (the general fact that the present government and political arrangement was a commonwealth without king or lords) and promising that the swearer would be "true and faithful" in not taking up arms against it. As I shall argue , the *Horatian Ode* makes a similarly de facto statement about Cromwell and the Rump being in charge,[47] even as it extends that de factoist point into a policy recommendation about religious toleration and the separation of the religious and the political – which is to say, about keeping de jure value judgments about divinity and morality out of loyalty oaths and other government business.

Thus, the historian Blair Worden's conclusion in 1974 that "the apologists for the engagement developed an amoral, secular, Hobbesian philosophy of subordination to a *de facto* government" still makes sense insofar as we understand "secular" to mean cautiously avoiding the issue of religion, as opposed to being defiantly non-religious or atheist.[48] As Worden suggests, the Engagement's lack of religious reference correlates with its lack of value judgment about the present government. Indeed, the government's newsbooks encouraged people to think of it "not as thing of Religion, but a civill action";[49] and a number of the Engagement's defenders underlined the Commonwealth's status as no more than a civil authority. Thomas Carre, for example, which may be the alias of the Catholic priest Miles Pinkney, went so far as to call the oath "secular." Glossing Romans 13:1 ("Let every soul be subject unto the higher powers"), the main tennis ball in the match between Engagers and anti-Engagers, Carre emphasized that this proof-text is "to be understood of the Civill, the secular Powers."[50] More tellingly perhaps, a number of Engagers and defenders of the Commonwealth, such as Dury, Parker, Milton, Gerrard Winstanley, George Wither, Lewis Du Moulin, and Enoch Grey, were essentially religious Independents of one sort or another and thus advocated some measure of church-state separation and toleration for peaceable Protestants.[51] The hostile Presbyterian John Vicars was onto something when he condemned several people for "Apostatiz[ing] to the Independent Faction" and then taking the Engagement.[52] Another Presbyterian opponent of Independency,

Clement Walker, similarly linked it to the Engagement. His arrest and the seizure of his papers in the fall of 1649 may have had something to do with his opposition to both.[53] Much later, Samuel Parker concurred with Vicars and Walker in his *Reproof to the Rehearsal Transprosed*.[54] For many, then, the Engagement bore the impress of Independency.[55]

As one of its most vociferous opponents, William Prynne, rightly observed, the Engagement's "chief Contrivers" supported "Liberty of Conscience" – or at least pretended to.[56] While Prynne could be accused of stating the obvious, given that the Republic was in part created by excluding intolerant Presbyterians such as himself from Parliament, there was considerable difference of opinion within the Rump about the shape of a future religious settlement. Its remaining Presbyterians did not see eye to eye with Independents of various stripes about issues such as whether there should be a tithe-supported state church, what form it should take, and what spectrum of religious practice should be allowed both within and without. We can say, though, that a large proportion of the Engagement's supporters in the Rump – especially those who sat on the committee empowered with tendering it to fellow MPs and writing the bill to make it compulsory for the nation at large – were Independents and sectarians interested in some degree of toleration and/or church-state separation.[57] While there were almost as many Presbyterians as Independents on the Engagement committee, some of them, such as Isaac Penington, William Gurdon, and Miles Corbet, were much less rigid than their co-religionists and could be labelled tolerant Presbyterians, somewhat open to Protestants other than the sects worshipping outside a state church.[58] A number of the committee's Independents, including the republicans Henry Marten, Thomas Challoner, Henry Neville, Bulstrode Whitelock, Edmund Ludlow, Algernon Sidney, and Sir Henry Vane Jr, wanted total church-state separation; and the first three on the list would probably have generalized that to the complete separation of religion and politics.[59]

But even more important as formative influences on Marvell in summer 1650 were Nedham and Hobbes.[60] No friend of Presbyterians like Prynne, Nedham had defended Independency and toleration in the 1640s and would defend them again in *The Case of the Common-Wealth*, a forceful exposition of the Engagement's de factoist principles that was in bookstalls by 8 May 1650, when George Thomason dated his copy. Throughout the notorious turns of his political coat, Nedham remained tolerationist and Independent, but open to a state church that indulged dissenters.[61] That, combined with his classical republicanism at this stage, would have seemed an irresistible model for the posture of irenic prudence Marvell strikes in the *Ode*. Nedham's neo-Roman republicanism in *The Case of the Common-Wealth* does not extinguish reference to God or religion, but it downplays them. In defending the Rump, Nedham argues that of the various forms of government, republics most effectively eliminate religious violence because they remove religious conflict from the public sphere. Nedham's tolerant Independency emerges in the 1640s, not just in a tract from his parliamentary phase, *Independencie No Schisme*, but even in his royalist *Case of the Kingdome*, where he argues that Independents and royalists can benefit from each other by allying against intolerant Presbyterians.[62] Back on the parliamentary side in 1650, Nedham pressed for toleration again in *The Case of the Common-Wealth*, stressing the separation of the civil and religious spheres and faulting the Presbyterians for encroaching on matters civil in pursuit of a virtual theocracy. In service of this point he used the word "secular": "the Reason why the *Presbytery* contended for is so destructive of *Liberty*, is because of the *Popish Trick* taken up by the *Presbyterian* Priests, in drawing all *Secular Affairs*, within the compasse of their *spirituall Jurisdiction*."[63] This sounds very much like the anti-clericalism with an accent on separate spheres in Marvell's *The Rehearsal Transpros'd* twenty years later.

The clincher is the section on religious toleration at the end of Nedham's book. In a chapter demonstrating the superiority of republics to monarchies, he argues that the former are more peaceful and prosperous because of their "*prudent*" "Toleration of different opinions in Religion."[64] Among his examples, non-Christian states such as Egypt, Turkey, and Japan rank high; among Christian states, he holds up the Protestant Netherlands. Tolerant countries, the argument goes, become successful empires. Crucially, Nedham is not finicky about the issue of a state church. There does not have to be one; but if there is, it should indulge, protect, and even honour people of faith outside it.[65] But the very fact that he praises, say, Turkey's tolerance of Christians and Jews but refuses to condemn Islam in any way demonstrates that Nedham himself models a toleration broader than one just for Protestants.

The other decisive influence on Marvell in summer 1650 was Hobbes. Along with the Hobbesian materialism already noted came the seeds of toleration, but toleration accomplished by Erastian means, which were not front and centre in Nedham's *Case of the Common-Wealth*. In the *Leviathan* (1651), Hobbes offers in its strongest form an argument that he knows will be understood as pro-Engagement in its immediate context and that while granting the civil magistrates supreme power in both civils and ecclesiasticals, nevertheless urges them to be involved in the latter as little as possible, with Independency as a kind of model for such forbearance. He admits that "the Independency of the Primitive Christians to follow Paul, or Cephas, or Apollos, every man as he liketh best . . . if it be without contention . . . is perhaps the best . . . because there ought to be no Power over the Consciences of men, but of the Word it selfe."[66] Thus, even Hobbes recommends Independency.[67] Now, of course this is a prelude to his condemnation of Catholic hierarchy later in the chapter, and of course other parts of *Leviathan* take issue with some Independent doctrines, but it is also part of an anticlerical preference for doctrinal and disciplinary minimalism in religion that would be expressed during the Restoration in his remarks against the abuse of the concept of heresy.[68] Jon Parkin thus rightly identifies points of contact between Hobbes and the Marvell of *The Rehearsal Transpros'd* (1672–3) on the questions of toleration and clerical hubris – even though they come at these issues from different angles (Hobbes from an Erastian one, Marvell from a non-Erastian).[69]

In Part II of *The Rehearsal,* Marvell takes a clearly non-Erastian stance.[70] If Part I of *The Rehearsal* is willing to entertain a top-down toleration issuing from the king, Part II – composed after Charles II had betrayed the cause of toleration by rescinding the Declaration of Indulgence and refusing to veto the Test Act, with its new anti-Catholic oath – becomes much more suspicious not just of royal (as opposed to parliamentary) toleration but of any state intervention in religion.[71] This is the part of *The Rehearsal* in which the comments about the state-clergy's intervention in civil affairs crescendo.[72] This is also the part where Tacitean warnings first appear about Nero's and Caligula's excesses, with the implication that not just clergymen like Parker but kings like Charles could become another Nero – suggesting that Marvell had begun to despair of the royal prerogative as the way forward to toleration.[73]

But what of 1650? Even then, in the months before Marvell's composition of the *Ode*, rehearsals of Hobbes's proto-tolerationist arguments in *Leviathan* were available in the publication in two parts of *The Elements of Law*: as *Humane Nature* (2 February 1650) and then *De Corpore Politico* (4 May 1650).[74] In fact, proto-tolerationist passages from the latter were collected by Nedham and advertised in a new "Appendix, added out of Salmasius, and M. Hobbs" to the second edition of *The Case of the Common-Wealth* no later than early July.[75]

Why would toleration and church-state separation be relevant issues to broach when speaking of and perhaps to Cromwell? For two reasons. First, Cromwell was widely understood to occupy a very tolerationist position on the spectrum of Independency.[76] Second, his identity and leadership of the largely Independent and sectarian New Model Army had been so bound up with toleration[77] that anyone seeking his patronage, as Marvell may have been doing, would want to pledge allegiance to toleration. Of course, Cromwell was not as tolerant as has been supposed; he was no modern tolerationist.[78] As Austin Woolrych puts it, "His ideal was not a plurality of sects tolerated out of indifference, but a community of all who 'had the root of the matter' in them [i.e., the godly], in a manner transcending differences over outward forms and rites." However, "although Cromwell was not a total tolerationist[,] he strove for a broader religious freedom than any parliament of the Interregnum would endorse – or indeed any parliament at all before 1689."[79] He had tolerated sectarians such as Baptists within his regiment before 1650 and would do so afterwards. As David L. Smith has argued, Cromwell's dismay at the intolerance of various Parliaments was an important factor in his decisions to dissolve them and to attempt something better, with or without their help.[80] If, after the excesses of potentially violent sects like Ranters and Fifth Monarchists became impossible to ignore, Cromwell did agree to a tithe-supported state church that regulated the composition of its ministry through boards of Triers and Ejectors, he also allowed pockets of Anglican and Catholic worship outside that church so long as they did not morph into royalist conspiracy. And he even readmitted the Jews to England, if with millenarian hopes of their conversion to Christianity.[81] In summer 1650, when Marvell probably wrote the *Ode*, all this was to come. But in the immediate future, Cromwell would write to the Scottish Covenanters in August 1650, protesting his support for some liberty of conscience. It was "no part of our business," he said, "to hinder any of them from worshipping God in that way they are satisfied in their consciences by the Word of God they ought, though different from us." Nedham summarized this letter in the next issue of *Mercurius Politicus*.[82] After Cromwell defeated the Covenanters at Dunbar in September, he sent recommendations for tolerationist reform back to the Parliament at Westminster, which duly passed a toleration act repealing the recusancy laws that had prescribed penalties for those who did not attend parish churches on Sunday.[83] Marvell would later elegize Cromwell as a defender of liberty of conscience:

"He first put arms into Religion's hand, / And tim'rous Conscience unto Courage manned."[84]

## An Horatian Oath to a Civil Polity

The *Horatian Ode* models the individual's right to bring some measure of religion, probably just Protestant religion, into public discourse (Taylor's Secularism 3), or to decide not to (Secularism 2). The poem's speaker introduces religion to the equation in a very general way by alluding vaguely to Providence in the phrase "angry heaven's flame" (26). While John Wallace's reading of the poem places great emphasis on this phrase,[85] the poem specifies nothing about religious doctrine or discipline. This is a studied absence, resulting not so much from neo-Stoic fear or circumspection,[86] as from a wish to model how public discourse might proceed. Religion does not have to play a big role in it. The poem's other model for public discourse and conduct is paradoxically Charles I. In Marvell's account of his last moments on the scaffold, Charles appears to leave religion out of whatever remarks he makes or does not make: he did not call "the Gods with vulgar spite / To vindicate his helpless right" (61–2). It is a secondary consideration that the word is "Gods" rather than "God," since no appeal is made to the divine at all. In this respect Charles is just another citizen, like Marvell or Cromwell; citizens can remain "reserved and austere" in their "private gardens" or leave those gardens to "urge their active stars" in public spaces (29–30, 12).[87] The "public" of line 90, before whose "skirt" Cromwell lays "his sword and spoils" (89), is not just the feminine Republic or its specific form of republican government in line 82, but also the public realm more generally. Horace's odes, the avowed model for Marvell's poem, make roughly the same distinction between public and private, though not the more absolute one emerging in the early modern period.[88]

The *Horatian Ode* also tackles the issue from the other side, modelling the state's need to show restraint and, within reason, to rise sublimely above religious niceties and keep specific religious doctrine and discipline out of its own deliberations and selection of personnel, as well as to keep itself out of public discussion and the practice of religion.[89] Different religious beliefs can coexist in the public sphere. The Engagement oath provides the key to both these points: 1) the individual takes it and makes a civil rather than religious commitment to a civil polity; 2) by omitting religion from the oath, the government stays out of the business of prescribing a specific religious doctrine or discipline. Again, within reason – nothing violently sectarian. The strictures against Fifth Monarchists in Marvell's *First Anniversary* make this abundantly clear.[90]

The *Horatian Ode* thus functions as a kind of Horatian Oath, if you will – a substitute for the Engagement that displays a dialectical process of coming to terms with the status quo and Cromwell, warts and all.[91] It admits the speaker's (and Marvell's) reservations and ambivalences, but after some thought arrives at acceptance of the Commonwealth's existence and the fact of Cromwell's rise to power, which may eventuate in either kingship or disaster. But the poem withholds a strong value judgment, a strong endorsement of Cromwell and Commonwealth. Like the Engagement, it merely accepts them and indicates that the speaker lacks a burning desire to avenge the "helpless right" of Charles I or II (l. 62). Like Robert Fletcher's *Mercurius Heliconicus*, it practises a religion only insofar as it is a religion of endurance, of surviving by accommodating itself to the powers that be, present or future: "He's secure / That makes it a Religion to endure."[92] In any case, the finer points of doctrine and discipline have little to no place in such a calculation. Providence has allowed the Commonwealth to assert itself and Cromwell to conquer Ireland, likely to be followed by Scotland in the next few months.

In pushing liberty of conscience, the *Horatian Ode* not only imitates the Independents but cannily anticipates Cromwell's own inclinations towards the relatively tolerant religious settlement he would achieve a few years later with the help of Independents such as his chaplain, John Owen. It should hardly surprise us that a poem about or directed to a potential patron should mimic that patron's Independency and tolerationism, and even insist that Cromwell live up to rather than betray his own professions of fighting for the people's civil and religious liberties. Yet Marvell also makes a bolder point. The *Ode* is on some level an alternative, personalized form of the Engagement like several ones offered by participants in the Engagement controversy,[93] and it is an oath not just to Cromwell but to the civil polity he represents, with its potential for religious toleration. But Marvell goes even further than that. The *Ode* is, in fact, more tolerationist and separationist than Cromwell himself (or Owen) turned out to be. Marvell joins Nedham in advising more than mere toleration outside a state church.[94] To not discuss religion or a state church, or to discuss them as little as Nedham does in *The Case of the Common-Wealth*; to adopt the republican idiom associated with pagan Romans and Greeks – in doing all of this,

Marvell deemphasizes religion's place in the public sphere while not banishing it entirely. Otherwise put, to speak the language of classical republicanism like Nedham is to speak the language of religious toleration and church-state separation. Indeed, it is to recommend the separation not just of church and state, but of religion and politics. Marvell's is a secular ode in insisting on these separations, not in denying belief in the divine. Whether Cromwell ever read it or not, such advice about toleration and the separation of the religious and political made pragmatic sense in the context of fusing together three kingdoms with very different religious traditions. The *Ode* thus shies away from a one-faith-fits-all solution such as the Solemn League and Covenant's imposition of a Presbyterian state-church on England, Scotland, and Ireland.

If the poem functions as a job application to Cromwell or perhaps to Fairfax (so haunted as the latter was by a former oath, the Solemn League and Covenant, and apparently reluctant about taking the Engagement),[95] it argues that religion should play little to no role in hiring for public offices. In saying that, it spins the fact that the Engagement was a requirement for public office into an interpretation of the oath in which its absence of religious reference is a policy recommendation: that religious views and practices not be a test for public office. Those offices would, of course, include the secretaryship for foreign tongues that Marvell would eventually secure with Milton's and presumably Cromwell's help. They might also include humbler posts like tutoring the children and wards of important generals, as Marvell was soon to do.

Whether the Marvell of the *Horatian Ode* is a royalist transitioning to some other position or not, he does not advocate an Anglican or Presbyterian union of church and state, as many royalists in the debate did. Religious thoughts are one's own, private, perhaps only to be shared with others when necessity demands. Nicholas von Maltzahn discerns this attitude in Marvell's Restoration writings,[96] and it is present even earlier in the *Ode*. The poem's apparently limited circulation – not printed until after his death, perhaps circulating in manuscript, perhaps only to Cromwell himself along with a letter of introduction – testifies to its own private status and thus to religious matters' private status and the separation of church and state. In the end Marvell's understanding of the Engagement oath, along with his re-presentation of its presuppositions in the eloquent silences of his poem, place him in the vanguard of oath theory, a vanguard leading towards a non-religious, or not primarily religious, understanding of oaths in general. For Marvell religion is a private matter that can be brought into the public sphere, but should not be forced into it by devices like the tests and picklocks of oaths. And the public sphere itself, as well as official government posts and other public offices, should not be barred to people by the device of doctrinally and disciplinarily specific loyalty oaths. Typical of this line of thinking is the U.S. Constitution's insistence that "no religious Test shall ever be required as a Qualification to any Office or public Trust."[97] The Marvell of the *Horatian Ode* is thus less cautious and more radical than we have supposed.

# 4 Samson's Cords: Imposing Oaths in *Eikonoklastes* and *Samson Agonistes*

*To* ADJU´RE. *v.a.* [*adjuro*, Lat.] To impose an oath upon another, prescribing the form in which he shall swear.

Thou know'st, the magistrates
And princes of my country came in person,
Solicited, commanded, threaten'd, urg'd,
*Adjur'd* by all the bonds of civil duty,
And of religion, press'd how just it was,
How honourable.

*Milton's Sampson's Agonistes, l.* 853

OATH. *n.s.* . . . An affirmation, negation, or promise, corroborated by the attestation of the Divine Being . . .

Those called to any office of trust, are bound by an *oath* to the faithful discharge of it: but an *oath* is an appeal to God, and therefore can have no influence, except upon those who believe that he is. *Swift*.

– Samuel Johnson, *A Dictionary of the English Language* (1755–6)

He went to university with a design of entering into the church, but in time altered his mind; for he declared that whoever become a clergyman must "subscribe slave, and take an oath withal, which, unless he took with a conscience that could retch, he must straight perjure himself. He thought it better to prefer a blameless silence before the office of speaking, bought and begun with servitude and forswearing."

These expressions are, I find, applied to the subscription of the Articles; but it seems more probable that they relate to canonical obedience. I know not any of the Articles which seem to thwart his opinions: but the thoughts of obedience, whether canonical or civil, raised his indignation.

– Samuel Johnson, *Life of Milton* (1779)[1]

*Sampson's Agonistes*? Whether careless or hostile, the work of Johnson or his compositor, this mispunctuation and misspelling of Milton's title do the poem a disservice by encouraging a misunderstanding of its second term, either rendering it ungrammatically meaningless or restricting the title's meaning to something like *Samson's Agon*. Moreover, put Johnson's *Life of Milton* together with his quotation from Swift, and you have an almost atheist Milton, not that far from the rabid king-killer many Tories considered him to be. Yet Johnson's ostensibly petty attention to oaths actually hits upon a crucial issue in the writings of the dissenting Milton, from the anti-prelatical and regicide tracts to *De Doctrina Christiana* and *Paradise Lost*. Like Johnson's Milton, Satan knows that if offered a chance to swear allegiance to a higher authority, he would "soon unsay / What feigned submission swore," soon "recant / Vows made in pain."[2] Prompted by Johnson's citation of Milton's Dalila as an example of adjuration, I will argue that via *Samson Agonistes*'s examination of sworn and unsworn vows Milton asks a number of questions about imposing state oaths: can one be bound by a forced oath? can one be bound by an oath someone else has sworn? must one keep an oath sworn in good faith but since regretted? Engaging these and related issues associated with the new seventeenth-century trope of oaths as Samson's cords, Milton's poem reproduces the crises of conscience and strategies of evasion associated with takers of state-mandated loyalty oaths in Stuart Britain. Samson must live with a vow imposed on him by someone else. This is the exact counterpart of the oaths imposed on subjects and officeholders in the decades before and after the Restoration, and it defines him. Yet both vow and identity are in some sense not his own.[3]

On two occasions in the early years of the Restoration, the influential exegete John Trapp seemed to compare Samson himself to an oath: "Men sport themselves with oaths, as the *Philistines* did with *Sampson:* which will at last pull the house about their ears."[4] But Milton does not go that far: rather than equating Samson with oaths, *Samson Agonistes* only associates him with them, painting him as a representative oath-taker. In his chapter on oaths and lots in *De Doctrina Christiana*, Milton offers the traditional definition of swearing as a "species of invocation . . . whereby we call God to witness the truth of what we say, with a curse upon ourselves, either implied or expressed, should it prove false."[5] While Milton opposes the hostility to all oaths exemplified by Quakers and cited by Sharon Achinstein as a context for *Samson Agonistes*,[6] and accepts their legality, he meets Quakers part way with the qualification that "It is only in important matters . . . that recourse should be had to the solemnity of an oath." Once sworn, however, "An oath involving a promise is to be observed, even contrary to our own interest, provided the promise itself be not unlawful."[7] Despite acknowledging a distinction between forced oaths required by robbers of their victims and forced oaths of allegiance required by conquerors of nations, the latter of which must be obeyed, Milton again hews to the consensus by eventually concluding that in the case of "unlawful oaths . . . oaths of which the purport is unlawful, or which are extracted from us by one to whom they cannot be lawfully taken," "the breach of such oaths is better than the performance."[8]

This discussion, like the preceding chapters on vows and covenants in *De Doctrina*,[9] addresses what we have seen to be a very live, very raw issue in the decades leading up to *Samson*'s publication in late 1670. Camille Slights has rightly argued that *Samson* is a poem about cases of conscience, but her reading does not mention oaths,[10] an important case that appeared in most of the period's conscience books: could an oath be taken at all, and if so, how far did it bind the swearer? Hence, Milton's own difficulties with oaths were hardly unique. In the much-anthologized passage from *The Reason of Church Government* that Johnson loosely quotes, Milton claims to have been "Church-outed" or prevented from taking orders in the Laudian church partly by the oath of office requiring assent not just to the episcopal hierarchy Johnson mentions but also to the Thirty-Nine Articles and Book of Common Prayer.[11] He took the oath of allegiance contained in the Solemn League and Covenant (1643) sometime before the publication of *Tetrachordon* in 1644, but later argued against the Covenant's binding force in several places, including the lines in the sonnet "On the New Forcers of Conscience" about the "stiff vows" with which Presbyterians had "adjure[d] the civil sword / To force our consciences."[12] In addition to the Covenant, he appears to have taken the Protestation (1641), the Vow and Covenant (1643), and the Engagement (1650), only the latter of which seems to have retained Milton's more or less unqualified support by the time of *The Readie and Easie Way to a Free Commonwealth*'s second edition (1660).[13] Two of his tracts in the year before the Restoration are not opposed in principle to civil rather than religious oaths of office, recommending them for both soldiers and MPs – and implicitly for anyone joining an organization or institution voluntarily, on the model of the religious oaths/covenants individuals swore to bind themselves to particular, non-national, Independent churches, always with the option of opting out.[14] But after 1660, discomfort over the state's forcing individual consciences in matters of religion[15] led him to oppose the Clarendon Code's oaths of office, with their abjurations of the Covenant, non-alteration clauses, and statements making commitments for people other than the swearers themselves.

Beginning with 1606, every debate over state oaths in the seventeenth century included some reference to the biblical figure of Samson, whose ability to break free of his cords was often compared, favourably or unfavourably, to the breaking of oaths. In the former case Samson deserved praise for breaking worthless oaths tyrannically imposed from outside; in the latter he was blamed for breaking his commitments to the community. The Presbyterian Richard Baxter provides examples of both modes. Like Milton, he claimed to have had misgivings about the clerical oath of office in the 1630s and 1640s, but unlike Milton, he swallowed them and entered the ministry.[16] Unlike Milton, he refused the Solemn League and Covenant, later urging others to do the same, including his flock at Kidderminster.[17] However, after being expelled from the restored Church of England in 1662 for refusing to swear the new oath of office and allegiance mandated by the Act of Uniformity,[18] Baxter concluded a 1664 account of his earlier campaigns against the Covenant and the Commonwealth's oath of Engagement by insisting that he had not wanted to force his parishioners to take oaths they could not keep, to become Samsons breaking their cords like flax or withes: "I could not judge it seemly for him that believed there is a God, to play *fast* and *loose* with a dreadful Oath, as if the Bonds of National and Personal Vows were as easily shak'd off as *Sampson*'s Cords."[19] This same trope had appeared many times before, not just in the Restoration debate over oaths, as in *Hudibras*, but in those over earlier state oaths, from the 1606 Oath of Allegiance, where it arguably originated, to the Protestation to the Covenant and Engagement. In addition to Baxter and Butler, a number of examples, including the *Eikon Basilike* and *Eikonoklastes*, suggest that it had become a commonplace by the time of the Restoration.[20]

## Oaths as Samson's Cords before *Samson Agonistes*

Despite Samson's often being cast as an exemplar of faith, the oaths-as-cords trope represents an alternate tradition in which he breaks faith. His cords had traditionally figured the enticements of the world, the flesh, the Devil and women.[21] But after 1606 a new trope emerged in England: in almost fifty books the strongman's cords became a way of talking about people's ties to others in the form of obligations, laws, vows, oaths, and covenants.[22] The groundwork had been laid centuries before in Hebrews 11:32's characterization of Samson as one of a number of heroes of faith, extraordinary citizen-saints whose faith in God "subdued kingdoms."[23] From the idea of keeping faith with God[24] it was not too big a step to that of keeping faith with fellow humans, the oath being a promise to keep such faith. Perhaps more important was the concept of the oath as a fetter for the soul (*vinculum animae*), which drew on Numbers 30's characterization of both vows and oaths as binding and fettering their takers' souls – itself a product of a broader, cross-cultural understanding of the oath as tie or bond.[25] The Hebrew words *issar* (bond) and *nephesh* (soul) in Numbers 30:2 and 13 became the Vulgate's *se constrinxerit* (chained himself) in its verses 3 and 14, with the concept of the soul left almost omitted, only appearing at the tail end of verse 14 (*animam suam*). This idea of vows and oaths binding the soul apparently fused at some point before the early modern period with the references in Judges 15:10–14 and 16:7–12 to Samson's being bound (the Hebrew verb *asar*) with ropes and cords (the Hebrew nouns *abothim, esura,* and *yetherim*), which the Vulgate renders as forms of the Latin verb for tying (*ligare*) and as the nouns *funibus, ligatus,* and *vincula*. Cicero had also referred to the oath as a *vinculum* in his famous discussion of Regulus's oath-keeping in *De Officiis*.[26] Hence, it seems to have become a commonplace by the late sixteenth century to refer to the oath as a chain or fetter of the soul (*vinculum animae*).[27] This made sense because while Judges 16:7–19 describes Samson as having seven locks of hair to cut off and as being bound by the Philistines with seven ropes (or *withes* in the Authorized Version), the Hebrew word for oath (*sheba*) is, as we will see shortly, cognate with the word for seven. Add to this the fact that, as we shall also see, Samson tenders an oath to the men of Judah in Judges 15. In any case, Milton's discussion of oaths in *De Doctrina* uses the term *vinculum* to describe the ties created by oaths.[28] Perhaps, then, Samson's seven locks and cords had allegorically referred to oaths in Judges – or so it began to seem to English polemicists after James promulgated the Oath of Allegiance.

They had been anticipated by rabbinical commentators who pursued some version of this line of thought and linked Samson to oaths. Scattered *midrashim* on texts other than Judges paint a general picture of Samson as an elemental, snake-like creature that feared and could be controlled by oaths. Take, for example, the gloss on Genesis 49:17, which mentions Samson's tribe of Dan (apropos Jacob's prophecy that

"Dan shall be a serpent in the way"): "As a serpent is bound by an oath, so was Samson the son of Manoah bound by an oath: And Samson said unto them: Swear unto me (Judg. XV, 12)." The modern editor adds that "This probably refers to the incantation of snake-charmers by which the serpent is rendered harmless."[29] In a commentary on the Judges story itself, the Babylonian Talmud details more connections between Samson and oaths. The Sotah Tractate claims in reference to Judges 13:5 ("and [Samson] shall begin to deliver Israel") that Samson's role as saviour of the Jews was a response to the Philistines' breaking the oath or league of non-aggression Abimelech swore with Abraham (Genesis 20–1, 26): "The oath of Abimelech became void, as it is written: That thou wilt not deal falsely with me, nor with my son, nor with my son's son." The fact that Samson uses foxes, supposedly backward animals, to burn the Philistines' fields is apparently fitting punishment for those who *go back on* their oaths: "Samson went and caught three hundred foxes. Why just foxes? . . . Samson declared: Let [the animal] come which turns backward and exact punishment of the Philistines who went back on their oath."[30]

In making these links to oaths, both Midrash and Talmud respond not just to Judges' depiction of Samson as vowed Nazir but also to the one clear oath in Judges, and an imposed oath at that. In Judges 15:12–13 Samson makes the men of Judah swear an oath not to kill him after they bind him with ropes to hand him over to the Philistines:

> And they said unto him, We are come down to bind thee, that we may deliver thee into the hand of the Philistines. And Samson said unto them, Swear unto me, that ye will not fall upon me yourselves. And they spake unto him, saying, No; but we will bind thee fast, and deliver thee into their hand: but surely we will not kill thee. And they bound him with two new cords, and brought him up from the rock.[31]

The passage may suggest an analogy between the ropes that bind Samson and the oaths that bind the men of Judah. Verse 12's "Swear" is a translation of the Hebrew *hishebu*, a verb related to the noun *sheba* or *shebua* (oath) and likely derived from the word *seven* (*sheba*).[32] Swearing in Hebrew may be "sevening" or "being sevened" for any number of reasons. The swearer may speak the formula of promise or assertion seven times for emphasis and strength.[33] Or "seven" may be a synecdoche for "a large number" of binding obligations created by an oath (compare the expression "the whole shebang").[34] According to another explanation, oath-takers bound themselves in the presence of seven (i.e., a large number of) witnesses or judges to speak truth or perform a future action.[35] Or seven may refer to the number of physical objects, such as stones or sacrificed animals, that witness and guarantee the swearer's promise.[36] Finally, it may refer to the swearer's risking seven years of curses for breaking the oath.[37]

While the English tradition of likening oaths to Samson's cords stems from a knowledge of these verses in the Hebrew of Judges, Milton's Samson story notably departs from Judges and from the English oaths-as-cords trope by substituting for the oath a league between the Philistines and Israelites, a league probably based on the oath/pact between Abraham and Abimelech mentioned by the Sotah Tractate.[38] Milton's Samson actually downplays the status of Judges 15:12–13's oath as perlocutionary speech-act by describing it merely as "some conditions" (line 258). But before we return to this passage, we must consider that trope's place in the English discourse of oaths.

We should by now be familiar with the veritable procession of state oaths in early modern England, including the Tudor Oaths of Succession and Supremacy, the Jacobean Oath of Allegiance, the Solemn League and Covenant and Engagement, the Clarendon subscriptions, and the Test oaths. In the wake of every oath's promulgation in the seventeenth century there appeared an attack or defence that alluded to Samson's cords, the breaking of which was recommended or condemned as occasion demanded. This new analogy provides a very precise index of the importance of state oaths in English culture, its frequency varying directly with the size of each controversy over state oaths. After James I was almost blown to bits by the Gunpowder Plotters, he imposed an additional oath of allegiance on Catholics from 1606 onwards, which eventually became the standard oath of allegiance for all subjects until 1689.[39] It was this oath that caused some English Catholics even more trouble than had the Tudor oaths, demanding that they renounce definitively the authority of the pope over the English state, if not the English church. In 1609 William Barlow's defence of James's new oath recalled the plotters' and other Jesuits' equivocating responses to the authorities' attempts to extort confessions from them, when it compared "Jesuited Catholics" to Samson:

> Indeede to be tied in bonds, is an *aggreeuance* to mans nature, which desireth libertie; but of all other vnto *Iesuited Catholikes* it can be none: who

> with their *Paganish Aequiuocation*, *vocally* swearing, but mentally distinguishing, can, with *Sampsons* slight, break *new* Cords, as a *threed of towe is broken when it feeleth fire*, though they be seuenfold, so is an *Oath*, & so to be reputed; by the *Hebrwes* therefore originally deriued from the number, *Seaven*, as being a bond multiplied and indefezible.[40]

Barlow warns that these Jesuits want to crush the pillars of the arguments Barlow and the king himself had made for the oath's necessity, but the message is that they will not succeed.[41] Donne's argument for the oath in *Pseudo-Martyr* (1610) – ironically opposed to that of his ancestor Thomas More – asserted that those Catholics who refused it were not really the martyrs for their faith they claimed to be, but only pseudo- or fake martyrs. Refuting their claim of being called by God to reject the oath, Donne adduced Samson as an example of a doubtful martyr, a man presumed by the Catholic Church to have been guided by God, but whose involvement with and guidance from God are basically unprovable.[42]

The international debate over the new Oath of Allegiance continued into the 1620s, involving such luminaries as Lancelot Andrewes, Cardinal Bellarmine, and the king himself. In 1620 the future primate of Armagh, James Ussher, suggested the Samson's cords analogy in a sermon to the House of Commons that concluded by emphasizing the need to take the Oath.[43] Moreover, the atmosphere created by some Catholics' refusing it had led Samuel Ward, minister of Ipswich and future Master of Sydney-Sussex, Cambridge, to preach an assizes sermon several years earlier that drew loosely upon Samson's identity as judge and likened him to corrupt judges and magistrates.[44] "Why then," he demanded, "what are oathes for Atheists and Papists, other then collers for monkies neckes, which slip them at pleasure? such neither are nor can be good subjects: muchlesse good Magistrates. Papists will keep no faith with Protestants, let Protestants give no trust to Papists, though they swear vpon all the books in the world."[45] Judges and magistrates took oaths of office that obliged them to mete out justice fairly and that included an oath of allegiance to the king. Bribed magistrates were thus nothing more than blinded Samsons whom God had abandoned because they had perjured themselves by not honouring their oaths' promise to serve justice.[46] In doing so, according to Ward, these men had only fallen into the condition of most men, who take and break oaths rashly, while "the land . . . mourne[s] for the contempt of oaths, and neglect of duties."[47] For oaths were more than empty formulas: "What are the nerues and sinewes of all gouernment, the bonds and commands of obedience, but an oath? and what are oaths to prophane men, but as Sampsons cords, which hee snapt asunder, as fast as they were offered him."[48]

If, then, individual oaths of office and allegiance were not to be "snapt asunder," neither were religious covenants sworn on the national level. Twenty years later, the Scots opposed the new Laudian prayerbook with riots and a national oath or covenant that led to two Bishops' Wars and two Civil Wars, arguably planting the idea for later state oaths such as the Solemn League and Covenant.[49] Scotland had a local tradition of likening itself and emblematic figures such as William Wallace to Samson as underdogs facing hostile outsiders, usually the neighbouring English, but occasionally the more distant French.[50] This tradition had begun in the reforming sixteenth century, when Scotland adopted Calvinist covenantalism – in this instance a welcome outside influence. Under figures like John Knox the Scots began swearing a series of domestic covenants, of which the National Covenant of 1638 was the most consequential, not only because it led to war among the three kingdoms but also because it was sworn by large numbers of women: in principle, all Scottish women.[51]

The diary of one of the Covenant's two authors, Archibald Johnston, Lord Warriston, states that he began the process of national subscription by reading the Covenant out to the assembled congregation in the Trinity Kirk, Edinburgh on 2 March 1638. This reading was prefaced by the minister, Henry Rollock, preaching a sermon that featured two texts – Jeremiah 3:4 and "Samsons mothers aunser to Manoah" (presumably Judges 13:23) – as parts of a "sensible exhortation" to swear the Covenant.[52] In the pulpit of the same church a few months later, the Aberdeen minister Andrew Cant identified two things as the pillars of Dagon's temple, a transparent reference to the Laudian church: 1) princes' (i.e., Charles I's) secular support for episcopacy; 2) bishops' own words, in sermons and in print, in support of themselves. Cant urged Scots to come to "this main pillar of Dagon's House [episcopacy] and apply all our Strength to pull it down."[53] In the same year George Lightbody defended the National Covenant as a last resort to be taken by the Scottish people in the absence of a godly magistrate (i.e., the English king), just as "*Iesus did scourge the buyers and sellers in the temple,* Samuell *killed king* Agag, Phineas *killed* Zimri *and* Cosbi, [and] Samson *slew the* Philistims."[54] And sometime before his death in 1653, the Glasgow minister Hugh Binning described oaths like the Scottish National Covenant and the Solemn League and Covenant as Samson's cords. Arguing that it would be unwise to allow covenant-breakers into positions of responsibility in Scotland because they would also break their oaths of office, he complained that "Oaths and Covenants are but like green Cords about *Samson* to bind these men . . . These whom that SACRED BOND OF COVENANT hath not tyed, what oath can bind?"[55] Charles I responded to the National Covenant by trying to convince the Scots to sign a counter-covenant, but with little success, and the Bishops' Wars soon followed. In 1640 a critic of the Scots characterized their breaking this counter-covenant, and by implication their oaths of allegiance to Charles, as Samson breaking his cords.[56]

In the runup to the War of the Three Kingdoms, critics of the Caroline regime, such as the future Presbyterians Cornelius Burges and Stephen Marshall (the latter a Smectymnuan), called for a national covenant in England and compared covenants to Samson's locks; an uncovenanted England would be like Samson without his hair.[57] Then in the spring of 1641 "news of an army plot" produced something like the covenant they had envisaged: the Protestation of May 1641, the English Parliament's oath to defend Church and king against popery.[58] Several writers would later refer to this and other parliamentary oaths as Samson's cords.[59] Almost two years later, in the months before Parliament promulgated two more state oaths in the midst of war – the Vow and Covenant (June 1643) and the Solemn League and Covenant (August–September 1643) – William Prynne clearly had in mind the Protestation (and at least one of the Covenants) when he argued for the inalienable powers of Parliament in its defensive war against the king, at whom Prynne now levelled the charge of oath-breaking.[60] In several *Remonstrances* around the time of and printed with the Nineteen Propositions of 1642, Parliament itself had strongly hinted that Charles had not just misinterpreted but actually broken his coronation oath.[61] In two printed petitions addressed to Parliament after the outbreak of war, *Samsons Fall* (January 1643) and *Samsons Legacie* (April 1643), the prophet of apocalyptic doom, Lady Eleanor Davies Douglas, pushed the argument further by painting the king as a Samsonian breaker of his coronation oath's cords.[62] Prynne picked up the metaphor at the end of March in his role as self-appointed spokesman for the Presbyterian-dominated Parliament. Pointing to the Magna Carta as an earlier example of just limitations on royal power, he claimed that the Great Charter had actually not been

> a sufficiant securitie to preserve [the Lords' and Commons'] Lawes and Liberties against the invasions of an, unconstant, willful foedifragous

> king ... whose *oaths and protestations* were but like Sampsons cords, broken all to pieces like a thread in a moment, by those who had Sampsons strength.[63]

"Foedifragous": the King had broken the covenant or pact implied by his coronation oath, which promised to uphold Parliament's laws, when he expanded his prerogative in the 1620s–1630s and went to war with his people in the 1640s.[64] Hence, Prynne argued, "the Kings Army of Papists and Malignants, invading the Parliaments or Subjects persons, goods, Lawes, Liberties, Religion may even in Conscience bee justly resisted with force," as proved "by many expresse Authorities recorded, and approved in Scripture," including the Samson story in Judges.[65] Samson figures both an oath-breaking king and his opponents.

The Solemn League and Covenant was the most important of all these state oaths because contested over so long a period: on and off from its inception in 1643 to the late 1660s, and even beyond.[66] What made it so controversial, and for so long – important enough for one of its early defenders to dub its opponents those who "grope at midday, blinde with light"?[67] On some level, it came to stand in for the Parliament's Good Old Cause in its entirety, in a way that other oaths, including the Republic's Engagement, never did. The Covenant arose from Parliament's need to turn the tide of battle against the king by seeking help from the Scots, whose national acts of resistance and covenanting had helped trigger the Civil War. The English obtained Scottish support in return for a promise to establish Presbyterianism in the three kingdoms. Not just a treaty between two kingdoms sealed by oath, the Solemn League and Covenant became in 1644 a required loyalty oath for all adult males in England and Scotland; as with the Scottish National Covenant, it was also subscribed by some women.[68] Over the next half-decade, it caused enormous qualms of conscience for royalists and anyone else who risked huge fines as well as loss of property and the protection of law if they refused to swear it. In comparison to the other oaths, it provoked the largest discussion in print, and the discussion re-emerged at the Restoration, when the Presbyterians who invited Charles II back to his native land tried to revive the Covenant and Presbyterianism, only to be met with a Cavalier Parliament that not only burned the Covenant but produced a series of oaths of office in the 1660s that explicitly repudiated it. In one way or another, it remained a feature of political controversy up through the Exclusion Crisis.[69]

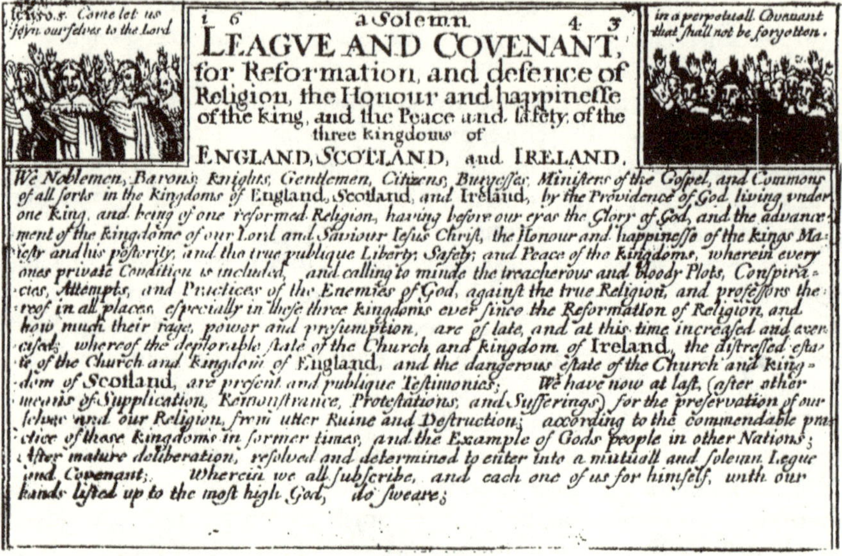

Ier. 50. 5. Come let us joyn ourselves to the Lord

1 6 a Solemn 4 3

LEAGVE AND COVENANT, for Reformation, and defence of Religion, the Honour and happinesse of the king, and the Peace and safety, of the three kingdoms of ENGLAND, SCOTLAND, and IRELAND.

in a perpetuall Covenant that shall not be forgotten.

We Noblemen, Barons, Knights, Gentlemen, Citizens, Burgesses, Ministers of the Gospel, and Commons of all sorts in the Kingdoms of England, Scotland, and Ireland, by the Providence of God living under one King, and being of one reformed Religion, having before our eyes the Glory of God, and the advancement of the Kingdome of our Lord and Saviour Iesus Christ, the Honour and happinesse of the kings Majesty and his posterity, and the true publique Liberty, Safety, and Peace of the Kingdoms, wherein every ones private Condition is included, and calling to minde the treacherous and bloody Plots, Conspiracies, Attempts, and Practices of the Enemies of God, against the true Religion, and professors thereof in all places, especially in these three kingdoms ever since the Reformation of Religion, and how much their rage, power and presumption, are of late, and at this time increased and exercised; whereof the deplorable state of the Church and kingdom of Ireland, the distressed estate of the Church and kingdom of England, and the dangerous estate of the Church and kingdom of Scotland, are present and publique Testimonies; We have now at last, (after other means of Supplication, Remonstrance, Protestations, and Sufferings) for the preservation of our selves and our Religion, from utter Ruine and Destruction; according to the commendable practice of those Kingdoms in former times, and the Example of Gods people in other Nations; After mature deliberation, resolved and determined to enter into a mutuall and solemn League and Covenant; Wherein we all subscribe, and each one of us for himself, with our hands lifted up to the most high God, do sweare;

Figure 2 Wenceslaus Hollar, illustration from *A Solemn League and Covenant* (1643), RB 124654, The Huntington Library, San Marino, California. Image produced by ProQuest as part of *Early English Books Online* (www.proquest.com) and published with permission of ProQuest. Further reproduction is prohibited without permission.

Many discussions of oaths after the Solemn League and Covenant included the trope of Samson's cords. One printed version of the Covenant was accompanied by illustrations, such as the one depicting its takers stretching their arms towards Heaven (Figure 2). The woodcut next to Article 5 of the Covenant promised that "we shall each one of us, according to place and interest, indeavour" "the happinesse of a blessed Peace between these kingdoms" so that "they may remain conioyned in a firm Peace an Union to all posterity." It featured three men, each representing one of the three kingdoms of England, Scotland, and Ireland, who hold a strand of a larger cord representing their union (see Figure 1 in my introduction).[70] The caption from Ecclesiastes 4:12 ("A threefold cord is not easily broken" in the Geneva translation) perfectly reinforces the idea of three kingdoms united by an oath's cord.

Ecclesiastes's threefold cord easily morphed into Judges' sevenfold ones. Edward Gee would later write of the Covenant and the other two parliamentary oaths preceding the Engagement (the Protestation and the Vow and Covenant) that "How light soever others make of these Oathes, though they bee to them as soluble and weake as *Samsons greene withs*; yet they are to us as a *three-fold Cord*, and [I] trust they will prove stronger in us than death."[71] Edmund Calamy built upon this semi-official trope of oaths-as-cords when he preached a sermon, *The Great Danger of Covenant-Refusing and Covenant-Breaking* to the Lord Mayor and Common Council of London in early 1646, specifying the cords as Samson's. For those who had taken and then broken the Solemn League and Covenant, it was never too late to renew it:

> So may the best Christian here present say: *Lord I am carnall, sold under sinne,* I have broken those golden cords of the Covenant with which I have tyed my selfe unto thee. Though I am *spirit,* yet am I *flesh* also: And therefore I come to binde my selfe anew. As *Dalilah* dealt with *Sampson,* &c. so do I desire to deale with my self, and to tye my self yet faster and faster to God, if by any meanes I might be kept firme to him.[72]

Covenant-takers were thus spiritual Samsons who might avoid the snares of the flesh and bind themselves by oath to God rather than Delilah.[73]

Two collections of apothegms appearing within a decade of the Covenant's signing responded to it with jaded cynicism: the royalist and future Archbishop of Canterbury William Sancroft's calling oaths hedges; the Parliamentarian Dudley, Lord North's dubbing them overused medicine – but both agreeing that oaths are as easily broken as Samson's cords.[74] In 1646 Bruno Ryves, a Covenant-refuser like Sancroft and one of Charles I's chaplains, complained in the royalist newsbook *Mercurius Rusticus* of parliamentary soldiers who apparently broke a truce with some of his fellow royalists, identifying them as "this generation of *Truce-breakers* . . . that keep Faith neither with God nor man, and break Oaths faster than ever *Sampson* did his Cords, whom nothing can tye fast but a Halter, the strongest Obligation for a Traytor."[75]

In the same year, John Lilburne levelled the same accusation at the Scots, who, he claimed, reputedly broke their Solemn League and Covenant like Samson's cords.[76] In 1647, however, Lilburne, while decidedly not a Catholic, turned himself into one of Donne's pseudo-martyrs by leaving the Army because, among other things, he refused to take the Solemn League and Covenant, which he called "the Divels fetters."[77] The title page of *The Resolved Man's Resolution*, one of the tracts he wrote in the Tower about refusing the Covenant and other matters, famously compares him to a Samson who will likely meet his death at Tyburn.[78] Another, *Rash Oaths Unwarrantable*, castigates Parliament not only for failing to keep its own oaths to govern well but for forcing others to perjure themselves by taking such conflicting oaths as the Covenant and the Oaths of Allegiance and Supremacy.[79] Yet in the face of his own opposition not just to the Covenant but to ex officio oaths in the 1630s and to all oaths when he became a Quaker at the end of his life in the 1650s, this same man would for mercenary reasons take the oath of Engagement to the Commonwealth three years later and defend it in print.[80] Moreover, given that the Engagement was attacked by Prynne (perhaps predictably) for being as frail as Samson's cords, is it possible that Richard Baxter's words against the cords of both Covenant and Engagement, though published much later, were written or formulated at the time of the Engagement?[81]

## The Cords of Coronation in *Eikon Basilike* and *Eikonoklastes*

Building on parliamentary accusations against the "foedifragous" king is the trope's appearance in the *Eikon Basilike*, the sacred book that contributed to the row over conflicting oaths in the wake of the Engagement and became a touchstone, even an obsession in much of Milton's later work. Probably the second most important book in seventeenth-century England after the Bible, and for many people a kind of second Bible, the *Eikon Basilike* offered a self-hagiography of Charles I that managed to appeal not just to Anglican royalists but to Presbyterians. For, among other things, it included a chapter on their Solemn League and Covenant. While emphatically condemning the Covenant as superfluous with respect to already existing oaths, such as (presumably) the Oaths of Allegiance and Supremacy and the Protestation, and as contrary to his vision of an episcopal Church of England, the Royal Martyr nevertheless allowed some room for the Church to reform itself under his guidance, and thus permitted takers of the Covenant to keep it insofar as it contravened neither previous obligations (sworn and unsworn) nor law and order more generally: "I willingly forgive such mens taking the Covenant, who keep it within such bounds of Piety, Law, and Loyalty, as can never hurt either the Church, My self, or the Publique Peace."[82] In making this point, Charles decried the fact that those previous oaths had been treated as "cords and wyths" that "will hold mens Consciences no longer then force attends and twists them: for every man soone growes his owne Pope, and easily absolves himselfe of those ties."[83] Charles clearly draws on traditions of, on the one hand, lambasting the pope for absolving English subjects of their oaths of allegiance to the monarch and, on the other, of slighting Presbyters for setting themselves up as popes in their local parishes. Yet equally clearly he invokes the Samson's cords metaphor, with his subjects as Samsons illegitimately breaking the bonds of oaths and commitments.[84] Otherwise, why mention both cords *and* withes in reference to the oath? Moreover, it is hard not to hear one of the final prayers in this chapter from *Eikon Basilike* as an extension of the cords metaphor that reverses its direction while complementing this first point. Charles asks his people to break the Covenant, at the very least the parts of the Covenant that compromise law and order: "Break in sunder, O Lord, all violent and sacrilegious Confederations, to doe wickedly and injuriously." In other words, Charles asks his subjects to become Samson by breaking the Covenant's cords.[85]

Charles's famous reference to himself as Samson appears in another chapter, the one on the Nineteen Propositions, which casts those parliamentary demands as unlawful restraints on the king's sovereignty. Vaguely referencing one of the Propositions, perhaps the Second, as binding him "to a generall and implicite consent, to what ever they [Parliament] shall desire, or propound," Charles represents agreeing to such infringement of the royal prerogative as allowing

> a latitude of blind obedience, as never was expected from any Free-man, nor fit to be required of any man, much lesse of a King, by His own Subjects . . . This were as if *Sampson* should have consented, not only to *binde* his own hands, and cut off his haire, but to put out his own eyes, that the *Philistins* might with the more safety mock, and abuse him; which they chose rather to doe, then quite to destroy him, when he was become so tame an object, and fit occasion for their sport and scorne.[86]

While Charles's final sentence here moves on to Samson's shearing and blinding, it crucially begins with his binding. Any of the Nineteen Propositions and any other devices that invade the monarch's power are the binding cords the royal Samson must break. Those devices may well include the king's coronation oath, as Milton's *Eikonoklastes* asserts in response to this passage.[87] Elsewhere in the *Eikon Basilike* Charles is adamant that his coronation oath does not bind him to accept (and thus not veto) all laws Parliament presents him. The king returns to the initial controversy over the Nineteen Propositions and their links to Parliament's insinuation in 1642 that his coronation oath binds Charles to consent to all laws "the people shall choose" – a phrase of which we shall hear more. Yet according to Charles, the oath binds him only to preserve royal government and the rights of the Episcopal Church.[88] Thus, the implication seems to be that Parliament's restrictive interpretation of the oath as forbidding vetoes is yet another cord this Samson must snap. If his subjects fail to take their oaths to him seriously – whether the Oaths of Allegiance and Supremacy or the almost redundant loyalty oaths imposed by Parliament in the 1640s – why should Charles not snap the oaths Parliament imposed without his permission? In fact, *Eikon Basilike* just barely avoids saying that the coronation oaths themselves, not just Parliament's restrictive interpretation of them, are Samson's cords waiting to be loosed or broken.

Milton calls the king out on exactly this issue in *Eikonoklastes*:

> if the Parlament . . . desir'd him [Charles I] to follow their advice and deliberation in things of public concernment [according to his coronation oaths], he accounts it the same proposition, as if *Sampson* had bin mov'd *to the putting out his eyes, that the Philistims might abuse him*. And thus out of an unwise, or pretended feare least others should make a scorn of him for yeilding to his Parlament, he regards not to give cause of worse suspicion, that he made a scorn of his regal Oath.[89]

That is why Milton returns to Samson in the famous passage later in the book, where he almost ignores what Charles has said in *Eikon Basilike* about his own words: that they should match his inner feelings and intentions and describe the truth, however unpopular. Instead of treating Charles's words as constative descriptions of inner states or truth, however, Milton seizes the opportunity to consider them as performative speech-acts: "*The words of a King,* as they are *full of power,* in the autority and strength of Law, so like *Sampson,* without the strength of that *Nazarites* lock, they have no more power in them then the words of another man."[90] The king's words only count as official speech-acts with a force that binds his subjects if those words are somehow spoken legally and backed by law.[91] And the reference to Samson revisits the issue of the coronation oath's cord-like breakability. According to Milton's paradigm, if the king swore his coronation oath to uphold "the laws the people shall choose"[92] but mentally reserved an understanding of the oath as allowing vetoes of bills on matters of "public concernment," his words would have no force, like a shorn Samson; they would be illegal, and he would almost cease to be king. At the very least, a veto of a public bill (via the words "Le Roy s'avisera" or any other veto formula) would have no legal force, and in that sense would be no different from the same words spoken by an ordinary person.[93] It becomes clear, then, that both *Eikon Basilike* and *Eikonoklastes* are marked by the cords analogy's place in the debate over state oaths, a debate that similarly marks *Samson Agonistes* and *Paradise Lost*.

## Samson's Cords in Restoration England

Perhaps most important for a consideration of Milton's treatment of oaths in the later poems, Samson's cords appeared in Restoration debates over state oaths: both the twenty-year-old Covenant and the Clarendon Code's new oaths of office and allegiance that repudiated it.[94] We can now see that by the early 1660s the metaphor had become so widespread and important as to be ripe for parody. Butler's reference in *Hudibras* (1662) to "Words and promises" as "Sampson's Cuffs" rather than Samson's cords is just that.[95] And we should recall that Baxter wrote his condemnation of breaking Samson's cords in 1664, while John Tabor's complaint that many people treated oaths of allegiance like the cords appeared a few years later.[96] In the early years of the Restoration, some Presbyterians like Thomas Hall used the figure to insist that covenants like the Solemn League and Covenant were still binding.[97] By contrast, an early biographer of George Monck, a prime architect of the Restoration, represented the Presbyterian general as urging the restored Long Parliament "that they had more need to repent of their former oathes than to take new" and "to be tender in imposing Oathes," for "men have used them [oaths] so commonly, that they can shake off their cords with as much ease as Sampson did his Withs."[98] But this advice went unheeded, for after the Presbyterians failed to achieve their Covenant-based Presbyterian settlement, the Cavalier Parliament that prevented it and reimposed the Church of England with a vengeance also promulgated many new oaths of office that required abjuration of the Covenant. These did not, however, quiet those Presbyterians who insisted that they were still bound by the Covenant's obligations to effect Presbyterian reformation and that those obligations did not conflict with their oaths of allegiance to the new monarch.

Hence the polemic over oaths continued hotly for the next few years, with Quakers playing an important role as refusers of all oaths, especially imposed ones. If Samson had "made the men of Judah swear" in Judges 15:12, said one Quaker, then Christ, "who is greater then Sampson," "ends the swearing, and ends the oaths." [99] John Gauden, who was not unsympathetic to Presbyterians and had helped portray Charles I as a Samsonian martyr in *Eikon Basilike,*[100] was, however, among the first to leap into the ring in 1660 and deny the Covenant's binding force,[101] and in 1661, after gaining a bishopric for his various services, attacked the Covenant once again in two books that used the image of Samson breaking his cords/oaths.[102] The writings of Robert Sanderson, the age's foremost authority on oaths and an opponent of the Covenant, were used after his death in 1663 to repudiate the Covenant yet once more. A passage on Samson's cords as oaths from a sermon Sanderson had preached to the Court in 1636 and published in 1656 was now excerpted to answer the question posed by the volume's editor: "Whether they that have taken the Covenant may renounce it?"[103] Sanderson's reply, now simultaneously proleptic and posthumous, was that if "a man hath bound himself rashly by some promise, vow, or covenant to do something he may not do, or not to do something he ought to do," "there is no way out again but one: even this, To loose his pledge, to break in sunder the bonds wherein he is tied, as Sampson did the green withs, and to cast away those cords from him."[104] On the other side, Presbyterian defences of the Covenant such as *The Covenanters Plea Against Absolvers* (1661), in which Baxter may have had a hand, protested that when various kinds of "sacred bonds" like the Solemn League and Covenant are "twisted into one cord, they must be stronger than Sampsons seven green withs, and like Solomons threefold cord which cannot be broken."[105]

When a large number of Presbyterian and other ministers, including Baxter, were ejected from the Church in 1662 for, among other reasons, refusing to swear the Clarendon Code's oaths and thus to reject the Covenant, some of them preached farewell sermons comparing themselves and fellow Presbyterians to Samson.[106] From the comparative safety of Holland, the Scots Presbyterian minister John Brown, in a book later burned with Milton's Regicide tracts at Oxford, protested the ejection of the Scottish ministers by comparing oath-breakers and covenant-breakers to Samson breaking his cords.[107] As we saw in chapter 2, in the same year that Milton's *Paradise Lost* was printed (1667), the English Presbyterian John Humfrey sensed an opening for parliamentary toleration after the Chatham disaster and initiated the toleration debate by urging Parliament to do away with the Clarendon Oaths, characterizing them as useless cords that anyone might break like Samson.[108] Tabor's condemnation of those who treat oaths of allegiance like Samson's cords made the opposite argument (that Nonconformists could not be trusted),[109] and many others joined him in using the trope against Nonconformists. In 1670 – the year in which both a second Conventicles Act put paid to toleration, and *Samson Agonistes* appeared as if in protest – Anglican royalists such as Thomas Pittis chastised their enemies for taking the wrong oaths in the past and disregarding legitimate oaths in the present.[110]

## Oaths, Vows, and Adjurations in *Samson Agonistes*

Curiously, *Samson Agonistes* goes out of its way to avoid both this tradition of comparing Samson's cords to oaths and one of the passages in Judges that may have suggested it. Judges 15:12–13 contains the one clear instance of an imposed oath in the narrative: the oath of non-violence that Samson requires of the men of Judah when they tie him up – the same oath Quakers invoked as an analogue to the state oaths they claimed Christ had forbidden.[111] Yet in contrast to the royalist Francis Quarles's 1631 poem *The Historie of Samson*, which magnifies this imposed speech-act into "a sacred oath" and "engage[ment of] plighted troth,"[112] Milton's treatment of the story refers to the incident without the word "oath." "I willingly on some conditions came / Into their hands," says the protagonist, not specifying how these "conditions" were arrived at and passing up the opportunity in the following lines to compare his cords to oaths (258–62).[113] However, the virtual elision of this oath, to which we will return, paradoxically contributes to focusing the poem even more on oaths, in this case the experience of taking rather than imposing state oaths.

For the dominant way in which the poem considers oath-taking is via the related speech-act of the vow. We should recall Satan's talking almost interchangeably of *swearing* submission and *vowing* submission to God in *Paradise Lost*. "How soon," he laments, "Would height . . . unsay / What feigned submission swore: ease would recant / Vows made in pain, as violent and void" (4.95–7). The various speech-acts designated as commissives by Searle (vows, oaths, covenants, promises, and so on) are related and often confused with each other. Generally speaking, in Milton's day those who chose their words carefully differentiated between swearing *by* God and vowing *to* God. The preposition marked the oath's involvement of God as witness of a transaction between humans, as opposed to the vow's promise on the part of an individual to give (up) something to God in return for services rendered – a meaning increasingly vestigial by Milton's time.[114] Yet despite this and other fine distinctions to be made between the two,[115] most people did not choose their words so carefully. Even in antiquity the difference was not ironclad. Vows and oaths are spoken of in the same breath in Numbers 30:2 and Psalm 132:20–5; and the Talmud's various tracts on vows and oaths, including Nedarim, Shebuoth, Nazir, and Eduyoth, sometimes conflate them. For example, the tract ostensibly on vows (or *nedarim*) mostly discusses oaths.[116]

In the early modern period, the oath-guru Robert Sanderson asserted that "oaths and vowes are in most things alike."[117] A popular conscience book of the 1650s by Milton's former antagonist Joseph Hall compared false or trivial vows to Samson's cords, and most early modern commentators would have agreed with Francis Taylor's sentiments: "I will not say that oathes, and vowes, and covenants, are all one in every circumstance: but certainly they are cousen germans at least, and can hardly be separated."[118] That vows and oaths were regarded as first cousins and even twins is confirmed not only by Shakespeare's Sonnet 152 ("all my vows are oaths but to misuse thee") and the line in *Hudibras* about "all the Oaths [that] to us they vow'd,"[119] but by Milton himself.

As we have seen, he defines the oath (Latin *iusiurandum*) as an act of "call[ing] God to witness that we are speaking the truth, and curs[ing] ourselves, either by implication or expressly, if we should be lying"; and he defines the vow (*votum*) as "a promise solemnly made to God" that "must concern some lawful thing."[120] For the Milton of *De Doctrina*, oaths and vows are thus two kinds of verbal commitment, the oath more assertory, the vow more promissory.[121] Yet the line between swearing by and vowing to God sometimes disappeared in his other writings. In *De Doctrina* itself, several of the proof texts in the discussion of vows only contain the words "oath" and "swear," and Milton notes that "in scripture" "a public vow . . . is usually called a covenant [foedus]."[122] In *Tetrachordon* he warns that while some call marriage "the Covnant of God," this is only so because "God is the witness thereof," and "this denomination [Covnant of God] adds nothing to the Covnant of Mariage, above any other civil and solemn contract." "Nor is it more indissoluble," he says, "then any other against the end of its own ordination, nor is any *vow or Oath* to God exacted with such a rigor, where superstition reignes not."[123]

In effect, the various commissive speech-acts (vows, oaths, and covenants) could blur into one another. They certainly seem equivalent in Parliament's descriptions of them. For example, Parliament's *Remonstrance* to the King's Answer to the Nineteen Propositions (18 June 1642) called the Protestation a "solemn vow and oath." The printed order for the Vow and Covenant of 1643 uses the phrases "Vow and Covenant" and "Oath and Covenant" interchangeably on its title page: *The Vow and Covenant . . . Ordered by the Lords and Commons assembled in Parliament, that this Oath and Covenant shall be forthwith printed.*[124] Moreover, in the *First Defence* Milton seems to refer to the Solemn League and Covenant, usually called an oath, as a vow.[125] At the very least, we could count both the Covenant and the Vow and Covenant among the Presbyterian loyalty oaths he characterizes as "stiff vows" in the sonnet "On the New Enforcers of Conscience."[126] Nor should we forget Baxter's warning, a propos the Covenant and the Engagement, that people not "play *fast* and *loose* with a dreadful *Oath*, as if the Bonds of National and Personal *Vows* were as easily shak'd off as *Sampson*'s Cords."[127]

In *Samson Agonistes* Milton both magnifies existing and implied vows in Judges and invents new ones, containing a total of eleven by my count.

### Vows in *Samson Agonistes*

1. Samson's vow of purity and deliverance as Nazarite (to avoid contact with unclean things or people and to deliver his people from the Philistines) (319, 1386, 1140–4, 1423–55; 22–39, 225–6, 292)
2. Samson's vow of bodily integrity as Nazarite (to keep his hair uncut) (1143–4)
3. Samson's vow of silence and secrecy (about the source of his strength) (377–99, 399, 428–9, 490–501, 1000–2)
4. Samson's vow of honesty or moral integrity (an avowal, oath, or protestation to Harapha that his strength comes from God rather than magic) (1149–51)
5. Samson's vow of marriage to the nameless woman of Timna (implied, 219–27, 382–7, 1018–23)
6. Samson's vow of marriage to Dalila (implied: 227, 382–8, 750, 1115)
7. Dalila's vow of fidelity and discretion in marriage (a marriage vow to be faithful and by implication not to betray Samson's secrets) (387–8, 750, 1115, 1022–3)
8. The Woman of Timna's vow of fidelity and discretion in marriage (227, 382–7, 1018–23)

9 The Israelites' vow of obedience and allegiance to the Philistines (in an alliance or league) (1182–91)
10 God's vow of reward/compensation (a promise to give Samson's parents a child) (633–5)
11 God's vow of deliverance (a promise to deliver Israel via the Nazarite Samson) (31–2, 38–9)

In this greater emphasis on taking vows, *Samson Agonistes* worries over the problem of living with imposed oaths, recreating the qualms of conscience experienced by members of the political nation confronted with the latest regime's demand for an expression of allegiance that invalidated previous ones. For Milton and other early modern English commentators on the Book of Judges,[128] the Samson narrative seemed particularly well suited to discussing the problematics of oath-taking because it features a man who does not choose his Nazarite vow but has it thrust upon him in the womb by God and a nameless mother. Nowhere does the Samson of Judges actually utter this vow to remain pure and deliver his people from the Philistines.[129] Moreover, it is abundantly clear that Samson has problems keeping his vow: he touches the unclean carcass of a lion and sleeps with presumably unclean women from the very enemy nation from which he must deliver his own. The fact that God makes exceptions in some of these cases stands at the centre of the story and of its relevance to early modern controversies over oaths, for a key bone of contention in such debates was the issue of when God could be said to have dispensed with his own laws on oaths, and to have dispensed in such a way as to allow someone to take a new oath that violated an old.[130]

My analysis of Milton's poem will focus on four things: an oath not taken (the Israelites' league with the Philistines), an oath possibly taken (the Nazarite vow), an oath almost certainly taken (Dalila's promise to the Philistine lords), and a pseudo-oath ambiguously taken (Samson's riddling penultimate speech).

To begin with, the league of obedience to the Philistines that Milton seemingly pulls out of nowhere in the Harapha episode involves a covenant or oath that Samson clearly hasn't subscribed but for which he is held responsible. While not in the Judges narrative itself, the idea most likely comes from Abraham and Isaac's league of non-aggression with Abimelech at Beersheba, the place of the oath (Genesis 21:22–4, 31–2; 26:28–33) – another instance of an oath that applies to people other than its initial subscribers.[131] Several sermons in the 1640s had compared

Samson to Malignant breakers of the Solemn League and Covenant.[132] But the controversy over oaths at the Restoration often touched upon the issue of the individual subject's autonomy in regard to oath-taking, with the argument sometimes advanced that subjects could be bound by oaths they had not personally sworn. In 1660, for example, a defence of the Oaths of Allegiance and Supremacy to the restored king claimed that these oaths, indeed all state oaths, bind every member of "the nation, not [just] those who have taken [them], and even [oblige] 'all their succeeding Posterity.'"[133] In the same year, the Presbyterian Zachary Crofton made a similar claim about the Covenant, declaring that it still bound not just those who had taken it but all members of the English nation, present and future: "it is a publick National Covenant, binding all the persons of this Nation (that swear, or swear not personally) and our posterity after us, in their particular places; and all that shall succeed into the publick places, and politick capacities of this Kingdom, to preserve and pursue the things therein promised, so long as it remains a Kingdom."[134] John Gauden and others objected that the Solemn League and Covenant did not bind people who had not sworn it.[135] Yet with an inconsistency not apparent to them, they also supported the oaths of office framed by the Cavalier Parliament[136] precisely to counter arguments like Crofton's, all of which required an abjuration of the Covenant and insisted that said abjuration apply even to people who had not sworn it.

What autonomy, then, does Samson have with regard to vows and leagues? When the giant Harapha, another of Milton's creations, visits Samson in his final hours, he asks accusingly, "Is not thy nation subject to our lords? / Their magistrates confessed [as much], when they took thee / As a league-breaker and delivered [thee] bound / Into our hands" (1182–5). Referring to the Israelites' attempts in Judges 15 to hand Samson over to the Philistines, Harapha seems to assume that they or their leaders have signed or verbally pledged to some agreement to ally with and thus obey this greater power; Samson has violated that league presumably by killing them and burning their fields (*SA* 1185–8; Judges 14:19; 15:8, 4–5). Since he has, as Harapha puts it, "broke[n] the league" individually, he alone is handed over to them for punishment: "The Philistines, when thou hadst broke the league, / Went up with armed powers thee only seeking, / To others did no violence or spoil" (*SA* 1189–91). In response to Harapha, Samson turns the accusation into a badge of honour, proudly admitting to being a "league-breaker" who "presumed / Single rebellion and did hostile acts" (1209–10), because, in effect, the Israelites had only agreed to the league under duress (1205–7) and, more importantly, I would argue, because Samson himself had never consented to the league by performing the appropriate speech-act.[137] As representatives of their people, Israel's magistrates may have made a league with the Philistines, but it does not necessarily bind him. Samson thus turns Crofton's argument for the Solemn League and Covenant on its head, using it now to justify Samson's removing himself from the league with the Philistines. As Barbara Lewalski has pointed out, the three appearances of the word "league" within the space of twenty-five lines would have recalled for many readers the Solemn League and Covenant.[138] My point is that Samson's league-breaking would also have recalled the various acts of resistance to this state oath by those forced to take or refuse it after its introduction in 1643 – a resistance that Milton had suggested or defended several times in the 1640s and 1650s.[139] Samson is right to have broken an invalid league – a position consonant with Milton's earlier printed views, with regard not just to the Solemn League and Covenant but to the covenant of marriage and the social contract, that because covenants are instrumental and conditional, they can be broken when they no longer serve their original purposes or contravene some greater one.[140] In effect, Milton takes the league-cum-implied-oath from the interpretive tradition and substitutes it for the oath that the Judges Samson imposes on the men of Judah.

We now return to a speech-act that Milton's Samson may have performed himself: the Nazarite vow. *Samson Agonistes* considerably amplifies but does not ultimately resolve the question of whether Samson takes it. As argued earlier, the Samson of Judges does not actually take this vow; his mother does it *for* him, her unborn child being incapable of assent or refusal. While Judges does not entirely rule out his performing this speech-act at some later date, it never mentions him doing so. *Samson Agonistes* comes closer to doing that in a number of passages, thereby foregrounding the issue of consent. Early on in the poem, Samson's "work from heaven imposed" is described as a "task," as "Breeding ordered and prescribed / As of a person separate to God, / Designed for great exploits," and more ambiguously as a "Promise . . . that I / Should Israel from Philistian yoke deliver" (565, 35, 30, 38).[141] This promise is most clearly God's to Samson's parents and nation (see Judges 13:3, 5, 7), possibly even to Samson himself, but the wording of the lines leaves open the possibility that Samson has made the promise. When he describes how Dalila has betrayed him, he admits to having wrongly broken his vow of silence about the source of his strength, calling it, in a formula more emphatic than redundant, "a pledge / Of vow" (378–9). "Pledge" may clarify the issue somewhat by suggesting that he has verbally taken the vow, and possibly at an age when he could have been expected to give informed consent. Yet even these lines do not definitively state that he has made the pledge himself, still casting doubt not only over whether he has, but also over whether he has done so voluntarily and continues to be satisfied with the obligations the vow entails. However, Manoa's later statement that Samson should come home with him and renew his "vows" (520) may imply that Samson has performed them himself, the plural form possibly suggesting either that he has performed them more than once before or that the Nazarite vow really consists of multiple vows. Manoa clearly regards Samson as having broken his vow or vows by marrying Dalila (and perhaps the nameless Timnite) and as capable of returning to his obligations and to something like a state of grace. Yet even here, the statement is not unequivocal: Samson could renew his vow simply by returning to its obligations rather than by repeating its formula orally. Samson's later claim that performing for the Philistines will not "stain" his "vow of Nazarite" (1385–6) – a statement not in Judges – merely indicates the existence of the vow, without stating definitively that he has taken it himself.[142]

Because Milton's Nazarite vow is not unquestionably voluntary, though somewhat moreso than its counterpart in Judges, the problem remains that it has been imposed. Whether Samson Agonistes has taken the vow himself or had it taken for him by his mother, it is still an imposed vow: his mother and God have imposed it on him.[143] It comes as no surprise that he has problems keeping the vow, repeatedly violating it, sometimes with God's permission, but crucially without it in the case of Dalila. And Milton's expansion of Dalila's role is crucial to the poem's examination of imposed oaths, for as Samuel Johnson recognized, the Philistines impose an oath on her as well. Early modern exegetes had imagined Delilah swearing an oath to Samson not to tell his secret – an oath not clearly in the text of Judges.[144] An important analogue of *Samson Agonistes*, Joost van den Vondel's play *Samson, Of Heilige Wraeck* (*Samson, Of Holy Revenge*) (1660), repeats this idea, with Delilah willingly taking money from Samson's unspecified "foes" to extract her husband's secret and, once she learns it, swearing a false oath to Samson not to betray it to anyone – in effect, a private, intra-marital oath, not a public one.[145] Milton's Dalila, on the other hand, excuses her "rash" breaking of her marriage vows (747, 750; cf. 907) by claiming that such a betrayal was forced on her by the Philistine authorities:

> the magistrates
> And princes of my country came in person,
> Solicited, commanded, threatened, urged,
> *Adjured* by all the bonds of civil duty
> And of religion, pressed how just it was,
> How honourable, how glorious to entrap
> A common enemy . . . (850–6, my italics)

In so many ways the double or mirror of Samson,[146] Dalila claims that her own patriotic espionage was also prompted by a public speech-act. The fifth in a series of verbs of coercion in lines 852–3 is "adjured," whose Latin etymology relates it to a number of English verbs involving the swearing of oaths in some way or another: "abjure," "perjure," even "conjure."[147] The word thus has a very precise and (since Johnson) little remarked meaning, both here and in the poem "On the New Forcers of Conscience," where the lines on "adjur[ing] the civil sword" refer to Presbyterians subordinating the civil power to themselves by forcing an oath upon the nation: the Solemn League and Covenant, one of the "stiff vows" referred to in the poem's opening.[148] Dalila's "adjured," then, is no dead metaphor but a very live reference to the Philistines' forcing her to swear an oath to break her marriage oath – much graver than the oath of secrecy in Vondel because not made privately to one person, her husband, but publicly to the Philistine authorities. Milton's discussion of oaths in *De Doctrina* allows for adjurations of subjects by magistrates, but only in lawful matters, especially inquiries after truth: "they must be complied with, in matters not contrary to religion or equity."[149] Yet in asking Dalila to betray her husband to them, the Philistine magistrates ask her to do something unlawful, something contrary to religion and equity, as Samson sees them.

There is an upside to this adjuration, however. Dalila certainly has her defenders,[150] and to the extent that I am one of them, it is because I take her seriously as a Philistine citizen, which is to say that I think Milton takes her seriously, elevating her to the status not just of wife but of political subject and political actor.[151] Dalila counts enough to be adjured, and adjured "in person" by "the magistrates / And princes of my country." She can be counted on to have enough of a sense of patriotism to take on this honourable, glorious mission against an enemy of the state – not the mercenary desire for gold that Samson imagines (831, 849–50). The fact that they adjure her "by all the bonds of civil duty / And of religion" may indicate one of three things: that these worthies 1) mentioned such bonds and obligations in the course of persuading her, 2) spoke to her a formula such as "We adjure you by all the bonds of civil duty and of religion to learn Samson's secret and disable him," or 3) coaxed her into taking an oath such as "I swear by all the bonds of civil duty and of religion that I will betray Samson" (apparently Johnson's interpretation). Whatever the case, Dalila matters; and her feelings matter as well.[152] She claims to have undergone a crisis of conscience akin to those faced by takers of mandatory state oaths, enjoined to place public above private good:

> Hear what assaults I had, what snares besides,
> What sieges girt me round, ere I consented . . .
> . . . what had I
> To oppose against such powerful arguments?
> Only my love of thee held long debate;
> And combated in silence all those reasons
> With hard contest: at length the grounded maxim
> So rife and celebrated in the mouths
> Of wisest men; that to the public good
> Private respects must yield; with grave authority
> Took full possession of me and prevailed;
> Virtue, as I thought, truth, duty so enjoining. (845–70)

In many ways Dalila's conflict mirrors Samson's repeated dilemma as husband of Philistine women he has married in order to gain access to the Philistines and bide his time till a Machiavellian *occasione* presents itself for him to liberate his people. When Dalila begs him to reveal his innermost secret, he must imitate her by weighing love against honour, private against public. Of course Milton intends such agonizing on Samson's and Dalila's parts to resemble the rarefied love-and-honour disputes of the heroic dramas that the poem decisively repudiates. But that is only to say that both the heroic drama and *Samson Agonistes* draw upon Restoration audiences' experiences of being adjured.

## Oaths, Covenants, and Riddles

While Dalila may be lying about being forced at oath-point to betray her husband,[153] she undoubtedly describes a process of magistrates imposing an action on someone with an oath, thereby foregrounding the issue of forced oaths in a way the Judges narrative does not. In the end the most agonized experience of living with imposed oaths is that of Samson, whose final two speeches in response to Philistine impositions evidence strategies of ambiguous evasion that Milton's contemporaries associated with oath-taking (1399–1409, esp. 1404–6; 1640–5).[154] In the penultimate speech, Samson announces that he will heed the Philistines' summons to perform for them in the theatre:

> I am content to go.
> Masters' commands come with a power resistless
> To such as owe them absolute subjection;
> And for a life who will not change his purpose?
> (So mutable are all the ways of men)
> Yet this be sure, in nothing to comply
> Scandalous or forbidden in our Law. (1403–9)

The equivocation in these lines has been much discussed.[155] Among a number of ambiguities present here is that while Samson seems to say that the Philistines are his masters and he owes them absolute subjection, he really says that God is his master and he will heed God's command by going to destroy the Philistines.

Yet similar equivocation is also characteristic of another form of compliance to a higher power: the state oath, both as drafted and as understood. Daniel Featley, for one, complained of the Solemn League and Covenant: "There being so many Amphibologies, Ambiguities, and riddles in this Oath, we must have some Oedipus of the Synod to read and clearly expound them, before we can safely engage our conscience by Oath to perform them."[156] To be sure, seventeenth-century loyalty oaths *were* often worded in the most general of terms to make them palatable to as many people as possible. This sometimes meant that generality became ambiguity,[157] allowing different swearers of the same oath to take or understand it in different senses – sometimes ones at variance with the intentions of the oath's designers.[158] So a subscriber to a forced oath could speak the words in such a way as to appear to comply with the government's demand for obedience and support for its objectives, yet mentally reserve some much more limited meaning, some much more limited feeling of support.

A case in point was the Commonwealth's oath of Engagement, perhaps the second most important state oath in this period after the

Solemn League and Covenant, and familiar to us as a context for Hobbes' *Leviathan* and Marvell's *Horatian Ode*. As understood by Robert Sanderson, the Engagement's promise "to be true and faithful to the Common-wealth of England, as it is now established without King or Lords" could allow his fellow royalists to pledge allegiance to the fledgling Commonwealth without compromising their previous oaths of allegiance to Charles I, and by extension to his son, Charles II, should he return.[159] Sanderson argued that there were, in fact, two distinct ways to interpret the oath: a de jure and a de facto reading. The de jure reading acknowledged the House of Commons and Council of State as the rightful rulers of England and renounced any and all allegiance to kings and lords.[160] The de facto one simply acknowledged the Council of State's status as sovereign power, not its right to that position, and promised not to rebel; it did not renounce previous allegiance to the rightful sovereign power, the king, who might return at any time and reclaim the swearer's allegiance.[161] Roughly speaking, then, the oath-taker could pledge loyalty to the Commonwealth as a legitimate authority, or as a temporary expedient, reserving allegiance to the higher power of the king. Samson's declaration that he will perform for the Philistines, while not precisely an oath, performs – or appears to perform – a loyalty oath's functions of submission, compliance, and obedience, recognizing an immediately higher power, just as performing feats of strength would make that submission even more visible. But like Sanderson's de facto reading of the Engagement, it reserves another allegiance to an even higher power, God.

A similar argument was made about the Solemn League and Covenant after the Restoration. In the same book in which John Gauden speaks of breaking oaths and covenants "like Sampsons cords and withes," he also says the following of the proper way to interpret the Covenant:

> the Covenant, as to the words and matter of it, may in some benign and charitable sense, be so far lawful, as it may consist with justice to God and man, with Laws Divine and Humane ... [Yet it] is not to be taken, as it is not to be kept[,] in any other sense then what is agreeable to the Laws of God and men, to Justice and Charity ... not any National Authority, which the Covenant never had, but onely the matter in it so far as it is lawful, doth binde any man who took it, yea, and so all that never did take it ... Whereas there is nothing in the Covenant that sounds either grace or vertue, equity or charity, true Religion or Loyalty, duty to God, Church, King,

> Countrey, but [I] willingly [allow] it, both as to the end and the means; [I judge] every man in their places and callings obliged to those rules and designs; not onely because there is such a Covenant of humane composure, to which some men have so far declared their consent, but from far higher authority, and more ancient bonds of morality. . . . there is no such charm or bond in any passages of [the Covenant], but that they may be easily undone by a juster and higher power than that which imposed it, or spontaniously took it in an unjust sense, and to ends unwarrantable.[162]

While on the opposite end of the politico-religious spectrum from Gauden, Milton would probably have agreed with his opposition to a rigid adherence to the Presbyterians' Covenant.

More important, however, is that Gauden insists on the non-binding or partially binding nature of covenants in order to claim that the Solemn League and Covenant does not bind its takers or the nation as a whole to extirpate episcopacy.[163] In reading the Covenant this way, Gauden resembles Milton's Samson because he essentially eviscerates the oath, making it say the opposite of what its framers intended. Article 2 of the Covenant quite clearly commits its takers to "endeavour the extirpation of Popery" and "Prelacy, (that is Church-government by Arch-bishops, Bishops, their Chancellours and Commissaries, Deanes, Deanes and Chapters, Archdeacons, and all other Ecclesiastical offices depending on that Hierarchy)."[164] For Gauden to claim that the Covenant actually does not advance the extirpation of episcopacy is to turn the oath on its head. Whereas Sanderson supplies two possible interpretations of the Engagement from which readers can choose – even though he clearly favours the de facto reading – Gauden dismisses all other interpretations and claims the Covenant says the opposite of what it so clearly says. His resistance to this "idol" of a state oath very much resembles that of Samson, who only intends to comply partially with the Philistines' commands and instead to obey what he regards as a higher command from God to destroy them. It is significant that while the commands are imposed, the oath-like utterance is not: Samson chooses to frame his assent in a form somewhat like that of state oaths and in an equivocal way capable of different constructions. Rewriting the formula for obedience is one of Samson's most significant acts of resistance.

To the extent that Samson's penultimate speech is a substitute for an oath pledging loyalty and implies allegiance to a higher authority than the Philistines currently in charge ("Masters' commands . . . with a power resistless / To such as owe them absolute subjection"), it also resembles the yea-and-nay kinds of affirmations or promises to the Restoration authorities that Quakers were willing to substitute for the Oaths of Allegiance and Supremacy and judicial oaths. See, for example, George Fox's response to the idea of reviving the Covenant and implicitly to swearing state oaths of any kind – entitled *Our Covenant with God* (1660):

> Our Covenant with God and with all men is Peace, and Life, and Light, and Salvation to the ends of the Earth . . . But to plot and confederate, or to raise insurrections, or to gather riotous meetings, or taking up arms outwardly, we utterly deny, and it is not our Principle, nor is it in our Covenant, for it is out of the Covenant . . . though we cannot swear to this; for he that hath all Power in Heaven and Earth given to him, commands us not to swear at all . . . And our yea is yea, and our nay is nay in that Doctrine of Christ who is the end of all Oaths in the Law and the first Covenant . . . and we are out of Covenants with men that doe change, and in the Covenant of God with him that remaineth and doth not change, and cannot be broken.[165]

In sum, Samuel Johnson was right to call attention to Milton's own Quaker-like refusal of an oath. Yet through Samson, who deals with the consequences of a vow he has not entirely taken and improvises his own pseudo-oath of loyalty to God disguised as submission to the Philistines, Milton does not just glance at the positions of Quakers and ejected Presbyterian ministers in the 1660s.[166] For the experiences of, on the one hand, resisting an imposed oath by not taking it or evading its provisions, and, on the other, carrying it out reluctantly and at great personal cost were not confined to Restoration Dissenters. In its consideration of the difficulties of living with forced oaths at a time when one's word was one's bond, the poem looks back over a series of state oaths that, from one regime to the next, tyrannized over the lives of Parliamentarians and royalists, Dissenters and Non-Dissenters alike – and even, if the Royal Martyr was to be believed, over kings.[167] Whether commanded by divine or human masters, oaths bound like cords and were to be struggled against and broken at great peril.

They bound fallen kings like Charles I and II no less than ordinary humans, and chapter 5 will examine the coronation oath in *Paradise Lost*, along with the crisis it creates, both for Satan and for readers of the poem. Chapter 6 then argues that Adam and Eve's untouchable fruit plays a role similar to Samson's untouchable hair. In both cases, renouncing the object (fruit or hair) is associated with swearing and the formation of subjectivity. In both cases, a man and a woman form different subjectivities in relation to the same forbidden object, just as swearers of state oaths were forced into widely varying subject positions by the command to renounce something designated as outside the nation and its values. The Tree of Knowledge's status as an oath-object thus raises the daring notion of female citizenship.

# 5 *Paradise Lost* I: God's Swearing by Himself: Milton's Troubling Coronation Oath

At a pivotal moment in British history, two visions of the Ancient Constitution faced off against each other in a courtroom.[1] Charles I had been indicted for something akin to crimes against humanity, which included breaking his coronation oath by trying to "overthrow the rights and liberties of the people" it had committed him to protect.[2] At the trial before his beheading in January 1649, Charles advocated a view of monarchy as hereditary and divine, in contrast to his accusers' understanding of it as elective and contractual (with subjects reserving an implicit right of refusal). When the president of the High Court of Justice, John Bradshaw, characterized him as an "elected king," Charles vigorously denied it, insisting that "England was never an elective kingdom but an hereditary kingdom for near these thousand years." Charles went on to stress the importance of his coronation oath: "*I am sworn* to keep the peace by that duty I owe God and my country, and I will do it to the last breath of my body . . . otherwise, I betray my trust and the liberties of the people."[3] Within days the *Eikon Basilike* would compare that oath to Samson's cords.

In response to Charles' self-defence at the trial, the prosecution lectured the King that

> your oath [and] the manner of your coronation doth show plainly that the Kings of England – although it's true by the law the next person in blood is designed – yet if there were just cause to refuse him, the people of England might do it. For there is a contract and bargain made between the King and his people, and your oath is taken. And certainly, Sir, the bond is reciprocal: for as you are the liege lord, so they are the liege subjects . . . This we know now – the one tie, the one bond, is the bond of protection that is due

> from the sovereign; the other is the bond of subjection which is due from the subject. Sir, if this bond be once broken, farewell sovereignty.[4]

In the short term, the elective principle won out, underpinned as it was by the notion of reciprocal oaths making a contract between ruler and ruled. Charles I was executed, and a Republic declared, accompanied, as we saw in chapter 3, by a new oath: the Engagement. This did not last, however, and the Republic soon gave way to yet another replacement: an unelected Lord Protector – not elected by the people at any rate, though possibly, in another sense, by God. Then the Restoration of 1660 seemed to provide a well-nigh unquestionable confirmation of the hereditary principle: Charles II was crowned king because his father had been king and because God had brought him back to England. The elective principle would not entirely reassert itself until the Glorious Revolution of 1688, when the English arguably cashiered a Catholic monarch who had encroached too far onto his subjects' liberties: James II. In his place they installed a double monarchy composed of James's Protestant daughter and son-in-law, William and Mary, who took new coronation oaths devised by Parliament. But heredity had not entirely vanished. Far from a Lockean withdrawal of the people from a social contract the monarch had broken, many saw these events as another Restoration, this time of the true blood heir to Charles II – "true" in the sense of Protestant. However, since the centre of gravity between king and Parliament had shifted (with the monarch eventually to dwindle into a figurehead), the issue became almost moot. Yes, the monarchy was still hereditary rather than elective, and kings were to be crowned and sworn in; but a process had been set in motion that by the nineteenth century would deprive the monarch of real executive power, ceding it to an elected prime minister.

Succession giving way to election: in this chapter I would like to suggest that the unabashed Whiggery of the foregoing account, with the significance it grants to the events of both 1649 and 1688, can help us to read *Paradise Lost*, a poem, after all, whose chronologically first event, the speech-act that touches off the revolt in Heaven, is a kind of coronation oath.[5] Addressing the assembled angels in Book 5, God announces,

> This day I have begot whom I declare
> My only Son, and on this holy hill
> Him have anointed, whom ye now behold
> At my right hand; your head I him appoint;

> And *by myself have sworn to him shall bow*
> *All knees in heaven, and shall confess him Lord.* (5.602–8)[6]

Critics have struggled to explain the details of God's dense speech, for example, glossing "begot" as "exalted," rather than as "created" or "given birth to" – a procedure complicated by the various acts of mediation at work in readers' access to it (the Narrator of *Paradise Lost* quotes Raphael quoting God quoting an oath he apparently swore previously). It should hardly surprise us that the powerful words of the Supreme Being come across as distant and hard to apprehend at first; indeed, the distance and the difficulty in part create that power. But even if the difficulty was not present in the original utterance and simply derives from the multiple acts of transmission, the poem's readers have no choice but to interpret the text they have on the page in front of them. In Raphael's version of God's speech, "begot" seems to mean two things: both that God created or gave birth to the Son and that God has promoted him on "This day," whatever span of time that refers to. Attention to the history of the English coronation oath can illuminate such ambiguities, which reflect the conflict between hereditary and elective theories of monarchy that characterizes that history. Before I explain fully how this is so, however, let us look at a few more important aspects of the speech's dense ambiguity and the questions it raises.

In general, the utterance's density stems from its layering of multiple speech-acts on top of one another. In a classic Austinian performative, similar to christening a ship or declaring war, God appoints the Son as head of the angels. Even the apparent constative, "I declare / My only Son," which purports to describe an existing fact, may function as a performative that brings something new into being as far as the assembled angels are concerned: to declare someone his "only Son," thereby excluding other candidates, is already to make him their head – a leader other than God, a leader they apparently did not know they had, and a leader who may or may not replace God. Thus, if there is ambiguity in the phrase "I declare" functioning as both constative and performative, there is even more in the amphibologies created by "your head I him appoint" and "by myself have sworn to him shall bow." In the first phrase, "your head" could function as an appositive to "I" (essentially "I, your head, appoint him . . ."). The phrase could thus mean several things: 1) "I, God, appoint the Son to be your head"; 2) "I, God, who am already your head, now appoint the Son to be your new head, replacing me"; 3) "I, God, appoint the Son, who is currently your immediate head but still subordinate to me, to the higher position of supreme head, supreme to all of us"; or 4) "I, God, appoint the Son, who is currently no one's head, to be your immediate head, but still subordinate to me, and I remain the supreme head." None of this would matter if Milton were a Trinitarian and believed God and the Son to be the same entity, but *De Doctrina Christiana* makes Milton's anti-Trinitarianism clear. This phrase in *Paradise Lost*, then, seems to raise a question about the exact relationship between God and the Son. Is it one of identity or of difference? Do the "I" and the "him," pronouns placed right next to each other, designate one person or two?

The second phrase might seem less troubling. "I . . . by myself have sworn to him shall bow . . ." could mean either that "I, God, have made a sworn promise to the Son that all angels shall bow down to him" or that "I, God, without any particular audience or without any audience at all, have sworn that all angels shall bow down to the Son." The difference between the two possibilities is comparatively slight, but the shorter phrase, "by myself have sworn," creates more divergent alternatives. God may have "sworn by himself" in at least three possible senses: first, in being the only one to swear; second, in doing so in the presence of no one else; third, in invoking himself, rather than someone else, as guarantor of his word. The first and third seem most likely.

The speech thus creates many problems, not just the ones outlined here.[7] Among the most important, however, is why God needs to swear at all. The same question had been asked by many students of the biblical texts on which Milton based this passage (Genesis 22, Isaiah 45, Psalm 110, Hebrews 6, Philippians 2, Romans 15, 1 Kings 1); God's oaths had also proved a troubling limit case for thinkers as various as Philo Judaeus and George Lawson.[8] William Ames, for example, had wondered whether God demeans himself in swearing, employing a speech-act made necessary by the unreliability of humans and their commitments.[9]

By contrast, many early modern apologists for state oaths (oaths of allegiance, oaths of office, courtroom oaths, coronation oaths) had made the fact of God's swearing in Genesis 22 and elsewhere part of an argument against Christ's apparent prohibition of all oaths in Matthew 5:33–7 ("Swear not at all").[10] Central to their case for the necessity of such public oaths was Hebrews 6:13–17's reminder that God had sworn the Abrahamic Covenant "by himself," which implied divine approval for oath-swearing that created peace and reconciliation: "an oath . . . is . . . an end of all strife." But even this passage was problematic because it implied that oaths are only sworn "by the greater" (6:16): by invoking some higher power that guarantees the swearer's promise or assertion. When God swears, there *is* no higher power, nothing outside God and his creation. Hence, he can only swear "by himself." This and other concerns led Ames to deny that God really swears.[11] Finally, if swearing usually ends strife, why does the oath of Milton's God create strife?

I would like to argue that Milton turned the problem of God's swearing to his own advantage in *Paradise Lost*, making it the centerpiece of this key episode, which should be seen as a modified coronation ritual. His God, in other words, swears a coronation oath – but crucially not for himself; and this is what sets the plot of the epic in motion. In the English version of the ceremony, the monarch's coronation oath had provided one of the clearest indications both of the social contract renewed there and thus of the limitations upon royal power. Almost from its inception the English coronation had included reminders not just of the divine right principle of succession (the crowning of the king in Westminster Abbey, the anointing of his body with holy oil) but of the contractualist principle of election and accountability (the king's swearing to rule well and preserve the Church in return for his subjects' obedience). In effect, the king swore a loyalty oath to his people.

However, even to call the ritual a coronation in the first place was to privilege one element at the expense of many others and play up the principle of divine right, for the coronation involved considerably more than crowning. At Charles II's coronation on 23 April 1661 – "the single most expensive and elaborate ceremony of Charles II's life" but one fairly representative of those during the Stuart era – the king processed in state from Westminster Hall to Westminster Abbey, accompanied by many notables carrying various ritual objects, including the regalia: the crown, orb, sceptre, and other royal accessories.[12] Among the four swords of state used in the rite, the blunted one known as the Curtana was borne by the Earl of Oxford.[13] After entering the Abbey, Charles was formally "acclaimed" or "recognized" as king when the Bishop of London turned to the four corners of the Abbey, each time asking the people if they were willing "to doe [their] Homage, service, & bounden duty"; they "signified their willingness by their loud Acclamations, all with one voice crying, God save King Charles."[14] Charles may even have broken precedent by addressing the people during the recognition.[15] He then took a multi-part oath to govern well, consisting of questions and answers and a hand on the Bible at the altar.[16] Later, he was anointed on the hands, arms, breast, shoulders, and head and compared to the anointed kings David and Solomon.[17] The formal crowning came next, as one part of the process of "investment": the donning of various garments and objects, including the sword of state and the spurs. When St Edward's crown was placed on his head, "the *People*, with *loud* and *repeated Shouts*, cried, GOD SAVE THE KING," and cannons were fired at the Tower of London.[18] After being formally enthroned, Charles received homage in the form of oaths of fealty from the bishops and nobles, punctuated by further shouts of approval from the audience.[19] He then pardoned all and sundry, took communion as part of the Mass, and left the Abbey for a banquet in Westminster Hall.[20] Interspersed throughout were prayers, blessings, anthems, and Bible readings. While Pepys, Evelyn, and company were predictably impressed, the republican Edmund Ludlow saw the spectacle as a "superstitious ceremony of anointing their idoll" and complained particularly of the acclamation: "the mocking of the people, in asking in a formall way, when they administered the oath to him, whether they would have this man to reigne over them."[21] It seems unlikely that these sentiments were not shared by the author of lines that prime the reader's perception of the Exaltation scene in *Paradise Lost* by condemning

the tedious pomp that waits
On princes, when their rich retinue long
Of horses led, and grooms besmeared with gold
Dazzles the crowd, and sets them all agape. (5.354–7)

In any case, the whole ritual at Westminster Abbey, preceded and followed as it was by such royal processions, could just as easily have been called an anointment, a consecration, an enthronement, an installation, or a swearing-in.

By contrast, the coronation of the Son in *Paradise Lost* consists solely of God's announcement to the assembled angels that he has already begotten the Son, already anointed him, already sworn an oath that they shall obey him. If most or all of these were ritual events, they appear to have taken place in the past, and with no audience. Raphael's description of God's proclamation offers nothing more: no ritual objects, no ritual words other than God's sixteen lines (5.600–15), no other ritual officers. Unlike English monarchs, who had for more than seven centuries sworn an elaborate coronation oath, the Son says exactly nothing. God swears the oath for him. Both the audience and the person at the centre of the ritual participate only insofar as they listen. By comparison, even the absolutist Charles II seems to have allowed a more contractualist coronation ceremony than that of Milton's God. What are we to make of all this?

Book 5's coronation of the Son seems both deeply troubling, a possible betrayal of Milton's republican principles, and a template for a reformed coronation oath and ceremony, not unlike those that would arrive after the Glorious Revolution. Students of Milton have become used to what I call the notion of the Divine Exception – that republicanism is appropriate for every state except that in Heaven. But after we compartmentalize and hive off the heavenly monarchy, recalling that monarchy only appears there because Milton's larger principle is that the best should govern and because God and the Son clearly possess more merit than anyone else, whereas no human could possibly be in that position on Earth – despite all this, we remain troubled – and well we should. Milton puts pressure on the Divine Exception, allowing a sense that this is all unfair to bleed over temporarily into our consideration of Heaven.

In order to gloss God's oath and decree, this chapter will first examine Milton's pronouncements on the English coronation ritual and oath in order to remind us that he was most interested in its contractual and consensualist aspects and condemned their opposites. Then it will revisit the history of the coronation and coronation oath and discern within it a struggle between contract and succession in which the former gains the upper hand. In light of this Whiggish or perhaps Miltonic history, *Paradise Lost*'s coronation oath and ceremony appear curiously truncated and retrograde, apparently privileging the succession principle. A look at *De Doctrina*'s discussion of the intertexts of God's self-oath only deepens the sense that it raises issues of voice, agency, and mediation that make God's role in the coronation ritual seem problematic because coercive and monopolistic. However, Milton's intention throughout is to provoke in the reader troubling thoughts not so much about God as about the system of reciprocal oaths underpinning the restored English monarchy. Such thoughts would only have been magnified by Satan's remarks against swearing obedience to God in Book 4 (93–8), which should be seen as Milton's attack not on God himself, or even on the Son, both of whom merit their posts, but on meritless earthly monarchs who style themselves gods and demand cringing loyalty oaths from their subjects – oaths contrary to religion and equity.

The next chapter will focus on the other oath in this reciprocal pair: the subject's oath of allegiance to the monarch. There we shall see that the prohibition against the fruit functions like an oath of allegiance to God and that the problems of loyalty it creates represent Milton's take on the English Oath of Allegiance and the "Superfoetation" of oaths of allegiance required of officeholders by the Clarendon Code. Milton's decision to evade censorship by discussing these oaths of allegiance in the obliquest of ways paradoxically shows how attuned his poem was to its immediate Restoration context in 1667. As chapter 6 will argue, *Paradise Lost* goes beyond both Vondel and Milton's own *Samson* and *Comus* in imagining women as full participants in the public sphere. To grant Eve a truly separate Fall that is really a breaking of an allegiance oath is to grant the first woman a status as an independent political subject and citizen – a status Englishwomen would not fully enjoy until the twentieth century.

## Milton and the Coronation Oath

In his prefatory poem to the second edition of *Paradise Lost* (1674), Marvell was the first to identify Book 5, lines 600–15 as a coronation of the Son: "Messiah *crowned*."[22] But Marvell's succinct phrase did not provide a full-blown reading of the Exaltation scene. In the 1980s Stevie Davies made a first pass at one, emphasizing the element of feudal fealty but paying insufficient attention to oaths as such and to changes in the coronation rite over its long history.[23] However, no subsequent critic, not even David Norbrook in his brilliant account of Milton's republicanism,[24] has pressed Marvell's insight to its logical conclusion and read Milton's coronation and oath in the immediate context of the Restoration of Charles II and the fierce debate over oaths of allegiance and oaths of all kinds that accompanied and lingered after his coronation. To do so would involve reviewing Milton's pronouncements on the coronation and oaths in the prose, as well as tracing the history of the English coronation rite up to and beyond the Restoration.

In 1660, at a time when he was also writing *Paradise Lost*, Milton's *Brief Notes upon a Late Sermon* emphasized the reciprocity between the monarch's coronation oath and the subject's oath of allegiance.[25] In response to Matthew Griffith's fulsome celebration of absolute monarchy in his sermon on *The Fear of God and the King*, Milton claimed that the only way even to consider monarchs legitimate would be to think of them as obliged by the coronation oath to represent their subjects' interests in return for their consent to be governed, as expressed in oaths of allegiance. But even that is not entirely satisfactory; nor does it make monarchs absolute:

> how could that person be absolutely supreme, who reignd, not under Law only, but under oath of his good demeanour given to the people at his coronation, ere the people gave him his Crown? And his principal oath was to maintain those Laws which the people should chuse? If then the Law it self, much more he who was but the keeper and minister of Law, was in thir choice; and both he subordinat to the performance of his duty sworn, and our sworn allegiance in order only to his performance.[26]

Better, in fact, to replace monarchy with the republic outlined in *The Readie and Easie Way to Establish a Free Commonwealth* (also of 1660) alongside its desperate appeal to Covenant-swearing Presbyterians added to the second edition, which appeared in the same month as the *Brief Notes* (April). While the first edition of *The Readie and Easie Way* (February 1660) had only glanced at the issue of state oaths in referring to the nation's abjuration of kingship in the Engagement of 1649–50 (a kingship now characterized as an "abjur'd and detested thraldom"), the second edition inserted a ten-page digression reminding Presbyterians and others of the oaths they had sworn, first to restrain an out-of-control king in the Protestation (1641) and Solemn League and Covenant (1643), and then to abolish kingship in the Engagement.[27] England was forced to end king and kingship, he implies, because Charles had broken the social contract to which he had sworn or covenanted at his coronation. The English people "took themselves [to be] not bound by the light of nature or religion, to any former covnant, from which the King himself by many forfeitures of a latter date or discoverie, and our own longer consideration thereon had more & more unbound us, both to himself and his posteritie."[28] While the Yale editors gloss "any former covnant" as the Solemn League and Covenant, it clearly has a much wider scope. Charles I was no party to that Covenant and thus could not have "forfeited" it. For the English, and especially English Presbyterians, "*any* former covnant" must have included the social contract or covenant that, according to one understanding of the laws of nature and nations, preceded but was made visible in the coronation ceremony, with its coronation oath for the king and oaths of fealty from lords spiritual and temporal, followed by subjects' Oaths of Allegiance and Supremacy to the king. If the parliamentary oaths of the 1640s and 1650s constituted elaborations of this implied original contract, Charles, strictly speaking, had only "forfeited" or broken his coronation oath, as Milton had insisted in the Regicide tracts.

But Milton had long been interested in the coronation oath and ritual. The *Brief Notes* and *Readie and Easie Way* merely pick up on similar lines of argument in the commonwealth tracts and commonplace book, arguments that focus on the oath's contents and position within the ceremony as a marker of the monarch's accountability to the social contract it instantiated. Even apparent minutiae, such as the name of a ceremonial sword (the Curtana), who was to carry it in the coronation, and why, matter a great deal to Milton.[29] The commonplace book's sections on laws, the king, and the subject cull passages from Holinshed, Stow, and Speed that cast the coronation ceremony as an oath-taking ceremony.[30] The oath must come before the crowning, and it primarily concerns upholding justice and the laws. "The crowning of K[ing]s in England," says Milton, is "not admitted till thire oath" is "receav'd of justice to be administerd, according to the laws."[31] If monarchs do not uphold the laws, they are subject to correction. According to Milton, the Curtana is to be carried before the monarch by the Earl of Chester "in token that he" has "the autority to correct the K[ing] if he should see him swerve from the limits of Justice."[32] As *The Tenure of Kings and Magistrates* and *The First Defence* put it, "that sword of St. Edward, called Curtana" is present in order "to mind them [monarchs] . . . that if they errd, the Sword had power to restraine them" and they are "liable to punishment."[33] These sentiments are congruent with the proposal in the Parliament's Nineteen Propositions to the king in 1642 that the medieval office of High Constable be revived so that the latter might "prosecute the King if he violated his coronation oath."[34]

Milton's commonwealth tracts defend the infant Republic by extending the argument about contract and reciprocity. In a paragraph in the final chapter of *Eikonoklastes*, Milton responds to Charles's meditations on death in the final chapter of the *Eikon Basilike* and discusses the contents of the coronation oath:

> Those objected Oaths of Allegiance and Supremacy [to which Charles refers in charging that his subjects have broken them by fighting and killing him] we swore, not to his Person, but as it was invested with his Autority; and his autority was by the People first giv'n him conditionally, in Law and under Law, and under Oath also for the Kingdoms good, and not otherwise: *the Oathes then were interchang'd, and mutual*; stood and fell together; he swore fidelity to his trust (not as a deluding ceremony, but as a real condition of thir admitting him for King; and [William] the Conqueror himself swore it ofter then at his Crowning) they swore Homage and

> Fealty to his Person in that trust. There was no reason why the Kingdom should be furder bound by Oaths to him, then he by his Coronation Oath to us, which he hath every way brok'n; and having brok'n, the ancient Crown-Oath of Alfred above mention'd, conceales not his penalty.[35]

According to Milton, the last clause of King Alfred's oath states that "the King should be as liable, and obedient to suffer right, as others of his people." For if the people are accountable to law, "the King should be [equally] accountable" and "answerable" to law, both in his courts and his great court of Parliament.[36] Milton's point is presumably that "right" and "penalty" mean "execution" in Charles's case. The paragraph rehearses Parliament's justification for the Civil War – that it was fighting the king's first body to save his second – with its insistence that this did not constitute a breach of subjects' oaths of allegiance to the king since they only applied to his second body, his body politic rather than his body natural.[37] To *Eikon Basilike*'s charge that Parliament had not only broken the oaths of allegiance but, in calling on Charles to consent to its abolition of episcopacy, had tried to force him to break the part of his coronation oath promising to preserve the Church, *Eikonoklastes* responds that the coronation oath was not that specific and, in fact, bound him to consent to any law made by his people, past, present, or future – in other words, not to veto legislation.[38]

Moreover, in its insistence that power "was first given him," and by extension all kings, "conditionally" by the people, and that the monarch's coronation oath is no "deluding ceremony, but . . . a real condition of thir admitting him for King" and thus the exact counterpart of subjects' oaths of allegiance in a mutual interchange of oaths, the paragraph suggests the same account of the coronation oath's genesis that had appeared some months earlier in *The Tenure of Kings and Magistrates*.[39] Thus, according to Milton's first *Defence of the People of England* (1651), the coronation highlights the people's expressed consent. Making a questionable case that ancient British kingship was not hereditary but by implication elective, Milton argues that this elective principle is enshrined in the current rite's *recognitio* or *acclamatio*, in which the people shout their approval of the king:

> I positively assert that their [the ancient Britons'] kingship was not hereditary, which is evident both from the succession of their kings, and from their way of creating them; for the approval of the people is asked [*petuntur*] in express words. When the king has taken [*dedit*] the accustomed

> oath, the archbishop, stepping to the four sides of the platform erected for the purpose, asks [*rogat*] the body of the people four several times in these words, "Will ye consent [*consentire*] to have this man your king?"[40]

Once the people have consented, the coronation oath, in Milton's expansive interpretation, binds the king to many things. He cannot dissolve Parliament until all grievances have been considered, nor can he veto laws it makes concerning public safety.[41] He must follow Parliament's advice and use the militia to defend the people.[42] Perhaps most important, he cannot make "a scorn of his regal Oath" by interpreting it selectively, "by his own will," "conscience[,] and reason" – contrary to Parliament's.[43] Milton repeats the charge Parliament had brought against Charles I that, after 1626, when he was first crowned in England, Charles had conspired with Archbishop Laud to alter his coronation oath at his 1633 coronation in Scotland by leaving out the "quas vulgus elegerit" clause (discussed below), thus opening the door to other violations of the people's rights, laws, and customs.[44] For if the king scorns his coronation oath as a merely ceremonial and "brutish formality," he breaks the contract with his subjects, whose obligations under their oaths of allegiance cease.[45]

Milton's insistence on contractual kingship – if there had to be any kingship at all – appears not to have wavered, for in his very last publication before his death in 1674 he emphasized the elective nature of Polish kingship as undergirded by a coronation oath. In his translation of the Polish lords' declaration accepting Jan III as king and describing the coronation ceremony, *A Declaration, or the Letters Patent of the Election of this Present King of Poland John the Third, Elected on the 22d of May . . . 1674*, forms of the word "elect" appear frequently, and the contractual nature of the kingship is stressed. The king, "the most Serene Elect," must consent to "bind himself by an Oath, to perform the conditions concluded with those persons sent by his Majesty, before the exhibition of this present Decree of Election" and to "provide in best manner for the performance of them by his authentick Letters." Indeed, he did as much when he took his "solemn Oath . . . on the 5th day of the Month of June, in the Palace at Warsaw, after the Letters Patent [were] delivered upon the Covenants, and Agreements, or Capitulations," presumably to the Polish lords' demands.[46] It is significant that the translation's title page downplays the coronation itself by calling attention to the lords' election of Jan "on the 22d of May," rather than to the date of the coronation the next month, June 5. Likewise, the tract's title calls attention to it as an act on the part of the lords rather than the king, *their* "Letters Patent" or articles, to which he had to agree in order to gain their support.

## A Whig or Miltonic History of the Coronation Oath

All these texts suggest a history of the English coronation ritual as part of a march towards the more obvious statement of the social contract after the Glorious Revolution, when a newly revised coronation oath threatened to reduce the monarch to the status of just another subject.[47] As Roy Strong shows, Charles II's coronation in 1661 hewed to the fourth version of the rite since its origins in the Middle Ages. The Glorious Revolution would produce the fifth and final one, used with relatively minor variations up through Elizabeth II's coronation in 1953 (see my **Table 1**).[48]

By the early modern period, the ceremony had become an amalgam of conflicting political principles: succession vs. election; royal vs. ecclesiastical power; and royal vs. parliamentary sovereignty. Did the ceremony mark the king's succession by divine right and patriarchal inheritance to a throne already his, or the people's choosing of him as one among a number of candidates? Did the Archbishop's anointing him with holy oil and placing the crown on his head signify the king's subordination to the Church, or his superiority to it? Did the presence of his subjects in a body at Westminster Abbey, along with their shouted "acclamation" of "God save the King!" and the oaths of fealty presented by the lords spiritual and temporal indicate their subordination or their superiority to the king? The answer was a little bit of both, or, more precisely, an oscillation between these principles at various points in the rite's history.[49] The coronation oath acted as a barometer of the balance of power within the English constitution – at the very least, of the monarch's perception of that balance.

The oath's form and position relative to other parts of the ceremony, particularly the acclamation, oaths of fealty, anointing, and crowning, reflected which principles had apparently gained ascendancy at a given time. We begin with the issue of the oath's placement, assuming that priority indicates priorities. In the first coronation order in the tenth century, the royal oath came at the very end – after anointing, crowning, and a form of popular acclamation (the prompted "God save the King!" from the Abbey's four corners) – and it was less an oath than a set of promises to rule well.[50] It came almost as an afterthought: the king had

Table 1. Essential Elements of English Coronations, 901–1953

| | | | | | | | | |
|---|---|---|---|---|---|---|---|---|
| 1st Recension (901–956) | | | | Anointing | Crowning | (Acclamation) | (Cor. Oath) | |
| 2nd Recension (973–1154) | | (Acclamation) | (Cor. Oath) | Anointing | Crowning | | | |
| 3rd Recension (1189–1274) | | (Cor. Oath) | Acclamation | Anointing | Crowning | | | |
| 4th Recension (1308–1685) | | Acclamation | Cor. Oath | Anointing | Crowning | Fealty Oaths | | |
| Charles I (1626) | | Acclamation | Cor. Oath | Anointing | Crowning | Fealty Oaths | | |
| Charles I (1633) | | Acclamation | Cor. Oath | Anointing | Crowning | Fealty Oaths 1 | People's Oaths | Fealty Oaths 2 |
| Charles II (1661) | | Acclamation | Cor. Oath | Anointing | Crowning | Fealty Oaths | | |
| Interregnum (1649–1660) | | | | | | | | |
| Charles II (1651) | Cor. Oath 1* | Acclamation | Cor. Oaths 2-3 | | Crowning | Fealty Oaths 1 | People's Oaths | Fealty Oaths 2 |
| O. Cromwell (1653) | | IG Read | Prot. Oath | | | | | |
| O. Cromwell (1657) | | SHC Oration | Prot. Oath | | | (Acclamation 1) | (Acclamation 2) | |
| R. Cromwell (1658) | | | Prot. Oath | | | | | |
| 5th Recension (1689–1953) | | Acclamation | Cor. Oath | Anointing | Crowning | Fealty Oaths | | |
| William & Mary (1689) | | Acclamation | Cor. Oath | Anointing | Crowning | Fealty Oaths | | |

Cor. Oath = Coronation Oath

Cor. Oath 1* = (in this order) Pre-Acclamation, Pre-Coronation Oath, Coronation Oath 1, Covenants (Scottish National Covenant, Solemn League and Covenant)

Prot. Oath = Protectoral Oath

IG Read = The Instrument of Government Read Out

SHC Oration = Oration by the Speaker of the House of Commons

(Parentheses indicate that the speech-act in question is the equivalent of a later or earlier one with the same title already become or been recognized as king via those three subrituals; the oath did not constitute a condition for becoming king. But from the Second Recension (973) onward, as Milton noted in the commonplace book and *Brief Notes*, the royal oath preceded the anointing and crowning (see Table 1), as if the latter two were contingent upon the royal oath and subjects reserved (at least nominally) the right to refuse this person as monarch.[51] This relative subordination of the crowning and anointing to the royal oath suggests a further wrinkle. With the brief exception of the Third Recension (1189–1274), the acclamation has always preceded the coronation oath, making the latter seem contingent upon the former. Moreover, the coronation oath and acclamation have always stuck together as a block relative to that formed by the anointing and crowning, thus stressing their reciprocal nature. By contrast, the new oaths of fealty sworn by the lords spiritual and temporal after the coronation oath and crowning from the Fourth Recension on (1308–1953) seem even more of an afterthought, a gloss on the general acclamation given by all the people earlier in the service, as well as a kind of oath of office by which these lords hold their titles and lands. Even so, the appearance of these oaths of fealty in 1308 strengthened the contractual element. It was strengthened even further by Charles I's Scottish coronation in 1633 (arguably a context for Milton's *Maske at Ludlow Castle* the following year), in which the people of that covenanting nation were granted their own separate oath of allegiance (see Table 1).[52]

Compared with the seventeenth century's other coronations, the unusual coronations or installations of the 1650s emphasized words more than objects, contract more than kinesthetics. In the absence of the anointment on all four occasions, and of the crowning on the last three, oaths loomed large. They were more swearings-in than coronations. Charles II's coronation by the Scots at Scone in 1651 trumped all others with its multitude of explicitly contractual and reciprocal oaths: not one but two sets of coronation oaths for the king, including his approval of the Scottish National Covenant and the Solemn League and Covenant; at least two acclamations; the oath for the whole people from his father's Scottish coronation; two sets of oaths for the lords temporal; and pointedly none for churchmen (Table 1).[53] Cromwell's first installation in 1653 stripped the rite down to little more than the Protector's oath of office preceded by an explanatory text: the Instrument of Government.[54] Addressing his first protectoral Parliament almost a year later (12 September 1654), Cromwell would revealingly characterize his installation as a "Solemnity" at which "I took the Oath to this Government." In that speech he repeatedly stressed that in everything he spoke, "I do not bear witness to myself" and to his own legitimacy as Protector because so many other people had already done so at the installation and afterwards. He ended by commanding MPs to express their consent to the constitution's "Fundamentals" by swearing an oath to "the Government, as it is settled in a Single Person and a Parliament."[55] We shall return to these comments.

Cromwell's more kingly second installation in 1657 still lacked a crowning and anointing but placed an investiture of robes, sceptre, sword, and Bible just before the oath and the two sets of pseudo-popular acclamations.[56] Once again, he would later refer to this ceremony as a swearing-in: "my Oath . . . to govern 'according to the Laws' that are now made" – the new constitution known as the Humble Petition and Advice.[57] When Cromwell died in 1658, his son Richard was proclaimed Lord Protector by the Privy Council throughout London by heralds and a procession and then sworn in at Whitehall with little ceremony other than acknowledgment of his new status by the Lord Mayor and aldermen of London. One of the Council's justifications for the transfer of power was that Oliver had "declared, and appointed" his son to "succeed him in the Government of these Nations." The official proclamation of Richard's succession, repeated four times in the streets of London, was accompanied by shouted acclamations and contained the words "We . . . do now hereby, with *one full voice*, and *consent of tongue and heart*, publish and declare the said Noble, and Illustrious Lord Richard to be rightfully protector of this Commonwealth."[58] In its omission of the crowning and its absence of the anointing (announced as having already taken place), as well as in its focus on issues of consent by tongue and heart, Milton's coronation of the Son in *Paradise Lost* is thus closest to those of the 1650s, particularly Cromwell's – and in certain respects even more to the swearing-in of his son Richard at the command of his father. While Gordon Campbell and Thomas Corns read the Exaltation scene as a test of the angels' loyalty and a reflection on Richard's coronation as a "dreadful example of how not to transfer power,"[59] I will concentrate on its reduction of the coronation rite to little more than God's oath, without meaningful interaction among the participants and thus without an opportunity to express genuine consent.

The contents of the coronation oath had also changed over time, reflecting different conceptions of the monarch's status relative to his subjects and church. In its first three recensions (901–1274), the oath consisted of three promises: 1) "that the Church of God and all Christian people preserve the peace at all times"; 2) "that [the king] forbid rapacity and all iniquities to all degrees" of people; 3) "that in all judgments [the king] enjoin equity and mercy."[60] With the Fourth Recension of 1308 (from Edward II to James II), the oath settled into a question-and-answer format.

**The Basic Form of the Coronation Oath, 1308–1685**

The Archbishop (or Bishop) goes to the King and in a moderate and distinct voice asks [*interroget*]:

ARCHBISHOP Sir, will you grant, keep, and by your oath confirm to the people of England the laws and customs granted to them by the Kings of England, your lawful and religious predecessors, and namely the laws, customs, and liberties granted to the clergy and to the people by the glorious king, St. Edward, your predecessor?
KING I grant and promise to keep them.

Then the Archbishop explains to him what he shall swear:

ARCHBISHOP Sir, will you keep peace and godly concord entirely (according to your powers), both to God, the holy Church, the clergy, and the people?
KING I will keep it.
ARCHBISHOP Sir, will you to your power cause law, justice, and discretion in mercy and truth to be executed in all your judgments?
KING I will.
ARCHBISHOP Sir, will you grant to hold and keep the just laws and customs [*iustas leges et consuetudines*] that the people shall have chosen [*quas vulgus elegerit*], and to defend and uphold them to the honor of God, so much as in you lies?
KING I grant and promise so to do.

[*The King then grants a pardon to the clergy.*]

With an oath/with the Eucharist [*sacramento*] upon the altar in front of everyone, the king confirms that he shall keep all these promises.

First, the Archbishop asked the monarch whether he wished to take an oath to preserve "the laws, customs, and liberties granted to the clergy and to the people by the glorious king, St. Edward [the Confessor]."[61] After agreeing, he was asked to swear three promises. When he had assented to each promise separately, he went to the altar to swear formally to keep them all, hand on Bible, and, in the early coronations, on or near the Eucharist. Two of the sworn promises were essentially the first and third provisions of the previous coronation oath: to preserve the peace and the Church; to see that justice and mercy were done throughout the realm. The provision against rapacity and iniquity, however, disappeared, to be replaced by what Roy Strong calls a "revolutionary" new one. Under great pressure from the barons, Edward II now swore to uphold the "just laws and customs . . . that the people shall have chosen" (*iustas leges et consuetudines . . . quas vulgus elegerit*).[62]

Until 1689 almost every subsequent oath, in Latin, French, or English, including those of Charles I and II, retained this wording and offered some kind of footnote to its fundamental ambiguity. The core issue was whether the future perfect *elegerit* (*shall have chosen*) in *quas vulgus elegerit* should be construed as *has chosen* (perfect tense, referring to laws the people have already chosen by the time of the coronation) or *shall choose* (future tense, laws the people shall choose after the coronation) – both meanings available in the Latin.[63] The former (*has chosen*) implies a balance of power in favour of the monarch, who is obliged only to respect existing laws at the time of the coronation, but not later ones. The latter (*shall choose*) suggests a balance in favour of Parliament, which reserves the option of making new laws that the monarch must not veto – an interpretation of the word that Milton broadcast in *Eikonoklastes* and the *First Defence*.[64]

After 1308, the meaning of *quas vulgus elegerit* tacked back and forth between these two poles. Many of the Tudors and Stuarts in particular tried to imprint the expanding power of the monarchy upon their coronation oaths, subordinating church to state and Parliament to sovereign (the *shall choose* to the *has chosen*). At his coronation in 1509, Henry VIII swore to preserve the laws and customs *quas vulgus elegerit*, with *elegerit* translated or at least understood as *shall be chosen*.[65] But in the late 1520s or early 1530s, as he began to declare independence from Rome and thus increase the monarchy's power, Henry contemplated revising the oath into English, possibly for a not unprecedented second coronation (perhaps with Anne Boleyn in 1533). In the event, however, he passed up the opportunity to be crowned a second time and never used the oath.[66] In Henry's own hand the document considers not only translating *elegerit* as "haue made and chosen," but adding language (see the italics) that limits the people's (i.e., Parliament's) power to make laws while increasing his own: the monarch "shall graunte to holde laws and *approvyd* customes of the realme *and lawfull and not preiudiciall to hys crowne or Imperiall Juris[diction;]* to his power kepe them and affirme them which the noblys and people *haue made and chosen w[ith] hys consent*."[67]

But Edward VI and Elizabeth apparently swore less absolutist oaths in the *shall choose* vein. Under the influence of his advisers, the young Edward swore in 1547 "to make no *newe lawes* but such as *shalbe* [shall be] to th[' h]onour and glory of God and to the good of the Common Wealth, and that the same *sh[a]lbe made by the cionsent [consent] of your people* as hath been accustomed" – which privileged the power of Parliament at the expense of the royal prerogative. William Prynne would print this oath in 1660, in the runup to Charles II's coronation.[68] We would like to know what Mary I swore in 1553, but in 1559 Elizabeth may have sworn Edward's oath with its future tense and reference to the people's consent, plus a new clause promising "to act 'according to the Laws of God, [and] the true profession of the Gospel established in this Kingdom.'"[69]

As an apostle of divine right, James I pulled decisively in the other direction in 1603, setting a precedent for his son and grandsons. He had the whole service translated into English and essentially returned to the *have chosen* interpretation Henry had considered, but with fewer absolutist qualifications, promising in English to preserve "the Lawes and rightfull Customes, which the Comminaltie of your Kingdom *haue*."[70] By removing the *chosen* from *have chosen*, he omitted the idea of the people or Parliament choosing laws at any time, let alone the future – avoiding, in fact, any reference to the origins of laws.[71] But the Stuarts added as well as subtracted. Either James or his son, Charles I, added something to another part of the oath: its preamble. The new clause (in italics below) mentioned the royal prerogative and the established Church:

> Will you grant and keepe, and by your oath confirme to the people of England the lawes and Customes to them granted by the Kinges of England your lawfull and Religiouse predecessors; and namely the Lawes, Customes and ffranchisez granted to the Clergie, and to the people by the gloriouse King Saint Edward your Predecessor *according to ye laws of God,*

> *ye true profession of the Gospell established in this Kingdome and agreeing to the Prerogative of the Kings thereof, and the ancient Customes of this Realm?*[72]

If James added the clause, it may have distinguished the established Church of England from Catholic and other Protestant churches abroad. If Charles added it, it may have had a domestic audience, distinguishing the established state church from Puritans and other dissenting Protestants. In both cases, it insisted on the king's prerogative powers vis-à-vis Parliament and Convocation.

Certain it is that in the runup to the Civil War, Parliament accused Charles I of breaking his coronation oath by allegedly tyrannical innovations in taxation and church government, and it specifically cited the *quas vulgus* clause. There was even false speculation that Charles and Archbishop Laud had conspired to omit the clause altogether, a charge Milton repeated in the *Defensio Prima*.[73] However, in 1626 Charles I seems to have kept the clause and his father's translation of *elegerit* as *have*, rather than *have chosen*: "the Lawes and rightfull Customes w[hi] ch ye Commonalty of this yo[u]r Kingdome *have*."[74] What Charles probably did leave out, with or without Laud's guidance, was the phrase "and to the people," which had appeared in James's preamble to the oath after "the Clergie":

> JAMES I: Will you grant and keepe, and by your oath confirme [A] to the people of England the lawes and Customes to them granted by the Kinges of England your lawfull and Religiouse predecessors; and [B] namely the Lawes, Customes and ffranchisez granted *to the Clergie, and to the people* by the glorious King Saint Edward your predecessor . . .
>
> CHARLES I: Will you grant and keep, and so by y[ou]r oath confirme [A] to the People of England the Lawes and Customes to them granted by the Kings of England yo[u]r lawfull and religious Predecessors; And [B] namely ye Laws, Customes, and Franchises granted *to ye Clergy* by ye glorious King St Edward yo[u]r Predecessor . . .[75]

Charles may just have been streamlining and clarifying matters by having himself grant "laws and customs to the people" in Clause A, while merely specifying the clergy as a subset of the people in Clause B, which begins with "namely."[76] But more hostile ears could have heard this as a calculated slight, in which he departed from his predecessors by not promising to keep and preserve the laws, customs, and franchises granted by St Edward to the people – only the ones to the clergy.

Hazy memories of this omission may have led to the mistaken charge about Charles and Laud's omitting the other clause containing the word *people* (*quas vulgus elegerit*) in 1626. In 1633, however, at Charles's second coronation in Scotland, scripted by Laud, the clause was indeed omitted – though likely more because of local Scottish precedents for the coronation oath, rather than an absolutist/imperialist English plot to deny the Scottish people their laws.[77]

In his son Charles II's first coronation at Scone in 1651 (the very last coronation of a monarch in Scotland), the Scots did their best to remove all ambiguity and to subordinate king to people. They replaced the ambiguous *quas vulgus elegerit* with very precise language amounting to the *shall choose* reading on steroids. Charles promised to obey and enforce all pre-existing Covenants and any law, civil or religious, that the Scottish Parliament should in future pass.[78] In Cromwell's first protectoral oath, multiple preambles stressed that he was accepting the reins of power offered by Parliament and people in the Instrument of Government (in effect, a written constitution); and he swore not to "violate, or infringe the matters and things contained therein, but, to my power, observe the same . . . And . . . in al other things, to the best of my understanding, govern these Nations according to the Laws, Statutes and Customs, seeking their Peace, and causing Justice and Law to be equally administred."[79] If the phrase "Laws, Statutes and Customs" failed to specify past or future, the rest of the text did appear to tie his hands in ways previous oaths had not. His second protectoral oath, repeated by his son the following year, likewise equivocated on the *quas vulgus* question. Despite identifying him as "chief Magistrate of these three nations," his oath returned to more monarchical language, promising to protect reformed Protestantism, govern "according to Law," and preserve the peace, safety, and "just Rights and Privileges of the people."[80]

In 1661 Charles II's orthodox second coronation returned to the language of the Fourth Recension that his father had used in England. The *elegerit* in the final question remained *have,* without the *chosen*; and the introduction retained the references to the prerogative and established Church.[81] However, the decisive break in the restored monarchical tradition came with William and Mary at the Revolution. Complaining of the "doubtfull Words and Expressions" in the former coronation oath, Parliament decided on new, more precise wording and fixed it in law for all future monarchs as part of the Fifth Recension.[82] Both monarchs were read the Declaration of Rights and offered the crowns by Parliament, which both revised the oath and attended the ceremony en masse.

William accepted the Declaration and the crown, acknowledging the monarchs' subordination to parliamentary law.[83] Swearing the oath in unison, both William and Mary agreed to "Governe the People of this Kingdome of England and the Dominions thereto belonging according to the Statues in Parlyament Agreed on and the Laws and Customs of the same" – that is, all parliamentary laws, both before and after the coronation.[84] Queen Anne's coronation oath in 1702 made the shift even clearer, adding language taken from loyalty oaths that subjects had sworn to various regimes in the seventeenth century, which bound her not to evade the oath through "equivocation, or mental reservation."[85] Never before had the coronation oath, even in Charles II's humiliating Scottish coronation, questioned the monarch's integrity and in effect reduced her to the status of subject in quite this way.

One might object that a Miltonic, contractualist understanding of the coronation oath and ceremony does not necessarily imply republican antimonarchism, perhaps just support for an elective monarchy of the kind mentioned by John Bradshaw and others at Charles I's trial.[86] Yet even Bradshaw was not defending monarchy per se at the trial, and *Paradise Lost*'s Heaven and heavenly coronation are clearly not elective. As some have pointed out in an effort to deradicalize the politics in *Paradise Lost*, this contractualist understanding is also consistent with limited monarchy and mixed government.[87] However, Milton's poetry, with all its intricacies, is not prose. It does not always present ideas straightforwardly; and apparent contradictions can arise between, say, the celebration of monarchy in Heaven and its denigration on Earth. Those contradictions are not to be resolved by assuming that Milton wants the same form of government in both places, thereby contorting his entire career by pegging him as a secret monarchist or mixed monarchist in *Paradise Lost*. Heaven is the exception that proves the rule that republics are the best governments. In any case, many clearly antimonarchist republicans, such as Algernon Sidney, Henry Vane, Henry Neville, Marchamont Nedham in his republican phases, and very likely Bradshaw and many others on the High Court of Justice, held views similar to Milton's about the reciprocal nature of the oaths of allegiance and coronation (something they shared with many monarchists), but more important, about the latter as a safeguard against absolutism and a temporary expedient on the road towards non-monarchical government.[88]

Even if one sticks to the prose and compares Milton's pronouncements on monarchy from 1649 onward, one must place most emphasis on the latest works in the sequence, those closest in time to *Paradise Lost*.

*The Readie and Easie Way* (1660) makes it unambiguously clear that God wants earthly polities to be republics in one way or another – republics in which the only king is God, not any single human.[89] While Milton's defenses of republicanism from *Tenure* to the *Second Defence* have been shown to allow some small room for righteous kings,[90] monarchy is clearly a second best, an anomaly, an expedient on the way to republicanism. This is the gesture of the *First Defence*, Milton's most forceful apologia for republican government and citizenship – republic first, king second and only if absolutely necessary – and it is certainly the gesture of his writings in 1660 and 1674. *The Readie and Easie Way* makes an increasingly desperate and dangerous case against the return of any kind of monarchy; and as monarchy's return becomes inevitable in April 1660, *Brief Notes upon a Late Sermon* only grudgingly concedes a limited, elective monarchy as the lesser of many evils – and unlikely to last.[91] There, as in the *First Defence*, he insists that while the occasional king can muster enough merit to rule well, most cannot.[92] *Letters Patent* (1674), published under the restored monarchy, in effect repeats that grudging admission in its implied support for elective monarchy in Poland and thus, by implication, for electing a non-Catholic king in England. And to return to 1660, most of Milton's writings in the months before the Restoration, including *A Letter to a Friend*, *Proposalls of Certaine Expedients*, *The Present Means and Brief Delineation of A Free Commonwealth*, and *The Readie and Easie Way*, entertain the idea of a loyalty oath of some kind that restates the Engagement's unconditional refusal of monarchy.[93] Focusing on oaths, then, demonstrates that Milton's heart was antimonarchist and that *Paradise Lost* best expresses this brand of republicanism.

## Intertexts of God's Oath

In order to appreciate God's oath as part of an unsatisfactory coronation ritual that robs participants of autonomy, we must scrutinize its dense intertextuality. While the self-referential oath of Milton's God appears to have no classical precedents, it has a few early modern and a host of biblical ones. To the extent that it involves granting power to someone else in a gnomic utterance, it resembles Richard II's heartbreaking abjuration and passing on of the crown to Bolingbroke in Shakespeare's play, accompanied by the notoriously opaque statement "Ay, no; no, ay" – all part of a quasi- or pre-coronation ceremony that releases his subjects from their oaths of allegiance and transfers them to Henry IV.[94]

By contrast, Milton's God does not so clearly give up all power or cancel his subjects' obligations to him; he remains omnipotent, even as he grants plenipotentiary powers to the Son. But in form rather than function, God's self-oath more closely resembles other Renaissance forebears, such as the oaths urged on Shakespeare's Romeo and Bassanio on the one hand and Donne's God on the other, in that it involves pressing someone else to make a commitment to action. Shakespeare's heroines, tragic and comic, ask their lovers to swear undying fidelity to them "by thy self." In "A Hymn to God the Father," the anxious Donne recklessly and punningly orders God to grant him life after death: "Swear by thyself that at my death thy *Sun* / Shall shine as it shines now, and heretofore."[95] For a Trinitarian like Donne, these lines only ask God to commit another part of himself (the Son) to save the poet (another of God's sons). But a non-Trinitarian might hear the lines differently: as committing God to commit a third party (the Son) to future action. In any case, of the three-plus people adjured (or urged to swear an oath) here, only one (Bassanio) clearly goes through with it.

More immediately, though, God's swearing for others in *Paradise Lost* resembles a set of statutory rather than literary oaths: the mandatory state-oaths enacted by the Cavalier Parliament after the Restoration. As the centerpiece of the Clarendon Code (1661–5), the Corporation, Uniformity, and Vestryman's Oaths required numerous officeholders to swear that other people were not bound by the Solemn League and Covenant of 1643 to change or reform the government: "I do declare that I do hold there lies *no Obligation* upon me *or any other person* from the Oath commonly called the Solemn League and Covenant *to endeavour any Change or Alteration of Government*, either in Church, or State."[96] They were thus forced not only to take an oath before entering office, but also, as we saw earlier, to take one that imposed commitments on other people without their permission. All these intertexts highlight the apparent arbitrariness and coercion involved in Milton's God committing others to do things without giving them a chance to object.

Attention to the scriptural models for God's self-oath in *Paradise Lost* reveals something more complex: its status as a coherent tissue of biblical quotations about exaltation and, crucially, mediation (Genesis 22:16, Isaiah 45:23, Psalm 110:4, Philippians 2:9–11, Romans 14:10–11, and 1 Kings 1:28–30). A survey of Milton's comments on these texts throughout *De Doctrina* in a number of different contexts demonstrates that, cumulatively, they problematize notions of voice and agency with respect to the words of God and his representatives. These comments are central to an understanding of Milton's at-times equivocal treatment of Arianism in Book 5 of *Paradise Lost*.[97] God's oath combines biblical quotations that make several points about the Son, his relationship to God, and both God and Son's relations to humankind. *De Doctrina* describes these relationships by outlining at least three roles or offices for the Son: prophet, priest, and king. Only the last two concern us, but all can be subsumed into Milton's scheme under the rubric of mediator.[98]

The Abrahamic Covenant is the main background for many of these offices and transactions. In Genesis 22:16, God swears for the first time by his own name, solidifying his earlier covenant to multiply Abraham's seed (Genesis 13:13–17). It is a curious moment because, like *Paradise Lost*, it involves an oath in the past tense now announced to one of God's creatures. In order to prevent Abraham from killing Isaac at the last minute, an angel announces that God has already sworn a promise that "in blessing will I bless thee, and in multiplying I will multiply thy seed as the stars of heaven." The oath is doubly distanced from Abraham by being announced by someone other than God (the angel) and by being phrased in the past tense: "By myself *have I sworn, saith the Lord*, for because thou hast done this thing, and hast not withheld thy son, thine only son."

In addition to being an oath-moment, and a self-referential oath-moment at that, it is also a father-son moment for Abraham and Isaac that anticipates God's relationship to his only begotten Son.[99] If Isaac (the type) is a near-sacrifice, the Son (the antitype) will become an actual sacrifice on the Cross. The difference is not only one of near-death vs. real death. In a sense the situations resemble each other in that neither son ultimately dies: Isaac is reprieved; Christ resurrected. Yet the two sons diverge in their knowledge of and agency in the sacrifice. Isaac remains ignorant of the sacrifice till the last moment; Abraham chooses it for him. As for Christ, this Son will later choose to sacrifice himself for humanity (*Paradise Lost* 3.236–41). In *Paradise Lost*'s Exaltation scene, the dynamic, like the wording ("by myself have sworn"), approaches that of Genesis 22:16 rather than Christ's crucifixion because God the Father chooses the Son's exaltation for him – and, I argue, swears his coronation oath for him. The Son seems to have no choice in the matter: his wishes are not discussed and seem irrelevant at this point. This would hardly figure as an issue in a Trinitarian understanding of the Son's relationship to God, but it looms large in Milton's Arian thinking. God has simply made him his successor, just as Abraham has paradoxically ensured by the attempted sacrifice that Isaac will be his successor to the status of covenanter with God, bearer of the promise.

Both Isaiah 45:23 and Hebrews 6:16 rehearse the Abrahamic Covenant and divine self-oath. Hebrews 6 offers the Son as a second guarantor of God's promise, yet another agent of his voice:

> For when God made promise to Abraham, because he could swear by no greater, he sware by himself . . . Wherein God, willing more abundantly to shew unto the heirs of promise the immutability of his counsel, confirmed it by an oath. That by two immutable things . . . we might have a strong consolation [hope] . . . as an anchor of the soul . . . the forerunner is . . . Jesus, made an high priest for ever after the order of Melchizedek. (13, 17–20)

The Son will continue to implement God's part of the covenant (i.e., to help Christians implement it) by mediating as a priest-king between them and God (Hebrews 6:20, 10–12).

A related passage from Psalm 110 (a coronation psalm like Psalm 2) raises the issues of agency and voice by featuring God's speaking through the psalmist David – it is, after all, prefaced by the title "A Psalm of David" – and apparently through a third party who speaks its opening line about the Israelite king: "The Lord said unto my lord: 'Sit thou at my right hand, until I make thine enemies thy footstool'" (110:1). When this speaker describes God crowning David in the coronation ceremony ("The Lord hath sworn, and will not repent, Thou art a priest for ever after the order of Melchizedek,'" 110:4), it involves another quotation of a quotation (David quoting the speaker quoting God). Hebrews adds yet another chain to the link when it quotes this verse throughout chapters 5–7; and in 6:13 it turns God's mere oath in Psalm 110:4 ("The Lord hath sworn") into the self-oath of the Abrahamic Covenant: "For when God made promise to Abraham, because he could swear by no greater, he sware by himself." Hebrews thus explicitly connects God's two oaths: the first and self-referential one that seals the Abrahamic Covenant (Genesis 22:16); the second and non-self-referential one that makes Christ the eternal mediator (Psalm 110:4; Hebrews 5–7). We can now see that the sources of *Paradise Lost* 5.607–8 relate the Abrahamic Covenant and the father-son relationship to the Son's succession, sacrifice, mediation, and coronation – all the while asking questions such as, who is speaking, and for whom? who is taking action, and for whom?

For Milton, Christ's resurrection from the dead and creation of the universe are both species of mediation, of doing tasks for God; and mediation is an instance of divided agency. *De Doctrina* sees Christ's Exaltation, referred to in *Paradise Lost* 5.602–15 and described by William Hunter in *Bright Essence*, as prefiguring his resurrection, and thus that of all believers, via Christ's sacrifice, at the end of time.[100] More important for our purposes, Christ mediates for God when, according to Milton, he creates the visible universe. *Paradise Lost*'s various narrators provide further echoes and even more mediation. In *De Doctrina*, Milton cites the coronation-like passages in Isaiah 45:23 and Philippians 2:9–11 – both sources of *Paradise Lost* 5.607–8 – as examples of Christ's roles as Creator, as the Word that emanates from God to create the universe and that is therefore an entity distinct from God.[101] In *De Doctrina*'s chapter on the Creation, Milton makes his anti-Trinitarian point that the Father and Son are separate beings by arguing that God created the world "per" or via his Son, who is the "less principal cause."[102] He refuses interpretations of Isaiah 45:23 that insist on the Son's doing the creating. Instead, Milton argues, God does it, not the Son – or only the Son as representative of but not part of God. Milton confronts Trinitarian arguments that the Son is part of God by contesting their use of Isaiah 45:23, one of our self-oath passages, as a proof-text:

> Another argument [Trinitarians offer] is brought from Isa. xlv. 12, 23. "I have made the earth . . . unto me every knee shall bow." It is contended that this is spoken of Christ, on the authority of St. Paul, Rom. xiv. 10, 11. "we shall all stand before the judgment seat of Christ: for it is written, As I live, saith the Lord, every knee shall bow to me." But it is evident from the parallel passage Philipp. ii. 9–11. that this is said of God the Father, by whose gift the Son has received that judgment seat, and all judgment, "that at the name of Jesus every knee should bow . . . to the glory of God the Father"; or, which means the same thing, "every tongue shall confess to God."[103]

Milton's invocation of Isaiah's self-oath and the passages from Romans and Philippians encourages us to see *Paradise Lost*'s Exaltation scene as an instance of creation by speech-act, a moment that looks forwards and backwards to the epic's other acts of creation. A speech-act, the Father's "decree" (5.602), creates the Son as king. It also informs the assembled angels that the Son was the Word by which God created them, and by which he will create humans and their universe, as well as the Hell necessary to punish the soon-to-be rebel angels, and, eventually, unregenerate humans. Hence, it also creates obedience and disobedience in God's creatures, if indirectly. Following the lead of Isaiah 45:23, Milton's God turns the event into a creation of loyalty and obedience in an imagined answering speech-act. *Paradise Lost* 5.607–8 sharpens this notion of an answering act of loyalty, but turns it into primarily a non-speech-act, a corporal gesture. Only the knees will bow and confess Christ Lord: "by myself have sworn to him shall bow / All knees in heaven, and shall confess him Lord." In a moment comparable to God's "den[ying]" "language of man . . . To beasts, whom God on their creation-day / Created mute to all articulate sound" (9.553–7), God virtually removes all opportunity for a verbal response. Instead, the response will be physical. In a conscious departure from the English coronation rite, in which the people expressed verbal consent or recognition of the new monarch, *Paradise Lost*'s coronation ceremony only allows God to perform a speech-act.

By having God in this moment create bodily obedience and basically silence all voices, Milton once again raises the whole issue of who is speaking, and for whom. In *De Doctrina*'s chapter on the Son of God, Milton returns to Genesis 22:16, the scene of God's first self-oath sealing the Abrahamic Covenant. There he confronts both this issue and the anti-Trinitarian view that the Son is not God, in spite of the fact that some scriptures refer to angels (and, by extension, Christ, as another representative of God) by his name:

> The name of God seems [at times] to be attributed to angels, because as heavenly messengers they bear the appearance of the divine glory and person, and even speak in the very words of the Deity. *Gen.* xxi. 17, 18. *xxii. 11, 12, 15, 16. "by myself have I sworn, saith Jehovah."* For the expression so frequently in the mouth of the prophets, and which is elsewhere often omitted, is here inserted, for the purpose of showing that angels and messengers do not declare their own words, but the commands of God who sends them, even though the speaker seems to bear the name and character of the Deity himself.[104]

Genesis 22:16 is thus for Milton one of several passages where "God said" really means "a representative of God said."[105] In another place, Milton amplifies the argument by making it a matter not just of words but of promises: "the name of Jehovah [sometimes] signifies two things, either the nature of God, or the completion of his words and promises."[106] This returns us to the issues of who is speaking in *Paradise Lost* 5.607–8 and who is an agent. For once, God seems to speak for himself – and yet he doesn't: he really speaks for the Son in the Exaltation scene. *De Doctrina*'s caution that sometimes the phrase "God speaks" means "an agent of God speaks" allows us to see the flicker of Trinitarianism that the Exaltation scene creates – a flicker quickly extinguished, but from Milton's point of view troubling all the same.[107] At a moment when an apparent transfer of power from Father to Son has taken place or is taking place, the urgent question arises of who's in charge.

The passage's notoriously slippery temporal markers ("This day," "I have begot," "I declare," "I have anointed," "I appoint," "I have sworn") simply underscore the problem of agency and mediation. When exactly did God do these things, or is he doing them as he speaks? And do the problems arise only because we hear his speech as mediated by Raphael for Adam and Eve, and thus by Milton for us? Did God in fact say something different? The tense of "I . . . by myself have sworn" has a hitherto unnoticed origin that solves one problem while creating others. The "I have sworn" of Milton's God does several things: 1) it honours the fact that in the Torah God is more frequently reported by an underling as having sworn in the past than as actually appearing to swear for himself in the present; 2) it constitutes a deliberate archaism, mimicking biblical Hebrew's propensity to use a past-tense verb, usually the perfect ("I have sworn"), to indicate actual swearing in the present; 3) it hints at the problem of pinning down origins, such as exactly when in the Torah God swears a covenant about land and a chosen status for the Jews; and, most important, 4) it creates a problem for Milton's English readers, who emphatically did and do not swear ceremonial oaths in the past tense.

First, we can conclude our discussion of *De Doctrina*'s treatment of God's indirect speech by noting that in the Torah he is always reported by someone else as swearing; it is always some version of "the Lord swore" or "'I have sworn,' saith the Lord." And in this indirect, quoted discourse, God sometimes does refer to his own swearing, but still in the past tense.[108] Second and more important, ancient Hebrew had what might be called a promissory perfect tense. For whatever reason, the way one swore official oaths at official oath ceremonies was to depart from the normal present tense and speak the past tense: literally "I swore to do X" or "I have sworn to do X," but understood as "I hereby swear to do X" and thus as a present-tense performative speech-act with binding force.[109] In effect, the perfect tense marks the utterance as a powerful performative that binds the swearer, making her accountable for non-performance.[110] Hence, the verb biblical speakers, human or divine, used to swear an oath in their own voice is usually *nishbati* ("I have sworn"), technically "I have been sworn."[111] For example, God's oath to Abraham in Genesis 22:16–17, as reported to him by the angel in the previous verse, is "By myself I have sworn, saith the Lord" (*b-i nishbati, nam Ieue*); and this is how everyone else swears for themselves in the Torah.[112] There are, as far as I can tell, no instances of the verb *shaba* (to swear) in the literal present tense, first-person active indicative. Hence, what the Authorized Version and most other translations, including the Septuagint and Vulgate, render as "I have sworn" may equally well be translated as "I swear." The angel may thus be saying to Abraham in Genesis 22:16, "The Lord says, I swear by myself that . . ."

Therefore, the perfect tense in *Paradise Lost*'s "I . . . by myself have sworn" plays the dual role of adhering to Hebrew practice in a Hebraic situation of oath-swearing – a studied archaism not all that different from the poem's epic Latinisms and Hellenisms – and of hinting at God's complete otherness with respect to time, when compared with humans: his oaths are simultaneously past and present, if not future. This is all well and good, especially for readers with a good knowledge of Hebrew. But the rest of us have little choice but to assume that "I . . . have sworn" straightforwardly indicates an action in the past – at the very least an action that began in the past. And if God indeed swore the oath in the past, why did he not do so in front of witnesses, and why does he only tell the angels now? Moreover, why does he swear an oath for other people, who will do the bowing and scraping he mentions? These problems create confusion and encourage us to ask whether we are actually reading God's original words, or even a half-way decent translation or approximation of them, especially of the sequence of events implied by the different tenses: past, present, and future. Milton does this to place us in the same position as the angels listening to God's announcement in Book 5, especially Satan: that of being overwhelmed by the dizzying alternatives. And it muddies the whole question of what exactly God says in this pivotal speech. For us the tense of God's oath compounds our sense of distance from him, a distance created not just by ontology (God and humans are different orders of being) but by transmission as well.

God's self-oath thus crystallizes the many problems of mediation created by his speaking to us through (a series of) his creatures. What things, and crucially what sequence of things, made it through undistorted? But if, according to Milton, the word "God" in various scriptures can denote angels speaking for God, the passage in Book 5 also raises the opposite question: for whom is God speaking here? Why should he speak for the angels, whom he requires to "speak" through their bodily gestures of submission to the Son, comparable to Adam and Eve's showing obedience by abstaining from the bodily act of eating the fruit? Or for that matter, should God speak for the Son himself, who, like a king in an earthly coronation ceremony, should do the swearing on his own?

## Republican Unease over the Son's Coronation

To help answer such questions, let us look at another source of God's self-oath (1 Kings 1:28–30) and then consider how the coronation ceremony in *Paradise Lost*, Book 5, responds to both the intertexts and the contractualist evolution of the English coronation oath's form and placement. The English ceremony had compared the anointing of the monarch to those of David and Solomon. As the bishop anointed Charles II's hands in 1661, for example, he drew on 1 Samuel 16:13 and intoned, "Let these Hands be anointed with Holy Oil, as Kings and Prophets have been anointed, and as Samuel did anoint David to be King." The choir followed with an anthem based on 1 Kings 1:34–40: "Sadoc the Priest, and Nathan the Prophet, anointed Solomon King: and all the People rejoiced, and said, GOD SAVE THE KING."[113] Book 5 of *Paradise Lost*, in turn, draws on both the English coronation and 1 Kings when God announces that he has already anointed the Son and already sworn "by myself" that "to him shall bow / All knees in heaven, and shall confess him Lord" (5.607–8). For in 1 Kings 1, in the verses just before those adapted by the English coronation, Nathan and Bathsheba prod David into formally declaring Solomon, rather than his older brother Adonijah, the heir apparent. They do so by telling David that he has already sworn an oath to this effect (13, 17). David immediately complies by renewing the oath:

> King David . . . swore, saying, "As the Lord Lives, who has redeemed my soul out of every adversity, as I swore to you by the Lord, the God of Israel, saying, 'Solomon your son shall reign after me, and he shall sit upon my throne in my stead'; even so will I do this day." (28–30)

On "this day" in Heaven, Milton's God basically quotes the Torah's David, saying that he has already sworn an oath, and an oath "by the Lord" – in other words, "by himself." His oath and thus David's oath both resemble the ancient Near Eastern "covenant of grant," in which a sitting king's oath designated one of his sons as heir so as to prevent future strife *or* granted land to a vassal king, sometimes adopted as his (metaphorical) son.[114] In the first instance the other sons were not always happy. Thus, just as Solomon has a rival for the kingship in Adonijah, so the Son has a kind of competitor in Lucifer/Satan, who considers himself passed over for promotion. The episode in *Paradise Lost* also recalls the fact that all of Israel's first three kings (Saul, David, and Solomon) are secretly anointed or appointed at first and only afterwards presented to the people in a formal ceremony (1 Samuel 10:1; 11:12–15; 16:13; 2 Samuel 2:4; 5:3; 7:12–13; 1 Kings 1:13–40; 1 Chronicles 17:11–14; 22:5–23:2; 28:1–10). Even more telling is the larger context: Israel's transition from an aristocratic republican form of government under the Judges to a monarchy – a monarchy explicitly condemned by both God and Samuel (1 Samuel 8:6–18; 10:17–19 cf. 12:6–20).[115] In the prose tracts Milton's comments on David's anointing in 2 Samuel 2:4 and 5:3 are conspicuously republican. *De Doctrina* lists it among several examples of magistrates being elected by the people; and *The Tenure of Kings and Magistrates* and *First Defence* emphasize David's making a mutual covenant with and being accountable to them.[116]

In this light, one thing would have stood out for Milton: the coronation of the Son in *Paradise Lost* is everything but a mutual contract. Succession beats out popular election as the animating principle, and Milton intends this absolutism to be seen as a problem. Without subscribing to the neo-Romantic argument that Satan is hero and God villain, I only contend that God's oath and speech are designed to raise a question like the one Satan asks later in Book 5: has God "by decree ... to himself engrossed / All power, and us eclipsed under the name / Of king anointed" (774–7)? There are in a sense two main questions here. Has God monopolized all roles in the coronation? And if so, what are we to think of it?

The Exaltation of the Son could be seen as either a reformed rite or a maimed rite. If reformed, it constitutes an attempt to imitate the installations of the 1650s by chucking out all the usual mummery and ceremony: the actual crowning, the oblations, the communion service, the Trinitarian hymns, the processions, most of the regalia, the proliferation of state apparatchiks performing menial duties with menial objects – possibly even the anointing (which God announces rather than displays).[117] By privileging the verbal over the visual and material, Milton strips away much of the ritual dimension of the ritual. Perhaps, he suggests, earthly transfers of executive power should be as sober and barebones as this, little more than the swearings-in of the Protectors. Preferably the leader will be not a monarch but an elected leader, sworn in.

However, it is much easier to see a rite maimed by its absolutism, even as it re-presents a maimed version of the English coronation. It thus offers no pattern for earthly ritual. How exactly is the Son's coronation so despotically monarchical, despite its excisions? First, it hardly counts as a participatory ceremony at all, more as an announcement or "decree" of a fait accompli: the earlier exaltation and anointment of the Son, which may be two actions or two descriptions of the same action (5.602, 605). Within this announcement lies the only classic speech-act in the present tense, the performative "your head I him appoint," which, in any case, seems merely to describe the previous closed-door activity (606). Hence, the oath, which usually preceded the anointing in the earthly rite, now trails it as an afterthought in a ceremony that seems an afterthought. Nor is it sworn in English's present tense, but rather announced in the problematic past tense as what appears to be another fait accompli, presumably one that happened after the exalting and anointing and before God's present announcement: "This day I have begot . . . have anointed . . . have sworn" (603–7). It is neither a sine qua non for the exalting or anointing to take place, nor part of a set of reciprocal oaths. Second, it conspicuously recalls Cromwell's speech to Parliament in September 1654, in which he recalled his first installation, then promised that "I do not bear witness to myself" (presumably because God was bearing witness), and finally required MPs to become further witnesses to his words by swearing an oath of obedience to him.[118] Oaths were understood to be acts of calling on God as witness, and Milton's God does bear witness to himself ("by myself have sworn"), even as he requires obedience from the angels.

Third, the self-oath replaces dialogue with monologue, God depriving almost everyone of a voice.[119] God plays the roles of all officiants in the English coronation ritual, including the archbishop who anoints and crowns the king; he even steals the role of king himself in swearing the oath for the Son, ostensibly the one proclaimed king.[120] The interactive call-and-response format, in which the Archbishop asked the monarch to swear the oath item by item, has gone missing. Moreover, whereas the coronation oath usually applied, like most oaths, only to its swearer, spelling out a commitment on the monarch's part about his or her own future behaviour, God's oath commits himself and the Son to almost nothing, amounting to little more than a command that others do something. There is no pretence of reciprocity, contract, popular election. Into a single speech he collapses the coronation oath, the oaths of fealty, and the Archbishop's call for the people's acclamation, putting the latter in the wrong place: after the oath.

The audience of angels presumably remains silent as God intones the decree, and his oath is worded in such a way as to command them to bow: "to him shall bow / All knees in heaven, and shall confess him Lord" (5.607–8). There is no indication that they disobey. Despite Stevie Davies's characterization of these actions as an oath of allegiance or obedience, the angels make no verbal oath at all.[121] Moreover, God's oath departs in a crucial way from its immediate sources. Isaiah 45:23 reads, "By myself I have sworn, from my mouth has gone forth in righteousness a word that shall not return: '*To me* every knee shall bow, every tongue shall swear.'"[122] Philippians 2:9–11 says of Christ, "God also hath highly exalted him, and given him the name which is above every name: That at the name of *Jesus* every knee should bow, of things in Heaven, and things on Earth, and things under the Earth; and that every tongue should confess that Jesus Christ is Lord." Romans 14:11 proclaims, "For it is written, *As I live*, saith the Lord, every knee shall bow *to me*, and every tongue shall confess to God." Where are the tongues in Milton's oath? "By myself [I] have sworn to him shall bow / All knees in heaven, and shall confess him Lord" (5.607–8): in *Paradise Lost* only the knees do the confessing, not the tongues, as emphasized by Satan's and Abdiel's later remarks about "knee tribute" rather than "tongue tribute" (5.782, 817). The assembled angels have no chance before the ceremony ends to consent verbally; and if their consent or acclamation appears in the bodily form of bowed knees, it departs from the English coronation ritual in coming conspicuously after God's oath, as do their later dancing and singing of unspecified hymns. Absent is the genuine verbal reciprocity of mutual oaths.[123]

I am emphatically not making an Empsonian argument that Milton encourages readers to reject God as tyrant and side with a victimized Satan – only a Norbrookian one that this passage provokes in readers a temporary republican dismay over a non-contractualist, non-republican ceremony in which God hogs all the roles. Even by the standards of the English monarchy, this truncated coronation and coronation oath conspicuously lack reciprocity and consent.[124] That dismay dissipates when readers recall that God and the Son deserve their offices because of their merit, their obvious superiority to all other candidates for them, as Books 3 and 6 make especially clear in the Son's case (3.236–8, 290;

6.806–92, esp. 814–22, 853, 887–8). But it lingers when applied to earthly candidates for rule, who do not so clearly excel all others in the capacity to rule well and thus should be elected by some form of popular consent, rather than succeed to supreme power by mere accident of birth. And this is what the open-ended dismay the episode should create in republican and other readers is designed to do. The troubling aspects of the episode sharpen rather than blunt the edge of Milton's earthly republicanism, which some historians of political thought have tried to downplay by ignoring the anti-monarchical force of texts such as *The Tenure of Kings and Magistrates* and *The Readie and Easie Way to a Free Commonwealth* while playing up Milton's grudging concession in the *First* and *Second Defences* (themselves clear arguments against kingship) that the occasional king can rule well and in the best interests of the people.[125]

In England Milton wishes an elected/selected Grand Council to rule "to perpetuitie," as *The Readie and Easie Way* puts it, until the Second Coming of Christ, the only man who really deserves to be king: "our true and rightfull and only to be expected King, only worthie as he is our only Saviour, the Messiah, the Christ, the only heir of his eternal father, the only by him anointed and ordaind."[126] Written at roughly the same time as *The Readie and Easie Way*, *Paradise Lost*'s account of God's troubling coronation oath "by himself," along with its depiction of Adam and Eve essentially breaking an oath of allegiance to God by eating the fruit, is part and parcel of his opposition to coronations and the oaths of office and allegiance required by the Restoration church-state in the Clarendon Code.[127]

# 6 *Paradise Lost* II: Of Apples, Oaths, and Women

The Engagement . . . gives a full liberty to all sort of people that are English men, and who are called upon by the State to subscribe the taking of it: to have their freedom in the choosing of their Representatives. . . . [The Engagement is prescribed by one of the Commonwealth's laws, which] restore England to their Creation right, as it was before any Conquest by sword came in. The meaning is this: That the Land of England shall be a common Treasury to all English men without respect of persons . . . [All who take this oath, even] the conquered Cavaleere party . . . are to have equall freedom with others, for they are Englishmen.

– Gerrard Winstanley, *Englands Spirit Unfoulded. Or An Encouragement to Take the Engagement* (1650)[1]

The previous chapter advanced English coronations and coronation oaths as contexts for God's truncated coronation of the Son in Book 5 of *Paradise Lost*. This one turns to the consequences of that coronation: Satan revolts; Abdiel stays loyal; Adam and Eve fall. As we shall see, these events are all connected to God's self-oath at the coronation, as contextualized by a contractualist understanding of both the English coronation rite and feudal land tenure. During the constitutional skirmishes of the 1620s, one of Milton's tutors at Cambridge, Joseph Mede, spoke of the fruit of the Tree of Knowledge as the "sign of [Adam's] *Fealty* unto the great Landlord of the whole Earth"; and an entry in the Engagement Debate compared the Engagement to the oath of fealty sworn by tenants to the lord of the manor.[2] The contractualist dimension lay in the common ancient constitutionalist and republican idea that subjects' fealty, their oaths of fidelity and obedience to the English monarch, often displayed at the coronation ceremony, provided an exact counterpart to his coronation oath. Subject and monarch swore obligations to each other. In this light the word "fealty" takes on special significance in *Paradise Lost*. In Milton's poem the prohibition against eating the apple functions very much like an imposed oath such as the Oath of Allegiance, the Oath of Supremacy, or the Clarendon subscriptions, themselves clear demonstrations of fealty.

Most significant for debates about women and gender in *Paradise Lost*, a consideration of the apple – or, rather, the abstention from the apple – as a kind of oath reveals that Eve's tragic eating of the fruit paradoxically grants her the status of full political subject, with, in Winstanley's terms, "equall freedom" and a "Creation right" to decide by herself and for herself where her loyalties lie.[3] The fact that Milton goes to such great lengths, within the constraints imposed by the Genesis narrative, to grant Eve a fully separate and independent Fall indicates that he considered women capable of taking state oaths, as they had done in the case of the Protestation of 1641, and perhaps even of voting for their own representatives, which Winstanley saw as a natural consequence of taking an oath such as the Engagement, at least for men. While less radical than the Digger Winstanley with respect to property, Milton proved more radical with respect to gender, extending the privilege of swearing oaths to women. Along with the obligation and even the right to take such oaths came the status of autonomous citizen, not subordinate to a husband. For Milton as for other republicans, citizens take oaths, and oaths make citizens.[4] Yet Milton outdid most early modern English republicans, and even a royalist like Margaret Cavendish, by recommending that women be active citizens in the ideal republic.

## Apples and Oaths

The Fall was probably the central moment in Christian thought on the problem of failed oaths.[5] After all, it was said, there had been no need for oaths before trust was broken by the Fall.[6] Only after the Fall did humans need to guarantee their commitments to action and truth by swearing to them.[7] Yet there were other ways to think of the Fall in relation to oaths. One might conceive of the apple itself as an oath, or as a metaphorical site of oath-making. To put it differently, one could consider the apple a surface for an inscribed oath, or a thing renounced or excluded, just like the outside or foreign elements invariably abjured by loyalty oaths.

Apples had been associated with oaths since antiquity in the myth of Cydippe. Most prominent in Ovid's *Heroides*, the maiden Cydippe inadvertently reads out the words of an oath inscribed on an apple's skin and is thereby forced to keep an oath to marry Acontius.[8] Given the ubiquity of Ovid in early modern curricula, as well as the allusion to Cydippe in Spenser's *Faerie Queene*,[9] we should hardly be surprised that this story of an oath on an apple was well-known throughout Europe and that political theorists such as Grotius and Pufendorf employed it to discuss the nature of political obligation and the scope of oaths and other social contracts, with the female Cydippe as a model for all subjects and citizens.[10] While Milton met Grotius and was clearly influenced by *De Jure Belli ac Pacis*, he would have found a discussion of Cydippe, apples, and oath-taking closer to hand in the foremost English treatise on promissory oaths: Robert Sanderson's *De Juramento* (1655).[11] Cydippe's plight thus became paradigmatic of the dilemmas faced by every subject forced, as it were, to marry the state by "swallowing oaths."[12] Indeed, one tract in the Engagement Debate, *The Grand Case of Conscience concerning the Engagement*, a tract once attributed to Milton, had described the reasons for taking the Solemn League and Covenant as an alluring golden apple.[13]

Nor should we be surprised that some saw Cydippe as an antitype of Eve, another woman who runs afoul of an apple. John Leech, for one, epigrammatized that

Cydyppen error similis delusit, & Euam:
Falsa etenim malis vtraque Nympha datis.
Nempe virum haec decepta capit: vir decipit illam.
Haec ludit, cupido luditur illa viro.

A similar error deluded Cydippe and Eve:
For evil apples both nymphs did deceive.
The latter, deceived, deceives her man, while a man deceives the maid.
The latter plays; the former by a lustful man is played.[14]

Before returning to the connections between the apple and the acts of renunciation in state oaths, the next two sections address the connections among, on the one hand, women, oaths, and politics and, on the other, coronations, oaths, and land tenure.

## Women, Oaths, and Politics

The idea of women as oath-taking citizens lies at the heart of one of the passages that provide an epigraph for this book. In the oft-cited passage from Margaret Cavendish's *Sociable Letters* (1664) discussed in the introduction, a fictional correspondent writes a letter to a female friend that decisively rejects this possibility:

> as for the matter of Governments, we Women understand them not, yet if we did, we are excluded from intermedling therewith, and almost from being subject thereto; we are not tied, nor bound to State or Crown; we are free, not Sworn to Allegiance, nor do we take the Oath of Supremacy; we are not made Citizens of the Commonwealth, we hold no Offices, nor bear we any Authority therein; we are accounted neither Useful in Peace, nor Serviceable in War; and if we be not Citizens in the Commonwealth, I know no reason we should be Subjects to the Commonwealth: And the truth is, we are no Subjects, unless it be to our Husbands, and not alwayes to them, for sometimes we usurp their Authority, or else by flattery we get their good wills to govern . . . they seem to govern the world, but we really govern the world, in that we govern men . . . yet men will not believe this, and 'tis the better for us, for by that we govern as it were by an insensible power, so as men perceive not how they are Led, Guided, and Rul'd by the Feminine Sex.[15]

While Cavendish's point is that women are not oath-taking citizens or even subjects of the polity, being "excluded" from and holding no offices within it, one marvels at the ease with which she turns clear exclusion into apparent domination.[16] Yet Sara Mendelson and Patricia Crawford have made the passage a springboard for a continuing investigation of the ways in which, despite their almost complete lack of the franchise, women actually did participate as something like citizens in the political process in seventeenth-century England.[17] Both Crawford and David Cressy have investigated the extent of women's participation in the swearing of state-mandated loyalty oaths such as the Protestation in the 1640s.[18] Recent studies of early modern women and politics have broadened the definition of participation so as to include many activities not usually recognized as overtly political in the modern world.[19] While this move is salutary, it should not cause us to neglect the clearly political activity of swearing loyalty oaths, an activity that involved large numbers of women at various points before the Restoration, especially in the 1640s, and that had a large but now underappreciated impact on women in life and literature. If cooking and embroidery are political acts, so is swearing.[20]

That women knew and cared about state oaths like the Solemn League and Covenant, which some of them took, seems obvious in the objections that Katherine Chidley, an Independent, printed in response to Thomas Edwards's remarks on that oath. Chidley had earlier pointed to the Protestation to make her case for Independency.[21] Despite the misogyny of Milton's later and strategic remarks on the role of women at courts, in his earlier *Apology against a Pamphlet* (1642) he spoke approvingly, and in virtually the same breath, of both the Protestation and the women and artisans delivering petitions to Parliament in its wake – a demonstrably public, political activity.[22] But petitioning was just one way for women to participate in politics in a world that denied most adult males and virtually all females the right to vote.[23] Others included preaching, prophesying, petitioning, joining a mob, writing, and, of course, taking oaths.[24] Swearing state oaths could thus be seen more as a right than a duty – as a mark of one's membership in the body politic as full citizen. Cavendish's 1662 closet drama *Bell in Campo* arguably fulfils such a dream in its depiction of an army of separatist women swearing allegiance to Lady Victoria in the Fifteen Commandments scene discussed in my introduction.[25] I will argue that Milton does something similar when he grants Eve the privilege of a completely separate Fall, a Fall that recalls the breaking of oaths of allegiance to English kings.[26] While Cavendish's women become sworn citizens only during an emergency, in *Paradise Lost* a woman functions as full citizen of the prelapsarian republic on the acropolis that is Eden.

## Coronations, Fealty, and Land Tenure

As long as there have been kings and gods, it has been possible to conceive of sworn allegiance to the latter in terms of sworn allegiance to the former. There was certainly a tradition of discussing the Judaeo-Christian Fall in terms of broken allegiance. In eighth- or ninth-century England, an anonymous Anglo-Saxon poem in the Junius Manuscript, had, in Watson Kirkconnell's translation, represented Adam and Eve as making "pledges" to God until Satan causes them to "wander away both in word and deed / From their allegiance to God," and thus to "break the command that He made with His word" – the prohibition against the fruit.[27] There is, however, no scene in which they swear an oath to God in the Austinian first person present active indicative. Satan himself has already fallen because he cannot find it in his heart to "give Allegiance to the Lord most high." The good angels who remain in Heaven after his Fall are those "whose love and allegiance were sure." All of this likely stems from a pre-feudal honour culture that shares with its feudal successor an emphasis on verbal ties of allegiance between warriors and overlords, ties sometimes cemented by bodily gestures and physical gifts or pledges. In the feudal period the series of oaths would have extended up to the king. In the Anglo-Saxon poem Eve tempts Adam by "pledging" him "her faith" – something close to a present tense oath – promising that God really wants them to do him "homage" in eating the apple.[28] On my reading, *Paradise Lost* does the opposite of what Eve claims here, making abstention from the fruit a sign of homage.

During the early Reformation, Luther and Calvin had forbidden profane swearing but supported oaths of allegiance to the local authorities rather than the pope.[29] This was especially true in Geneva, the epicentre of a covenantal theology that asked citizens to swear explicit allegiance to the polity and thus to God. English translations of Calvin's *Institutes* and commentaries on Job and Galatians had represented sin as something like an act of breaking one's oath of allegiance to God and confederating with the Devil.[30] The commentary on Job argued that if humans had kept their allegiance to God, they would have been princes of the world: "we should haue reigned peasably ouer all beasts, if we had not beene vnthankefull to our God, in *breaking the allegeance* which wee ought [owed] vnto him. That then is the cause why wee be bereft of the Lordship and souerayntie which was giuen vs ouer all beasts."[31]

The idea of obeying God as keeping an oath of allegiance had become commonplace.[32] Marlowe's tragedy *Dr. Faustus*, which features its title character abjuring God by swearing allegiance to the Devil, makes obvious use of it, reflecting upon the crises of conscience created by the Elizabethan Oath of Allegiance to queen rather than pope.[33] In Milton's time George Lawson made such a comparison explicit, likening the individual Christian's oath of obedience to God in baptism to the subject's oath of allegiance to the sovereign: "We[,] not only by God's command, but also by our promise so solemnly confirmed by Baptism, are bound to observe [his] commandments: A loyal Subject will obey his Sovereigns command, and will remember his Oath of Allegiance and Fidelity . . . and shall not we obey our Saviour's Laws, written and confirmed with his own blood?"[34] In a similar vein John Bunyan asserted that youthful sinners such as his own adolescent self are "such as once were under subjection to their Prince, even those who after they have sworn subjection to his Government, have taken up arms against him."[35] This becomes even more explicit in Part I of *Pilgrim's Progress*, where Pilgrim tells an avatar of Satan, "I have given [God] my faith, and sworn my Allegiance to him; how then can I go back from this, and not be hanged as a Traitor?"[36] Such a position may emphasize Bunyan's affinities with Baptists, especially the antijurist kind.

In *Paradise Lost* Milton's God discusses the fruit of the Tree of Knowledge in terms that recall oaths of allegiance to the English king, as at least one contemporary commentator observed. The Council in Heaven in Book 3 allows God to articulate the terms of the quasi-contract by which Adam and Eve remain in Eden, a contract underpinned by the concept of fealty. "Man disobeying," proclaims God, "Disloyal breaks his fealty, and sins / Against the high supremacy of Heav'n" (3.203–5). Glossing these lines, Milton's earliest printed annotator, Patrick Hume, explained in 1695 that the word "fealty" means "an Oath of Fidelity" (or faith) and, etymologically speaking, is an abbreviation of the word "fidelity."[37] Support for Hume's reading comes from Milton's own reference to "Oaths of Fealty and Allegeance" in *The Tenure of Kings and Magistrates*, where he stresses that even though the Israelites swore these oaths to Eglon, King of Moab, Ehud was justified in killing the tyrant.[38] Hume goes on to specify fealty's place in medieval land law: "There is a double Fealty, one General, due from every Subject to his Prince; the other Special, owing by every Tenant to the Lord of the Fee of whom he holds . . . The Fealty God required of *Adam*, the first great Tenant of the Universe, seem'd as reasonable as it was easie."[39] According to Hume, then, Adam and Eve hold their land, the Earth, as vassals swearing fealty to God.

In the English coronation ceremony lay traces of medieval land law: the reciprocal oaths king and subjects swore to emphasize the renewal of the social contract. The king swore an oath of office, promising to rule well and uphold the laws, while some of the lords temporal and spiritual did homage to the king and swore oaths of fealty to him in order to retain their own lands and offices. The common people were prompted to chime in with shouts of "God save the King!" – in effect, their promise of fealty – a promise echoed in the oaths of allegiance, supremacy, and office many of them swore to the king after the Restoration.[40] Moreover, as we saw in chapter 5, Charles I's and Charles II's Scottish coronations also demanded an explicit oath from the people, with hands raised to Heaven.[41] Some medieval monarchs had also required oaths of fealty and allegiance of the populace around the time of their coronations.[42]

The oaths of fealty the bishops and peers swore at Charles II's coronation are worth quoting because they cement the connection between allegiance and land tenure. First, the bishops swore to "be Faithful, and True, and Faith, and Truth bear unto you, Our Sovereign Lord, and Your Heirs, Kings of England, and shall do, and truly acknowledg [*sic*] the Service of the Land, which I claim to hold of You, in light of the Church: So help me God." Second, the nobles swore to "become your Liege-man, of Life and Limb, and of Earthly Worship: and Faith and Truth I shall bear unto You, to live and die against all manner of Folk: So God me help." Later, they "ascended the Throne" and reached out to touch "the King's Crown, promising by that Ceremony to be ever ready to support it with all their power."[43]

But lest one forget that the coronation ceremony involved land tenure for the nobility as well, we should note that the feudal notion of land tenure was still somewhat in force, even though Parliament had formally abolished it at the Restoration. By this arrangement the king was understood to have originally owned all land in the kingdom and merely to have granted use or possession of it in exchange for subjects' allegiance, usually manifested in oaths and military service.[44] Thus, the royal proclamation requesting nobles' attendance at Charles's coronation offered the following reason: "by ancient Customes and Usages of this Realm, as also in regard of divers Tenures of sundry Mannors, Lands, and other Hereditaments, many of Our Loving Subjects do claim and are bound to do and perform divers several services on the said day and at the time of the Coronation, as in times precedent their Ancestors and those from whom they claim, have done."[45] That is, the service at the coronation – holding a sword or bearing a ring – was both a sign of and substitute for the original military service, but more generally for the allegiance to the monarch that that service expressed. Descriptions of coronations like that of Charles II bring this point to the fore by naming specific nobles who performed services at the coronation in exchange for specific lands. For example, after Charles received the crown, "Mr. Henry Howard (Brother to Thomas Duke of Norfolk) delivered, by virtue of his Tenure of the Manour of Wirksop, in the County of Norfolk, to the King a rich Glove for his right Hand." Likewise, at the coronation banquet that followed, the manors of Lord Allington, Sir Edward Dymocke, and Thomas Leigh, Esquire, are adduced by name and county to explain these men's rites of obeisance.[46] On the one hand, the tenure of a specific piece of land entitled these nobles to the honour of being seen to do an important job in the ceremony, thus creating and maintaining cultural/political capital. On the other, the function in the ceremony was a service that (nominally) earned them title to the land in the first place.

In Book 8 of *Paradise Lost*, the animals offer fealty to Adam as subjects did to the English monarch. God grants Adam the tenure of Earth, which includes the right to receive fealty from the animals:

> Not only these fair bounds, but all the earth
> To thee and to thy race I give; as lords
> Possess it, and all things that therein live . . .
> In sign whereof each bird and beast behold
> After their kinds; I bring them to receive
> From thee their names, and pay thee *fealty*
> *With low subjection* . . .
> As thus he spake, each bird and beast behold
> Approaching two and two, these *cowering low*
> *With blandishment*, each bird stooped on his wing. (338–51, my emphasis)

Here is Patrick Hume's gloss on the passage:

> *Fealty with low subjection; Moses Barcepha,* in his Book of *Paradise,* seats *Adam* on its highest Eminency with awful and majestic look, and his Face shining like *Moses*'s, Exod. 34. 29. naming the Animals Terrestrial, passing by in pairs, beneath him, *Cowring low with blandishment,* cringing before him; and the Birds humbly stooping on Wing paying their Fealty, as at. V[erse]. 350. *Fealty,* Bo[ok]. III. V[erse]. 204.[47]

The idea of Adam sitting on high suggests a throne, and the animals' paying Adam fealty reminds Hume of his own annotation of the word in Book 3 as "oath of fidelity." God thus crowns Adam king of Earth without requiring him to swear a coronation oath to his subjects; Adam must only abjure, as we have seen, "the tree whose operation brings / Knowledge of good and ill, which I have set / The pledge of thy obedience and thy faith" (8.323–5).[48] Adam and Eve, as we have seen, pledge their obedience and faith to God not by speaking the words of a formal oath but by abstaining from the fruit. His tacit agreement to God's terms and his abstention from the fruit thus seem closer to a subject's oath of allegiance, even as his joint position as receiver of the animals' fealty in the pseudo-coronation ceremony suggests that his actions double as a coronation oath. He is God's vassal as much as the animals are his. Yet the more explicit reciprocity of the English coronation's multiple oaths is absent. Eve comes to share his status and pledge. The next section treats the loyalty oaths that subjects pledged outside the English coronation ceremony, for in a crucial respect they resembled God's prohibition against the fruit in Milton's poem.

## Loyalty Oaths, Abjuration, and the Apple

English loyalty oaths, especially Restoration ones, almost always involved rejection or renunciation of something. In effect, to swear was always to forswear, to swear off.[49]

### Loyalty Oaths as Abjurations

Henrician Oath to the Succession (abjures pope and other foreign rulers) (1534)
Henrician Oath to the Supremacy (abjures pope and other foreign rulers) (1535)
Elizabethan Oath of Supremacy (abjures pope and other foreign rulers) (1559)
Jacobean Oath of Allegiance (abjures pope and other foreign rulers, as well as treason) (1606)
Scottish National Covenant (abjures "popish" innovations in the Scottish Church) (1638)
Etcetera Oath (abjures Catholicism) (1640)
Protestation (abjures Catholicism and "popish innovations" in the Anglican Church) (1641)
Vow and Covenant (abjures "popish" plots against Protestantism) (June 1643)
Oath of Abjuration (abjures transubstantiation, idolatry, purgatory, & justification by works) (Aug. 1643)
Solemn League and Covenant (abjures "popish" plots and innovations) (SLC) (September 1643)
Negative Oath (abjures King Charles I) (1645)
Engagement (abjures kingship and the House of Lords) (1649)
The Clarendon Code's Loyalty Oaths (1661–5)
Corporation Oath (abjures fighting against King Charles II) (1661)

Militia Oath (abjures fighting against King Charles II) (1662)
Uniformity Oath (abjures SLC, as well as fighting against King Charles II) (1662)
Schoolmaster's Oath (abjures SLC, as well as fighting against King Charles II) (1662)
Vestryman's Oath (abjures SLC, as well as fighting against King Charles II) (1663)
Oxford Oath (abjures SLC, as well as any attempt to alter the government of church and state) (1665)
First Test Oath (abjures transubstantiation) (1673)
Second Test Oath (abjures transubstantiation and Mariolatry) (1678)
William and Mary's Oaths of Allegiance and Supremacy (abjure pope and other foreign powers) (1689)
Oath of Abjuration (abjures the Pretender) (1701)

The Oaths of Allegiance and Supremacy sworn by subjects to the monarch since at least 1606 explicitly renounced allegiance to other rulers, temporal and spiritual, the pope chief among them; and implicitly renounced republicanism.[50] In the Civil War years, Parliament forced defeated royalists to forswear fighting for the king in the Negative Oath (1645), and Catholics to deny transubstantiation, idolatry, purgatory, and justification by works in the Oath of Abjuration (1643).[51] The Commonwealth's Engagement oath (1649) committed the swearer to a polity without a king and House of Lords; and after the Restoration the Cavalier Parliament set about overturning all of the Long Parliament's oaths in the Clarendon Code, which required public officeholders to swear oaths of office rejecting not just the idea of rebelling against the king but the Solemn League and Covenant (1643).[52] In this light a renunciation of an apple as a way of showing allegiance and obedience to God looks very much like an English loyalty oath. Adam and Eve abjure a fruit rather than the pope or the Covenant.

Given that near indistinguishability of swearing and forswearing, we now return to Patrick Hume's understanding of the word "fealty" in *Paradise Lost*. In Book 9 Adam predicts that Satan's "first design" against them may "be to withdraw / Our fealty from God" – just as Satan himself "dissolve[d] / Allegiance to th' acknowledged power supreme," as Gabriel puts it in Book 4 (9.261–2; 4.955–6). If Hume correctly glosses "fealty" in Book 3 as "oath of fidelity," then we must examine humans' original agreement with God, who granted tenure of the Earth and its resources to Adam in return for fealty and allegiance. In Book 4 Adam reminds Eve that God

requires
From us no other service than to keep
This one, this easy charge, of all the trees
In Paradise . . . not to taste that only Tree
Of Knowledge . . .
The only sign of our obedience left
Among so many signs of power and rule
Conferred upon us, and dominion giv'n
Over all other creatures that possess
Earth, air, and sea. (4.419–32)

Forbearance from the fruit is merely a "sign" of Adam and Eve's "obedience," as well as of their God-given "power," "rule," and "dominion" over Earth. As we have seen, in Books 3 and 8 both God and Adam call this a "pledge of obedience" to God (3.94; 8.325) – a pledge that must be given freely, God stresses, if it is to mean anything:

Not free, what proof could they have giv'n sincere
Of true allegiance, constant faith or love,
Where only what needs must do, appeared,
Not what they would? What praise could they receive?
What pleasure I from such obedience paid,
When will and reason . . . had served necessity,
Not me. (3.103–11)

Hume's commentary on the phrase "true allegiance" in these lines reads as follows: "True Obedience, constant Trust and Love: *Allegiance*, of the word *Alligare*, Lat. to bind to, the Faith we swear to our King being the highest Bond and Obligation imaginable."[53] In other words, he understands "Allegiance" to be an abbreviation of "Oath of Allegiance," just as "fealty" is one for "Oath of Fidelity." And what was the seventeenth-century Oath of Allegiance if not an oath of fidelity, the same oath of fidelity to the king contained in the many oaths of office proliferated after the Restoration? In many of the British colonies in North America the counterpart of the Oath of Allegiance was called the Oath of Fidelity (increasingly to the colony itself rather than the king).[54]

To adapt Stephen Greenblatt, there seemed to be oaths after the Restoration, no end of oaths, but not for women. Margaret Cavendish's claim that women could not swear oaths of allegiance and oaths of office was not strictly true. As Mendelson, Crawford, and others have shown, some women did swear the former, and in rare cases the latter – when they took up office at Court, for example. But from the perspective of the early Restoration, when Cavendish published the *Sociable Letters* and when a debate raged about oaths in general, and judicial oaths and oaths of office and allegiance in particular, her larger point strikes home: women were not subject to the oaths of office taken by clergymen and most officeholders. While the *Commons' Journal* contains a few instances of women swearing Oaths of Allegiance and Supremacy in order to become naturalized subjects in 1660,[55] women's duty and right to pledge loyalty must have seemed conspicuously absent from the debate that took place over the next few years. In fact, from this perspective, the Restoration could easily have looked like a period in which women's right to swear had been snatched away after gains made in the 1640s, when many women had sworn both the Protestation and Solemn League and Covenant.

## Oaths, Divided Loyalties, and Citizenship

Choices in the face of conflicting loyalties are the stuff of both Milton's epic and seventeenth-century loyalty oaths, and *Paradise Lost* as a whole can be profitably read as a drama of conflicting loyalties. I choose to focus on Eve's. In the broadest sense her choice to eat the apple privileges loyalty to herself over loyalty to God and Adam. But the salient point is that on the Edenic acropolis that loyalty is hers to grant. She is not under Adam's control, nor is her Fall the same as his. Milton goes to great lengths to demonstrate that, *pace* comments like the following from Philo ("it is a matter of necessity that when she ate, the man too should eat"),[56] the two Falls are separate and Adam still has free will even after Eve brings him the fruit. They both independently conceive of the possibility of his remaining unfallen and asking Eve to be replaced by a second Eve (9.828, 911). Adam could very well choose not to eat. Eve's Fall is thus her own, not his. In opting to fall with his wife, however, Adam shows his loyalty and love not to any old woman but to this one.[57]

There has been much discussion of republicanism in both early modern England and Milton's works.[58] However, for all of its attention to the differences among republicanism, civic humanism, and liberalism; negative and positive liberties; the varieties of republicanism (classical and non-classical, constitutional and ethical/religious); their Greek, Roman, and Hebrew origins; and the local and national dimensions of citizenship[59] – for all this attention, studies of English republicanism have often neglected gender.[60] The omission is understandable given women's virtual exclusion from full citizenship in republican theory and practice up to Milton's time. It is telling, for example, that in Machiavelli's *Discourses* the opposite of masculine republican *virtù* is passive effeminacy and the female Fortuna. Among English republicans Algernon Sidney offers in his *Discourses Concerning Government* a fairly typical sentiment in speaking of the male citizens of Athens bravely leaving their wives and children in order to fight the Persians.[61] And it would be easy to read Milton as consigning Eve to the role of effeminating obstruction to Adam's realization of his manly republican virtue. Milton, however, swerves from this paradigm by making Eve a full participant in Eden's affairs.[62]

If the apple and its prohibition have been functioning like loyalty oaths, the original pair have also been acting like citizens of an Edenic republic. The very loss of Eden proves that they were citizens in the first place. If Philo had described Adam as the world's first citizen (*kosmopolites*),[63] Milton takes pains to include Eve. Again, his comments in *De Doctrina Christiana* offer guidance. Earlier, his *First* and *Second Defences* of a commonwealth without kings had displayed a language of republican citizenship deployed to represent Milton himself as a good citizen or *civis*, trying, like Cicero, to preserve the commonwealth with his oratory and counter-oratory.[64] These Latin tracts had also modelled the role of citizen as selfless public servant for a continental audience. However, until recently, the presence of the word *civis*, and thus of the Roman idea of citizenship, if not classical citizenship more generally, has been insufficiently acknowledged in translation, though Claire Gruzelier's edition of the *First Defence* corrects many of the problems.[65] This inattention to the language of citizenship especially bedeviled previous translations of *De Doctrina* until the most recent Oxford edition, which restores that language to its proper place.

The issue becomes crucial in *De Doctrina*'s chapter on the Fall, which resonates with matters of politics and citizenship that fade away if *civis* is not rendered as "citizen." An important part of the chapter dilates upon the notion of the collateral damage caused by our parents' original sin, defending the justice of this idea by adducing examples of other people rightly punished for crimes they did not commit. We are told – unconvincingly to my mind – that "Sometimes a whole nation is punished for the sin of one citizen [*civis*] . . . and the offence of a single person is imputed to all" and that "Citizens [*cives*] have to pay a penalty, too, for the sins of their king, as all Egypt did for Pharaoh's sins. Even king David, who thought it unjust that citizens [*cives*] should suffer in this way, also thought it quite equitable that sons should be punished for and with their fathers."[66] The section ends with a comparison of the Fall to the crime of treason:

> Immo vel laesae maiestatis humanae reus, non sibi tantum, sed et posteris omnibus *fundum aut civitatem* amittit; aliaque haud absimilia decernunt etiam Iurisconsulti: et quid sit ius belli non in auctores tantum, verum etiam in eos omnes qui modo in ditione hostium sunt, foeminas puta atque etiam infantes, quique nihil neque opis neque voluntatis ad bellum contulerunt, quis ignorat?

> More than that, even a person convicted of high treason forfeits – not just for himself but for all his descendants too – his *lands and citizenship*, and Jurists also make other not dissimilar decrees. And who is not aware what the right of war is, not just against its perpetrators but also against all those who are just now in their enemies' power, such as women and even infants, and those who have contributed nothing – no support, either material or moral – to the war?[67]

In the pivotal phrase "fundum aut civitatem," the second term clarifies that the traitor will lose the status of citizen (*civis*) of a state (*civitas*): in other words, citizenship (perhaps the original meaning of *civitas* for Romans).[68]

Yet all translators to date fail to acknowledge the full force of the other word in the phrase that taps into the classical republican tradition: "*fundum* aut civitatem." While Sumner translates *fundum* as "possessions" or property, Carey and the Oxford team more accurately render it as "estate."[69] I translate *fundum* as "lands" for the following reason. The latter two translations elide what must be emphasized in the context of a Fall both from grace and from occupation of the Garden: the idea of *fundus* as real estate, ground, soil, farm (a word related to *latifundium*), not as moveable property. Milton's *fundus* thus conjures up the idea of landed citizens with a stake in defending the *patria* and their patrimonies. Even more important, *fundus* seems also to have referred to

Roman citizenship granted after the Social War (90–88 BCE) to allies on the Italian peninsula whose city-states eventually became part of the territory of greater Rome.[70] Hence, Milton's "fundum aut civitatem" should really be seen as the hendiadys it is: two different words yoked together to describe the same concept – land- or territory-based citizenship. We can now see that Milton thought of Adam and Eve as landed citizens of Eden – probably in light of James Harrington's insistence in *Oceana* (1656) that a landowning and armed citizenry should be the heart of a republican body politic.[71] Not vassals (in the medieval sense) to any other human, they answer only to God. The issue then becomes whether Adam and Eve both enjoy that status in equal measure. In other words, is Eve a full citizen before the Fall – and even after the Fall?

## Oaths and Spheres in *Paradise Lost* and the Divorce Tracts

Oaths are just one part of Milton's case in *Paradise Lost* that Eve is a full citizen of Eden and that women should therefore be full citizens of England. Eve is fully involved in Eden's politics, both in Book 9 and before.[72] In the separation debate, for example, she gives as good as she gets, holding her own and convincing Adam to allow her to work separately from him (9.205–384).[73] It is worth pausing over the related but not identical questions of whether Eve is inferior to Adam and whether she participates in Eden's politics. Much ink has been spilt over Milton's portrayal of Eve: misogynistic or not? does Eve have a subjectivity and agency separate from Adam's? is Eve equal to Adam? The issue of subjectivity, especially in the various "first sight" scenes in Books 4 and 8 (to which we shall return), has well-nigh monopolized our critical attention, at the expense of the passages on loyalty and fealty in Books 3, 4, and 9.[74] The critical spotlight has privileged the existence and origins of Eve's subjectivity rather than its effects: her agency and actions. Some critics think she has little to no subjectivity independent of Adam's and thus little agency – or that she does, but in ways subordinate to, supportive of, lesser than Adam's.[75] Others believe that she does have independent, if somewhat different, but nevertheless equal subjectivity and agency.[76] Part of the problem is whether there exists a separation of private and public spheres before the Fall, with Eve confined to the former and Adam moving freely between the two. Does only Adam engage in politics and political discussion, leaving Eve to cultivate the affective and domestic? Most critics, with the exception of

David Norbrook, Laura Knoppers, and a few others, accept the idea of a separation of spheres in *Paradise Lost*.[77] If Eve cannot leave the private sphere and participate in politics, understood as exclusively public, she can hardly count as a full citizen of the Edenic commonwealth whose opinions and actions have a force independent of and not countermandable by Adam.

A brief comparison of *Paradise Lost* and the divorce tracts will demonstrate that the poem conflates the private and public spheres, the household and the state. Whereas in the divorce tracts, the household is *like* the state, in *Paradise Lost* it *is* the state.[78] Identity replaces analogy, and from this insight everything else flows. The analogy between marriage and government was well-worn by 1660,[79] and Milton had actually rejected it for strategic reasons in the *First Defence* (1651): in order to resist its royalist implications.[80] But it had occupied a central place in his argument for no-fault divorce in the 1640s. Essentially, the analogy cut both ways. The state could be compared to a household (with king as father, and people as wife, children, servants), or the household could be compared to a state (with the ties between man and wife referred to as leagues, covenants, charters, and oaths of allegiance).[81] Milton takes the latter tack in the divorce tracts, especially *The Doctrine and Discipline of Divorce* and *Tetrachordon*. State and household are different things. For Milton as for Aristotle, the state is the sum of many different households. Paradoxically, it is just this difference that allows the one to stand in for the other in thought or speech.

Oaths feature prominently in Milton's case in *The Doctrine and Discipline of Divorce* that the household and state are clean different things. In various ways Milton argues that peace and love are as necessary to a household as to a state, and in their absence the household or marriage should break up. A seminal passage in the Preface makes this point by likening the marriage vows to oaths of allegiance:

> *He who marries, intends as little to conspire his own ruine, as he that swears Allegiance*: and as a whole people is in proportion to an ill Government, so is one man to an ill marriage. If they against any authority, Covnant, or Statute, may by the soveraign edict of charity, save not only their lives, but honest liberties from unworthy bondage, as well may he against any private Covnant, which hee never enter'd to his mischief, redeem himself from unsupportable disturbances to honest peace, and just contentment.[82]

And oaths are an important part of Milton's larger case for divorce in both *The Doctrine and Discipline of Divorce* and *Tetrachordon*. First, he shows his own loyalty to Parliament and the nation by reminding them that he has taken two of Parliament's loyalty oaths (the Protestation and the Covenant). Second, he characterizes rigidly literalist interpretation of scripture as an unwarranted act of swearing to its letter rather than its spirit. Third, he contests the rigidly literalist interpretation of Christ's apparent prohibition of divorce by comparing it to his apparent prohibition of swearing in the next few verses (Matthew 5:31–7). In both cases, a charitable, context-sensitive interpretation of Christ's words in Matthew 5 reveals that Christ left loopholes for divorce and for swearing in some cases. Finally, Milton dismantles a similarly literalist analogy between oaths and marriage in which both were thought to be indissoluble once entered into. Instead, Milton claims, both are conditional and revocable covenants.[83]

Milton's views on divorce contributed to his defence of tyrannicide as part of a justified withdrawal from the social contract in *The Tenure of Kings and Magistrates*. Yet the point of the earlier passage from *The Doctrine and Discipline of Divorce* is the *limitations* of the analogy between family and state. It continues:

> to resist the highest Magistrat though tyrannizing, God never gave us expresse allowance, only he gave us reason, charity, nature and good example to bear us out; but in this economical misfortune [i.e., a bad marriage], thus to demean our selves, besides the warrant of those foure great directors [reason, charity, nature and good example], which doth as justly belong hither, we have an expresse law of *God*, and such a law, as whereof our Saviour with a threat forbid the abrogating. For no effect of tyranny can sit more heavy on the Commonwealth, then this household unhappiness on the family.[84]

At this point in his career, Milton publicly resists the idea that subjects of a tyrant can proceed beyond mere passive resistance and self-defence into active rebellion. The defence of active resistance would arrive five years later in *Tenure*.[85] In *The Doctrine and Discipline*, then, the limited nature of the analogy is part of Milton's case that household is not identical to state. His account of Eden and Edenic marriage in the divorce tracts bolsters this partial picture of the household as a mini-state that must be governed justly and well but that is nevertheless separate from *the* state. If it is governed well, the man can leave the household and serve the commonwealth as a good citizen.[86] The woman stays at home and is presumably not a citizen of the commonwealth, or at least not a fully fledged one. There is a clear distinction between "private" and "publick employment."[87] And to allow the continuance of a bad, soulless marriage, a marriage characterized by sexual rather than spiritual union, would be to dispirit the man and thus interfere with his "publick employments" as, in effect, a citizen of the commonwealth. It would be figuratively to make sin "a free Citizen of the Common-wealth" of marriage.[88]

Things look quite different in *Paradise Lost*, where the spheres hardly diverge.[89] To be sure, Eve does appear at the door of the Bower when Raphael arrives in Book 5. Eve is the one in charge of the food stores and "studies household good" (5.303–7, 313–27; 9.233). Eve does not speak during Adam's conversation with Raphael and withdraws for part of it (8.40–57). Eve, like Adam, speaks of a short time just after her creation before she saw or spoke with another sentient being – a time that could be labelled private or pre-public (4.449–65; 8.250–91). But for all intents and purposes the household and the nation are coterminous before the Fall.[90] The Bower is a bounded space to which the first couple retreats temporarily for rest and sex, probably not for eating. Yet Eve works every day, doing the same physical labour as Adam outside the Bower (9.205–12). There is no real distinction between public and private as far as Adam and Eve are concerned – that is, in their relations with each other, rather than with other intelligent beings such as God, the Son, and angels. We must stress the issue of the first pair's internal relations because those are at stake in any consideration of their equality or inequality. If one wants to make the case for their being unequal because Adam can move to a public sphere denied to Eve, then what or where is that public sphere exactly? If the unit of analysis is Adam and Eve as the Edenic body politic, then there is no separate public place, literal or figurative, where Eve is denied the right to speak and act on issues of joint concern. Both Adam and Eve go in and outside the Bower; both Adam and Eve discuss the nature of the universe; both Adam and Eve work. Other intelligent beings enter the Garden on rare occasions (Raphael, as we have already seen; the Son or God after each person's creation); and the guardian angels are there constantly but do not appear to have interacted at all with our first parents (4.677–88). Raphael's visit is the first angelic contact. The Bower is obviously accessible to God and the Son at any time and thus not really private in relation to them.

The Garden is a bounded entity in which Adam and Eve converse and deliberate with each other for the most part. Despite some of the Narrator's remarks to the contrary (4.296–310, 446–7, 488–91, 635–8; 8.540–6, 568–75), when we see them before the Fall, Adam and Eve interact mostly on a level of equality. Eden is the equivalent of a bounded community or nation that only occasionally receives visitors from the outside. Eve's curiosity about the night sky sparks Adam's question to Raphael about whether the universe is Copernican or Ptolemaic (4.657–8; 8.13–38). Adam and Eve discuss whether to do the same work separately in Book 9, and the former does not limit the latter's talk or actions. What could be more public, of more general concern, than the issues of temptation and expulsion raised by the proposal to work apart? Eve's voice and vote prove decisive here.

In comparison to the divorce tracts, then, *Paradise Lost* downplays gender hierarchy. Hierarchy there clearly is, with the man on top, but considerably less of it.[91] Adam is less dominant over Eve, and both engage in essentially the same work of dressing and keeping the Garden.[92] Is the fact that Eve takes care of roses and other flowers (8.44–7; 9.218–19, 424–31) a material difference from the couple's joint reformation of the whole Garden, through which both move freely? The only real specialization of labour appears in the preparation of food, which seems to be Eve's province (though not wholly hers, as Laura Knoppers reminds us).[93] This may prefigure a postlapsarian domestic identity for women, at least as suggested by Adam, who expresses his own opinion rather than Milton's (232–4). Yet not definitively – he does not make the claim that women should never leave the house and participate directly in public affairs as relative equals. The joke is on Adam when he reveals that he has not bestirred himself enough beforehand to know how to feed a guest like Raphael, mistakenly thinking that they have a separate larder or "store" of fruits and vegetables (5.313–25).

In general, Adam and Eve appear not to do substantially different work among themselves, or even to differentiate roles in the work of intellectual inquiry, until Raphael arrives. For example, Eve is the one who initiates the line of inquiry into whether the universe is geocentric, as we have seen, and into whether angels can eat human food (4.656–7; 5.327–30).[94] Eve is the one who initiates and has her way in the one discussion of separating, but crucially not *differentiating*, "our day's work" in the Garden (9.205–25). Her argument in the separation debate is hardly that they should do different work, but that they should do the same work in different places. To the extent that physical separation may involve different tasks, she implies, it is because "divid[ing] our labors" will allow Adam and Eve to go "where choice / Leads thee, or most needs" (214–15) – a choice presumably open to them both. Tellingly, Adam's description of the work they have shared up to this point at God's behest stresses the first person plural and refuses to parcel out different tasks:

> These paths and bowers doubt not but *our joint hands*
> Will keep from the wilderness with ease, as wide
> As *we* need walk, till younger hands ere long
> Assist *us*. (244–7, my emphasis)

If there is a home in Eden to leave, a home marked off from their workplace, they *both* leave and return to it each day. This is much more egalitarian than the relationship between man and woman in the divorce tracts. Both Adam and Eve are essentially Harringtonian citizens of a republic in that they are freeholders: they own and defend their land (if ultimately unsuccessfully). Yet Eve seems to play a much greater role in her polity than Harrington's women[95] – a point underscored by *Paradise Lost*'s use of classical rather than English materials.

## Eve's Oath-Breaking Autonomy and Citizenship

If we return for a moment to the scene so fetishized by earlier gender critics (Eve's first sight of herself), we find it liberating rather than subjugating Citizen Eve. Eve's gazing at herself in the pool of water (4.449–91) clearly recalls Narcissus and has rightly prompted a number of Lacanian questions about mirrors, maturity, and autonomy.[96] However, we need to address all three of the episode's main sources as identified by Fowler: not just Ovid's Narcissus, but Spenser's Britomart and Plato's Cavedweller.[97] The episode's point is that Eve is *not* Narcissus: she avoids his fate and *is* persuaded to tear herself away from her lovely image. Like Britomart, she is strong and independent enough to leave her mirror behind and search for a mate over whom she can exert some measure of control – even if she differs from Britomart and imitates Narcissus in causing her partner's demise. Most important, however, is the earliest of the three sources: Plato's *Republic* – arguably a source for Ovid and Spenser too.[98] Not only does Plato's Cavedweller reject his own image on the wall of the cave; outside, he encounters the "likenesses or *reflections in water* of men and other things," but learns to recognize "the things themselves"; later "the heavens and heaven itself"; and "finally ... to look upon the sun itself and see its true nature, not by *reflections in water* or phantasms of it in an alien setting."[99] Milton hints at his episode's debt to Plato when Eve describes her pool of water as having "issued from a *cave*" (*Paradise Lost*, 4.454, my emphasis). Moreover, lest we get lost in the episode's metaphysical/epistemological implications (the need to learn by sceptically questioning present appearances and moving up a ladder of knowledge towards the Divine), we should remember its political ones. Plato employs the Allegory of the Cave as an argument for educating the ruling class of Guardians, who will progress beyond their more limited fellow citizens and acquire the skills, however reluctantly, to guide them: "the philosophers who arise among us" will "take charge of the other citizens."[100] Eve is thus being groomed to enter the ruling elite of humans in contrast to the animals. Even if she takes more time than Adam to free herself from the images, she eventually succeeds, and then continues to engage in the process of learning by asking questions about such things as the heavens. Even if she occupies a slightly lower place in that elite than Adam before other humans arrive, she is still a member of it. Nothing could be more Platonic than a woman learning to be a citizen and Guardian.[101]

For the most part, though, both Adam and Eve display a broadly Greco-Roman brand of citizenship characterized by active participation in the public affairs of a self-governing republic.[102] Eden is for the moment a self-contained, non-expanding Greek *polis*. Yet as revealed by the collocation of the Roman terms *civis* and *natio* in *De Doctrina*'s analysis of the Fall, Milton certainly conceived of citizenship in the context of the nation rather than just the city or city-state, which sets him apart from Marvell and other early modern civic humanists and participants in local government who conceived of themselves as an elite of citizens acting at the local level.[103] Because his Adam and Eve are landowners, freeholders from a largely non-interfering God in a way that makes them something more than medieval vassals, they meet not just Harrington's requirements for political participation but those of Cromwell and Ireton at the Putney Debates as well: they have "a permanent fixed interest" to defend in the polity – their land.[104] They are also good republican citizens in that they have solved Plato's and Aristotle's problem of seeing manual work as antithetical to citizenship. Adam and Eve choose leisurely work that allows them enough time to reflect upon matters of joint concern – a solution hinted at in Harrington's *Oceana* but not extended to women.[105]

This is half my point. The other is that Milton represents Eve as having full autonomy as citizen of the Edenic commonwealth by allowing her the option of leaving it, whether she knows she is doing it or not. Despite her slight inferiority to Adam in some faculties of mind and body (4.296–310),[106] she can fall separate from him. Some inequality exists between them but does not ultimately count for much in terms of her status as public citizen. She can and does work and talk. She can and does withdraw her fealty from God, however unwittingly – her fealty functioning, as we have seen, like an English oath of allegiance. In fact, her greater influence over her own life and community gives her an influence proportionally greater than that of an MP, let alone someone who could elect or select one in the restricted early modern franchise.

Why is prelapsarian *Paradise Lost* not an example of the typical republican account of states' origins, as in Harrington's *Politicaster* and *Art of Lawgiving* or Sidney's *Discourses*, where patriarchal families, each dominated by a man, eventually band together as brotherly tribes and appoint a few virtuous men as magistrates over their equal brethren?[107] For two reasons: because in Milton's poem the woman cannot be completely overruled by the nearest male in an important matter, as she could be in the ancient Hebrew context that Harrington and others invoked to underwrite their visions of republican commonwealths (not to mention the Greek and Roman contexts); and because she has the option to refuse. Milton gives Eve her own Fall. Unlike Harrington's women, who merely assist the man of the house in his voting other men into office, and even more than Cavendish's women, who are ready to "swear to obey . . . whatsoever" Lady Victoria pleases,[108] Milton's Eve votes for herself in every sense.

The fact that Eve can break her oath and withdraw her fealty from God means that she is solely in charge of it, and in the most meaningful sense equal to Adam in public, political terms. Breaking her pledge of allegiance is thus paradoxical evidence of Eve's full membership in the Edenic body politic.[109] It means that she enjoys not just agency but autonomy. She abjures the realm, but it is hers to abjure. The conventional wisdom about oaths, vows, and covenants, dating back at least to the Pentateuch and making an appearance around the time of the Engagement Controversy, had it that virgins and married women could not swear vows or oaths for themselves and that their fathers or husbands could reverse them if they did (Numbers 30:2–15).[110] Milton registers awareness of this idea both in the divorce tracts and in his discussion of vows in *De Doctrina Christiana*, whose conclusions apply to the following section on oaths.[111] Yet *Paradise Lost* offers something quite different: Adam clearly cannot undo the effect of his wife's eating the apple. All he can do is not join in, which would allow him to live and then ask for a second, different wife. Eve's action cannot be erased, nullified, invalidated by her husband. Their relationship thus cannot have been as unequal as the ones between men and women in the Pentateuch, Milton's earlier writings, and the mainstream of English republicanism.

Even though the Fall intensifies the gender hierarchy, it still does not preclude women's continuing to act as fully virtuous, active citizens outside the household – the self-contained, separate household postdating the Fall, along with the public/private division. Both *Samson Agonistes* and *Paradise Regained* exhibit this division between private and public precisely because they treat postlapsarian humanity. The fact that Eve is shown to have been a citizen before the Fall means that women could be once again, even though they are not in the England of 1667. The point is that woman has not just the interest in and capacity to understand extra-domestic politics, but also the right to participate in them.[112] If she has shown herself capable of both ruling and being ruled in Eden, in obeying Adam but sometimes taking the initiative and leading deliberations about matters of joint concern, she has shown herself to be a Platonic (and Aristotelian) citizen. That example remains to guide postlapsarian humanity as an ideal. We can never go back to Eden, but we can recover some of its behaviours and political procedures, even on a larger scale; and these include women participating actively in the polity outside the home. Eve and her daughters up to Milton's day are urged, like everyone else, to earn their way into an active role in public life as full, oath-swearing citizens. This does not, of course, guarantee that they will be selected for public office, or that they will or even should dominate government – the various councils recommended by *The Readie and Easie Way* are decidedly select.[113] It only guarantees women greater access to and voice in government, without being excluded from participation in public deliberations in the street, in print, and in elections for various representative assemblies, when those occur.

Milton has in effect created a fifth column within English republicanism, making a case for women to be full political subjects and citizens by allowing the first woman to take and break state oaths of allegiance and participate in prelapsarian politics. *Paradise Lost*'s republican citizenship thus looks back to the gains of the 1640s, when women were asked to swear the Protestation and Covenant; and forward perhaps to the twentieth century, when women gained the right to vote. Almost no one besides Cavendish and Milton appeared to be complaining about the virtual exclusion of women from public oath-taking in the 1660s, and from the right to participate in the public sphere and political nation that it implied.[114] But in granting women the privilege of swearing oaths, Milton clearly outgoes the royalist Cavendish. He swims against the tide of republican theory and practice, classical and contemporary, in imagining women as full citizens. By drawing on classical, medieval, and early modern materials, Milton's oath-like apple thus creates two ironies. While Adam and Eve are clearly at fault for breaking an oath of allegiance, both God and the Restoration authorities are also to blame for demanding oaths in the first place. While Eve behaves like a citizen in *Paradise Lost*, the best proof of her citizenship arrives at the very moment when she loses both Paradise and citizenship.

## Samson's Cords Cast Off

I hope to have demonstrated the centrality of oaths to Restoration England and to the work of Milton, Marvell, and Butler, and to have suggested why gender deserves more attention in studies of English oaths and republicanism. With *Paradise Lost* we have moved from texts overtly about oaths, such as *Hudibras* and *The Rehearsal Transpros'd*, to texts that treat them more obliquely. Like *Samson Agonistes*, *Paradise Lost* demonstrates the difficulty of pledging, keeping, and breaking allegiance, but also the ways in which these actions create subjectivity in the modern sense. Roughly speaking, Butler employs oaths as a subject matter in order to interpellate subjects; Marvell and Milton, to interpellate citizens. *Hudibras* seeks to create an obedient if quirkily genial subject of the king who will keep order in the provinces. *The Rehearsal Transpros'd* seeks to shape a genially tolerant citizen who will refrain from persecuting his neighbours and mix affably with all sorts of people in an urban setting. Both *Samson* and *Paradise Lost* attempt to fashion an independent, inquisitive, anxiously self-questioning citizen – female or male – who will fight for what is right and suffer patiently but expectantly when nothing else can be done.[115]

Most important, however, *Paradise Lost* abandons the support for loyalty oaths so evident in Milton's writings in the months before the Restoration, especially in the second edition of *The Readie and Easie Way to a Free Commonwealth*, which pounds into the heads of its audience of covenanting Presbyterians the Engagement's eschewal of government "without a King or House of Lords."[116] It seems that in the ensuing years, as composition of *Paradise Lost* continued apace, the Clarendon Code soured him on oaths. What that strongest of readers, William Blake, got right about Milton was that he ultimately rejected oaths. In *Milton: A Poem* Blake depicted his eponymous character, but also the poet, rising up "from the heavens of Albion ardorous," taking off "the robe of the promise," and ungirding himself "from the oath of God" (**Figure 3**).[117]

This episode has been read as a reference to Milton's opposition to the Anglican Church's Thirty-Nine Articles, to which Milton, like Marvell, had to "subscribe slave" at Cambridge, as Johnson noted.[118] Yet no better description could be given of what Milton accomplishes in *Paradise Lost*. Blake has changed the metaphor somewhat (oath as belt or clothing rather than mere cords), but the sense of liberation is clear.[119] Untying the belt that surrounded the "robe of the promise" and tied it in place around the waist is not so much an act of breaking an oath as of rejecting oaths altogether, of casting off the restrictions of others' commands in the fetters of oaths. Blair Worden is wrong to say that "Milton showed little interest in the imposition of outward tests and oaths of loyalty."[120] Milton's great Restoration poems are in fact polemics against them. Both Blake and Milton insist that oaths do not work and should be replaced by something better. There are other ways of expressing love and loyalty and creating community.

That oaths often fail to produce these things emerges from various events in *Paradise Lost*. Almost every scene in which rulers test someone for loyalty (as opposed to knowledge and understanding, as God does to Adam in Book 8) harms the testee in some way. Although God's self-oath prompts Abdiel to become an emblem of loyalty ("His loyalty he kept," 5.900), it prompts Satan to rebel. Satan's "conjúring" or tendering an oath of conspiracy to his followers (2.692–3) leads them to defeat and Hell. In so doing, Satan breaks his "discipline and faith *engaged*, / [His] military obedience" to God and "dissolve[s] / Allegiance to the acknowledged power supreme" (4.954–6) – in effect, breaking an oath very much like the Commonwealth's oath of Engagement, touted by its defenders as a mere acknowledgment of the supreme power in England. If George Wither warned at the Restoration against Charles II's "imposing oaths" on his subjects,[121] Milton's God "imposes" rigid laws on Heaven and Earth, embodied in the oath-like Tree of Knowledge (5.679, 8.333–4, 12.397–8); and it is Satan who demands that the Son fall down and pledge loyalty to him in *Paradise Regained* (4.166–7) and considers swearing verbal loyalty to God in *Paradise Lost*. Milton agrees with Satan's subsequent rejection of

Figure 3 William Blake, *Milton a Poem*, Copy C. The New York Public Library, image courtesy of The William Blake Trust.

swearing "feigned submission," of "Vows made in pain" (4.96–7). Satan, then, becomes a magnet for most of these poems' explicit references to English loyalty oaths, giving them a negative valence.

God's testing humans' loyalty by asking them to abstain from an arbitrarily prohibited fruit leads to the Fall and Expulsion. If Eve breaks the bond with God by showing loyalty only to herself, she tests Adam by asking him to Fall with her, a test he passes with flying colours because he shows her the highest possible love and loyalty.[122] Tragic as the Fall is, it proves that action rather than words – self-sacrificial action, freely chosen – is the firmest expression of loyalty:

> Not free, what proof could they have given sincere
> Of true allegiance, constant faith or love,
> Where only what they needs must do appeared,
> Not what they would? (3.103–6)

There can be no greater expression of sincere love and loyalty than the Son's freely sacrificing himself for humanity. But after the Fall, Adam rightly warns, "Let none henceforth seek *needless* cause to approve / The faith they owe; when earnestly they seek / Such proof, conclude they then begin to fail" (9.1140–2). "The faith they owe": this could refer to the allegiance someone owes to someone else or to the allegiance someone demands of another. In the second case especially, such needless demands must be refused, as Christ does repeatedly in *Paradise Regained*. *De Doctrina* allows that "An adjuration must be obeyed" only "in those matters which are not contrary to religion or fairness."[123] All of this constitutes a plea not to use mandatory verbal oaths to create community by exclusion and coercion, a plea to do away with the mere professions of loyalty in the Clarendon subscriptions and Oaths of Allegiance and Supremacy. In Milton's mind these oaths were contrary to both religion and equity and could be broken if imposed; but the best course was to avoid them altogether. Both *Samson* and *Paradise Lost* dramatize the costs of unavoidable, imposed oaths, while *Paradise Regained* rewards Christ for holding out against them. Such a polemic would have met with the approval of Quakers like Thomas Ellwood. Marvell, for his part, approached this antijurist position in both *The Rehearsal* and the *Horatian Ode*, where his various pronouncements on oaths indicate essentially the position Milton had reached in 1659–60: that no loyalty oaths should involve matters of religion, only civil obedience. To reject state oaths altogether was but one step farther.

# Appendix

## A Proposal for Emending One of Marvell's Letters

In Marvell's letter to William Popple of 24 July 1675, the phrase "A new popish Test for Book-Houses, else to be incapable" has given scholars pause, since the rare word "book-house" has, according to the *OED*, most often referred to a library.[1] It seems odd that a "test," let alone a "Popish test," should be given to a library, private or public, which would become "incapable" of something if it failed. Incapable of what exactly? Pierre Legouis tries to resolve the problem by taking "Book-Houses" to refer to bookshops, a judgment with which the *OED* concurs, citing as its sole exemplar of this meaning this very phrase from Marvell's letter in Oxford's 1971 edition of Marvell's *Poems and Letters* with Legouis's commentary.[2] If Legouis and the *OED* are right, then, Marvell would seem to refer to a new government order to censor bookshops, either forcing them not to sell Catholic books or censoring them in various ways, some of them sympathetic to Catholics, with the institution of censorship itself understood as papist – most notoriously manifest in the Index of prohibited books. However, no such order has been found, and it seems odd that Marvell would refer to it as a "Test." Instead, I suggest that "Book-Houses" is a mistaken eighteenth-century transcription of the phrase "Both-Houses" and that it refers to a 1675 bill to apply a new anti-Catholic Test oath to members of both Houses of Parliament.

As argued in chapter 2 above, doubt about religious tests informs Marvell's last half-decade of letters. They assiduously note the various proposals for new Tests, of which there were at least six, including the bill that would become law soon after his death in 1678.[3]

**Proposals for New Test Oaths (1675–8)**

Test Bill 1: a Bill to Prevent Catholics from Sitting in Parliament (1675) (eventually to become the 1678 Test)
Test Bill 2: a Bill to Suppress Popery by Speedier Conviction of Catholics (1675)
Test Bill 3: Danby's Bill for a Non-Resistance and Non-Alteration Test (1675)
Test Bill 4: a Bill to Explain (and Tighten Enforcement of) the 1673 Test (1675)
Test Bill 5: a Bill to Tender an Anti-Catholic Test to the King and Bishops (1677)
Test Bill 6: a proposal for an Anti-Bribery Test Oath for MPs (1678)

Test Bill 1, the Test for all members of Parliament, was passed in 1678 but first broached in 1675 as the "Act for the more effectuall preserving the Kings Person and Government by disableing Papists from sitting *in either House of Parlyament.*" It included a more detailed renunciation of Catholicism: a rejection not just of transubstantiation but of Mariolatry and the Mass.[4] As we shall see in a moment, this bill provides an important context for rereading Marvell's letter to William Popple. But it was not the only test bill floated in these years. Chapter 2 considers Marvell's opposition in the *Account of the Growth of Popery and Arbitrary Government* to Test Bills 3 and 5: Danby's Test (1675) and the Test for Bishops and the King (1677). In addition to these, there were two other failed bills in 1675, making a total of four failed bills. Test Bill 2, first mentioned by Marvell in 1675, wanted to use an unspecified Test to distinguish between Protestant and Catholic Dissenters so as to exempt the former from laws aimed at the latter (the Bill for Speedier Conviction of Papists).[5] Test Bill 6 sought to make an oath denying bribery a qualification for sitting in the House of Commons.[6] Marvell only seems to have supported Test Bill 6. He shows contempt for the 1673 Test in both the *Account*, as we have seen, and in a letter from January 1675 that scorns the Duke of Lauderdale's taking it for mercenary reasons, merely to gain a pension, rather than to display principled religious belief.[7]

His candid letter to his nephew William Popple that summer (ca. 24 July 1675) discloses reservations about all of the different Tests that failed in the spring session (listed here in the order in which they appear in the letter).[8]

## Marvell's Reservations about Proposed Test Oaths

Reservation 1: "an Act for taking the popish Test," in which the Duke of York "should be exempted by a particular Proviso" (Test Bill 4: the bill to explain and amplify the 1673 Test)
Reservation 2: "a politic Test to be inacted, and then taken by all Members of Parliament, and all Officers"; "after such an Act they thought another Parliament might safely be called, if this proved refractory"; "Never were poor Men exposed and abused, all the Session, as the Bishops were by the *Duke of Buckingham*, upon the Test; never the like, nor so infinitely pleasant: and no Men were ever grown so odiously ridiculous" (Test Bill 3: Danby's Test for both Houses of Parliament)
Reservation 3: "A new popish Test for Book-Houses, else to be incapable" (Test Bill 1: the precursor of the 1678 Test)
Reservation 4: a "New Test, and Way of Proceeding, for speedyer Conviction of Papists" (Test Bill 2: the Test to distinguish between Protestants and Catholics).

The various and confusing references to "Tests" in the letter denote different measures, and untangling them will help us see why an important emendation should be made in the standard text of the letter. Reservation 1 (to "the popish Test") is distinct from the others ("a new popish Test"; "a politic Test to be inacted"; "a New Test"), because it seems to refer to an existing, already passed Test, not a new one to *be* passed; the only candidate for it is the 1673 Test. "Popish," here and in the third instance, seems to be shorthand for "anti-popish," but it also suggests that any kind of Test oath, however much directed against Catholics, is actually "popish" in the sense of restrictive, arbitrary, absolutist, intended to weed Parliament of people and opinions inimical to the bishops and the Court. Reservation 2, about a bill to "to be inacted" in order to ensure a new, "safer," more reliably Court-friendly Parliament, must be Danby's non-resistance Test; to swear not to resist or alter government in any way is to agree to be a Court toady. Reservations 3–4 are part of a list of almost ten bills considered by Parliament in spring 1675, each summarized quickly by Marvell. They come in quick succession and do not refer to the same bill. Reservation 4's reference to a "New Test" as part of a bill "for speedyer Conviction of Papists" uses the words applied by the Commons to a measure "for more easy and speedy discovery and conviction of Papists."

Despite its puzzling phrase ("Book-Houses"), Reservation 3 ("A new popish Test for Book-Houses, else to be incapable") really seems to be a description of the measure that would eventually pass as the 1678 Test. The holograph of this letter has not survived, and the only record we have of it is Thomas Cooke's transcription in his edition of Marvell's works in 1726.[9] H.M. Margoliouth's twentieth-century edition of the letters reprints the phrase verbatim, and Pierre Legouis's 1971 note to this edition glosses "Book-Houses" as "book-shops."[10] To my knowledge no subsequent critic has questioned this interpretation. Yet we have no contemporary record of a bill to give "a new popish Test" to bookshops, whatever that might mean: to prevent them from selling Catholic books? to regulate or censor their inventories in some way, which could be considered "popish" in itself, comparable with the compilation of the Index of books forbidden to Catholics? Hence, it makes much more sense to assume that Cooke mistranscribed the phrase "Both-Houses" as "Book-Houses," perhaps because it appeared near the end of the line in the original manuscript of the letter.[11] Surely "A popish Test for Both-Houses" would refer to "a bill to prevent/hinder Papists from sitting in Parliament" (i.e., both Houses of Parliament), as it was called when introduced in the Commons on 16 April 1675 (three months before the letter in question) and eventually passed as the 1678 Test Act, also known as "An Act for the more effectuall preserving the Kings Person and Government by disableing Papists from sitting *in either House* of Parlyament."[12] So if the line reads "A new popish Test for Both-Houses, else to be incapable," Marvell refers to what would become the 1678 Test as "popish" either because it would weed Catholics from Parliament or because any attempt to weed out MPs based on religion would be as arbitrary and absolutist as the Papal Court and its censorship of books. This sentence, then, may be a practice run for the *Account of the Growth of Popery and Arbitrary Government*'s conspiracy theory. The new "popish Test" for "Both-Houses" of Parliament would be only the first step in the Conspirators' drive to pack Parliament with sycophants by purging it of refractory members and opinions, Catholic or otherwise, thereby tightening the stranglehold of French-style absolutism on England.

That Marvell looks askance at virtually all of these oaths is obvious in the case of Danby's Test (Test Bill 3), later to be lambasted in the *Account*, but also evident in the other three cases. To call Tests *about* popery "popish," as Marvell does in the first and third instances, is to cast doubt not just on the oaths' contents but on the very act of imposing oaths on officeholders. The bill to amplify the 1673 Test (Test Bill 1) appears suspect because the product of a cabal formed by Lauderdale, Danby, "the Bishops, and the entire old Cavalier Party," who have "persuaded" the Duke of York that he "should be exempted" from it "by particular Proviso" in the new bill. Lauderdale, Danby, and York have "had, as they generally have, the great Stroke in our Counsels" – which sounds ominous, absolutist, conspiratorial.[13] But most surprising is the last instance. One might expect Marvell to stand fully behind a measure to relieve Protestant Dissenters from penalties levelled against Catholics and to convict the latter more speedily, and yet the full sentence in which it appears does not quite say that: "New Test, and Way of Proceeding, for speedyer Conviction of Papists; and, which is worse, for appropriating the King's Customs to the Use of the Navy; and, worse of all, [the Commons] voted one Morning to proceed on no more Bills before the Recess."[14] Surely, the negatives in the latter two parts of the sentence (". . . which is worse . . . worse of all . . .") imply that the first item in the sentence, separate from the other two, is bad enough. What we have here is a suggestion that speedier conviction of Catholics is a bad thing, not outweighed by the potential benefits to Protestant Nonconformists – too high a price for sparing the latter. In a sense, this anti-anti-Catholicism, however small, is of a piece with his arguably *un*ironic distaste for, even dismay over, pope-burning processions in his last letter to Sir Edward Harley in 1677 ("I am afraid they burne Popes to night"),[15] and with his praise in the *Account* for Catholics who honourably gave up their offices after the 1673 Test Act to avoid perjury. I address this apparent sympathy for Catholics in chapter 2 above.

# Notes

## Introduction

1 Turner, *James II*, 190. Unless otherwise indicated, all emphases, here and elsewhere, are those of the original text.
2 Spurr, "Perjury, Profanity and Politics," esp. 36–7, 41; Harris, *Restoration*, 46; Matchinske, *Women Writing History*, 124, 128; Webster, *Performing Libertinism*. On profane swearing in Restoration literature, see Montagu, *The Anatomy of Swearing*, 172–87; Hughes, *Swearing*, 139–42, and "The Restoration," in *An Encyclopedia of Swearing*, 392–4; McEnery, *Swearing in English*, 79–116. In contrast to the chaste Caroline court, which imposed judicial oaths on the godly and oaths of office on the clergy but policed profane swearing within its own precincts, the Restoration court proliferated oaths of all kinds, promissory and profane.
3 For a Quaker woman said to have died in jail after refusing the Oath of Allegiance, see Whitehead, *A Brief Account*, 121–2.
4 Strictly speaking, the active part of the oath is an interjection or grammatical supplement ("I swear that" or "Hell") that claims to intensify the truth or emotional value of an existing utterance ("I will fight you at dawn tomorrow"). For a pre-Derridean account of the oath as supplement, see Hobbes, *The Elements of Law*, 86.
5 Church of England, *Articles*, 24–5 (Article 39).
6 Condren, *Argument and Authority*, 253. Cf. Ames, *The Marrow of Sacred Divinity*, 293.
7 For speech-acts, felicitous and infelicitous, illocutionary and perlocutionary, see Austin, *How To Do Things With Words* – the main implications of which are worked out in a series of books by John R. Searle: *Speech Acts*; *Expression and Meaning*; *Intentionality*, 4–13, 26–9, 160–96; and Searle and Vanderveken, *Foundations of Illocutionary Logic*.

8 See, for example, Bowles, *The Dutie and Danger of Swearing*, 15; Sanderson, *De Juramento*, 265–6.

9 For example, Hawes, *The Co[n]uercyon of Swearers*; Becon, *An Inuectyue*; Coverdale, *A Christen Exhortacion*; Bicknoll, *A Svvoord agaynst Swearyng*; Downame, *Fovre Treatises*, 1–76; Gibson, *The Lands Mourning*; White, *Of Oathes*; Strode, *A Sermon*; Powell, *A Summons*; Bowles, *The Dutie and Danger of Swearing*; Boyle, *A Free Discourse*; Hammond, *Gods Judgements*; Smallwood, *A Sermon*; Collier, *A Short View*.

10 D.M. Jones, *Conscience and Allegiance*, 270–1; McAlindon, "Swearing." The best account of oaths in Henry's reign is Gray, *Oaths and the English Reformation*.

11 D.M. Jones, *Conscience and Allegiance*, 271–2; McAlindon, "Swearing," 211.

12 Tabor, *Seasonable Thoughts in Sad Times*, 50.

13 Spurr, "Perjury, Profanity, and Politics"; "A Profane History of Early Modern Oaths"; and "'The Strongest Bond of Conscience'"; Hill, *Society and Puritanism*, 328–61; Robbins, "Selden's Pills"; Staves, *Players' Scepters*, 191–251; Vallance, *Revolutionary England*; D.M. Jones, *Conscience and Allegiance*; Condren, *Argument and Authority*; Tutino, *Law and Conscience*, 6–8, 12–18, 117–222; *Thomas White and the Blackloists*, 3, 44–68; *Empire of Souls*, 127–58, 180–4, 220–34; and *Shadows of Doubt*, 9, 149–90; Gray, *Oaths and the English Reformation*; Cressy, "The Protestation Protested, 1641 and 1642"; Sommerville, "The 'New Art of Lying,'" esp. 160, 177–81; as well as the issue of *Etudes Epistémè: Revue de Littérature et de Civilisation (XVIe –XVIIe Siècles)* 24 (2013) devoted to early modern English oaths. Andrew Hadfield's *Lying in Early Modern English Culture: From the Oath of Supremacy to the Oath of Allegiance* (2017) appeared too late for consideration.

14 To arrive at the figure of "perhaps a dozen" loyalty oaths, I begin with the figure of 10 in Hill, *Society and Puritanism*, 352, which applies to the period before the Restoration, and add the roughly 2+ new oaths from 1660 to 1688.

15 D.M. Jones, *Conscience and Allegiance*, 14, 116, 129, 147, 279; Vallance, *Revolutionary England*, 4, 110, 160; Cressy, "Protestation Protested," 251, 265, 278–9; Battigelli, *Margaret Cavendish*, 159.

16 For some self-described conscience books from the early modern period that discuss oaths, see Perkins, *The Whole Treatise of the Cases of Conscience*, 379–99; Ames, *Conscience*, 7, 27, 43, and *The Marrow of Sacred Divinity*, 290–6; Joseph Hall, *Cases of Conscience*, 54–60, 108–16; Wolleb, *The Abridgment of Christian Divinitie*, 175, 358–65; Jeremy Taylor, *Ductor Dubitantium*, 1:188–208; Ives, *The Great Case of Conscience*; John Crook, *Twenty Cases of Conscience*, esp. 2–3; Baxter, *A Christian Directory*, 1:414–21, 700–13; Sanderson, *Eight Cases of Conscience*, 107–33. About this casuistry of oaths, see, for example, D.M. Jones, *Conscience and Allegiance*, 63–103.

17 Kenyon, *The Stuart Constitution*, 169; Vallance, *Revolutionary England*, 125, 161, 169, 189.

18 See n. 3 above.

19 Austin, *How To Do Things*, 158–9, 162; Searle and Vanderveken, *Foundations*, 188, 194. Cf. Bach and Harnish's similar classification of oaths as both "commissives" and "effectives" in *Linguistic Communication and Speech Acts*, 50, 111.

20 On this deconstruction, see J. Hillis Miller, *Speech Acts in Literature*, 16.

21 Austin, *How To Do Things*, 3–7, 46–7, 54–5, 64–5, 67, 145–7, 150 (constative vs. performative); 98–111, 121 (locution, illocution, perlocution). Early in his career, Quentin Skinner made much of these distinctions with respect to literature and its speech-acts, as well as writing an important article on the Engagement oath but he has not, to my knowledge, discussed oaths as speech-acts in any sustained way. See, for example, Skinner's contributions to *Meaning and Context*, esp. 59–64, 73–7, 83–91, 103–11, 122, 128–9, 265–7, 270–1, 276–85; as well as "Conventions and the Understanding of Speech-Acts"; "On Performing and Explaining Linguistic Actions"; "Hermeneutics and the Role of History"; and "Conquest and Consent."

22 Austin, *How To Do Things*, 148.

23 See the discussion of the famous line from Euripides's *Hippolytus*, "My tongue swore, but my heart did not," in *How To Do Things*, 9–10; cf. 158–9.

24 Ibid., 6, 105 n. 1. For the opposite view, see J. Hillis Miller, *Speech Acts in Literature*, 135.

25 Austin, *How To Do Things*, 122, 162.

26 Derrida, "Signature Event Context"; cf. Austin, *How To Do Things*, 22, 9, 104.

27 Searle, *Expression and Meaning*, viii, 12–17; Loxley, *Performativity*, 49. Instead of "expressives," Reddy, *The Navigation of Feeling*, prefers the term "emotives."

28 Searle, *Expression and Meaning*, 29; Searle and Vanderveken, *Foundations*, 188; cf. 194; Loxley, *Performativity*, 50.

29 Allan and Burridge, *Euphemism & Dysphemism*, 117.

30 See also Austin, "Performative Utterances," 246; Searle, *Expression and Meaning*, 5, 13, 23, 127 (a jokey example about the Presidential oath of office); cf. 8. The passing references to oaths or swearing in the following represent no significant advance beyond Austin's and Searle's work on the subject: Ohmann, "Speech, Action, and Style," 248, 253; Ohmann, "'Instrumental Style,'" 119; Fish, "How To Do Things with Austin and Searle: Speech-Act Theory and Literary Criticism," in *Is There A Text in This Class?* 219; Bach and Harnish, *Linguistic Communication and Speech Acts*,

50, 111; Katz, *Propositional Structure and Illocutionary Force*, 216; Felman, *The Scandal of the Speaking Body*, 7, 66; Petrey, *Speech Acts and Literary Theory*, 13, 25, 43, 46; J. Hillis Miller, *Speech Acts*, 51, 135; Allan, *Natural Language Semantics*, 16.

31 See, for example, Derrida, *Adieu to Emmanuel Levinas*, 33–4.

32 Derrida, *Without Alibi*, 172–3, 231, 245, 247–8, 259, 263–4; Derrida, *Acts of Religion*, 57, 64. But see Derrida's essay on the Declaration of Independence in *Negotiations*, 46–54. For a recent account of English contract theory, see Kahn, *Wayward Contracts*.

33 Derrida, *Politics of Friendship*, 149, 138, 168 n. 26, 180–1, 191, 236, 240, 268, 273, 289, 305; Schmitt, *Political Theology*. Cf. neighbour theory's positing of the neighbour as both friend and potential foe, or something in-between: Kenneth Reinhard, "Toward a Political Theory of the Neighbor," in Zizek, Santner, and Reinhard, *The Neighbor*, 13–14, 16–19, 26, 32, esp. 19, 32.

34 Derrida, *Acts of Religion*, 83; *A Derrida Reader*, 584, 592, 594.

35 Derrida, *Sovereignties in Question*, 75–6; *Acts of Religion*, 56–7, 64–71, 80, 95–6, 98–9, 223, 388. See also his *Adieu to Emmanuel Levinas*.

36 See, for example, *A Derrida Reader*, 478–9, on the oath as speech and presence.

37 Derrida, *Without Alibi*, 97, 111–12, 194; *Sovereignties in Question*, 79, 165; *Acts of Religion*, 80, 98, 100, 350, 388.

38 Derrida, *Acts of Religion*, 64–5, 70; Derrida, *Sovereignties in Question*, 82; Derrida, *Without Alibi*, 141, 277; Derrida, "Signature Event Context." Cf. John Kerrigan, *Shakespeare's Binding Language*, 68 on oaths and the formation of groups.

39 Derrida, "Signature Event Context"; cf. Skinner, "Afterword," in *Meaning and Context*, 276.

40 Agamben, *The Sacrament of Language*, 33, 49–50, 58–9, 65–6, 69. Cf. Agamben, *Homo Sacer*, 11, 21, 71, 79–89, 98–9.

41 See Westermarck, *The Origin and Development of the Moral Ideas*, 2:118; Tylor, "Oaths," 939–40. Cf. Silving, "The Oath," 1329–30, 1337.

42 Katz, *Propositional Structure and Illocutionary Force*, 14, 21, 24.

43 Friesenhahn, *Der Politische Eid*, 10, 14–15, 114–15, 121, 127, 132, 137–8. Schmitt himself actually has little to say about oaths in *Political Theology* and *The Concept of the Political*, but *Constitutional Theory* makes a few remarks in passing (69, 81, 97, 99, 118, 122, 334).

44 See n. 92 below.

45 Judith Butler, *Undoing Gender*.

46 Catherine Bell, *Ritual*, 252; Rappaport, *Ritual and Religion*, 103, 119–23, 134.

47 Cf. Schalkwyk, "Shakespeare's Speech," 379–80, 396.

48 Van Gennep, *The Rites of Passage*, 8, 29–30, 94, 20; Victor Turner, *Dramas, Fields, and Metaphors*, 176–7; Rappaport, *Ritual and Religion*, 131, 151; Schechner, *Performance Studies*, 65–6, 124. Cf. Condren, *Argument and Authority*, 25, 328–9, on oaths as rites of passages into specific offices, although he basically claims that in the early modern period all social roles were conceived of as offices.

49 Catherine Bell, *Ritual*, 52, 84, 87, 129–30, 148–50, 155–6 and n. 67, 193–4, 201, 229–31, 239, 242; Rappaport, *Ritual and Religion*, 34–5, 131, 144, 151–2, 155, 270, 315–16, 318–20, 326; Schechner, *Between Theater & Anthropology*, 165–99.

50 Elizabeth Bell, *Theories of Performance*, 19, 30–1, 128; cf. 59, 188. Cf. D.M. Jones, *Conscience and Allegiance*, 15.

51 Rappaport, *Ritual and Religion*, 57–8, 67, 76–7, 80–1, 107–8, 320, 122.

52 Ibid., 34–5, 113–16, 144, 152, 155, 279, 315–16, 318–20, 326, 372, 415, 427.

53 This work (by William Robertson Smith, Max Müller, Edward Tylor, and others) is best summed up by Tylor, "Oaths," 939–43; Crawley, "Oath," 9:430–4. Cf. Agamben, *Sacrament of Language*, 11–12.

54 For Hellenists, see Kitts, *Sanctified Violence in Homeric Society*; Sommerstein and Fletcher, *Horkos*; the issue of *Mètis* ns 10 (2012), entitled *Dossier: Serments et Paroles Efficaces*; Judith Fletcher, *Performing Oaths in Classical Greek Drama*; Paul Cartledge, *After Thermopylae*; Sommerstein and Bayliss, *Oath and State in Ancient Greece*; Sommerstein, Torrance, et al., *Oaths and Swearing in Ancient Greece*. For Hebraists, see Ziegler, *Promises to Keep*; Conklin, *Oath Formulas in Biblical Hebrew*; Strine, *Sworn Enemies*.

55 Wither, *Speculum Speculativum*, 115.

56 Hill, "From Oaths to Interest," in *Society and Puritanism in Pre-Revolutionary England*, 328–61. See also Robbins, "Selden's Pills." Hyman's *To Try Men's Souls*, is especially marked by the McCarthyite context.

57 Matchinske, *Women Writing History*, 104.

58 Spurr, "Perjury, Profanity and Politics," 32, 46.

59 D.M. Jones, *Conscience and Allegiance*, passim; Vallance, *Revolutionary England*, 17, 31–2; Gray, *Oaths and the English Reformation*.

60 Spurr, "Perjury, Profanity and Politics," "Profane History," and "'Virtue, Religion and Government,'" 35, 39; D.M. Jones, *Conscience and Allegiance*, 169–227, 267. See also Vallance, *Revolutionary England*, 4; Condren, *Argument and Authority*, 1, 26.

61 D.M. Jones, *Conscience and Allegiance*, 169–227, 265–6.

62 Vallance, *Revolutionary England*, 199–216, 222; Spurr, "Perjury, Profanity and Politics," 46.

63 D.M. Jones, *Conscience and Allegiance*, 269, 270–2; Vallance, *Revolutionary England*, 17, 20, 31–2; Evans, *Oaths of Allegiance in Colonial New England*,

9–11, 15, 19–21, 25, 31–3, 35, 43, 45, 48–9, 52–3, 56, 63; Hyman, *To Try Men's Souls*, 21, 40–6.

64 Cressy, "Protestation Protested"; Vallance, *Revolutionary England*, 4–5, 17; D.M. Jones, *Conscience and Allegiance*, 116, 129; Knights, *Representation and Misrepresentation*, 4, 28, 118, 154–60.

65 In this regard the Engagement is the exception rather than the rule. For the inclusion of religious beliefs in state oaths after the Reformation, see John Kerrigan, *Shakespeare's Binding Language*, 378. For Schmitt and his followers, see notes 33 and 43 above.

66 Condren, *Argument and Authority*, 27, 290–342 (esp. 328–9). Cf. D.M. Jones, *Conscience and Allegiance*, 6, 264.

67 Hughes, *Swearing*, 237, 248–9, and his introduction to *Encyclopedia of Swearing*, xxi. Cf. Montagu, *Anatomy of Swearing*, 300–3.

68 Mohr, *Holy Sh*t*; McEnery, *Swearing in English*; Jay, *Cursing in America*, 74–5. Cf. Friesenhahn, *Der Politische Eid*, 10–12.

69 Hughes, *Swearing*, 4, 248–9.

70 For versions of such a holistic perspective, see Spurr, "Perjury, Profanity and Politics," "Profane History," 61, and "The Strongest Bond of Conscience," 152, 157; Mohr, *Holy Sh*t*; and n. 92 below. For judicial oaths, see Silving, "The Oath"; Shapiro, "Oaths, Credibility and the Legal Process," esp. 152–8, 166; Staves, *Players' Scepters*, 220–34.

71 For Shakespeare studies, see Shirley, *Swearing & Perjury in Shakespeare's Plays*; Hamilton, *Shakespeare and the Politics of Protestant England*, 128–62; William Kerrigan, *Shakespeare's Promises*; and John Kerrigan, *Shakespeare's Binding Language*. For Marlowe studies, see Preedy, *Marlowe's Literary Scepticism*, 20, 92–120. See also n. 47 above.

72 Canfield, *Word as Bond*, esp. xi–xvii. The heroic drama's significance may lie not just in its service of this aristocratic honour code but also in its attention to dilemmas of oath- and promise-keeping that spoke directly to the non-aristocrats forced to take state oaths in Restoration England.

73 Staves, *Players' Scepters*, 191–251.

74 Matchinske, *Women Writing History*, 103–35, esp. 120–5; Cressy, "Protestation Protested," 251, 265, 278–9, and *England on Edge*, 243; cf. 158, 209, 211–12, 224, 226, 228, 241–6, 266, 305–6, 325, 373, 382, 386–7, 396–7, 412 n. 102. See also n. 91 below. John Kerrigan's *Shakespeare's Binding Language*, however, does shine light on women and oaths (7, 25–30, 34, 97–113, 371, 446, 459, 468).

75 Gauden, *A Discourse*, 9, qtd. in Staves, *Players' Sceptres*, 203; Marvell, *The Rehearsal Transpros'd*, in *The Prose Works of Andrew Marvell*, 1:195.

76 Tabor, *Seasonable Thoughts*, 52. See also Jordan, *A Cure for the Tongue-Evill*,, esp. 4, 10.

77 Collier, *Short View*, 56–7, 59, and passim.

78 Wilmot, *The Complete Poems*, 40–1, 60, 130–1, 139; Bunyan, *Pilgrim's Progress*, ed. Cynthia Wall, 47–8, 67, 70, 106, and *The Life and Death of Mr. Badman*, 212, 35, 207.

79 Pepys, *The Diary*, 4:181; 8:384, 508; 9:200.

80 Howard, *The Committee*, 1.1.63, 139, 282; 2.3.60; 2.4.134; 3.4.51, in *The Broadview Anthology of Restoration & Early Eighteenth-Century Drama*, 474, 476, 478, 486, 489, 500. All subsequent references are to act, scene, and line numbers.

81 Ibid., 1.1.21, 75; 3.2.134, 144, 177; 4.3.157, 177.

82 Ibid., 2.4.222–3.

83 Ibid., 2.4.115, 236; 3.1.93; 3.2.172; 3.4.157; 4.1.64; 5.2.29, 83–4.

84 Cavendish, *Sociable Letters*, 61.

85 Cavendish, *Bell in Campo*, Part I, 2.10–3.13, in *The Convent of Pleasure*, 120–6. Cf. Aristophanes, *Lysistrata*, 212–36; *Thesmophoriazusae*, 81–3, 269–74; *Ecclesiazusae*, 427–30, 455–64, 516–18, 590–724, 797–8, 1160 (cf. 263–7, 296–9), in *Aristophanes III*, 24–5, 138–9, 154–7, 270–3, 284–7, 292–3, 300–17, 322–3, 354–5; and John Harington's translation of Ariosto's *Orlando Furioso*, 37.115–20: *Orlando Fvrioso in English Heroical Verse*, 313 (37.97–101).

86 Given that many electors took oaths of allegiance in order to vote in Stuart England, this may represent a fantasy of female suffrage centuries before Mrs Pankhurst. Cf. Vallance, *Revolutionary England*, 4–5 ("Individuals whose wealth or sex excluded them from participating in elections were brought into the political process through the swearing to . . . covenants" such as the Protestation); Harris, *Restoration*, 228.

87 Staves, *Players' Scepters*, 196.

88 *The Book of Oaths* (1689), 233 (cf. 234); Staves, *Players' Scepters*, 203. Cf. Vallance, *Revolutionary England*, 180.

89 Robbins, "Selden's Pills," 316; Staves, *Players' Scepters*, 203; Vallance, *Revolutionary England*, 179-80.

90 *The Book of Oaths* (1689), 235; Robbins, "Selden's Pills," 316; D.M. Jones, *Conscience and Allegiance*, 263–4. The infamous Etcetera Oath of 1640 had contained similar language but had not applied it to the civil state. See D.M. Jones, *Conscience and Allegiance*, 273.

91 Stevenson, "The National Covenant, 259, 269; and *The Scottish Revolution 1637–1644*, 83, 92, 164–5, 173; Houston, *Scottish Literacy*, 287; D.M. Jones, *Conscience and Allegiance*, 261. Thanks to Professor Stevenson for assistance with this subject.

92 Benson, *A Second Testimony*, 4 (my emphasis), 5 (Jacob's pillar of stones in Genesis 31:44–54). See also Lawson, *Theo-Politica*, 172–3; Anthony Burgess, *An Expository Comment*, 664; Tombes, *Sephersheba*, 1:26; Baxter, *A Paraphrase*, C3r. Cf. the relevant remarks about pledges, the body, fixity, and more generally on externalizing and making oaths physical, even performing them without words, in John Kerrigan, *Shakespeare's Binding Language*, 19, 37–8, 58, 63, 75, 113, 126, 132, 224.

Benson's definition of the oath as an appeal to externality or otherness suggests a new approach to swearing that can only be gestured at here but that would involve neuroscience and biocultural criticism more generally. There are hints of such an approach in Burkert, *Creation of the Sacred*, 171; Ziegler, *Promises to Keep*, 90 n. 21; Ibrahim, "Oaths in the Qur'an," 488; Schalkwyk, "Shakespeare's Speech," 375, 380, 382, 387; and John Kerrigan, *Shakespeare's Binding Language*. It would take a holistic view of both assertory and promissory oaths (including cussing), paying attention, among other things, to the way the human brain processes things and people it designates taboo or outside itself or its group in religious, cultural, and bodily terms. See, for example, Hughes, *Swearing*, 248–9; Allan and Burridge, *Forbidden Words*, 1, 77, 89, 249; Jay, *Why We Curse*, 41, 56–7, 72, 74, 126, 175, 179, 185–7, 192; Bergen, *What the F*, 87–96, 198–211; Adams, *In Praise of Profanity*, 50, 59, 103–4, 129–30. The oath thus becomes a principle of division that unites a *me* to an *us* by separating an *us* from a *them*, sometimes gesturing towards an *it*.

93 For example, Crowne's comedy *City Politiques* (1682).

94 See Gary S. De Krey's *ODNB* entries on Bethel and Cornish. I thank John Spurr for calling my attention to them.

95 Vallance, *Revolutionary England*, 179, 194, 196; Harris, *Restoration*, 200, 239, 242, 277–83, 320, 392, 409.

96 Harris, *Restoration*, 54, 74–5, 237.

97 D.M. Jones, *Conscience and Allegiance*, 281.

98 Condren, *Argument and Authority*, 314–42.

99 For these debates see Sommerville, *Politics and Ideology*, 195–9, and "Papalist Political Thought"; Condren, *Argument and Authority*, 269–342; Vallance, *Revolutionary England*, 70–4; Skinner, "Conquest and Consent," 80–95.

100 A search of EEBO (Early English Books Online) for books whose titles contain the words "oath" and "swear" from 1660 to 1664 yields roughly 86 hits, which, shorn of duplicates and red herrings and supplemented conservatively by titles not containing these words but clearly focusing on oaths, comes to roughly 88.

101 For Presbyterian views on the Covenant and oaths more generally, see *The Covenanters Plea Against Absolvers*; *The Anatomy of Dr. Gauden's Idolized Non-sence and Blasphemy*; Crofton, *Analepsis*, *Analepsis Anelephthe*, and *Berith Anti-Baal*; and Guthrie, *A Sermon . . . upon Breach of Covenant*.

102 For Baptist arguments against oaths, see Adis, *A Fanatick's Testimony*. For Baptist arguments for oaths, see Denne, *An Epistle Recommended to All the Prisons*; Tombes, *A Serious Consideration of the Oath of the Kings Supremacy*, *A Supplement to the Serious Consideration of the Oaths of the Kings Supremacy*, and *Sephersheba*; Ives, *The Great Case of Conscience Opened*.

103 For the Quaker position against oaths, see Fox, *Our Covenant with God*; Hubberthorn and Fox the Younger, *Something Against Swearing*; Caton, *An Epistle to King Charles*; Fisher, *One Antidote More*; John Crook, *The Case of Swearing* and *Sixteen Reasons*; and Hookes, *The Spirit of Christ*.

104 The royal proclamation, dated 5 December 1662, prefaces a surviving copy from York: Richard Mocket, *God and the King: or, A Dialogue Shewing that Our Soueraigne Lord the King . . . Doth Rightly Claim Whatsoever Is Required by the Oath of Allegiance* (York, 1663), ¶2r–¶3r.

105 Catholics: Sergeant, *Reflexions*, esp. 4, 20ff., 48; Winter, *Observations upon . . . the Oath of Supremacy*; Peter Walsh, *Some Few Questions concerning the Oath of Allegiance*.

106 For the Anglican position against the Solemn League and Covenant and in favour of the new oaths, see Bramhall, *A Fair Warning*; Rowland, *A Reply*; *The Scotch Covenant Condemned*; Womock, *The Solemn League*; Brabourn, *Of the Lawfulness of the Oath of Allegiance*; Tomkins, *Short Strictures*; Gauden, *Analysis*, *Certain Doubts*, *Anti-Baal Berith*, and *A Discourse Concering Publick Oaths*; [Stileman], *A Discourse*; Cressener, *Anti-Baal-Berith Justified*; Fullwood, *The Grand Case*; and Tickell, *A Serious Enquiry*.

## 1 Conjuring Oaths and Identities in *Hudibras*

1 Wasserman, *Butler*, 53; Braverman, *Plots and Counterplots*, 59. Cf. Miner, *The Restoration*, 188–9, who considers and then rejects the possibility of the Widow representing the English state, and Seidel, *Satiric Inheritance*, 101, who identifies the Widow's estate, rather than the Widow herself, with the state. Blanford Parker, *The Triumph of Augustan Poetics*, 49, identifies the Widow as a metonym for Mother England. However, as I argue below, Butler deliberately made the poem's historical allegory as partial, discontinuous, careless, and incomplete as its prosody and story.

2 Ashley Marshall, "The Aims of Butler's Satire in *Hudibras*," esp. 637, 641, 646, 649, 660, 665; cf. 647–8, reprised in *The Practice of Satire in England*, 92–7; Wasserman, *Butler*, 130 (*Hudibras* was "the most popular poem of the Restoration"). Marshall makes a very persuasive general case for the poem as an immediate, polemical contribution to early Restoration debates about Dissenters and toleration, but she has little to say about oaths or the debate about oaths.

3 Cf. Ashley Marshall, *Practice of Satire*, 93 ("the rigorous enforcement of uniformity").

4 For the failure of narrative in *Hudibras*, see Miner, *Restoration Mode*, 167. For the centrality of oaths and vows to the poem, see Staves, *Players' Scepters*, 218.

5 This and all subsequent references are to Butler, *Hudibras*, ed. John Wilders and will appear by line numbers in parentheses in my text.

6 Exodus 20:7; Matthew 5:34; Hebrews 6:16.

7 Cf. *Hudibras*, 2.3.87–8; "The Ladies Answer to the Knight," 176–80; and the character of A Knight of the Post, in Butler, *Characters*, 205–6.

8 See n. 58 below.

9 In 1660, for example, Basier, *The History of the English and Scotch Presbytery*, 141, compared the Scottish National Covenant of 1638 to Catiline's "Conjuration" or conspiracy against the Roman Republic. For plots and conjurations in Shakespeare, see John Kerrigan, *Shakespeare's Binding Language*, 313–21.

10 Scot, *Scot's Discovery of VVitchcraft*, 278–310, esp. 285–6, 305; and *Hudibras*, 1.3.937–42 (Trulla for her compatriots); cf. 1.2.1041–94 (Ralpho for Hudibras).

11 Scot, *Discovery of VVitchcraft*, for example, retails one account of five spirits allegedly swearing to do the conjurer's will, and another of "Promises and oaths interchangeably made betweene the conjuror and the spirit." In the latter, the conjurer visits a dying person or a prisoner about to be hanged and swears he will pray for his salvation. In return, the dying man swears "that my spirit that is within my body now, shall not ascend [to Heaven], nor descend [to Hell], nor go to any place of rest, but shall come to thee [the conjurer]" and do his bidding "all the dayes of thy life." See 294, 305–6, 285–6. Cf. *A Whip for the Devil*, 123–5, 134.

12 Indeed, the iambic tetrameter of *Hudibras*'s couplets demands that just about every instance of the word in the poem be stressed on the first syllable. Nevertheless, virtually all meanings of the word in early modern English and in *Hudibras* have something to do with oaths.

13 Wharton, *A Vindication of Mercurius Elencticus*, 6; *Lilly Lash't with His Own Rod*, 1.
14 Butler, "An Hermetic Philosopher," in *Genuine Remains*, 1:232, 251.
15 See n. 22 below for the virtual equivalence of the terms "oath" and "vow" in Butler's vocabulary.
16 Butler, "An Hermetic Philosopher," in *Genuine Remains*, 1:238–9 (my emphasis).
17 *Constitutional Documents of the Puritan Revolution*, 391 (my emphasis).
18 Compare the similar pun on "conjure" in the character of A Bowler in Butler, *Characters*, 250.
19 Cf. Hudibras's later words to Sidrophel about the latter's "*Metonymie*; / Your words of second hand intention, / When things by wrongful names you mention, / The Mystick sense of all your *Terms*, / That are indeed but *Magick Charms*, / To raise the Devil, and mean one thing, / And that is, down-right *Conjuring*: / And in it self's more warrantable, / Then *Cheat*, or *Canting* to a Rabble" (2.3.588–96).
20 Cf. another reference to Sidrophel as "conjurer" in a discussion of oaths, this time judicial oaths and perjury, in Part III (3.3.724–72, esp. 742), as well as to Hudibras himself as "Conjured into Raving fits" (which could be read as "addled by oaths") in a *disjectum membrum* that never made it into *Hudibras*, 3.1 (Butler, *Satires*, 456).
21 E.g., Butler, *Genuine Remains*, 1:399; 2:282, 320, 427; *Characters*, 260; and *Prose Observations*, 79.
22 For example, see Butler, *Hudibras*, 2.1.892–5; 2.3.54; as well as 2.2.119–89, 268–96; 2.3.44–8; 3.1.966, 1237, 1281. See also "An Heroical Epistle," 19–82, 169–72, 329–30; and "The Ladies Answer," 20–6.
23 Cf. Seidel, *Satiric Inheritance*, 111 (for Butler, talk is action); Nussbaum, *The Brink of All We Hate*, 55 (there is more debate than action in *Hudibras*); Braverman, *Plots and Counterplots*, 60 ("the word fails" in *Hudibras*).
24 Interestingly, the poem may describe swearing in gendered terms. While generally equating oaths and vows, it tends to describe women's commissive speech-acts as vows and men's as oaths; and with some notable exceptions, women tend to impose these commissives, while men take them. See also Butler's own footnote to some lines he added in 1674: 1.2.383–6.
25 See, for example, 1.2.544; 1.1.651–2n., 730; 3.2.1269–74; cf. 2.2.78–80.
26 Staves, *Players' Scepters*, 208.
27 Butler simply wants to keep civil war and republicanism at bay and to limit Presbyterian, Independent, and sectarian influence on the English Church, particularly by preventing a Presbyterian-friendly church

settlement – a not-so-distant prospect in 1662–3, even after the Cavalier Parliament had tried to put an end to the question with the Clarendon Code and its oaths. Oaths were the most effective means of keeping Presbyterian ministers, and many of their congregants, out of the Church and out of state offices. Perhaps their misguided flocks would return to the Anglican fold if not misled by their flawed pastors.

28 Snider, "By Equivocation Swear," 158, 171, expanded in *Origin and Authority*, 218–19.

29 See n. 2 above.

30 *The Book of Oaths* (1689), 232–3; *Statutes of the Realm*, 5:308–9 (1661 Act), 361 (1662 Act) (14 Charles II c. 3, 1662) (sections XVII–XVIII).

31 *The Book of Oaths* (1689), 232–3; *Statutes of the Realm*, 5:322.

32 *The Book of Oaths* (1689), 233–4; *Statutes of the Realm*, 5:365–6.

33 *The Book of Oaths* (1689), 234; *Statutes of the Realm*, 5:446–7.

34 *Statues of the Realm*, 5:350–1.

35 *Statues of the Realm*, 5:516–20 (esp. section XVII).

36 *Statues of the Realm*, 5:575.

37 Staves, *Players' Scepters*, 203.

38 The ambiguity of "don't" is telling. Primarily it means "done it," but a silent reader could also construe it in haste as "do not." In other words, the couplet could be mistakenly read as "Bring me an oath when you *don't* have yourself whipped." So the Widow could be seen to express doubts about his getting the whipping and bringing her a valid oath of confirmation; cf. 2.1.411–14. While this might reflect badly on the Widow herself in that she could be asking Hudibras to swear an oath that she knows will be false, it reflects even more badly on the knight himself, since his reputation for making and breaking oaths precedes him and virtually guarantees that he will perjure himself.

39 Cf. Miner, *Restoration Mode*, 162–3, on jailed Quakers as context for *Hudibras*.

40 Lilly, *History of His Life and Times*, 92.

41 Cf. Wasserman, *Butler*, 65–6, on the Widow as romance rescuer.

42 He is, of course, unlike a phallic sword in not being able to sleep with her.

43 Cf. the Fradubio episode (1.2.28–44) in Spenser, *The Faerie Queene*, 49–53.

44 On early modern notions of office and the oaths that allow people to enter it, see Condren, *Argument and Authority*.

45 Marshall, "Aims of Butler's Satire," 643–5.

46 Staves, *Players' Scepters*, 208–9, 193–4 (but see 217); Snider, "By Equivocation Swear"; Ashley Marshall, "Aims of Butler's Satire," e.g., 643–7, 649.

47 For Buckingham as Butler's associate and patron, see Grey's life of Butler in his edition of *Hudibras*, vii; Wasserman, *Butler*, 10–14; Hugh De Quehen's entry on Butler in the *ODNB*; De Beer, "The Later Life of Samuel Butler," 163–4; Quintana, "Samuel Butler," 9.

48 Butler, *Genuine Remains*, 2:351, 354–6, 278–9, 363, 155, 48, 51, 41, 35–6; 1:133–6. For the dating of the *Characters* to 1667–9, see Thyer's note in *Genuine Remains*, 2:iv, which modern editors have accepted as authoritative: Butler, *Characters*, 4.

49 Butler, *The Transproser Rehears'd*, 108; *Characters*, 45–55. For Butler's authorship of this tract, see von Maltzahn, "Samuel Butler's Milton," 482–6.

50 Butler, *Hudibras*, 3.2.164–208. The fact that Parts I–II of *Hudibras* (1662–3) do not contain such an obvious endorsement of good oath-behaviour, as some critics have noted, is no proof that Butler opposed it, or the oaths at which it was directed, the Oaths of Allegiance and Supremacy. See notes to Ashley Marshall, "Aims of Butler's Satire," 639–40. Cf. Wilding, *Dragons Teeth*, 192; Selden, *English Verse Satire*, 90–1. For more examples of Butler's refusal to criticize, and even his endorsement of, the Oaths of Allegiance and Supremacy, see Butler, *Hudibras*, 3.2.267–76; *Genuine Remains*, 1:36, 269, 427; *Satires*, 264.

51 Butler, *Prose Observations*, 6 (first published in 1759 in *Genuine Remains*, 2:485); *Satires*, 441 (my emphasis); *Hudibras*, 3.1.230–4. The first of these three passages comes from a notebook, British Library Add. MS 32625, which, according to Hugh De Quehen, postdates October 1665: see De Quehen's introduction to Butler, *Prose Observations*, xxxix, xxvi. Cf., however, De Quehen's caveats about dating (xxvii).

52 For example, the *OED*'s entry for "test," n.[1], 3, lists only one example from earlier than 1673: from the *Journal of the House of Lords*, 31 October 1665.

53 Further confirmation that Butler supported royalist oaths at least as early as Parts I–II of *Hudibras* may come in a prose satire from the same period that bears Butler's idiosyncratic marks, defends the Uniformity Oaths, and complains of Dissenters who "refuse all manner of Oaths, of Allegiance and Supremacy, or in Cases Civil and Criminal": *A Proposall Humbly Offered for the Farming of Liberty of Conscience* (London, 1663), esp. 5. While Butler's editors disagree as to whether this satire really is his, there are a number of reasons for following his earliest editors and restoring it to his canon, reasons that considerations of space only allow me to sketch. Numerous similarities of phrase and image suggest that one person wrote *Hudibras*, the contents of Butler's *Genuine Remains* (including the *Characters*), and the *Proposall*: the obsession with oaths

and state oaths; tax farming and "rates"; cropped or missing ears; Babel/Babylonian confusion of tongues; bears and humans in bearskins; the hangman Edward Dun; and the phrase "Blood and Rapine." See *A Proposall*, 2–3, 5–6, 8–9; Butler, *Genuine Remains*, 1:14, 20, 23, 84, 131–3, 136, 142, 172, 240, 243, 260, 282, 285–8, 289, 298, 300, 304, 306, 309, 335–7, 346, 360, 427; 2:6, 36, 137–8, 155, 171, 191, 274, 278–9, 282, 315–16, 351, 354–6, 363–5, 485; *Characters*, 260, 276, 286–7, 289, 292, 299, 308, 314; *Satires*, 278, 447, 490; *Prose Observations*, 156; *Hudibras*, 1.1.91–102 and notes, 789–94, 1098; 1.2.503–26, 625–52; 1.3.142–68 and note; 2.1.32–476; 3.1.125–272 (esp. 135–7, 151), 338, 1144, 1155; 3.2.Argument.1–4; 3.2.1663–4; 3.3.393–772 (esp. 601); "An Heroic Epistle of Hudibras to Sidrophel," ll. 9–16; "An Heroical Epistle of Hudibras to his Lady," ll. 19–88 (esp. 25–6, 49–56); "The Ladies Answer to the Knight," ll. 21–6, 97–8, 155–84; *Hudibras*, ed. Grey, 2:340 (3.2.1534n.).

54 See chapter 2, n. 86 below. For Buckingham and the Test, see O'Neill, *George Villiers*, 16, 44–5, 114 (Andrew Marvell's reference in a constituency letter to Buckingham's attacking Danby's proposed Test in 1675); Chapman, *Great Villiers*, 202, 220–2, 231; and Bruce Yardley's biography of Buckingham in the *ODNB*. In the 1660s Buckingham had supported Charles II's attempts (ultimately unsuccessful) to rescind the Act of Uniformity, with its similar requirement that officeholders swear allegiance to the state church; see Webster, *Performing Libertinism*, 47.

55 *Journal of the House of Lords*, 12:560–1.

56 See De Quehen's entry on Butler in the *ODNB*; cf. Wasserman, *Butler*, 10, 14, who hazards the dates 1669/70–1674.

57 *Hudibras*, 3.2.164–208, 267–76.

58 In *The Daring Muse*, 50, 52, Margaret Doody neatly summarizes many characterizations of *Hudibras* as burlesque by defining the genre as one in which, in violation of literary decorum, a subject is deprived of its appropriate style, so that burlesque in essence produces a style that opposes its subject. See also Grey, preface to *Hudibras*, 1:xviii–xix, and *Critical, Historical, and Explanatory Notes upon Hudibras*, 1; Samuel Johnson, *Life of Butler*, in *Prefaces, Biographical and Critical*, 2:38; Nash, introduction to *Hudibras*, 1:xx, xxiii; Bond, *English Burlesque Poetry*, 6; Edward A. Richards, *Hudibras in the Burlesque Tradition*, x, 20, 25; Nevo, *The Dial of Virtue*, 227; Farley-Hills, *The Benevolence of Laughter*, 33, 46, 71; Selden, *English Verse Satire*, 100; Staves, *Players' Scepters*, 207; Yadav, "Fractured Meanings," 530; Parker, *Triumph of Augustan Poetics*, 53.

59 For the courting of widows as low subject matter, see the *Grub Street Journal* 39 (1730–1), qtd. in Bond, *English Burlesque Poetry*, 45.

60 As recent work has shown, royalism was hardly monolithic; and even Anglican, as opposed to Presbyterian, royalism varied considerably on issues such as the relative strength of king and parliament in an ideal polity, the conduct of the war in the 1640s, and the strategies the king's party should pursue in the wake of the Regicide. See, for example, Donagan, "Varieties of Royalism."

61 In a later portrait of his patron, the rakish Duke of Buckingham, Butler complained of the Duke's addiction to "Continual Wine, Women, and Music," a charge repeated in Butler's notebooks along with the countervailing idea of Butler's own "plain downrightness of sense." See Butler, "A Duke of Bucks," in *Characters*, 66. But Butler was not only distinguishing his Horatian and Virgilian homeliness from other varieties of royalism, such as this libertinism; he was probably also hitting out against the homely plainness of Dissenting speech, clothes, and houses, as well as against the homely plainness of the New Science's language, as exemplified by the Royal Society and Robert Boyle, whose works frequently employ the term "homely."

62 Butler, *Genuine Remains*, 1:69–80, esp. 69 (ll. 7–8), and Table of Contents. Cf. Miller's argument that *Hudibras* began as an anti-royalist allegory ("Allegory," 326).

63 Cousins, "The Idea of a 'Restoration,'" 134.

64 Ibid., 135–6.

65 For the notion of the scapegoat, see Frazer, *The Golden Bough*, 626–68, 651–79; Girard, *Violence and the Sacred* and *The Scapegoat*. In Butler's case the scapegoating is conscious and overt.

66 Lilly, *The Starry Messenger*, *2v, referred to Cavaliers as "dam-boyes."

67 "Parole, n.[1]," 1a-c, *OED*.

68 For royalists being given the Negative Oath to be parolled, see *Hudibras*, ed. Grey, 1:188 (1.2.1111–12n.).

69 In the 1674 edition. The 1663 edition reads "elenctique case," pulling his situation closer to that of people facing cases of conscience in opposition ("elenctique") to some problem or evil, or possibly to that of someone refuting someone else's argument by cross-examination.

70 Butler, *Genuine Remains*, 2:285.

71 Butler, *Genuine Remains*, 2:90.

72 Marvell, *Last Instructions*, l. 393, in *The Poems of Andrew Marvell*, ed. Smith, 380; cf. Butler, *Hudibras*, 2.2.585–712.

73 See, for example, Samuel Johnson, *Life of Butler*, in *Lives*, 2:15, 25; James Hannay, *Satire and Satirists* (1854), qtd. in Moulton, *The Library of Literary Criticism*, 2:332; Veldkamp, *Samuel Butler*, 83; Jack, *Augustan Satire*, 32;

W.O.S. Sutherland, *The Art of the Satirist*, 60; and James Sutherland, *English Literature*, 158.

74 "Homely, a.," "Homely, adv.," *OED*.

75 And perhaps even "English," given the references to "home" as England in opposition to France (2.3.751, 771). Cf. Yadav, "Fractured Meanings" on *Hudibras*'s nationalism. For *Hudibras*'s exuberance and carelessness, see Johnson's *Life of Prior*, qtd. in Bond, *English Burlesque Poetry*, 293–4.

76 Cf. Blanford Parker, *Triumph of Augustan Poetics*, 26; cf. 15.

77 See John Dryden, John Dennis, and William Coward, qtd. in Bond, *English Burlesque Poetry*, 30, 31, 38; William Warburton, qtd. in Moulton, *Library of Literary Criticism*, 2:334; Gibson, "Samuel Butler," 331; Jack, *Augustan Satire*, 32; Nevo, *Dial of Virtue*, 218 (cf. 239); James Sutherland, *English Literature*, 160; Farley-Hills, *Benevolence of Laughter*, 50, 53; Wasserman, *Butler*, 73, 91 (cf. 127); Yadav, "Fractured Meanings," 543–4; Parker, *Triumph of Augustan Poetics*, 6, 11, 18.

78 Cf. Wasserman, *Butler*, 5 ("a rustic poem"). See n. 73 above.

79 *Hudibras*, 1.1.277, 384, 508, 606, 784–8, 842; 1.2.200, 453–64, 471–2, 714; 1.3.115; 2.3.113, 115, 250.

80 Ibid., 1.3.1073; 2.3.8, 403–8.

81 Ibid., 1.3.248.

82 Ibid., 1.1.843–4 and n.; 2.1.171, 356; 2.2.645.

83 Braddick, *State Formation*, 30–4, 167, 321–3, 327–30.

84 Johnson, *Life of Butler*, in *Lives*, 2:29; Dixon, *English Epic and Heroic Poetry*, 261; Engler, "*Hudibras* and the Problem of Satirical Distance,"443.

85 Staves, *Players' Scepters*, 212.

86 De Quehen, "Butler," *ODNB*.

87 Butler, *Characters*, 107, 168, 261, 286, 261; D.M. Jones, *Conscience and Allegiance*, 60. By contrast, Grey, Johnson, and other early critics were very conscious of Hudibras's status as commissioned JP: *Hudibras. The Second Part*, ed. Wasserman, 23; Grey, preface to *Hudibras*, 1:ii–iii, xix; Johnson, *Life of Butler*, in *Lives*, 2:17, 20; and the Militia Acts of 1661–2's commissions for lieutenants in the militias (*Statutes of the Realm*, 5:308–9, esp. sections I, II, and V, and 358–64, esp. section I and sections IV, X–XI, which mention judicial oaths militia officers may tender to soldiers and other officers). See also *Hudibras* 1.1.23's hint that as someone who occupies a bench ("Great on the Bench"), Hudibras may also be a local judge. He is thus a composite of various kinds of local official.

88 The anonymous, unauthorized *Hudibras: The Second Part* in effect delivers an analysis of what the author(s) thought Butler was trying to do in his first instalment. For in addition to pointing out Butler's turn to low subject

matter and form, it focuses on Hudibras's activities as a local official, a JP who clamps down on the wrong activities (other merry sports such as maypoles and puppet shows) and allows real problems, such as robbery, to continue unchecked. In fact, Hudibras and his squire become robbers themselves, making away with both the puppets and the proceeds of the show. It is no accident that Hudibras turns thief after the personification of Justice, which has accompanied him through the first half of the poem, finally departs at the end of the second canto. See *Hudibras. The Second Part* (1663), ed. Wasserman, 88, 41; cf. Wasserman's introduction, 8. The point of the later cantos would seem to be that here there is no Astraea Redux, no justice, precisely because there are no competent officials. Both Wasserman's introduction to this edition and his "'That Paultry Story'" give too much credit to the abilities of the hack or hacks who produced the spurious sequel. Wasserman maintains that rather than simply capitalizing on the market for Butler's kind of poem and producing "a counterfeit poem that would pass as Butler's" – as I think – it parodies and critiques Butler's first book from within the royalist camp (introduction, 3–4; "'That Paultry Story,'" 461, 463, 467–8).

89 *Statutes of the Realm*, 5:358–64 (section XVIII).

90 *Statutes of the Realm*, 5:364–70 (esp. sections V, XVII).

91 *Statutes of the Realm*, 5:321–3 (esp. sections I, III, VII–VIII). The later Conventicles and Five Mile Acts (1664 and 1665 respectively) contained similar provisions for involving JPs in their enforcement and in the administration of oaths: *Statutes of the Realm*, 5:648–51 (esp. sections I–II, XIV, XVII), 575 (esp. sections II, IV).

92 Butler concedes that oaths are imperfect instruments for purging church and state of Dissenters at the local level, but they are the most effective tools the kingdom has and should be fully used.

93 *Hudibras*, ed. Nash, 3.23 (1.1.255n.); *Hudibras*, ed. Grey, 1:32–3 (1.1.241n., 257n.); Butler [?], "The Tale of the Cobler and the Vicar of Bray," in Butler, *Posthumous Works*, 3:285. For the literary precedents, see Veldkamp, *Butler*, 168–71. Hudibras's beard was also connected in Butler's mind to that of the Independent minister Philip Nye, which the knight mentions in his Epistle to the Widow in Book III (l. 188) and is the subject of several poems Butler left in manuscript. One of Butler's first editors hastened to mention Nye's early advocacy of the Presbyterians' signature "strict vow" or oath, the Solemn League and Covenant. See Butler, "Upon Philip Nye's Thanksgiving Beard," in *Genuine Remains*, 1:177–84 and Thyer's notes thereto.

94 Subsequent lines gloss the "Words and Promises" as the New Model Army's code of military conduct and justice (1.2.1095–8).

95 *Hudibras*, ed. Grey, 1:187 (1.2.1094–5n.), refers the reader solely to Judges 15. While Samson is shackled in "fetters of brass" in Judges 16:21, there is no mention of their being on his hands, his directing that they be there, or his breaking them.
96 *Hudibras*, ed. Grey, 1:33 (1.1.260n.).

## 2 Testing the Tests in *The Rehearsal Transpros'd*

1 Marvell, *The Loyal Scot*, ll. 218, 226, in *The Poems of Andrew Marvell*, ed. Smith, 410; Anchitell Grey, *Debates of the House of Commons*, 4:324. All further citations of Marvell's poetry are to Smith's edition.
2 Marvell, *The Rehearsal Transpros'd* (hereafter *RT*), in *The Prose Works of Andrew Marvell* [hereafter *PWAM*], ed. Annabel Patterson et al., 1:66; cf. 313–14.
3 Hickeringill, *Gregory, Father-Greybeard*, 29.
4 On drolling and drolleries, see Raylor, *Cavaliers, Clubs, and Literary Culture*, 152.
5 Castrop, *Die Varronische Satire in England 1660–1690*, 126–77, 186–200. See also my essay on *The Rehearsal Transpros'd* in the forthcoming *Oxford Handbook of Andrew Marvell*.
6 Cf. Nevo, *Dial of Virtue*, 200.
7 Von Maltzahn, *An Andrew Marvell Chronology* (hereafter *AMC*), 22, 24; Kelliher, *Andrew Marvell*, 23. For matriculation oaths as context for *Love's Labour's Lost*, see John Kerrigan, *Shakespeare's Binding Language*, 69, 399.
8 Kelliher, *Andrew Marvell*, 22. And possibly even five years earlier, along with his oath of admission to Cambridge on 14 December 1633 (19–20; *AMC*, 21).
9 *AMC*, 26; Kelliher, *Andrew Marvell*, 25; Smith, *Andrew Marvell*, 35–6, 41; Marvell, *RT*, 262 (my emphasis).
10 See the *ODNB* entry on Parker about the timing of his MA. It is, of course, possible that Parker did at some point before July 1663 leave Trinity temporarily because of the oaths, only to return sometime later, take the oaths, and receive the MA. But this does not rule out the possibility of Marvell's confessing his own reluctance about the oaths in *The Rehearsal Transpros'd*.
11 Kelliher, *Andrew Marvell*, 31; *AMC*, 29, 30.
12 Wallace, *Destiny His Choice*, 69–105; Condren, "Marvell's 'Horation Ode on Cromwell's Return from Ireland.'" Nigel Smith, *Andrew Marvell*, 83–4, thinks that he must have taken it and that the *Horatian Ode* is written from the perspective of someone who has. See also Worden, *Literature and Politics*, 85.

13 *The Poems and Letters of Andrew Marvell* (hereafter *P&L*), 2:43 (27 October 1666).

14 *AMC*, 209; von Maltzahn, "Milton, Marvell and Toleration," 95.

15 *AMC*, 19 (13 October 1627), 75 (30 July 1663); Kelliher, *Andrew Marvell*, 32; Legouis, *André Marvell*, 421 n. 270; Marvell, *RT*, 186. According to Withington, "Andrew Marvell's Citizenship," 116, Popple "paid the fine in full" and was thus "relieved from holding office (and so reneging on the Covenant [by abjuring it])"; "the election to replace Popple as alderman" took place in early January 1664. So Popple appears to have sacrificed not only the office but a sizable sum of money, perhaps £150, to avoid renouncing the Covenant. In the case of the Forced Loan of 1626–7, in addition to an oath about other payers and shirkers of the Loan, there was also "An oath to accuracy of valuation . . . required of payers for the first time since 1563": see Hirst, "The Privy Council," 52. After the Restoration, Marvell showed frequent sympathy for wine merchants tendered similar forensic oaths about their cargoes: Marvell, *P&L*, 2:103 (19 March 1670), 319 (17 December 1670), 186 (8 March 1677). Cf. Marvell's like sympathy for a Scot's refusal of another forensic oath, this time of a religious nature: Marvell, *P&L*, 2:356 (7 August 1677).

16 Marvell, *RT*, 221 (title page of Part II); 197, 422, 358, 393, 360; 392, 371, 380, 409, 262, 186, 374, 296. All but the passages on pp. 186 and 197 come from Part II, showing that Marvell stepped up his attack on oaths after the Test Act. Apropos the "Dutch" oath of "Sacraments, Sacraments" (393), see Vernon's *Letter to a Friend*, 70, which accuses Owen of being one who "(Dutchman like) could Sail with every wind" when it came to religious and political issues – i.e., trim sails and change views. By "Dutch" oaths, then, Marvell would seem to mean oaths one will not keep or oaths whose obligations one regards as flexible. Apropos conjuring, see Marvell's *Last Instructions*, l. 667 and *Loyal Scot*, l. 33.

17 By the 1670s Marvell's religious views appear to have moved towards voluntarism, the idea of reason tempering revelation and grace, and the minimum of doctrine expressed in the Apostles' Creed and the roughly thirty-six doctrinal Articles (the Thirty-Nine Articles minus Numbers 20, 34, 36, and part of 21). In *The Rehearsal Transpros'd* Marvell implies his support for Elizabeth's requiring "the Puritans . . . *only* [to] subscribe the Articles of Doctrine," rather than discipline (409, my italics). In the *Essay* and *Mr. Smirke*, the Apostles' Creed seems to represent Marvell's ne plus ultra with regard to Christianity's minimum beliefs: a bare affirmation of "the holy Catholic [i.e., universal] church, the Communion of Saints, the forgiveness of sins, the resurrection of the body," "the life everlasting,"

and the existence and divinity of Christ and the Holy Spirit, as the catechism of the Book of Common Prayer put it in 1662. See *The Book of Common-Prayer* (London, 1662) (Wing B3622), aa2v; Marvell, *Mr. Smirke, PWAM*, 2:69–70 (Apostles' Creed); 77–8, 80, 107, 109 (Thirty-Nine Articles); Marvell, *A Short Historical Essay Touching General Councils, PWAM*, 2:143–4, 148, 160 (Apostles' Creed); 129, 143, 173 (Thirty-Nine Articles). For John Owen's support for swearing to the Thirty-Nine Articles, see *A Discourse Concerning Evangelical Love*, 214; cf. Owen's *A Peace-Offering*, 10 (support for the doctrinal parts of the Thirty-Nine Articles), 13–14. There is thus a case to be made for Marvell as Independent.

18 Spurr, *England in the 1670s*, 35–6; Spurr, "The Church of England, Comprehension," 935.

19 Marvell, *RT*, 99. Cf., in the context of Richard Lee's abjuration of the Solemn League and Covenant, these verses from the broadside *A Rod for the Fools back: or, An Answer to a Scurrilous Libel, called The Changeling*, 1: "Bishops beware, these Pick-locks of an *Oath*, / Long for your *Birth-right*, though they hate your *Broth*."

20 Marvell, *P&L*, 2:342 (24 July 1675).

21 Marvell, *Remarks upon a Late Ingenious Discourse*, in *PWAM*, 2:427.

22 Marvell, *An Account of the Growth of Popery* [hereafter *AGP*], *PWAM*, 2:281–7; 310, 313–23; 268–70, 239–40, 374–5.

23 Marvell, *AGP*, 281.

24 The Bill to Prevent Dangers from Disaffected Persons (Persons Disaffected to the Government): Marvell, *AGP*, 281–7. Cf. Marvell, *P&L* 2:147–52, 155, 157–9; *Journal of the House of Lords* (hereafter *JHL*), 12:659, 665–6, 691–2 (15, 21, and 23 April 1675; 14 May 1675). See also Marvell, *AGP*, 282; cf. *Mr. Smirke*, 79. "*Foreboding* the Alteration of Religion, or Government" probably puns on the oath's attempt to "*forbid* the alteration of religion or government."

25 Marvell, *AGP*, 313–19 and von Maltzahn's comments in his introduction and notes; Nicholas McDowell, *Poetry and Allegiance*.

26 Grey, *Debates*, 4:336 (4 April 1677) (mentioned by Marvell and von Maltzahn in *AGP*, 311 and n. 442). Presumably this added to his less doctrinally specific coronation oath.

27 Grey, *Debates*, 4:323–4 (27 March 1677).

28 Marvell, *AGP*, 268–9.

29 Ibid., 269.

30 Marvell takes a cheap shot at Parliament by adding that by giving itself control over who enters which office, a control not unlike the political patronage that allowed patrons to sell offices (or their reversion),

Parliament had become no better than corrupt political patrons – in a sense a natural outgrowth of its own position as 5/6 bribed and coerced placemen or potential placemen. See Marvell, *AGP*, 269, 299–304.

31 Marvell, *AGP*, 270 and n. 257, 269.

32 Marvell, *AGP*, 239–40, 269–70, 374–5.

33 Though see Marvell, *AGP*, 291–2, and von Maltzahn's introduction to it, 181 and n. 6.

34 Marvell, *AGP*, 374, 269. One of the many ironies Marvell presents is that the Test inadvertently ejected from office one of Protestantism's greatest supporters: the Earl of Shaftesbury (Marvell, *AGP*, 268).

35 Marvell, *Mr. Smirke*, 41.

36 Marvell, *RT*, 44–6 (which laments censorship and compares books to conventicles); cf. *P&L*, 2:314–15 (21 March 1670), 318 (28 November 1670).

37 Marvell, *A Short Historical Essay*, in *PWAM*, 2:145, 160.

38 Ibid., 173.

39 Ibid., 144–5.

40 Marvell, *Mr. Smirke*, 79.

41 See the Yale editors' quotation from Francis Turner's *Animadversions upon a Late Pamphlet* about university graduates subscribing "Articles," not just the Oaths of Allegiance and Supremacy (Marvell, *Mr. Smirke*, 79 n. 251).

42 Ibid., 77–8.

43 Ibid., 78.

44 Ibid.

45 On the Vestry Act, see Seaward, "Gilbert Sheldon, the London Vestries, and the Defence of the Church." Marvell has in effect attacked all of the Clarendon Code's oaths of office, not just the Uniformity oaths. In doing so, he resembles his patron Shaftesbury. See the latter's speech to the House of Lords (20 October 1675) in *Two Speeches*, 11; and *A Letter from a Person of Quality to his Friend in the Country*, 1–3.

46 *The Manner of the Solemnity of the Coronation of His Most Sacred Majesty King Charles*, 1.

47 *Mr. Smirke*'s passage about Charles's taking a subject's oath, rather than a king's oath, recalls the conceit of the poem *Upon his Majesty's being made Free of the City* (1674): that the citizens or freemen of London have essentially made the king one of their own in a citizenship ceremony – a ceremony that usually involved the candidate for freeman status taking an oath promising allegiance to the monarch and obedience to the City's norms: "Ye shall swear, That ye shall be good and true to our Soveraign Lord King Charles . . . and obedient . . . to the Mayor and Ministers of this City, the Franchises and Customes thereof . . . Ye shall colour no Foreign Goods under or in your name, whereby

the King or this City might or may lose Customes or Advantages." See *POAS*, 1:237–42; *The Book of Oaths* (1689), 13–14; cf. *The Book of Oaths* (1649), 22–3. Marvell's or pseudo-Marvell's *Upon his Majesty's being Made Free of the City*, in *POAS*, 1:242 quotes this oath at ll. 116–17. Although Charles apparently took no freeman's oath that day, a day on which he attended the installation of Sir Robert Viner as Lord Mayor, the poem cheekily refers to Charles's coronation oath as the equivalent of an apprentice's or freeman's oath and thus as a similar moment of contract or "indentures." To be "bound" as a freeman is "the same [as] to be crown'd" king (ll. 28–9; cf. 73–8). If neither the king's "Word nor his Oath" can "bind him to troth," then is Charles (or, for that matter, James, Duke of York, the heir apparent) really "fit . . . to govern" (ll. 67–8, 111), let alone be a citizen of London? The similarity between *Mr. Smirke* and *Upon his Majesty's being Made Free of the City* thus strengthens the case for Marvell's authorship of the latter. For that case, see *POAS*, 1:237; George deF. Lord's edition of Marvell's *Complete Poetry*, 196–201; *PWAM*, 2:xv.

48 Marvell, *P&L*, 2:241–2.

49 *Book of Oaths* (1689), 36–8.

50 Ibid., 38–9.

51 *Journal of the House of Commons* (hereafter *JHC*), 9:280–1 (29 March 1673) (my emphasis).

52 *AMC*, 93 (27 October 1666); Marvell, *P&L*, 2:42–3 (27 October 1666) ("dedimus potestatem" to JPs to tender the oaths; also mentions Anglican Communion as a litmus test). Cf. the references to *dedimus potestatems* a year later: 2:58–9 (8 & 26 October 1667), 62 (26 November 1667). These admittedly could be bare passings-on of orders, but the addition of reasons why the orders are necessary seems to argue against it.

53 *AMC*, 162 (8 May 1675), 167 (16 November 1675). Cf. Marvell's letters to the Hull Corporation on this issue: Marvell, *P&L*, 2:60 (14 November 1667), 120 (3 December 1670), 123 (17 December 1670); 2:189 (15 March 1677); cf. 191. On naturalization policies after the Restoration, see Robbins, "A Note on General Naturalization." A bill for general naturalization was also being considered in the 1673 session that passed the Test Act: e.g., *JHC*, 9:274–5 (24 March 1672/3).

54 Marvell, *RT*, 195.

55 Marvell, *P&L*, 2:31–2 (17 June 1661), 313–15 (21 March 1670); Marvell, *AGP*, passim.

56 Marvell, *P&L*, 2:33 (27 June 1661).

57 *AMC*, 112–13. Cf. Marvell, *P&L*, 2:330 (24 October 1674) on the oaths of Edinburgh's electors. The case of the disputed York election of 1673, which found Marvell's friend and relative Sir Henry Thompson in a situation

apparently similar to Rolle's, is actually different in that the dispute over electors concerned whether they were freemen, rather than Corporation members as in Rolle's case, and so did not involve Corporation oaths at all. See Marvell, *P&L*, 2:335, 380n.

58 It is also worth noting that Marvell refers at least twice to the oath required of Nonconformist ministers by the Five Mile Act of 1665 as the "Corporation Oath," even though contemporaries usually referred to it as the "Oxford Oath" (Marvell, *P&L*, 2:147 [20 April 1675], 346 [1 July 1676]). This may provide further evidence of animus towards the Corporation oaths.

59 Marvell, *P&L*, 2:356 (17 November 1677). On Taunton's Nonconformity, see William Gibson, *Religion and the Enlightenment*, 101–2, 97–9, 13, 66, 116.

60 Marvell, *P&L*, 2:356.

61 Marvell, *P&L*, 2:69 (12 March 1668), 72 (11 April 1668), 103 (10 March 1670). Cf. Grey, *Debates*, 1:229–30. Catholics like Peter Walsh even called for the omission from the Oath of Allegiance of the denial of the pope's indirect deposing power (also part of the Clarendon Code's requirements). See Walsh, *The Advocate of Conscience*, 139–43, 127; cf. 176–93. See also the Baptist physician Peter Chamberlen's manuscript revision of the Oaths of Allegiance and Supremacy, ca. 1661–2, which excised the royal supremacy in religious matters: printed in Michael Adams, "Peter Chamberlen's Case of Conscience," 305–6.

62 Marvell, *P&L* 2:363 (11 March 1668), 72 (11 April 1668), 104 (14 April 1670), 146 (17 April 1675), 175 (18 November 1675); cf. 139–40 (on the expected "Act of Grace" or royal indulgence, 13 & 18 April 1671); *AMC*, 61, 62 (a bill to ease tender consciences by making the Worcester House Declaration law),106 (?7–9 March 1668); Bate, *The Declaration of Indulgence*, 14, 38–9, 45, 65, 139; Sykes, *From Sheldon to Secker*, 70–1, 78–81, 83, 89; Whiteman, "The Restoration of the Church of England," 80, 83; Thomas, "Comprehension and Indulgence," 195, 212–21, 223–31, 240–8; Spurr, "Comprehension and the Toleration Act of 1689," 931–45.

63 Samuel Parker, *A Reproof to the Rehearsal Transprosed*, 157.

64 For references to oaths and toleration in this group of poems, see Marvell, *The Loyal Scot*, l. 226 ("New oaths 'tis necessary to invent"); *Third Advice to a Painter*, ll. 243–4 (the St Bartholomew's Day ejection in 1662 and massacre in 1572); *Last Instructions*, ll. 287–8 ("A gross of English gentry, nobly born, / Of clear estates, and to no faction *sworn*"). See also pseudo-Marvell, *Nostradamus' Prophecy* (1672), in *POAS*, 1:187 ("When declarations lie, and ev'ry oath / Shall be in use at court, but faith and troth").

65 And not just Catholics, but Protestant Dissenters as well. See George Bishop, *The Warnings of the Lord* ([London], 1667), 19, cited in *Poems of*

*Andrew Marvell*, ed. Smith, 329. See Baxter, *Reliquiae Baxterianae* (hereafter *RB*), Part III, 2:1; Part II, 1:448.

66 Marvell, *P&L*, 2:57 (3 October 1667); *AMC*, 99.

67 Greaves, *Enemies under His Feet*, 142–51; Martin Dzelzainis and Annabel Patterson, introduction to *PWAM*, 1:6. Cf. von Maltzahn, "The First Reception of *Paradise Lost*)."

68 Humfrey, *A Proposition*, 8, 20–1, 54, 68, 91.

69 Tomkins, *The Inconveniencies of Toleration*, 4–5, 9–10, 13–15; Perrinchief, *A Discourse of Toleration*, 7, 25, 33, 38, 40–1, 42–4; idem, *Indulgence Not Justified*, 2–3; Patrick, *A Friendly Debate*, 102–5, 107, 109, 208, 220; idem, *A Continuation of the Friendly Debate*, 44–52, 55, 94, 414–15, 422, 442, 455; idem, *A Further Continuation and Defence*, 249; and idem, *An Appendix to the Third Part of the Friendly Debate*, 36, 80–90, 171–2, 205. See also *The Toleration Intolerable*, 13; Assheton, preface to *Toleration Disapprov'd and Condemn'd*, 1, 3–6, 12–13, 18, 21; Pittis, *A Private Conference*, 37–40; Fullwood, *The Doctrine of Schism*, 47–8 (test). See also Thorndike, "The True Principle of Comprehension: Or a Petition against the Presbyterian Request for a Comprehensive Act" (1667) and "The Plea of Weakness and Tender Consciences Discussed and Answered" (1668), in *The Theological Works of Herbert Thorndike*, 5:299–344, 345–80, esp. 333, 348.

70 Locke's manuscript "Essay on Toleration" (1667) and Milton's *Of True Religion* (1673) also defended toleration using the category of things indifferent, but with less attention to oaths. It was at this time (1667) that Locke reversed his position on things indifferent, arguing that they were not the jurisdiction of the state church. See Locke, *Political Essays*, 136, 139, 141–2, 145 (perjury), 151, 152 (oaths dispensed by pope), as well as the references to "assent" (142, 155, 159), which, in light of his strictures against religious uniformity in the "Essay" (157, 159) and his more or less contemporary annotations of Samuel Parker's *Ecclesiastical Politie* (212 [assent and consent to the magistrate's opinions]), seem to refer to the 1662 Uniformity Act's "assent and consent" oath; Milton, *Of True Religion, Haeresie, Schism, Toleration, and What Best Means May Be Us'd against the Growth of Popery*, in *Complete Prose Works* (hereafter *YP*), 8:427–9 (on adiaphora but not oaths).

71 Humfrey, *Proposition*, 19–25, 54–5, 64–5, 73–4, 76, 81, 88–9; Owen, *Indulgence and Toleration Considered*, 4–5, 15; idem, *A Peace-Offering*, 9, 12, 24; idem, *Truth and Innocence Vindicated*, 143, 266–8 (esp. 267), 322–4, 365–6; idem, *A Discourse*, 171–81, 202–14; Wolseley, *Liberty of Conscience*, 26, 40, 47, 58, 63, 66; Corbet, *A Discourse*, 24, 30–2, 34, 37–9, 41; [John Norton], *An Humble Apology*, A2r–v, A8r, 4–5, 7, 39, 47, 51, 94, 120, 123–5, 150; [Samuel Rolls], *A Sober*

*Answer*, 4–5, 103–4, "240–1," "257–9"; Baxter, *An Apology for Nonconformists Ministry*, 111–13, 136–7, 154, 183; idem, *Sacrilegious Desertion*, 8, 31, 38, 65, 96, 136; Humfrey, *Case of Conscience*, 7, 13–17, 19–20; and Milton, *Of True Religion*, *YP*, 8:427–9. See also *A Letter to a Member of this Present Parliament*, 9; *A Second Letter to a Member of this Present Parliament*, 6, 7–8; *Indulgence Not to Be Refused*, 2, 6, 20, 22, 24.

72 [David Jenkin], preface to *The Judgment of Richard Baxter*, 3–4; Humfrey, *Proposition*, 19; Humfrey, *Case of Conscience*, 7, 19; Patrick, *Friendly Debate*, 208–9; [Norton], *Humble Apology*, 120, 128; [Rolls], *Sober Answer*, "257"; Baxter, *Apology*, 111–13; Samuel Parker, *A Discourse of Ecclesiastical Politie*, 239–40. Cf. Robbins, "The Oxford Session," 223–4; Spurr, "Comprehension and the Toleration Act of 1689," 931; Whiteman, "Restoration," 73; and Nuttall, "The First Nonconformists," 158–9, 184, who claims that oaths like the abjuration of the Solemn League and Covenant were not the main issue, at least for Richard Baxter.

73 See, e.g., *A Letter to a Member of this Present Parliament*; *A Second Letter to a Member of this Present Parliament*, 15; Humfrey, *Proposition*, 90–1, 54, 68; Norton, *Humble Apology*, 125, 150; Baxter, *RB*, Part III, 1.43. Vernon, *Letter to a Friend*, 66, charged that Owen had distributed one of his own pro-toleration books, possibly *Truth and Innocence Vindicated*, among MPs in time for the 1670 session – a charge that Owen, however, denied in *An Expostulatory Letter*, 18. But it was at least plausible to suggest that Owen's book was relevant to Parliament's deliberations about Dissent. See also von Maltzahn, "The First Reception of *Paradise Lost*," 484–5; Spurr, "Comprehension and the Toleration Act of 1689," 942; *AMC*, 112, 163. On these legislative attempts, see Spurr, "Comprehension and the Toleration Act of 1689," 933–4; Sykes, *From Sheldon to Secker*, 71–5; Bate, *Declaration of Indulgence*, 54, 56–61; Thomas, "Comprehension and Indulgence," 196–203.

74 Marvell, *P&L*, 2:69 ([12 March] 1668), 72 (11 April 1668); see also the letter to Sir Edward Harley of 17 November 1677 (2:356).

75 Von Maltzahn, "Marvell and the Lord Wharton," 252 n. 2, 253.

76 Marvell, *P&L*, 2:103 (10 March 1670); Grey, *Debates*, 1:228–9 (9–10 March 1670).

77 Bate, *Declaration of Indulgence*, 82 (the Declaration of Indulgence required no oaths).

78 De Krey, *London and the Restoration*, 123–5; Lacey, *Dissent and Parliamentary Politics*, 66–7.

79 *JHC* 9:259 (27 February 1673); Spurr, *England in the 1670s*, 39 (just the Oaths of Allegiance and Supremacy and the Thirty-Nine Articles).

80 At roughly the same time, Humfrey's *Comprehension Promoted* called on Parliament to bring about comprehension not only by rolling back the Uniformity oaths (the declaration of "assent and consent" to the Book of Common Prayer and the abjuration of the Solemn League and Covenant – leaving, at most, a subscription to the Thirty-Nine Articles), but by repealing the Five Mile Act's so-called Oxford Oath as well. See Humfrey, *Comprehension Promoted*. Cf. Baxter, *RB*, Part III, 110–11. See Lacey, *Dissent*, 67–8, on Baxter's and Humfrey's attempts to influence the Ease Bill. In the course of debating it, there was a proposal for it to include a Test to exclude Protestant Dissenters from Parliament: see Lacey, *Dissent*, 68 and n. 102; Grey, *Debates*, 2:93–6 (10 March 1673); *JHC*, 9:266 (10 March 1673); Dering, *Parliamentary Diary*, 135.

81 The majority of the bishops opposed toleration of any kind; the Court and the Lords wanted indulgence, and royal indulgence, rather than mere comprehension; and Charles was probably more interested in easing Catholics than Protestant Dissenters. See, among others, Bate, *Declaration of Indulgence*, 127–9; Sykes, *From Sheldon to Secker*, 78; Swatland, *The House of Lords*, 182–3, 186.

82 See Grey, *Debates*, 2:157 (25 March 1673): "The Earl of *Anglesea* only managed the Conference" between the two Houses over the Ease Bill, and "he told us how ready the Lords were to comply with us in so important, good, and seasonable a Bill, sent them by this House." On the issue of oaths, see *JHC*, 9:279–81 (28–9 March 1673), esp. 280–1 (29 March). Cf. 274–5 (24 March 1672/3). Why Charles should have intervened when this process was only days away from completion is an open question. Perhaps he refused to grant toleration to Protestants if they could not share it with Catholics; perhaps he preferred a royal indulgence to a parliamentary one, a royal indulgence that would make Dissenters beholden to him; perhaps both.

83 Parker, *Discourse*, 1–4, ch. 3 (87–110, esp. 87–9, 94–6), ch. 4 (111–34, esp. 115–20, 131–2), ch. 5 (135–70, esp. 143), ch. 6 (171–223, esp. 171–7, 182, 203 [surplice], 218–19 [Oath of Allegiance]), ch. 7 (224–64, esp. 239–41), ch. 8 (265–326, esp. 265–7 [kneeling]); Parker, *A Defence*, 80, 605, 628–30, 637, 659–60, 682, 718; Parker, *Preface*, c6r–v, c8r; Parker, *Reproof*, 12–13, 304–8, 315, 320, 415–16, 421, 424–6, 431–2, 449, 458–9.

84 Cf. Tomkins, *Inconveniencies*, 25; Vernon, *Letter to a Friend*, 11–31.

85 Parker, *Reproof*, 449, 458–9; cf. 12–13, 158, 291–4, 304–8, 315, 320, 415–16, 424–6. See also Parker, *Preface*, a4v, a7r, c1v, c6r–c8r, d2v, e4v–e5r.

86 Parker, *Defence*, 628–30, 637–9; cf. 659–60, 682, 562, 577, 584 (emphasis mine). He most likely refers to the Oaths of Allegiance and Supremacy, Protestation, and Covenant.

87 See, e.g., Parker, *Defence*, 629: "Men that own the peculiar and distinguishing Principle of your [John Owen's] Party, are not fit to be trusted or endured in any Commonwealth." "Trusted" might refer just to holding public office, but "endured in any Commonwealth" seems to call for expulsion from the British polity.

88 Parker, *Defence*, 637–9.

89 E.g., Hickeringill, *Gregory, Father-Greybeard*, 55, 58, 140–5.

90 Parker, *Reproof*, 309–10, 427, 429–35, 442–3, 443ff.

91 Marvell, *RT*, 248.

92 *A Common-Place-Book out of The Rehearsal Transpros'd*, 43–4, 52. For the appearance of the relevant clause in the oaths required by the Corporation, Uniformity, Vestry, Militia, and Five Mile Acts, see *Book of Oaths* (1689), 232–4, 238. MPs like Marvell did not have to take these oaths unless they held other public office; they merely took the Oaths of Allegiance and Supremacy, which contained language promising to defend the monarch against rebellions (36–7).

93 Hickeringill, *Gregory, Father-Greybeard*, 55, 23, 143.

94 Butler, *The Transproser Rehears'd*, 108. For earlier evocations of "King Conscience," see Wild, *The Loyal Nonconformist*, line 18, and the anonymous reply, *Swearing and Lying* (1666), line 16, both in *POAS*, 1:303, 308.

95 Marvell, *RT*, 276; Legouis, *Andrew Marvell*, 145 ("Marvell, even if he did not join in 'remonstrating the Declaration', as his arch-enemy was soon to accuse him of having done, no doubt welcomed the Test Bill."); Legouis, *André Marvell*, 273 and n. 180 ("Quelle fut l'attitude de Marvell lorsque ce projet de loi vint en discussion devant les Communes [the Test Bill]? Très probablement il lui donna son approbation silencieuse," because "La majorité en faveur de l'*Epreuve* était si écrasante qu'il n'y eut pas de vote par division"). Marvell probably took the Test after 28 April 1673, when the Test certificates were printed (*AMC*, 142–3). He admits taking it in *RT*, 276. Cf. John Patrick Montaño's claim in *Courting the Moderates*, 172, that Marvell "denounced the Declaration [of Indulgence] solely on constitutional grounds in his brilliant piece of mockery, *The Rehearsal Transpros'd*. He considered it, as he had the Conventicles Act of 1670, 'the Quintessence of Arbitrary Malice.'" But "denounced" is not quite right: Marvell wanted indulgence and might have accepted a royal one if it was the only option. In fact, he had already accepted it in Part I of *The Rehearsal Transpros'd*. Montaño's claim is a better description of Part II, which does hint at doubts about the royal prerogative and indulging power and does suggest that a parliamentary indulgence would be preferable.

96 Wallace, *Destiny His Choice*, 191.

97 Ibid.

98 Spurr, *England in the 1670s*, 19; *JHC*, 9:217 (11 March 71): "The ingrossed Bill to prevent the Growth of Popery was read. A Clause, for an Oath to be taken, for not taking up Arms, by Pretence of the King's Authority, against His Person, was thrice read. The Question being put, That this Clause be made Part of the Bill; It was resolved in the Affirmative. *Resolved*, &c. That the Bill do pass: And that the Title be, An Act to prevent the Growth of Popery: And Sir *Thomas Meres* is to carry up the Bill to the Lords." The precise target of this oath is not entirely clear – perhaps all adult male Catholics, perhaps officeholders, perhaps the entire adult male population. There was supposed to be a conference with the Lords on the bill on 13 March, but if it took place, no record of its results appears in the *JHL* 12:453 (13 March 1671); the Lords read the bill for the first time on 17 March and sent it to committee on 24 March, where it appears to have died (12:460–1, 468–9). The *JHL* 12:453–4 (11 and 13 March 1671) and *JHC* 9:217–18 (13 March 1671) mention a parliamentary petition against the growth of popery that was presented to Charles on 13 March; the king replied "That He would presently issue out His Proclamation for the banishing of Popish Priests and Jesuits, and give Charge that the Laws against Popery should be put in Execution; and that He would take all the Care He could, for suppressing the Growth of Popery." A new Test oath for MPs alone had been envisaged by the Anglican royalists in Parliament as early as 1669 but seems never to have made it to the floor. See Montaño, *Courting the Moderates*, 255, 263.

99 Humfrey, *Comprehension Promoted*; Baxter, *RB*, Part III, 110–11.

100 Marvell, *The Loyal Scot*, ll. 218, 226.

101 Parker, *Discourse*, 308.

102 Parker, *Discourse*, ch. 8 (265–326, esp. 308–9); cf. ch. 1 (1–64), ch. 3 (87–110), ch. 6 (171–223).

103 Marvell, *RT*, 99 (I have italicized "he").

104 *Book of Oaths* (1689), 233–4.

105 Marvell, *RT*, 193.

106 Ibid., 104. As the Yale editors mention, "the March-Licenses" were the permissions granted to Nonconformist ministers to preach after the Declaration of Indulgence in March 1672.

107 Patrick, *Friendly Debate*, 107, 111–12, 116, 233; Patrick, *Further Continuation*, 3–4, 9, 278–9, 349–51; Patrick, *Appendix*, 123–33; Fullwood, *Doctrine of Schism*, 167–8; Parker, *Discourse*, iv, xiii–xviii, "xxv–xxvi," 76, 225–8,

240–53; Parker, *Defence*, ch.1 (1–99, esp. 2–3, 27, 41, 46, 81, 86), ch. 2 (100–213), 495, 584, 607; Parker, *Preface*, a7v, c6r, d5v; Parker, *Reproof*, 306–8, 342–3, 393–7; *Common-Place-Book*, 4, 55; Butler, *Transproser Rehears'd*, 13–14, 102–4; Hickeringill, *Gregory, Father-Greybeard*, 25, 57, 63–76, 218, 236–313.

108 These defenses of his own loyalty are not just, as Chernaik, *The Poet's Time*, 92, argues,"blinds to avoid prosecution or get round the censorship."

109 Marvell, *RT*, 81–2.

110 Ibid., 82.

111 Ibid., 116.

112 Martin Dzelzainis and Annabel Patterson, introduction to Part II of *The Rehearsal Transpros'd*, in *PWAM*, 1:210; Marvell, *P&L*, 2:120. Cf. the text of the Second Conventicles Act: "Charles II, 1670: An Act to prevent and suppresse Seditious Conventicles," in *Statutes of the Realm*, 5:648–51.

113 Marvell, *RT*, 82.

114 This may be why, after 1673 and before the prose tracts of 1676–7, Catholics like Roger Palmer celebrated Marvell's achievement in the book; see *AMC*, 149. Marvell's opposition to the anti-Catholic Test was perhaps much clearer to them than it is to us.

115 Wolseley, *Liberty of Conscience*, 66, 58; Norton, *Humble Apology*, 123; Baxter, *Sacrilegious Desertion*, 136; Walsh, *The Advocate of Conscience*, 139–43, 127; cf. 176–93. See also Owen's near-paraphrase of the Oaths of Allegiance and Supremacy in *Peace-Offering*, 13–14.

116 Norton, *Humble Apology*, 124.

117 Norton, *Humble Apology*, A2r–v; Baxter, *Sacrilegious Desertion*, 136.

118 Norton, *Humble Apology*, A8r.

119 [Rolls], *Sober Answer*, 5; Humfrey, *Comprehension Promoted*, 7.

120 Wild, *The Loyal Nonconformist* (1666) lists various things that Wild will swear and not swear. He will swear to defend the king; he admits that he "owe[s] assistance to the King by oath." See Wild, *The Loyal Nonconformist*, ll. 29, 81, in *POAS*, 1:303. This position is attacked in the anonymous reply to Wild's poem: *Swearing and Lying*, l. 77 ("In fine you must not sever Church and State"), *POAS*, 1:311. He will not, however, swear approval of the ecclesiastical courts and the clerical surplice. And in stanza 4, he alters the non-alteration clause of the Five Mile oath, which read, "I A.B. do swear, That it is not Lawful upon any pretence whatsoever, to take Arms against the King, And that *I do abhor the Traiterous position of taking Arms by his Authority against his Person, or against those that are Commissioned by him, in pursuance of such Commissions;*

And that *I will not at any time endeavour any Alteration of Government either in Church or State*. So help me God" (emphasis mine). In Wild's poem this becomes "I never will endeavour alteration / Of monarchy nor of that royal name / Which God hath chosen to command this nation, / But will maintain his person, crown, and fame." See the *Book of Oaths* (1689), 238; Wild, *The Loyal Nonconformist*, ll. 13–16. Not only does this mix in a bit of the Oath of Allegiance (see the *Book of Oaths* [1689], 37), it essentially swears the clauses common to the Five Mile, Uniformity, Corporation, and Militia oaths (the italicized passage above), while leaving out the promise never to take up arms against the king. In the next stanza he specifies that if the king commands something contrary to conscience, Wild will only obey passively (ll. 17–20). Perhaps most important is the fact that what Wild endeavours never to alter is "monarchy" and "that royal name / Which God hath chosen to command this nation." This is much more restricted than the Five Mile oath's promise never to alter anything at all in church or state. He has left out the church, most obviously; and he has left out the "any" in "any Alteration," which leaves room for attempts to reform both church and state in modest ways; it is not a blanket condemnation of any and all attempts to change them. Over all, Wild separates church from state, promising, "The civil government I will obey" (l. 29).

121 Sturgion, *A Plea for Tolleration*, 8. Cf. JVCO, *Amsterdam: Toleration, or No Toleration*, 36: "*Non-conformists* [request:] 'May it please your Majesty that we have liberty to joyn with our people in pure Worship and Ordinances, giving good security that we neither speak nor do anything publickly against the established order of the Kingdom'"; "giving good security" presumably implies "without oaths." Quakers, of course, attacked all oaths.

122 Parker, *Defence*, 637–9.

123 Marvell, *RT*, 161–2.

124 Ibid., 117.

125 Ibid., 117 n. 422.

126 Ibid., 181–8.

127 Ibid., 186. The quotation marks are Marvell's.

128 Rushworth, *Historical Collections*, 434–55ff.; Marvell, *RT*, 188.

129 The full passage in Rushworth, *Historical Collections*, 455, reads, "But when I saw the Instructions, the Refusers should be sent away for Soldiers to the King of *Denmark*, I began to remember *Urias*, that was set in the fore-front of the Battel; and to speak truth, I durst not be tender in it. And when afterwards I saw, that men were to be put to their Oath,

with whom they had conference, and whether any did disswade them? And yet further beheld, that divers were to be imprisoned: I thought this was somewhat a New World."

130 Marvell, *RT*, 276.

131 Indeed, his quotation of Parker's quotation of the Declaration's reference to "*several Statutes and Acts of Parliament*" may signal that Marvell regards the king's powers, in both religious and civil affairs, as given or delegated to him by Parliament.

132 Marvell, *Flecknoe, an English Priest at Rome* (ca. 1646), ll. 51–62, 97–101, in *Poems*, ed. Smith, 171–2. Cf. *The Loyal Scot* (ca. 1667–73), ll. 120–1, in the same volume.

133 Marvell, *RT*, 248. In quoting this passage, I have retained the words that the Yale editors' copytext for *The Rehearsal Transpros'd* (no. 72a) cancelled from the previous impression (no. 72), removing the brackets they place around the words.

134 *A Common-Place-Book out of The Rehearsal Transpros'd*, 52.

135 Ibid., 428.

136 Marvell, *RT*, 428.

137 Ibid., 279.

138 Ibid., 280.

139 Ibid., 278 n. 292.

140 Ibid., 279–80.

141 Marvell, *The Loyal Scot*, ll. 216–26, in *Poems*, ed. Smith, 410 (the epigraph for this chapter).

142 Marvell, *P&L*, 2:226.

143 An Act for Exempting their Majestyes Protestant Subjects dissenting from the Church of England from the Penalties of certaine Lawes (1689), *Statutes of the Realm*, 6:75 ("I A B doe *sincerely promise* and *solemnely declare* before God and the World that I will be true and faithfull to King William and Queene Mary").

144 Parker, *Reasons for Abrogating the Test*. On this odd book, mostly taken up with arguments about transsubstantiation and idolatry, see Schochet, "Between Lambeth and Leviathan," 206–8.

145 They place the issue of secular allegiance in an oath separate from the one about the king's civil and religious supremacies. A major point of the Oath of Allegiance is that the pope cannot interfere in subjects' allegiance to the English king. The Oath of Supremacy, while saying nothing about religious doctrine, only speaks to religious discipline in naming the king as final arbiter of religious issues, just as he is of civil ones; it does not mention an episcopal church or say unequivocally that the civil and

religious realms are identical. Chapter 3 will put the term "secular" under some pressure.

146 *JHC*, 9:280–1 (29 March 1673).

147 Montaño, *Courting the Moderates*, 215, 271, 277 and 277n. 13. Marvell refers to the "Test for the Members that they had not been bribed": Marvell, *P&L*, 2:242 (18 June 1678); *JHC*, 9:500–1 (18 June 1678); Grey, *Debates*, 6:103–5 (18 June 1678). It failed to go to committee on a vote of 100 to 86.

148 Everett, "The Shooting of the Bears," 68.

### 3 An Horatian Oath: The *Horatian Ode*, Secularism, and Toleration

1 Marvell, *P&L*, 1:295 (Margoliouth's commentary).

2 Legouis, *André Marvell*, 34 ("il n'y a rien de chrétien dans cette ode"), and *Andrew Marvell*, 15 ("There is nothing Christian in this ode"), 17 n. 1 ("the pagan character" of the *Ode*); Marvell, *P&L*, 1:301 (Legouis's commentary). Cf. Brooks, "Criticism and Literary History," 205; Bush, "Marvell's Horatian Ode," 367.

3 Mazzeo, "Cromwell as Davidic King," 55. Cf. his earlier "Cromwell as Machiavellian Prince," 2, 9.

4 Warren Chernaik, "Was Marvell a Republican?" 90, which repeats his earlier discussion of the poem's "classical, secular framework," a framework "secular rather than Christian," in *The Poet's Time*, 18, 43–5. Cf. Norbrook, *Writing the English Republic*, 265–6.

5 See, e.g., Worden, "The Question of Secularism," 20–40, and *God's Instruments*, 325.

6 Wallace, *Destiny His Choice*, 43–105.

7 Cf. Everett, "Shooting of the Bears," 86; Bush, "Marvell's Horatian Ode," 367–8; Judith Richards, "Literary History," 33–9.

8 McDowell, *Poetry and Allegiance*, 208–37, and "Marvell among the Cromwellians," 482–3, 488. While I largely agree with Nicholas von Maltzahn's claim in "Milton, Marvell, and Toleration," 86, that Marvell's brand of toleration during the Restoration has it "that contending faiths might agree to disagree, or even turn a blind eye on each other, with religion increasingly construed as a private practice tolerable within a secular state," I do not see Marvell and Milton as so far apart in this respect.

9 Cooper, *Thesaurus Linguae Latinae & Britannicae*, s.v. *seculum*.

10 "Secular," *OED*; Edward Phillips, *The New World of English Words*, s.v. *secular*; Blount, *Glossographia*, s.v. *secular* and *secular priests*; Miege, *A New Dictionary English and French*, s.v. *seculier* and *seculierement*; Wilkins, *An Essay towards a Real Character*, 284–5 and Index under *secular* and *temporal*.

11 See, e.g., "Secular Humanism," *OED*.

12 Dryden, *The Secular Masque*, in *John Dryden: Selected Poems*, 515–18; Horace, *Carmen Saeculare*, lines 21–2, in *The Odes and Epodes*, 352–3. Cf. Syfret, "Marvell's 'Horatian Ode,'" 169, 171; Everett, "Shooting of the Bears," 80.

13 Horace, *Odes*, 4.6.41–4 and 4.2.41–4.

14 Horace, *Odes*, 1.37.21–32; 4.2.33–48; 4.5.1–16. See Syfret, "Marvell's 'Horatian Ode,'" 169–70; Coolidge, "Marvell and Horace," 113, 116–17.

15 Dryden, *Secular Masque*, ll. 91–2.

16 Danet, *A Complete Dictionary*, s.v. "Seculares Ludi" (Qqq4v, Rrr1r). For a similar modern argument, see Landmann, "Die Aufteilung der Chöre," 179. For an opposing view, see Putnam, *Horace's Carmen Saeculare*, 97.

17 Hobbes, *Leviathan*, 555, 561, 589, 633.

18 Hobbes, *De Cive*, translated by Charles Cotton as *Philosophicall Rudiments Concerning Government and Society. Or, A Dissertation Conerning Man in his Severall Habitudes and Respects, as the Member of a Society, first Secular, and then Sacred*, title page, 208, 215, 254 (quotation), 256, 266, 330, 341. Cf. the original Latin edition of *De Cive* (1642), 155, 159, 188–90, 197, 249, 258.

19 The Civil War-era bookseller and book collector George Thomason's dates for the two parts of Hobbes's *The Elements of Law* are 2 February 1650 (the first thirteen chapters, entitled *Humane Nature*) and 4 May 1650 (the rest of it, entitled *De Corpore Politico*). When I supply specific dates in subsequent notes, they are either the days on which Thomason bought the text or the ones mentioned in the texts or on their title pages themselves as the time of completion – whichever comes first.

20 Hobbes, *De Cive* (*Philosophicall Rudiments*), 226–7. Cf. *Leviathan*, 203, 395–6, 401.

21 Connell, "Marvell, Milton, and the Protectoral Church Settlement," 563; McDowell, *Poetry and Allegiance*, 234, 237 (Marvell as Erastian).

22 Marvell, *RT*, 414, 329, 162; cf. 58, 182, 198, 250, 347, 357, 371, 390, 392. Milton sounds a similar note in *Paradise Lost*, lamenting priests who exercise "Secular power" and "force" "Spiritual laws . . . On every conscience." See Milton, *Paradise Lost*, ed. Alastair Fowler, 12.517–21. All subsequent references are to this edition and appear in-text. Cf. his unpublished sonnet to Cromwell (1652), ll. 11–12 ("new foes arise / Threat'ning to bind our souls with secular chains"), in *John Milton: The Complete Poems*, ed. Leonard, 114.

23 Marvell, *AGP*, 233.

24 Marvell, *RT*, 296. Marvell's "&" probably parodies the infamous Etcetera Oath of 1640. Sarah Barber assumes that the Engagement was meant to be taken by all adults, including women. See her *Regicide and Republicanism*, 180 and n. 22. Cf. Vallance, *Revolutionary England*, 169.

25 With apologies to Taylor, for reasons of coherence I reverse the order of his first two categories and substitute the term "secularism" for his "secularity" in all three cases.
26 Charles Taylor, *A Secular Age*, 2. In Taylor's taxonomy this is "Secularity 2."
27 Taylor, *Secular Age*, 1–2. In Taylor's taxonomy this is "Secularity 1."
28 Taylor, *Secular Age*, 3.
29 Schmitt, *The Concept of the Political* and *Political Theology*.
30 See my introduction above, n. 43.
31 Taylor's unacknowledged Marxist point is that secularism is no less an ideology than religion; it has simply replaced one ideology with another.
32 We might see this as a kind of tolerationism originating from a place opposite to that of its counterpart in seventeenth-century England. Instead of opening the public sphere, jobs, and education to a wider range of religious believers (still Protestant in the rather limited Toleration Act of 1689), Taylor would have modern states open themselves up beyond their secular elites to welcome a plurality of secular and religious voices in public deliberations. Even if the state remains secular, society does not have to, although Taylor disagrees with Habermas and others about how far religion should extend into public life. Should parliamentary debates, texts of laws, and official government declarations include (substantial) religious content, for example? See Charles Taylor, "Why We Need a Radical Redefinition of Secularism," 35, 49–50, 56, 57–8 n. 11, and "Western Secularity," 36; Jürgen Habermas, "'The Political'" and "Dialogue," 23, 26, 64–6.
33 Garganigo, "Mourning the Headless Body Politic."
34 For Hobbes's materialist account of forces and force, see *The Elements of Law*, 24–6, 43–4, 48–60, 70–3, 77–81; *De Cive* (*Philosophicall Rudiments*), B4v, 6, 8–15; *Leviathan*, Part I, esp. 81–99, 108–9, 118–19, 150–68, 185–8.
35 See n. 6 above. Cf. Worden, "Andrew Marvell, Oliver Cromwell, and the Horatian Ode," 158–9, 169, 176.
36 Wallace, "The Engagement Controversy."
37 James I, *Triplici Nodo*, 26–7, qtd. in Ascham, *Of the Confusions and Revolutions*, 125. Cf. Ascham, *A Reply*, 15, which employs the word "secular" in relation to the same passage in James's *Apologie*. Earlier versions of the Engagement apparently had contained references to God as witness and thus to its own oathiness. See Barber, *Regicide and Republicanism*, 181–2, and "The Engagement," 53.
38 Dury, *Just Reproposals* (before 7 January 1650), 17–18, *The Unchanged, Constant and Single-hearted Peace-Maker* (30 May 1650), 16, and *Objections . . . Answered (9 June 1650)*, 16–17, A2v. See also T.B., *The Engagement Vindicated* (7 January

1649/50), 8–9; Ascham, *Of the Confusions and Revolutions*, 125, 158–9, and *A Reply*, 2, 15, 17–18; Warren, *The Royalist Reform'd* (26 November 1649), 28, 15; Goodwin, *Englands Apology* (17 February 1651), 35; Saunders, *Plenary Possession* (19 May 1651), 2–3, 8, 20; Rocket, *The Christian Subject* (16 November 1651), 43, 65, 78; Osborne, *A Perswasive* (1 January 1651/2), 40.

39 T.B., *The Engagement Vindicated*, 3, 7–9.

40 Nedham, *Case of the Common-Wealth*, 1st ed. (8 May 1650), 25–32 (although he does also refer to oaths as religious); Henry Parker, *Scotlands Holy War* (17 January 1650/1), 70.

41 Henry Hall, *Digitus Testium* (12 January 1651), 19. Cf. *Severall Proceedings in Parliament* 14 (28 December 1649–4 January 1650), 180; Crouch, *The Man in the Moon* 48 (13–20 March 1650), 372. Aucher, *Arguments and Reasons* (14 February 1650), 8, regarded the Engagement as a religious, if sinful, act precisely because it was an oath.

42 Wallace, *Destiny His Choice*, 43–68; Zagorin, *A History of Political Thought*, 62–7, 70; Skinner, "History and Ideology," and "The Ideological Context," 295, 298–9, 301, 303–15. For qualified confirmation of Skinner's argument about the Engagers' de factoism, see Barber, *Regicide and Republicanism*, 187–9, though she, like Vallance, acknowledges the diversity of arguments for and against the Engagement. See also Scott, *Commonwealth Principles*, 259.

43 Condren, *Argument and Authority*, 295–308, 313, and "Marvell's 'Horatian Ode,'" 258–65 (quotations on 263–5).

44 Burgess, "Usurpation," 515–16; Vallance, *Revolutionary England*, 161–78. The importance of Providence in the Engagement debate had, of course, already been acknowledged by Wallace, "Engagement Controversy," 384, 387, 395–6, 399, 401–4.

45 For *pro-Engagement* texts that make *both* de facto and de jure arguments, see Rous, *Lavvfulnes of Obeying the Present Government*, 2nd ed. (after 25 July 1649), 6, 9–11, 15, 20–2, 25; Ascham, *Of the Confusions and Revolutions* (November 1649), 115–18, 131, 137, 157, 159; Dury, *Considerations Concerning the Engagement* (4 November 1649), 14–20; Dury, *Just Reproposals* (before 7 January 1650), 3, 13; T.B., *Engagement Vindicated* (7 January 1650), title page, 7, 9–10; Ascham, *A Reply to a Paper of Dr Sandersons* (9 January 1650), 4–6, 11–12; N.W., *A Discourse Concerning the Engagement* (29 January 1650), 5, 7–8, 14, 20; *A Logical Demonstration* (30 January 1650), 4–5; [Dury,] *A Disingag'd Survey of the Engagement* (7 February 16450), 1, 20–2; Du Moulin, *The Power of the Christian Magistrate* (before 25 February 1650), 21, 25, 27, 62–3; [Charles Herle,] *The Exercitation Answered* (3 April 1650), title page, 1, 36–8, 42–55; Nedham, *Case of the Common-Wealth*, 1st ed. (8 May 1650), 6, 18–19, 21, 23–4, 30; Dury, *Two Treatises* (24 May 1650), 61,

24, 34, 60–1; Nedham, *Case of the Common-Wealth*, 2nd ed. (4 July 1650), 103, 108, 110; Dury, *A Second Parcel* (ca. 19 October 1650), 22, 25; Henry Parker, *Scotlands Holy War* (17 January 1651), 67–8; Saunders, *Plenary Possession Makes a Lawfull Power* (19 May 1651), title page, 2, 6, 9, 21; Drew, *The Northern Subscribers Plea* (August 1651), 7, 10, 25, 29, 33, 36, 43, 45, 59–61; Thomas Carre (Miles Pinkney?), *A Treatise of Subjection* (1651), 4, 6–7, 11, 15, 17, 35, 50–1, 55. I present these texts in chronological order with dates in order to demonstrate which ones Marvell could have read before writing the *Horatian Ode* in June–July 1650. For the date of the second edition of Nedham's *Case of the Common-Wealth*, see n. 75 below.

For *anti-Engagement* texts that make *both* de facto and de jure arguments, see Ward, *Grand Case of Conscience* (22 June 1649), 3–9; Gee, *Exercitation* (18 December 1649), title page, 1, 12, 48–51; Reynolds, *Humble Proposals* (19 December 1649), 1–2, 4; Aucher, *Arguments and Reasons* (14 February 1650), title page, 3; Gee, *Vindication* (14 February 1650), 40–2; Ward, *Discolliminium* (15 February 1650), 32–3; *Pack of Old Puritans* (22 February 1650), title page, 17, 23; Gee, *Plea for Non-Scribers* (11 June 1650), 1:11–12, 19, 29, 37–9; 2:24, 26, 30–1, 47–9.

46 Condren, *Argument and Authority*, 298, is right to say that "there was no *de facto* camp of theorists" in the Engagement controversy, "but there was . . . an increasingly shared *de facto* idiom of accusation." Yet there was a difference of emphasis, the Engagers accenting the de facto.

Engagers: Rous, *Lavvfulnes*, 2nd ed., 1, 6, 9–11, 15, 20–2, 25; Ascham, *Of the Confusions and Revolutions*, 3, 10, 47–50, 115–18, 131, 137, 157–9; Ascham, *A Combate* (2 July 1649), 11, 17; Ascham, *Bounds & Bonds of Publique Obedience* (27 August 1649), 2–3, 16, 18–19, 24, 30–1, 66; Ascham, *Reply*, 4, 6, 10–12; Dury, *Considerations*, 14–20; Dury, *Just Reproposals*, 3, 13; Dury, *Disingag'd Survey*, 4, 6, 20–2; Dury, *Two Treatises Concerning the Matter of the Engagement* (24 May 1650), 34, 50–1, 60; Dury, *Objections against the Taking of the Engagement Answered* (9 June 1650), 2–5, 15–16, 21, 23; Nedham, *Case of the Common-Wealth*, 1st ed., 6; Warren, *Royalist Reform'd*, 8, 26, 28, 42; *A Brief Resolution of That Grand Case of Conscience* (probably after 9 January 1650), 5–6. Cf. the Anti-Engager Edward Gee, *Plea*, 1:34 on the rhetorical strategy of the Engagers, esp. Ascham: "the principall Advocates for this Power [the Commonwealth] argue for submission and obedience to it, under the notion of unlawfull."

Anti-Engagers: Gee, *Exercitation*, title page, 1, 12, 48-51; Gee, *Vindication*, 40–2; Gee, *Plea*, 1:11–12, 19, 26, 29, 34, 37–9; 2:24, 26, 30–1, 47–9; Ward, *Grand Case of Conscience*, 3–9; Ward, *Discolliminium*, 32–3; Ward, *A Religious Demurrer* (4 May 1649), 2–3, 5, 7; *Vox Veritatis*, 31.

47 Cf. Patterson, *Marvell: The Writer in Public Life*, 36 ("Truthful evaluation").

48 Worden, *The Rump Parliament*, 229. Cf. Barber, *Regicide and Republicanism*, 181–3.

49 E.g., *Severall Proceedings in Parliament* 14 (28 December 1649–4 January 1650), 180; Warren, *Royalist Reform'd*, 4, 8, 15, 22, 26, 28; Ascham, *Of the Confusions and Revolutions*, 19, 22, 24, 106, 124–5, 135, 139, 159; Ascham, *Reply*, 2, 5–6, 12, 15, 17; Ascham, *Genesis kai Telos Exousias: The Original and End of Civil Power* (8 May 1649), title page; Goodwin, *Englands Apology*, 35; Saunders, *Plenary Possession*, 2–3, 8, 20; Rocket, *Christian Subject*, 43, 65, 78, 124, 149; Carre (Pinkney?), *Treatise of Subjection*, 42, 51–2; Drew, *Northern Subscribers Plea*, 9, 33, 56; Dury, *Case of Conscience Resolved* (15 March 1649), title page, 28; Grey, *Vox Coeli* (23 July 1649), 6, 37; R[obert] Fletcher, *Radius Heliconicus* (28 February 1650), 1. See McCrea, "Reason's Muse," 665 n. 39, for the identification of Fletcher as the author of *Radius Heliconicus*. Of Carre, we should, however, note Wallace's caution in "Engagement Controversy," 405, that "This Carre should not be confused, as he is in Wing, with the pseudonym for Miles Pinckney."

50 Carre (Pinkney?), *A Treatise of Subjection*, 14.

51 See their *ODNB* entries, as well as their writings in support of the Rump and the Engagement: Winstanley, *Englands Spirit Unfoulded. Or an Incouragement to Take the Engagement*, in *The Complete Works of Gerrard Winstanley*, 2:161–7; cf. 1:51; George Wither, *Respublica Anglicana* (28 October 1650) (which responds to Clement Walker's latest salvo against Independents), title page, 14, 31; Du Moulin, *The Power of the Christian Magistrate*, 5, 74; Grey, *Vox Coeli* (dedicated to Fairfax and Cromwell), 8–9, 47. Du Moulin would go on to write a number of tracts in support of Independency, with a toleration for Presbyterianism and Episcopacy, and to enjoy the support of Cromwell and his chaplain, John Owen, whom he knew as a fellow professor at Oxford in the 1650s. For Milton, see, e.g., his 1652 sonnets to Cromwell ("Cromwell, our chief of men"), ll. 12–14, and Sir Henry Vane ("Vane, young in years"), ll. 9–14, in *John Milton: The Complete Poems*, 113–14, and the remarks on separation of church and state from the early 1650s in his commonplace book, in *YP*, 1:476. Milton may, in fact, echo the *Horatian Ode* in this sonnet (see Hirst and Zwicker, *Andrew Marvell: Orphan of the Hurricane*, 171 n. 23 and the arguments cited there), and thus its tolerationist argument.

As for Dury, while William Prynne, *The Time-Serving Proteus*, title page, called him an Independent, Dury represented himself in *The Unchanged, Constant and Single-hearted Peace-Maker* as a supporter of the broad, pan-European Protestant cause, with great tolerance for differences in non-essentials: "Ceremonies . . . ought not to be made a matter of strife, but might harmlessly be used, or also inoffensively not used according to circumstances, because *circumstantials* are by the Apostle *left free to every church*" (6, my emphasis). Overall, he resisted labels: "It is most false that I have been metamorphosed from a *Prelaticall* to a *Presbyterian*, and from that to an *Independent* Professor. I have ever endeavoured and professed my self to be *extra partes*" (11). For a different opinion about Dury's religious beliefs ("basically a Presbyterian"), see Wallace, "Engagement Controversy," 399.

Francis Rous, provost of Eton, where Marvell would soon encounter a number of Independent divines, was, according to the title page of both editions of his *Lawfulness of Obeying the Present Government* (1649), a Presbyterian. But soon thereafter he turned Independent, according to the *ODNB*.

52 Vicars, *Dagon Demolished*, 8, 12 (quotation on 12); cf. 11. Thomason dates *Dagon Demolished* to 12 April 1660, a time when some in Parliament were clearly trying to prevent the Restoration by reviving the Engagement with its rejection of monarchy. But *Dagon Demolished* must have been written before Vicars's death in 1652.

53 Clement Walker, *The High Court of Justice*, 15–17, 30 ("these engaged, Independent Comissioners of the High Court of Justice"). Cf. T.M.'s continuation of Walker: *The History of Independency*, 10–11. For Walker's imprisonment, see his entry in the *ODNB*. For other anti-Engagers who attacked the new regime as dominated by Independents, see *Vox Veritatis* (16 November 1650), 3–5.

54 Parker, *Reproof*, 420. See also the royalist newsbook writer John Crouch's more immediate response to the dissemination of the Engagement in 1650: *The Man in the Moon* 37 (2–9 January 1650): 293, 297.

55 One critic even alleged that the Engagement was friendly to Catholics: Henry Hall, *Digitus Testium*, 29.

56 Prynne, *A Brief Apologie* (18 February 1650), 11.

57 For the composition of the Rump's Engagement committee, see *JHC*, 6:307, 321, 326, 337–9; cf. the other Independents mentioned in connection with the Engagement at 6:370, 413, 432. For their religious views, see the *ODNB* entries for everyone in the following two lists, as well as Worden, *Rump Parliament*, 128–9, 206, 297, 299.

Independents: Daniel Blagrave, Thomas Challoner, Lord Grey of Groby, Sir Arthur Hesilrige, Cornelius Holland, John Hutchinson, Edmund Ludlow, Henry Marten, Herbert Morley, Richard Salwey, Algernon Sidney, Anthony Stapley, Sir Henry Vane the Younger, John Venn, John Weaver, Bulstrode Whitelocke.

Sectaries or MPs favourable to them: John Fry, Thomas Harrison, John Jones, Nathaniel Rich, Walter Strickland.

58 See their *ODNB* entries, as well as Worden, *Rump Parliament*, 123. Since Worden describes Corbet as oscillating between Presbyterianism and Independency, I place him in the category of tolerant Presbyterians.

59 See their *ODNB* biographies, as well as Worden, *Rump Parliament*, 128–9, 132. On Sidney in particular, see his *Court Maxims*, 95, 105, and Winship, "Algernon Sidney's Calvinist Republicanism," 755–7, 760–2, 764.

60 Hirst and Zwicker, *Andrew Marvell*, 12 n. 5, suggest a date of August 1650. On similarities between between Nedham's writing and the *Horatian Ode*, see Duncan Jones, "The Erect Sword"; Worden, *Literature and Politics*, 66–9, 86–100. For Hobbes and the *Ode*, see, for example, Worden, *Literature and Politics*, 104–5; Wortham, "Marvell's Cromwell Poems," 24–9.

61 As Joad Raymond puts it in his *ODNB* article on Nedham, in the latter's political thought, "Fundamental to stability" under a republic with a mixed constitution "was a separation between church and state, and he was prepared to endorse a national church and tithes provided liberty of conscience was simultaneously protected; he rarely wrote about religion, perhaps because it was a divisive topic." Cf. Raymond, "Marchamont Nedham," 389, 378, 383.

62 Nedham, *Independencie No Schisme*, 2–3, and *Case of the Kingdom Stated*, A2r–v, 4–5, 8 10–11.

63 Nedham, *Case of the Common-Wealth*, 1st ed., 61–8 (quotation on 67).

64 Ibid., 89, 91.

65 Ibid., 90–1. Cf. Worden, *Literature and Politics*, 347: Nedham "occasionally suspended, under the Rump, his normal Erastian posture."

66 Hobbes, *Leviathan*, 711.

67 Richard Tuck, introduction to the Cambridge edition of Hobbes's *Leviathan*, xxiii–xxiv, and "The Civil Religion of Thomas Hobbes," 137; Jeffrey Collins, *The Allegiance of Thomas Hobbes*, 4–7, 123–30, 143, 145–6; Curley, "Hobbes and the Cause of Religious Toleration," 309–10, 322–6; Parkin, *Taming the Leviathan*, 92. For the opposite view, see Sommerville, "Hobbes and Independency."

68 Hobbes, *Leviathan*, 712–13, 524, 530, 577–86, 537, 575–6, 609–26, 663, 700; *A Dialogue between a Philosopher and a Student of the Common Laws of England*, in *The English Works of Thomas Hobbes*, 6:96–129; Sommerville, "Hobbes and Independency," 166–70.

69 Jon Parkin, "Liberty Transpros'd," 269–70, 275, 279–83.

70 Marvell, *RT*, 208 (editors' introduction), 275. For a different view, see McDowell, "Marvell among the Cromwellians," 491.

71 Marvell, *RT*, 275, 277, 316–17, 324–30, 334–5, 341–6. Marvell insinuates his suspicions of the royal prerogative in matters spiritual, despite protesting

that "I despair not [yet] of seeing" toleration arrive "by Gods goodness and the influence of his Majesty, upon the prudence and moderation of my Lords the Bishops" (435).

72 Marvell, *RT*, 301–2, 329–30, 333, 420.

73 Marvell, *RT*, 302–12, 317, 343, 379–81. It seems that Marvell was willing to make common cause with but not commit himself wholly to whoever might forward the cause of toleration: Cromwell, Presbyterians, the king, the Commons, or the Lords.

74 Hobbes, *Elements of Law*, 69–70, 142–51, 153, 159–60, 180–1; *De Cive* (*Philosophicall Rudiments*), 179–80, 194, 197–9, 211–15, 244, 250, 255, 286, 296–7, 310–11, 334, 342–3, 347–57.

75 Nedham, *Case of the Common-Wealth*, 2nd ed., 110–11. We can date the second edition to July 4 because Nedham advertised it in *Mercurius Politicus* 4 (27 June–4 July 1650), 64.

76 Hill, *God's Englishman*, 121, 185, 188, 190, 206, 213–14, 257; Gaunt, *Oliver Cromwell*, 54–5, 57–8, 62–3, 69–70, 107–8, 121, 125–6, 129–30, 173, 179, 186, 191, 195, 197, 205, 235–8; Worden, *The English Civil Wars*, 116, 128–33, 135–6; Coward, *The Stuart Age*, 255–7, 266–70, 273–4.

77 Moore, "The Irony of Marvell's Horatian Ode," 40–1, hears the *Ode*'s account of "temples" being "rent" in ll. 21–2 as a reference to Cromwell's Independency.

78 Foxley, "Oliver Cromwell on Religion and Resistance," 226; Worden, *God's Instruments*, 72, 79, 82, 85.

79 Woolrych, *Britain in Revolution*, 586, 610.

80 David L. Smith, "Oliver Cromwell, the First Protectorate, and Religious Reform," esp. 46–7.

81 Woolrych, *Britain in Revolution*, 638–40.

82 *Oliver Cromwell's Letters and Speeches*, 3:29; *Mercurius Politicus* 12 (22–9 August 1650), 181.

83 Woolrych, *Britain in Revolution*, 487, 453. See also Worden, *Rump Parliament*, 238–9.

84 Marvell, *A Poem upon the Death of his Late Highness the Lord Protector*, ll. 179–80, in *Poems*, ed. Smith, 308.

85 Wallace, *Destiny His Choice*, 70, 72, 74–5, 105.

86 See McCrea, "Reason's Muse," 673–80.

87 Cf. Marvell, *A Poem upon the Death of his Late Highness the Lord Protector*, ll. 309–12; Nedham, *Excellencie of a Free-State*, 26.

88 Ode 3.8 advises Maecenas to "Dismiss the cares of state [*civiles super urbe curas*] . . . Be for the nonce a private man [*privatus*], care-free, and cease to be too much concerned lest in any way the people suffer!" Ode 2.15

reminds us that in the times of "Romulus and unshorn Cato . . . private estates [*privatus*] were small, and great was the common good [*commune*]. No private man [*privatis*] had a portico measuring its tens of feet, lying open to the shady north; nor did the laws permit our fathers to scorn the chance turf, but bade them at public cost [*publico sumptu*] adorn their towns and the temples of the gods with marbles rare." The remark about adorning "towns" and "temples" specifies nothing about religious beliefs, practices, or institutional structures, or for that matter about political forms. Horace harks back to the simple virtues of the early Roman Republic even as he addresses the officials of the new Empire. His references to "public" things are not necessarily an endorsement of the republican form of government. For the early modern separation between public and private spheres, see, for example, McKeon, *The Secret History of Domesticity*, xix–xx.

89 Komorowski, "Public Verse and Property," 334–5, 320–2, 316–18, rightly directs our attention to the poem's consideration of the state/government and "foundational social institutions," rather than just Cromwell.

90 Marvell, *The First Anniversary of the Government under H.H. the Lord Protector*, ll. 293–308, in *Poems*, ed. Smith, 295.

91 Cf. Everett, "Shooting of the Bears," 81 and 71–90 on time and process in the *Ode*.

92 R[obert]. Fletcher, *Mercurius Heliconicus* (3 February 1651), p. 6.

93 E.g., *The Old Protestant His Consciencious Queries about the New Engagement*, 7: an Engagement to be "in all things . . . true and faithful under this present power, so far as is consistent with former Engagements."

94 On the *Horatian Ode* as advice, see Patterson, *Marvell and the Civic Crown*, 63.

95 Zwicker, "Passions and Occasions," 294–6, an argument somewhat qualified by Hirst and Zwicker, *Andrew Marvell*, 156. See also McDowell, "Marvell among the Cromwellians," 483. Cf. H.M. Margoliouth's commentary in Marvell, *P&L*, 1:295. Rumors of Fairfax's not taking the Engagement had to be dispelled by an official declaration of the Rump: *JHC* 6:369 (20 February 1650), cited in Barber, "Engagement for the Council of State," 54.

96 See n. 8 above.

97 U.S. Constitution, Article VI, clause 3.

## 4 Samson's Cords: Imposing Oaths in *Eikonoklastes* and *Samson Agonistes*

1 Samuel Johnson, *A Dictionary of the English Language*, and *The Lives of the Most Eminent English Poets*, 245. The Swift quotation is from *On The Testimony of Conscience*, 8:231.

2 Milton, *Paradise Lost*, 4.95–7.

3 Cf. Richard Sibbes's earlier commentary on the significance of Samson's hair as sign of his dependence on someone else (God) and thus of his strength being fundamentally not his own: *A Learned Commentary . . . upon . . . Corinthians*, 435, 457; *The Bruised Reede*, 307. See also Trapp's insistence in *A Commentary . . . upon the Four Evangelists and the Acts of the Apostles*, 163, that "when . . . an oath is required of us, then it is not our communication, but anothers."

4 Trapp, *A Commentary . . . upon . . . Proverbs*, 2:239 (on Jeremiah 5:7), repeated almost verbatim in his annotation on Judges 16:30: *Annotations upon the Old and New Testament*, 93. From the late 1640s onward, Trapp's influential if at times idiosyncratic exegeses came as close as anything to codifying the association between Samson and swearing that had become so popular in that decade's controversy over state oaths. The analogy between Samson's cords and state-imposed loyalty oaths made its first appearance in Trapp's exegetical corpus in a 1647 volume's annotations of Matthew 5:33 and 2 Peter 2:14. It rears its head again in other annotations in 1654 and 1657: on Hosea 4:2; Jonah 2:9; and Ezra 10:10. The annotations on Ecclesiastes 10:8–9 and Jeremiah 5:4 in 1660 and on Judges 16:30 in 1662 simply crown an effort spanning fifteen years and eight different biblical passages to broadcast the cords metaphor. See Trapp, *A Commentary . . . upon the Four Evangelists and the Acts of the Apostles*, 152–3, 460; *A Commentary . . . upon the XII Minor Prophets*, 57, 318; *A Commentary . . . upon the Books of Ezra, Nehemiah, Esther, Job and Psalms*, 40; John Trapp, *A Commentary . . . upon . . . Proverbs*, 1:292, 2:239; *Annotations upon the Old and New Testament*, 93.

5 Milton, *De Doctrina Christiana*, in *The Works of John Milton* (hereafter *CM*), 17:119. I accept the arguments for Milton's authorship of *De Doctrina* advanced in Campbell et al., *Milton and the Manuscript of De Doctrina Christiana*, esp. 155–61.

6 Achinstein, "*Samson Agonistes* and the Drama of Dissent," 133–4, 148; cf. 139, 140, 145–6 and n. 29. As Achinstein explains, she uses the Quaker Thomas Ellwood's refusal of an oath as a way of "set[ting] the [more general] dissenting dilemma before us," a dilemma that revolved around the issue of consent (137, 148). See also Wittreich, *Shifting Contexts*, 207, 273; Achinstein's discussion of *Eikonoklastes* within the context of the Commonwealth's oath of Engagement (1650): "Milton Catches the Conscience of the King"; idem, "Milton and King Charles," 141, 157; as well as Togashi, "Milton and the Presbyterian Opposition."

7 Milton, *De Doctrina*, *CM*, 17:121.

8 Ibid., 17:127, 129.

9 Ibid., 15:113–15, 173–5; 16:79, 99–111, 165–219.
10 Slights, *The Casuistical Tradition*, 259–96; but see 107–9 (on *Macbeth*, Father Garnet, and equivocation).
11 Milton, *The Reason of Church Government*, *CM*, 3:242. Following the Yale editor's note on this passage (Milton, *YP*, 1:823 n. 161), Lares, *Milton and the Preaching Arts*, 16–28, argues that the oath in question is not the oath of office prescribed by the Canons of 1604 but the infamous Etcetera Oath of 1640.
12 Milton, *Tetrachordon*, *CM*, 4:63 ("your [i.e., Parliament's] Vows and solemne Covenants," which may also include the Vow and Covenant of June 1643); Lewalski, *Life of John Milton*, 162; Milton, "On the New Forcers of Conscience under the Long Parliament," lines 2, 5–6, in John *Milton: Complete Shorter Poems*, ed. Carey, 298. See also *The Tenure of Kings and Magistrates*, in *The Oxford Authors: John Milton*, 292–4; *Eikonoklastes*, *CM*, 5:304–5, 307–8, 161–2, 209; *The First Defence of the English People*, *CM*, 7:499. Cf. Milton, *The Readie and Easie Way to Establish a Free Commonwealth*, 2nd ed., *YP*, 7:409–20. For Milton's other remarks on oaths and covenants of various kinds, see, for example, *Tenure*, in *The Oxford Authors: John Milton*, 278, 280, 284, 285, 288, 291–2; *CM*, 3:326; 7:411–13, 417–19, 439, 535–43; 10:212–17, 255, 264, 304, 315.
13 *Readie and Easie Way*, *YP*, 7:411–20; *Tetrachordon*, *YP*, 2:578; Lewalski, *Life*, 249. Edward Jones, however, casts some doubt on the issue of Milton's taking the Protestation: "The Loyalty and Subsidy Returns," 239–40. For Milton's earlier, unqualified support for the Engagement, see his state letter to the Hamburg Senate (*YP*, 5:2.496–8). We should, however, admit the possibility that this official letter only expresses the Council of State's view and not his own.
14 Milton, *Proposalls for Certain Expedients* and *Letter to a Friend*, *YP*, 7:337, 330–1; see also *The Readie and Easie Way*'s and *The Present Means and Brief Delineation of a Free Commonwealth*'s paraphrases of the Engagement, *YP*, 7:367–8, 431–2, 392–3. Cf. *De Doctrina*, *CM*, 16:323.
15 *CM*, 16:281, 333–5; 17:129, 131–3, 397–9, 401–5.
16 Baxter, *RB*, 1:13–14; cf. 1:234, 241; Nuttall, *Richard Baxter*, 21.
17 Baxter, *RB*, 1:48–53, 63–4, 387.
18 Ibid., 1:384; cf. 409–22. Baxter was later imprisoned for refusing the Oxford Oath required by the Five Mile Act of 1666: Baxter, *RB*, 2:48–50; cf. 4–15.
19 Baxter, *RB*, 1:64; a heading in the "Breviate of the Contents of the Ensuing Narrative, Which was Written by Parts, at different Times," d2r, states that Part I of *Reliquiae* was "Written for the most part in 1664."

20 See, for example, *The Spiritual Bee*, 114–15 (covenants/vows as Samson's withes). This particular Samson tradition is not discussed in Joseph Wittreich's *Interpreting Samson Agonistes* and *Shifting Contexts*.

21 See Krouse, *Milton's Samson*, 22–79.

22 My claim of novelty only applies to England. The trope of oaths as Samson's cords may have appeared earlier on the Continent.

23 Hebrews 11:32's spelling of Samson's name as Σαμψων with a *psi* (ψ), as opposed to the Hebrew's *Shimshun* (שִׁמְשׁוֹן), accounts for the alternate spelling of "Sampson" with a "p" in the early modern period. For the term "citizen-saints" see Lupton, *Citizen-Saints*, esp. the chapter on *Samson Agonistes* (181–203).

24 E.g., Jeremiah Burroughs on Samson, faith, and the covenant with God in *Moses His Self-Denyall*, 188–9.

25 For a general characterization of oaths as social ties and as involving material objects that symbolize social ties, see Fezas, "Le Serment," and Testart, "Le Lien et Le Liant," both in *Le Serment*, ed. Verdier, 1:223–35, 2:245–55; Carastro, "Fabriquer du Lien." The idea of the oath as tie or bond is obviously central to Kerrigan's *Shakespeare's Binding Language*, esp. 14, 42, 49, 315, 350–1; see also his section on Jews and oaths (175–89).

26 Cicero, *De Officiis*, 390 (3:31): "Nullum enim *vinculum* ad astringendam fidem iure iurando maiores artius esse voluerunt." Cf. Augustine, *City of God*, 1:68–75, 102–7 (1.15, 24).

27 Lancelot Andrewes's appendix to Cosin, *An Apologie*, 249, 244 (citing Numbers 30:13); Elizabeth Grymeston, *Miscellanea* (1604–6), 116. Cf. Strode, *A Sermon*, 18.

28 Milton, *De Doctrina*, in *The Complete Works of John Milton* [hereafter *Oxford Milton*], 8: pt 2, 1002.

29 *Midrash Rabbah*, 1: Pt 2, 963 (on Genesis 49:17). See also the commentaries on Leviticus 16:1 and Ecclesiastes 9:2 (both of which reference Judges 15:12): 4:251; 8:2.227.

30 *The Babylonian Talmud: Sotah*, 44–5. Although there is a substantial body of recent criticism on Milton and rabbinical lore, none of it to my knowledge discusses rabbinical commentary on Samson and oaths.

31 *The Holy Bible . . . Authorized King James Version*, 1:233. Unless otherwise indicated, all further citations are from this edition. For divergent opinions on this passage's relevance to the issue of imposed oaths, see Richard Rogers, *A Commentary*, 712, 714 (cf. 553); Richardson, Ussher, and Gataker, *Choice Observations*, 434–5; Tombes, *Sephersheba*, 2:62; Prynne, *Concordia Discors*, 15; Hubberthorn, *Antichristianism Reproved*, 17–18.

32 See Lehmann, "Biblical Oaths," 78–80. The etymology from seven has not gained universal acceptance, however. See Ziegler, *Promises to Keep*,

5–6 and nn. 41–5, which mention alternatives, such as the idea that seven connotes satisfaction, satiety, completion.

33 "Shaba" (עַבָשׁ), in Brown, Driver, and Briggs, *A Hebrew and English Lexikon.* Cf. Richard Knolles's early modern account of Turks demanding that oaths be sworn seven times in *The Generall Historie of the Turkes*, 913.

34 Barlow, *Answer*, 17–18.

35 Anthony Burgess, *An Expository Comment . . . upon . . . Corinthianst*, 659 (on 2 Corinthians 1:23); Ainsworth, *Annotations upon the Five Bookes of Moses*, 82–3 (on Genesis 21:31); Leigh, *Critica Sacra*, 241.

36 Genesis 21:27–31; Fitzmyer, "Aramaic Inscriptions," 185, 208; Herodotus, *The Histories*, book 3, sect. 8, p. 205; Bristow, *A Reply to Fulke*, 354.

37 Cf. Markus Zehnder, "Building on Stone?" 523. Or possibly a curse on his own family down to the seventh generation: cf. Genesis 4:15.

38 *The Babylonian Talmud: Sotah*, 44–5.

39 Kenyon, *Stuart Constitution*, 167.

40 Barlow, *Answer*, 17–18; cf. 184. See also Ireland, *The Oath of Allegeance Defended*, F2r; Yates, *A Modell of Divinitie*, 289–90. It also worth noting that Richard Rogers's *Commentary vpon the VVhole Booke of Iudges*, with its discussion of oaths and covenants as Samson's cords and its reservations about imposed oaths (709–10), also appeared during the years in which the international debate raged over the Jacobean Oath of Allegiance (roughly 1606–23).

41 Cf. Featley, *Virtumnus Romanus*, **1v; Heyrick, *Three Sermons*, 158.

42 Donne, *Pseudo-Martyr*, 35.

43 Ussher, *A Sermon Preached before the Commo[n]s*, 49 ("If matters now be come vnto this passe, that such as are addicted to the Pope, will account the Oath of Allegeance to haue lesse force to binde them then a rope of straw").

44 Ward, *Iethro's Iustice of Peace*, 32, 5–6, 24, 29, 48; Masson, *The Life of John Milton*, 2:225.

45 Ward, *Iethro's Iustice of Peace*, 33–4.

46 Ibid., 48, 29.

47 Ibid., 33.

48 Ibid., 32.

49 Rowland, *A Reply*, 46.

50 Sempill, *The Kingis Complaint*, 1; idem, *The Testament and Tragedie*, 1; idem, *The Sempill Ballates*, 1–3 (the French-educated Mary Queen of Scots as Delilah/Dalyday to Darnley's Samson); Alexander Hume, *A Treatise of the Felicitie*, 43; Colvill, *The Palinod of Iohn Coluill*, C2v; Barbour, *The Actes and*, ¶5v (William Wallace as Samson vs. the English); Spottiswoode, *The*

*History of the Church of Scotland*), 464; Hume, *The History of the Houses of Douglas and Angus*, 22 (William Wallace). Cf. Archibald Johnston, Lord Warriston's poem "The Unconquerable!", ll. 12–18, p. 88.

51 Stevenson, "The National Covenant," 259, 269; idem, *The Scottish Revolution*, 83, 92, 164–5, 173; Houston, *Scottish Literacy*, 287.

52 Johnston, *Diary of Sir Archibald Johnston*, 323.

53 Cant, *A Sermon*, 12–13.

54 Lightbody, *Against the Apple*, 78–9. For later instances of the Scots Presbyterian Samson vs. foreign Philistines and Delilahs like the English and the Catholics, see, among others, *The Doctrine and Discipline of the Kirke of Scotland*, A2v; Gillespie, *An Assertion*, ¶4r–v; Rutherford, *Joshua Redivivus*, 554; Ker, *The Sober Conformists Answer*, 24.

55 Binning, *An Useful Case of Conscience*, 24, 12, 21.

56 John Corbet, *The Epistle Congratulatorie*, 54–5. Cf. Lilburne, *An Vnhappy Game*, 18; Phil-Alethio, *A Brief Resolution*, 19.

57 Burges, *The First Sermon*, 55; Stephen Marshall, *A Sermon*, 15–16, 9.

58 Coward, *The Stuart Age*, 520; Vallance, *Revolutionary England*, 51.

59 Edmund Calamy, *Gods Free Mercy to England*, 14; Smith, *The Three Kingdomes Healing-Plaister*, 14; Swadlin, *A Letter of an Independent*, 1.

60 Prynne, *The Soveraigne Povver*, 4:21, 30; see also 3:2, 85.

61 *A Remonstrance or Declaration of the Lords and Commons Now Assembled in Parliament, 26. of May. 1642*, 5–7, 24; *A Remonstrance of the Lords and Commons Now Assembled in Parliament*, 25–39.

62 Lady Eleanor Davies Douglas, *Samsons Fall* (London, 3 January 1643), 14, 304; *Samsons Legacie* (London, 14 April 1643), 2–3 (a prefatory section entitled "To the Most Honourable the High Court of Parliament"), 5. The dates in each case are George Thomason's. For a discussion of both tracts, see Cope, *Handmaid of the Holy Spirit*, 107–9, esp. 107. For a further instance of the Samson cords trope, see Lady Eleanor's *A Prayer or Petition for Peace. November 22. 1644* (rpt. London, 1649), 4–5, which extends the metaphor to include breaking the ties that bind nations in alliances, including the ties binding the three kingdoms of Great Britain, ties clearly broken by the War of the Three Kingdoms.

63 Prynne, *Soveraigne Povver*, 2:18 (my emphases; cf. 17); on its separate title page, Part II of *Soveraigne Povver* has an imprimatur from the House of Commons' Committee on Printing, dated 28 March 1643. Milton's first references to Samson as Charles I and/or the body politic in *The Reason of Church Government* and *Areopagitica* (*CM*, 3:276; 4:344) should be seen as responding to and participating in a similar kind of argument.

64 Prynne, *Soveraigne Povver*, 2:34–5.

65 Ibid., 3:73, 75. Also in the wake of the Protestation, see the apothegms collected in Clarke, *The Saints Nosegay*, 181–2. Cf. Joseph Hall, *Resolutions and Decisions*, 260–1.
66 Vallance, *Revolutionary England*, 60. On the Covenant, see also Vallance, *Revolutionary England*, 57–9, 70–4, 119–28; Jones, *Conscience and Allegiance*, 125–46.
67 Woodward, *The Solemne League and Covenant*, A2r.
68 Jones, *Conscience and Allegiance*, 116, 129; Hutchinson, *Memoirs of the Life of Colonel Hutchinson*, 216.
69 Vallance, *Revolutionary England*, 60.
70 *A Solemn League and Covenant*, 7.
71 Gee, *A Plea for Non-Scribers*, 55 (my emphases). See also Prynne, *Concors Discordia*, 29 ("If *a threefold cord be not easily broken*, Eccles. 4. 12. much more then *a sevenfold Oath* successively renued, should not easily or quicklie be broken, but remain inviolable to all posteritie").
72 Calamy, *The Great Danger*, 3; cf. 23, 8.
73 For other comparisons of the Solemn League and Covenant to Samson's cords, see, George Smith, *The Three Kingdomes Healing-Plaister*, 14; Case, *Sermon III*, 368; Heyrick, *Queen Esthers Resolves*, 26. Cf. Walwyn, *A Word in Season*, 7–8. For the Covenant as Samson's locks, see Caryl, *The Nature . . . of a Sacred Covenant*, 26; Stephen Marshall, *A Tvvo-Edged Svvord*, 5.
74 [William Sancroft?], *Modern Policies*, F2r–v; North, *A Forest of Varieties*, 241. Cf. John Selden on oaths as bitter pills: *Table Talk*, 113.
75 Ryves, *Mercurius Rusticus*, 78; cf. Vallance, *Revolutionary England*, 125.
76 Lilburne, *An Unhappy Game*, 18.
77 Gregg, *Free-Born John*, 111; Jones, *Conscience and Allegiance*, 140; Vallance, *Revolutionary England*, 154; Lilburne, *Ionahs Cry out of the Belly*, 15.
78 Lilburne, *The Resolved Man's Resolution*, title page and 27.
79 Lilburne, *Rash Oaths*, 9, 13–14, 17. Cf. *Resolved Man's Resolution*, 5, on MPs' oaths; and the very different uses of the cords trope in Lilburne, *An Answer*, 8, and *The Prisoner's Plea*, B2r.
80 Gregg, *Free-Born John*, 56–61, 63, 66, 76, 340–4; Lilburne, *The Engagement Vindicated*, esp. 2, 5. Cf. Binning, *Useful Case*, 24.
81 Prynne, *A Summary Collection*, 53. See also Baxter's comments on national oaths published around the same time as Milton's *Samson*: Baxter, *Christian Directory*, 1:702.
82 Charles I and John Gauden, *Eikon Basilike*, 115–16.
83 Ibid., 113–14.
84 For Charles as Samson, see Clay Daniel, "Royal Samson," which discusses the coronation oath in passing on 137.

85 Charles I and John Gauden, *Eikon Basilike*, 121.

86 Ibid., 76–7. Both Wittreich, *Interpreting Samson Agonistes*, 347–8, and Daniel, "Royal Samson," 133, discuss this passage in *Eikon Basilike* without referring to the Nineteen Propositions or oaths.

87 Milton, *Eikonoklastes*, 102–3.

88 Ibid., 36, 59, 160–2.

89 Ibid., 103; cf. Milton's hammering this point in many other passages: 222, 226, 57–9, 83–4, 156–7, 190. See also Joseph Jane's response in *ΕΙΚΩΝ ΑΚΛΑΣΤΟΣ* (*Eikon Aklastos*), 180–1 and the more detailed treatment of the coronation oath without reference to Samson in the anonymous *ΕΙΚΩΝ ΑΛΗΘΙΝΗ* (*Eikon Alethine*), 33–6 (esp. 35–6), 62. The anonymous author of *ΕΙΚΩΝ Η ΠΙΣΤΕ (Eikon Hē Pistē*) defended the king as Samson and insisted that if Charles had broken his coronation oath, it did not matter (3–4, 74–6; cf. 30, 44–5, 50).

90 Charles I and John Gauden, *Eikon Basilike*, 199; Milton, *Eikonoklastes*, 179. In *Eikon Aklastos*, 238, Jane refuses the analogy between the law and Samson's locks and falls back on the notion that the king's words have power because he has been anointed; the anointing was, of course, a key part of the English coronation ceremony. In this context Jane comes close to downplaying the coronation oath's part in the ceremony at the expense of the anointing.

91 Cf. Daniel, "Royal Samson," 126.

92 Cf. *Eikon Alethine*, 33–6's response to *Eikon Basilike*'s pronouncements on the coronation oath, esp. its *quas vulgus elegerit* (which the people shall have chosen) formula – a response Milton would surely have read in preparing *Eikonoklastes*. The *Eikon Hē Pistē*, 30, anticipates Milton's line of argument in some respects. We will hear much more of this formula in the next chapter.

93 Since my reading of *Samson Agonistes* limns the perplexities of subjects taking state oaths, I lack the space to develop the potential argument that the poem also treats Samson as a penitent king sorry for breaking his coronation oath to his people and now trying to atone with one final act of self-sacrificial violence. For a different approach, see Daniel, "Royal Samson."

94 The Corporation, Uniformity, and Five Mile Acts (1661, 1662, 1665) all required the following abjuration: "I do declare that I do hold there lies no obligation upon me or on any other person from the oath commonly called the Solemn League and Covenant to endeavour any change or alteration of government either in Church or State" (excerpted in Kenyon, *Stuart Constitution*, 355; see also Staves, *Players' Sceptres*, 196).

95 Butler, *Hudibras*, 1.2.1091–4.
96 Baxter, *RB*, 1:64; Tabor, *Seasonable Thoughts*, 50.
97 Thomas Hall, *Samarias Downfall*, 79.
98 Lloyd, *Modern Policy Compleated*, 2:40–2. See also his *Never Faile*, 40–1.
99 Hubberthorn, *Antichristianism Reproved*, 17–18.
100 Perhaps in response to Milton's comparison of Charles to Samson in *The Reason of Church Government* and *Areopagitica* (*CM*, 3:276; 4:344)?
101 John Gauden, *Analysis*. Gauden's controversial *Analysis* spoke of the Solemn League and Covenant's "withes and cords" (15) and circulated widely the notion of a state oath, such as the Covenant, as a band or bond to be loosened or broken, as two of Zachary Crofton's responses testify: *Analepsis*, esp. 28–9, 34, and *Analepsis Anelephthe*, 37, 156. As Janel Mueller has pointed out in "The Figure and the Ground," 140, Crofton later represented his 1661–2 imprisonment in the Tower for preaching the binding force of the Covenant as a Samsonian struggle with death: Crofton, *Defence against the Dread of Death*, 24–7. For a clearly anti-Presbyterian, anti-Covenant use of the cords trope, see Phil-Alethio, *A Brief Resolution*, 19–20.
102 Gauden, *Anti Baal-Berith*, 83 (misnumbered 82), and *A Pillar of Gratitude*, 33.
103 D.F., *Reason and Judgement*, 82.
104 Ibid., 83.
105 Timorcus [probably Richard Vines, Richard Baxter, Thomas Gataker], *The Covenanters Plea*, 7–8.
106 Jacomb, *Forenoon Sermon*, 82, 92–3; and Watson, *Sermon against Popery*, Hhhh4v; Lye (or Leigh), *Second Sermon*, Aa1r; William Cooper, *A Farewell Sermon*, Aaaa1r. If the John Collins who preached a farewell sermon on Jude 5:3 is the same as the moderate Presbyterian minister, John Collinges, rather than the Independent minister John Collins, then he should also be included. See John Collins, *Farewell Sermon*, 367.
107 John Brown, *An Apologeticall Relation*, 337; cf. 268.
108 Humfrey, *A Proposition*, 20–1. For some of the many later instances of the Samson's cords trope, see Vernon, *A Letter to a Friend*, 12; Settle, *Absalom Senior*, 30; Ferguson, *A Representation*, 30; *A New Protestant Litany*, 3.
109 Tabor, *Seasonable Thoughts*, 50. Rolls, *Londons Resurrection*, 176, makes the same point about Catholics.
110 Pittis, *A Private Conference*, 239. Cf. *The Cloud Opened*, 44 (a slight variation, with Delilah as the oaths: "The *Sampsons*, who had been bound and blinded by deceitful *Dalilahs*, false Oaths, and foolish Ingagements, though with their own dissolution can be content to pluck down the house of the Philistians so long devoted to the Idols folly").

111 Hubberthorn, *Antichristianism Reproved*, 17–18.
112 Quarles, *The Historie of Samson*, 2:159.
113 All references to *Samson Agonistes* will be to Carey's edition in *John Milton: Complete Shorter Poems*, 349–413, and cited by line numbers in the text.
114 For the earlier definition of the vow as a conditional promise to a god that will be fulfilled in return for the god's carrying out his/her separate promise to the mortal, see Tony Cartledge, *Vows in the Hebrew Bible*, 33. Cf. Benveniste, *Indo-European Language*, 489–98.
115 Martinez, "Achilleus' Vow of Abstinence," 47, explains that a Hebrew *issar* vow differed from an oath in that while both involved a self-curse of the taker's part, the curse was spoken and came first in vows but came second in oaths and was sometimes left unspoken.
116 According to Cartledge, *Vows in the Hebrew Bible*, 26, the Nedarim Tractate is mostly about oaths.
117 Sanderson, *De Juramento*, 183. See also Samuel Pepys's *Diary*, 3:294. Cf. Kerrigan, *Shakespeare's Binding Language*, 16, 290.
118 Hall, *Cases of Conscience*, 197–8; Francis Taylor, *The Danger of Vowes Neglected*, 15; cf. *The English-man's Allegiance*, 2.
119 Shakespeare, Sonnet 152, l. 8; Butler, *Hudibras*, 3.1.966. See also Shakespeare, *2 Henry VI*, 3.2.159–60; 5.1.180–8; *Titus Andronicus*, 5.1.78–83; *A Midsummer Night's Dream*, 3.2.124, 130–4, 154; *1 Henry IV*, 4.3.62–7, 77–8; *Henry V*, 4.7.116–27; *Measure for Measure*, 1.4.9–10; *Antony and Cleopatra*, 1.3.27–31; and Butler, *Hudibras*, 2.1.892–5; 2.3.54; as well as 2.2.119–89, 268–96; 2.3.44–8; 3.1.1237, 1281; "An Heroical Epistle," 19–82, 169–72, 329–30; "The Ladies Answer," 20–6.
120 Milton, *De Doctrina Christiana*, *YP*, 6:684 ("JUSJURANDUM est quo DEUM TESTEM APPELLAMUS VERA NOS DICERE, CUM EXECRATIONE VEL TACITA VEL EXPRESSA SI MENTIAMUR"), 679–80 ("Votum est pollicitatio de re licita Deo sancte").
121 Much of *De Doctrina* is based on the Swiss theologian Johannes Wolleb's *Compendium Theologiae Christianae* (1626), which distinguishes between private and public oaths, but *not* between private and public vows. Milton does the opposite, transferring the sentence about the private/public distinction from Wolleb's discussion of oaths almost verbatim to his own discussion of vows. In Milton's terms Samson's Nazirite vow would thus qualify as a special private vow. See Johannes Wolleb, *Compendium Theologiae Christianae*, 277; Milton, *De Doctrina*, in *Oxford Milton*, 8, pt 2, 990–3.
122 *De Doctrina Christiana*, *YP*, 6:680–2.

123 *Tetrachordon*, *YP*, 2:624 (my emphasis). For other instances of oaths, vows, and covenants spoken of in the same breath, see *CM*, 4:63; 14:133, 17:109–11.

124 Parliament's *Remonstrance* (London, 18 June 1642), 14; *The Vow and Covenant Appointed by the Lords and Commons Assembled in Parliament* (London, 1643). The Protestation of 1641 actually contained the word "vow": "I, A. B., . . . in the presence of Almighty God, promise, *vow*, and protest to maintain and defend . . . the true Reformed Protestant Religion . . . and neither for hope, fear, nor any other respects shall relinquish this promise, *vow*, and protestation."

125 Milton, *First Defence*, in *Milton: Political Writings*, 233. After mentioning the Solemn League and Covenant (232), Milton admonishes, "You Presbyterians . . . fulfil your vows [*vota*] to God: love your brothers who liberated you" (233). He also tells all his "countrymen [*Cives*]," including presumably Presbyterians, with whom the Covenant was closely identified, that "Your vows [*vota*] and burnings prayers God kindly granted when you fled to him for refuge, crushed by more than one kind of slavery" (252). Cf. his reference in *The Tenure of Kings and Magistrates* to the Vow and Covenant of 1643 as belonging to or insisted upon by the Presbyterians: "*thir* Vow and Covenant." See Milton, *The Tenure of Kings and Magistrates*, in *Milton: Political Writings*, 27.

126 Cf. Wither, *The British Appeals*, 57; *The Scotch Riddle Unfolded*, 1. At least one Scot referred to the Solemn League and Covenant as a "vow": see Stevenson, "The Solemn League and Covenant," 160.

127 Baxter, *RB*, 1:64 (my emphases). It was not unusual to summarize Samson's relationship with God as a covenant made, broken, and then renewed. See Pynchon, *The Covenant of Nature*, 120.

128 On Samson and oaths, see Richard Rogers, *A Commentary Vpon the Whole Booke of Ivdges*, 712–14; Diodati, *Pious Annotations*, 155; Richardson, Ussher, and Gataker, *Choice Observations*, D4v, 434–5; Downame et al., *Annotations* (1657), Ii4r; Trapp, *Annotations*, 93. On Samson, covenants, and vows, see John Downame et al., *Annotations* (1645), Bb2r, Cc1v, Cc2r; Downame et al., *Annotations* (1657), Ff3r, Ii2r–v, Ii3v, Kk1r; Haak, *The Dutch Annotations*, Ss2r–v.

129 See Jackson, *Annotations*, 161; Ainsworth, *Annotations*, 4:35; Lightfoot, *Horae Hebraicae & Talmudicae*, in *Works*, 384. As the Talmud's Nazir Tractate puts it, "we are not aware that Samson personally ever pronounced a nazirite vow." See *The Babylonian Talmud: Nazir*, 11. Mieke Bal goes so far as to call the vow his mother's, not Samson's: *Death and Dissymmetry*, 146–7, 200. Moses Maimonides, *The Code of Maimonides*,

*Book Six: The Book of Asseverations*, 132, 239 n. 13, attributes the vow to the angel "who commanded [Samson's] mother to eat no unclean thing." In contrast, Sir Thomas Browne distinguishes between Nazarites by vow, by birth, and by education, but classifies Samson as the first: *Pseudodoxia Epidemica*, 245.

130 See, for example, Perkins, *Whole Treatise*, 397; Hall, *Cases of Conscience*, 199–200 (apropos vows); Jeremy Taylor, *Ductor Dubitantium*, 1:201, 440, 442, 444, 488; Tombes, *A Supplement*, 20; Baxter, *Christian Directory*, 1:702, 709, 710. In Gauden's *Anti Baal-Berith*, which speaks of the need to break oaths and covenants "like Sampsons cords and withes" (83 [misnumbered 82]), dispensation of oaths for various reasons is a frequent topic: e.g., 123 (misnumbered 115), 184, 193, 270, 288.

131 As the Talmud's Sotah Tractate stresses (see n. 38 above). See also the discussion of this covenant/league by Rogers, *Commentary*, 662.

132 Francis Taylor, *Danger of Vowes Neglected*, 11–12, 14; Case, *The Quarrell of the Covenant*, 95, 57.

133 W[armestry], *The Oaths of Allegiance and Supremacy*, 5–7, 11 – mentioned in Spurr, "Perjury, Profanity, and Politics," 34; cf. Spurr's citation ("Profane History," 61) of a similar passage in the works of Sir Edward Coke.

134 Crofton, *Analepsis Anelephthe*, 145 (cf. 133–4), cited in Vallance, *Revolutionary England*, 182–3.

135 Gauden, *Certain Scruples and Doubts*, A2r–v; Gauden, *Anti Baal-Berith*, 80, 109; J.D., *A Discourse*, 5.

136 Stileman, *Discourse*, 1–2; and by implication the references to "uniformity" in John Gauden, *A Discourse*, A3v, a3r.

137 Cf. the argument by opponents of the Solemn League and Covenant that forced oaths do not bind: Sanderson et al., *Reasons of the Present Judgement*, 2–3; not to mention Milton himself in *De Doctrina*, *CM*, 17:123–9, and *The Doctrine and Discipline of Divorce*, in *The Riverside Milton*, 937, 948.

138 Lewalski, *Life*, 532. Knoppers, "'League with You I Seek,'" 276, argues that "Samson responds [to Harapha] by reasserting his errand in a higher covenant than the political league between Israel and Philistia."

139 See n. 15 above.

140 *YP*, 7:409–11; *CM*, 5:134, 210, 300–1, 304–5; *Doctrine and Discipline of Divorce*, 937, 948; *CM*, 4:118, 119, 171; *Tenure*, 281, 293, 278; *CM*, 6:268; 7:265, 267, 379, 385, 499, 539; 8:167; 17:123–9. Lewalski, *Life*, 532, says the following of the Harapha episode: "Harapha declares Samson a rebel covenant-breaker and murderer, echoing royalist denunciations of the Puritans before and after the Restoration for rebellion, breaking the Solemn League and Covenant, and regicide. Samson echoes the Miltonic

justifications for those actions: natural law which always allows armed resistance to those enslaved – 'force with force / Is well ejected when the Conquer'd can' (1,206–7) [*sic*] – and a vocation confirmed by divine mandate and evidenced by superior strength, recalling Milton's defenses of the Rump and the army in *Tenure*, the *Defensio*, and especially the *Readie & Easie Way*."

141 Cf. the other instances of the word "impose" in the poem: ll. 1343, 1640.

142 If Samson has, in fact, taken the Nazarite vow, it would seem to fit Milton's definition of the private general vow because it "relate[s] to things which God has commanded" and "is vowed by an individual" who has "arrived at the full use of his judgment" and is thus "his own master" (*De Doctrina*, *CM*, 17:111, 115). Perhaps the ambiguity in both Judges and Milton's own poem about Samson's consent to and keeping of the vow is the reason for Milton's not including Samson or Judges in the many citations of Scripture in this consideration of vows, even though he cites Numbers 6, which discusses Nazarite vows (115).

143 In *De Doctrina*'s discussion of vows, Milton insists that all vows, but especially the private special vow that is the Nazarite vow, must be voluntary, not sworn by someone else. See Milton, *De Doctrina*, in *Oxford Milton*, 8, pt 2.992–3: "No one can make a special vow unless he is a free agent, not in someone else's power . . . No one . . . can declare either a general or a special vow who, on grounds of age, is not yet endowed with reason and judgement."

144 Ness, *A Compleat History*, 1:145 (on Judges 14), 154 (on Judges 16; it imagines the Philistines offering Delilah £1000!); cf. Ness, *A Chrystal Mirour*, 75–6.

145 Vondel, *Samson, Of Heilige Wraeck*, Act 2, 89.

146 See, for example, Sypniewski and MacMaster, "Double Motivation," 148, 152; Mollenkott, "Milton and Women's Liberation," 102 (Milton "has taken a woman customarily treated as a stock villain and has raised her to a human stature fully equal to that of Samson").

147 Sumner's notes to the chapter on oaths in *De Doctrina* cite Dalila's "adjure" speech in connection with the problem of whether coerced oaths to thieves are binding: *CM*, 17:572, 123.

148 Milton, "On the New Forcers of Conscience," ll. 5, 2. "Adjure," which Carey glosses as "charge, entreat" (298 n.5), is defined by the *OED*, in a usage that hearkens back to its Latin root of "adiurare" (to swear to or to confirm or promise by oath), as "To put (one) to his oath; 'to impose an oath upon another, prescribing the form in which he shall swear,'" quoting Johnson's definition of "adjure" but offering as example not

*Samson* but *The Doctrine and Discipline of Divorce*. By making the Solemn League and Covenant a test of loyalty to the parliamentary regime, Milton's sonnet implies, the Presbyterians had in effect used an oath to make state interfere with church. For other instances of the word "adjure," see *CM*, 3:193; 7:541; 17:131, 133.

149 *De Doctrina*, *CM*, 17:131–3, 129; cf. 17:395–9.

150 See Empson, "A Defense of Delilah"; Landy, "Character Portrayal in *Samson Agonistes*," 244–7; Revard, "Dalila as Euripidean Heroine," 296–302; Ulreich,"'Incident to All Our Sex.'"

151 On Dalila as political subject, see McKeon, *The Secret History of Domesticity*, 393 ("Dalila spurns the private subjection of the *feme covert* in favor of political and public subjecthood"). Cf. Paula Loscocco's focus on Dalila as a response to royalist depictions of powerful women such as Jael and Judith in "'Not Less Renown'd than Jael,'" esp. 186. Chapter 6 will have more to say about women as citizens as opposed to subjects.

152 See the remarks about Dalila's conflicting allegiances in Landy, "Character Portrayal in *Samson Agonistes*," 239, 243, 246; Revard, "Dalila as Euripidean Heroine," 296; DiSalvo, "Intestine Thorn," 219.

153 In contrast, Quarles's Delilah mentions a more or less voluntary vow to the Philistine lords (*Historie of Samson*, 163).

154 In the latter speech Michael Lieb hears echoes, especially in "of my own accord" (1643), of God's formula for swearing oaths by Himself: *Theological Milton*, 201–3. Achinstein, "*Samson Agonistes*," 148, reads the former in light of the Quaker Thomas Ellwood's refusal of the Oath of Allegiance.

155 E.g., Lewalski, *Life*, 533.

156 Featley, *The League Illegal*, 23. See also Gauden, *Certain Doubts and Scruples*, A2r; Sanderson et al., *Reasons of the Present* Judgement, 19. Crofton, *Anelepsis Anelephthe*, 128, responded to charges like Featley's by saying that the Covenant was not an ambiguous riddle.

157 See, for example, Vallance, *Revolutionary England*, 133.

158 However, Crofton argued that while ambiguities can invalidate an oath like the Covenant, they have to be in the text itself, not in the mind of its swearer: Crofton, *Analepsis Anelephthe*, 127.

159 Sanderson, *Of Engagement*, 112–29 (misnumbered 131).

160 Ibid., 123.

161 Ibid., 123–4; see also 126–9, 113–14.

162 Gauden, *Anti Baal-Berith*, 83 (misnumbered 82), 108, 74, 110, 263–4.

163 Ibid., A2v–A3r, and passim.

164 See the reprint of the Covenant entitled *England Uniting to Her Sovereign*, 4.

165 Fox, *Our Covenant with God*, 1.

166 Compare, for example, Achinstein, "*Samson Agonistes*," 138–40, and *Literature and Dissent*, 139–40, on the position of ministers forced to take oaths of allegiance and abjuration after the Restoration.
167 The coronation cords trope appeared once again in the 1680s, when Robert Ferguson complained that with the Declaration of Indulgence James II was breaking his own coronation oath like Samson's cords. See Ferguson, *A Representation of the Threatning Dangers*, 30.

## 5 *Paradise Lost* I: God's Swearing by Himself: Milton's Troubling Coronation Oath

1 For the Ancient Constitution, see Pocock, *The Ancient Constituion and Feudal Law*. For the relevance of ancient constitutionalism to Milton, see Herman, *Destabilizing Milton*, 61–81.
2 Qtd. in *The Trial of Charles I*, 61.
3 Qtd. in ibid., 65, 66.
4 Qtd. in ibid., 124; cf. 120, 123.
5 For speech-acts such as creation and naming (but not swearing) in *Paradise Lost*, see Esterhammer, *Creating States*, 88–110.
6 Milton, *Paradise Lost*, ed. Fowler, 319–20 (emphasis mine). All subsequent references are to this edition and appear by book and line number in-text.
7 See, for example, Empson, *Milton's God*, 27, 71, 98–104; Bryson, *The Tyranny of Heaven*, 27, 83, 92–6; Herman, *Destabilizing Milton*, 54–7, 85, 99–104. Of the three, Herman's reading comes closest to my own in emphasizing the troubling absolutism of the speech. However, I pull back slightly towards something closer to the positions of Stevie Davies and David Norbrook, which are by no means identical: see Davies, *Images of Kingship*, 148, 143; Norbrook, *Writing the English Republic*, 480.
8 Philo, *Allegorical Interpretation of Genesis II, III* and *On the Birth of Abel and the Sacrifices Offered by Him and by His Brother Cain*, in *Philo*, 1:438–43, 2:162–7, 136–7; Lawson, *Theo-Politica*, 172–3. Cf. Tutino, *Shadows of Doubt*, 157, 170.
9 Ames, *Marrow*, 290–1.
10 E.g., Cosin, *An Apologie*, 3:8–9; Perkins, *The Whole Treatise*, 382, 384; Andrewes, *XCVI. Sermons*, 2:40; Wolleb, *The Abridgment of Christian Divinitie*, 359; Sanderson, *De Juramento*, 19–20; Grotius, *Of the Law, of Warre and Peace* 224; Tombes, *A Serious Consideration*, 13; Gauden, *A Discourse*, 21, 37.
11 Ames, *Marrow*, 290–1.
12 Keay, *The Magnificent Monarch*, 4–8 (quotation on 7); Ashmole and Sandford, *Ceremonies*, 4–7; Edward Walker, *Account*, 83–91; Ogilby, *The Entertainment*, 169–73.

13 Ashmole and Sandford, *Ceremonies*, 4, 6; Edward Walker, *Account*, 86; Ogilby, *Entertainment*, 171.
14 Walker, *Account*, 92–3; Ashmole and Sandford, *Ceremonies*, 8; Ogilby, *Entertainment*, 173.
15 Heath, *Glories and Magnificent Triumphs*, 199; Sharpe, *Rebranding Rule*, 162.
16 Ashmole and Sandford, *Ceremonies*, 12; Walker, *Account*, 95–8; Ogilby, *Entertainment*, 176.
17 Ashmole and Sandford, *Ceremonies*, 15–16; Walker, *Account*, 99–100; Ogilby, *Entertainment*, 177–8.
18 Ashmole and Sandford, *Ceremonies*, 17–19 (quotation on 19; emphases in the text); Walker, *Account*, 101–3; Ogilby, *Entertainment*, 178–81.
19 Ashmole and Sandford, *Ceremonies*, 22–3; Walker, *Account*, 105–13; Ogilby, *Entertainment*, 182–3.
20 Ashmole and Sandford, *Ceremonies*, 23–8; Walker, *Account*, 113–21; Ogilby, *Entertainment*, 183–6.
21 Pepys, *Diary*, 2:88 (23 April 1661); Evelyn, *Diary*, 5:278–84; Heath, *Glories and Magnificent Triumphs*, 197 (misnumbered 183); Ludlow, *A Voyce*, 286. Cf. Joyce's parody of the coronation ritual and oath in *Ulysses*, 391–4. There were also complaints about expense. See Andrew Marvell and John Ramsden's relief that new tax money did not have to be collected to pay for the coronation and that a scheme for strongly encouraging voluntary contributions to defray its costs ("benevolences") also came to nothing. Otherwise, they said, "the peoples good will" toward the king might have been "indanger[ed] . . . by *taking* their benevolence." See Marvell, *P&L*, 2:13 (25 December 1660) (my italics).
22 Marvell, "On Mr. Milton's *Paradise Lost*," l. 3, in *The Poems of Andrew Marvell*, 182.
23 Davies, *Images of Kingship*, 127–63. See also Fallon, *Divided Empire*, 50; Corns, *Regaining Paradise Lost*, 182; Condren, *Argument and Authority*, 159–62. There is a whiff of this line of argument in Empson, *Milton's God*, 101.
24 Norbrook, *Writing the English Republic*, 433–91, esp. 445–6, 474–80.
25 On the notion of reciprocity and reciprocal oaths, see Percy Schramm, *A History of the English Coronation*, 182–3; Dury, *Considerations*, 2 ("as you were sworn to the King, so he was sworne to you"); Grey, *Vox Coeli*, 44; Vane, *Tryal*, 100–1, 107–8. Cf. Davies, *Images of Kingship*, 135–6.
26 Milton, *Brief Notes upon a Late Sermon*, *YP*, 7:484.
27 Milton, *Readie and Easie Way*, *YP*, 7:356–7, 409–20, esp. 409, 411.
28 Ibid., 409.

29 Milton, *Commonplace Book*, *YP*, 1:447, 427–8, 435–6; *Tenure of Kings and Magistrates*, in *The Oxford Authors: John Milton*, 287; *First Defence*, in *Milton: Political Writings*, 212.
30 The same idea reappears in Mike Bartlett's recent play *Charles III*, which climaxes with the coronation ceremony of a future William V. The excerpt from the coronation consists mostly of the coronation oath followed by the crowning. See *King Charles III*, 121 (5.2).
31 Worden, "Milton's Republicanism," 232, finds Milton's interest in the coronation oath in his commonplace book "precocious."
32 Milton, *Commonplace Book*, *YP*, 1:427–9, 435, 447.
33 Milton, *Tenure of Kings and Magistrates* and *First Defence*, qtd. in notes 15–16 of *YP*, 1:447.
34 D.M. Jones, *Conscience and Allegiance*, 114. Cf. 3, where Jones quotes Henry Parker's *Observations upon some of his Majesties late Answers and Expresses* (1642) with regard to the king's being bound by his coronation oath to protect the people.
35 Milton, *Eikonoklastes*, *CM*, 5:300. Cf. Sharon Achinstein's comments on this passage in "Milton and King Charles," 157.
36 Ibid., *CM*, 5:299.
37 On the body natural versus the body politic, see Kantorowicz, *The King's Two Bodies*.
38 Milton, *Eikonoklastes*, *CM*, 5:234; confirmed by Milton's *Defence of the People of England*, *CM*, 7:539 (which mentions the *quas vulgus elegerit* clause).
39 See also the first *Defence* for the idea of reciprocal oaths: *CM*, 7:81; as well as *Brief Notes on a Late Sermon*, *YP*, 7:484.
40 Milton, *Defence of the People of England*, *CM*, 7:411. The present tense "rogat," which Sumner translates as "asks," after the perfect tense "dedit," which he renders as the present perfect "has taken" (literally "has given," for "Postquam enim rex consuetum juramentum dedit" can be literally translated as "After, in fact, the king has given the customary oath"), makes it clear that Milton is referring to the current coronation rite as a survival of ancient principles.
41 Milton, *Eikonoklastes*, *CM*, 5:121; *Defence of the People of England*, *CM*, 7:453.
42 Milton, *Eikonoklastes*, *CM*, 5:267–8, 181, 179, 172–3.
43 Ibid., *CM*, 5:179, 134–5, 234.
44 Milton, *Defence of the People of England*, *CM*, 7:535–9.
45 Ibid., *CM*, 7:541–3; *Eikonoklastes*, *CM*, 5:134, 300; *Tenure*, in *The Oxford Authors: John Milton*, 293, 291, 296, 281, 283, 305, and passim.
46 Milton, *Letters Patent*, *YP*, 8:451–3.

47 Cf. Condren's remarks on the coronation oath in *Argument and Authority*, ch. 12 (254–68); Reeves, *Considerations on the Coronation Oath*, 52–3; and Catherine Bell's discussion of the coronation as ritual in *Ritual*, 83–8.
48 Strong, *Coronation* 299–309 and passim. The classic study of the British coronation as collective ritual is Shils and Young, "The Meaning of the Coronation."
49 Cf. Schramm, *Coronation*, 214, 229; Churchill, *The Story of the Coronation*, 73.
50 Strong, *Coronation*, 25–6.
51 Ibid., 25–6, 28–30, 5, 17, 22, 44–5, 84–8, 379–81, 489–90. Cf. Hunt, *The Drama of Coronation*, 26. For the opposite view, see Heyrick, *A Sermon*, 21–3, 29.
52 Balfour, *The Historical Works*, 4:399: "We sueare, and by the holding wpe our hands, doe promisse all subiectione and loyaltie to him, Charles, our dread souerane; and as wee visch God to be mercifull to ws, shall be to his Ma[jes]tie treu and faithfull, and be euer redey to bestow our landis, liues and quhat els God hath giuen ws for the defence of his sacred persone and croune." See also Wordsworth, *The Manner of the Coronation*, 103–4; Prynne, *Singla Loyalty*, 2:314; *The Ceremonies . . . at the Coronation*, 19. Milton's *Maske at Ludlow Castle* (1634) responds to the Scottish coronation in its focus on the sea deities' "sapphire crowns," the Lady's throne-like chair, Sabrina's anointing of the Lady's body with sprinkled water, Comus's sceptre-like wand, and the reference to the Earl of Bridgewater's "new-entrusted scepter" as Lord President of the Council of Wales and Lord Lieutenant of Wales and the Marches (ll. 26, 36, 658SD, 659, 911–19).
53 *Form and Order of the Coronation*, 67–8; cf. 3–4, 69–70.
54 *Severall Proceedings of State Affaires*, 3499 (misnumbered 3498); Hilliam, *Crown, Orb & Sceptre*, 131–2. Sherwood, *Oliver Cromwell*, 7–12, however, insists that it retained regal elements.
55 Cromwell, *Cromwell's Letters and Speeches*, 3:373–4, 383–4, 386, 388, 400–1.
56 Nedham, *Mercurius Politicus* 369 (25 June–2 July 1657), 7882–3; Prestwich, *Respublica*, 17–19; Sherwood, *The Court of Oliver Cromwell*, 160–2, and *Oliver Cromwell*, 95–104.
57 Cromwell, *Cromwell's Letters and Speeches*, 4:360–1.
58 Nedham, *Mercurius Politicus* 432 (2–9 September 1658), 803–8 (quotation on 806, my emphasis).
59 Campbell and Corns, *John Milton*, 345.
60 Strong, *Coronation*, 26. This is Strong's summary of the three promises, rather than their exact wording.
61 Hoyt, "Coronation Oath of 1308," 355–6; *Liber Regalis*, 6–7 (I translate this source's original Latin, as I do in Table 1).

62 Hoyt, "Coronation Oath of 1308," 356; *Liber Regalis*, 7–8; Strong, *Coronation*, 92; Condren, *Argument and Authority*, 260–3; Hunt, *Drama of Coronation*, 94, 156.
63 Strong, *Coronation*, 240.
64 Milton, *CM*, 5:234; 7:539. Cf. Zachary Crofton's similar interpretation of *quas vulgus elegerit* as *shall choose*, indicating the monarch's being bound to the laws: *Analepsis Anelephthe*, 99–100, 121.
65 Leopold Wickham Legg, ed., *English Coronation Records*, 230; Hunt, *Drama of Coronation*, 27, 47.
66 Strong, *Coronation*, 185–6; L. Wickham Legg, *English Coronation Records*, 240–1; Hunt, *Drama of Coronation*, 39, 47–50.
67 L. Wickham Legg, *English Coronation Records*, 251 (my emphases).
68 Strong, *Coronation*, 200 (my emphases); Hunt, *Drama of Coronation*, 88–9; Prynne, *Signal Loyalty*, 2:251.
69 Strong, *Coronation*, 240; Hoak, "The Case of Edward VI," 115, 149–50; Hunt, *Drama of Coronation*, 128, 146, 157. Strong comments, "In effect, the oath was Protestantised before the country was" (240).
70 J. Wickham Legg, *Coronation Order of James I*, 16; Strong, *Coronation*, 238–40.
71 Peck, "Kingship," 81–2.
72 J. Wickham Legg, *Coronation Order of James I*, 15, combined with Wordsworth, *The Manner of the Coronation of Charles I*, 19 (my emphases). See the sources mentioned in J. Wickham Legg, *Coronation Order of James I*, 89–90, xcix. He uses as his main text for this edition a manuscript that does not have the new clause about the prerogative and the established profession of the Gospel (13–15). While Schramm, *Coronation*, 218–19, and Strong, *Coronation*, 239–40, think that James I introduced the clause, Madway, "'The Most Conspicuous Solemnity,'" 147 and nn. 29–30, assumes that it was Charles I.
73 Schramm, *Coronation*, 219; Milton, *Defense of the People of England*, *CM*, 7:535–9.
74 Wordsworth, *Manner of the Coronation of Charles I*, 23.
75 J. Wickham Legg, *Coronation Order of James I*, 15 (my emphases); Wordsworth, *Manner of the Coronation of Charles I*, 19 (my emphases); L.Wickham Legg, *English Coronation Records*, 250–1; Peck, "Kingship, Counsel, and Law," 115 n. 131.
76 Later, the revised coronation oath for William and Mary in 1689 seems to acknowledge this clarification by further separating the two statements. Clause A and Clause B now become separate sets of questions: the former about the people and civil affairs; the latter about the clergy and

ecclesiastical ones. A new third set of questions is inserted between them to make the separation clear. See An Act for Establishing the Coronation Oath, 1 William III and Mary II, chapter 6, *Statutes of the Realm*, 6:56–7.

77 Balfour, *Historical Works*, 4:392–3; Wordsworth, *Manner of the Coronation of Charles I*, 98–9; Prynne, *Signal Loyalty*, 2:307–9, 16–17. Compare the relevant portion of the coronation oath in 1633, in either of its two variants in these sources ("to reule the people subiecte to you according to the lawes and constitutions receaued within this realme"; "to rule this People subject to you, and committed to your Charge, according to the Laws, Constitutions and Customes of this your kingdom"), with its counterpart in the previous Scottish coronation, James VI's in 1567 ("s[h]all rewle the people committit to my charge, according to the will and command of God, revelit in His foirsaid Word, and according to the lovabill lawis and constitutionis resavit in this realme, na wayis repugnant to the said Word of the Eternall, my God"), and it becomes evident that in this part of the oath at least, Charles and Laud were merely adapting local Scottish tradition, not trying to expand the royal prerogative at the expense of the Scottish parliament. See *The Register of the Privy Council of Scotland*, 1:542. While the word "subject" is new in 1633, it emphasizes that Scots are subject to the king according to laws – a stronger statement of social contract than in the 1626 English coronation oath ("Will you grant to hold and keep the Lawes & rightfull Customes w[hi]ch ye Commonalty of this yo[u]r Kingdome *have* . . . ?"). In 1567 those "laws," along with those "constitutions," had been described as "received in this realm," but it was not specified who received them (king? parliament/people? both?) or when (before the coronation? after it? both?). 1633 does not remove this ambiguity and thus does not fix those laws as the present laws that the parliament/commons already "have" (and thus not future ones). More strikingly, 1633 removes other potential restrictions on which laws are meant. 1567 had specified "the *lovabill* lawis and constitutionis *resavit* in this realme, *na wayis repugnant to the said Word of the Eternall, my God*" (my italics), leaving open the possibility that James might ignore laws and constitutions that were not "lovable" (or "allowable"?) and that were "repugnant" to the Bible. In 1633 Charles left out these (religious) qualifications.

78 *The Form and Order of the Coronation of Charles the Second*, 67–8: "I, for my self and my Successors, shall consent and agree, to all Acts of Parliament enjoyning the National Covenant, and the Solemn League and Covenant, and fully establishing Presbyterial Government, the Directory of Worship, Confession of Faith, and Catechisms in the Kingdom of Scotland, as they are approven by the General Assembly of this Kirk and Parliament of this

Kingdom; And that I shall give [my] Royal Assent, to Acts and Ordinances of Parliament passed, or *to be passed*, enjoyning the same in my other Dominions: And that I shall observe in my own Practise and Family, and shall never make Opposition to any of these, or endeavour any change thereof." Cf. 3–4, 69–70.

79 *The Government of the Commonwealth*, 19–20.

80 Nedham, *Mercurius Politicus* 369 (25 June-2 July 1657), 7882–3 and 432 (2–9 September 1658), 808.

81 Ashmole and Sandford, *Ceremonies*, 12–13; Walker, *Account*, 95–8; Ogilby, *Entertainment*, 176.

82 An Act for Establishing the Coronation Oath, *Statutes of the Realm*, 6:56.

83 Strong, *Coronation*, 278.

84 An Act for Establishing the Coronation Oath, *Statutes of the Realm*, 6:56; Strong, *Coronation*, 286; Nenner, "Loyalty and the Law," 865–6.

85 Hilliam, *Crown, Orb & Sceptre*, 153–4 (quotation on 154); Strong, *Coronation*, 286–7.

86 Worden, "Republicanism, Regicide and Republic," 1:314, and *Literature and Politics*, 227–33 (esp. 231); Nigel Smith, *Literature and Revolution*, 181.

87 Condren, *Argument and Authority*, 149–52; William Walker, "*Paradise Lost* and the Forms of Government," 270–99, esp. 283, 286, 288–90; Rahe, "Classical Republicanism," 243–75, esp. 251–2, 256–7, 268. For the idea of "deradicalization," see Corns, "Milton and the Characteristics," 42.

88 Sidney, *Discourses Concerning Government*, 248, 297–8, 311, 322–9 (esp. 327–9), 338, 341, 363, 375, 391, 414–16, 444, 459, 461, and *The Very Copy of a Paper*, 2; Vane, *The Tryal of Sir Henry Vane*, 8 (Preface to Reader), 13–15, 100, 107–8; Neville, *Plato Redivivus*, 128–30, 227–8; Nedham, *Excellencie of a Free-State*, 13–14, 122–3, 162. For the general importance of oaths to English republicans, see Worden, "English Republicanism," 468.

89 Milton, *Readie and Easie Way*, *YP*, 7:424, 449–50. Cf. Milton, *First Defence*, in *Milton: Political Writings*, 80–1, 83, 85, 88–90, 92, 101–2.

90 Worden, "Milton's Republicanism," 228; Dzelzainis, "Milton's Classical Republicanism" and "Milton and the Protectorate in 1658"; Corns, "Milton and the Characteristics," 19, 205, 31, 33, 35; Lovett, "Milton's Case for a Free Commonwealth," 466, 469; as well as the arguments in n. 125 below. Cf. Nedham, *Mercurius Politicus* 87 (29 January–5 February 1652): "if any Kingly Form be tollerable, it must be that which is by Election; and herein as Kings are tolerable only upon this Account of being Elective, so these Elective Kings are as intolerable upon another Account, because their present greatness gives them opportunity ever to practice such Sleights, that in a short time, the Government which they received only for their

own lives, will become entailed upon their Families, whereby the Peoples Election will be made of no effect, farther than for fashion, to mock the poor People, and adorn the Triumphs of aspiring Tyranny."

91 Milton, *Readie and Easie Way*, *YP*, 7:407-63; *Brief Notes*, *YP*, 7:482: for "the space of a raign or two we may chance to live happily anough, or tolerably" under kings – but *only* for a reign or two, not permanently.

92 Milton, *Brief Notes*, *YP*, 7:469, 475–6, 481–2, 484; *First Defence*, in *Milton: Political Writings*, 99, 153, 94.

93 See the virtual repetition of the Engagement's formula ("the Commonwealth . . . without a King . . .") in *YP*, 7:330–1, 337–8, 368, 392–3, 431–2.

94 Shakespeare, *Richard II*, 4.1.190–211, esp. 191; for the releasing of subjects' oaths, see 200–1 ("With mine own breath [I] release all duteous oaths. / All pomp and majesty I do forswear"), 204–5. A literary coronation scene more contemporary to *Paradise Lost* appeared in the final scene (5.7) of Roger Boyle, Earl of Orrery's *Henry the Fifth* (1664), in which Betterton, Harris, and Smith appeared in the actual robes worn by Charles II, the Duke of York, and the Earl of Oxford at the 1661 coronation. See Boyle, *The History of Henry the Fifth*, in *The Broadview Anthology of Restoration and Early Eighteenth-Century Drama*, 2, 36–7; Pepys, *Diary*, 5:240 and n. 3.

95 Shakespeare, *Romeo and Juliet*, 2.1.155 ("swear by thy gracious self"), and *The Merchant of Venice*, 5.1.243–7 ("Swear by your double self"; "by my soul I swear / I never more will break an oath with thee") (cf. 4.1.35–6, 235–7), in *The Norton Shakespeare*, 926, 1174, 1160, 1164; Donne, "A Hymn to God the Father," 15–16, in *The Oxford Authors: John Donne*, 333. Cf. William W.E. Slights, "'Swear By Thy Gracious Self.'" See also John Harington's translation of Ariosto's *Orlando Furioso*, 29.28–9: *Orlando Fvrioso in English Heroical Verse*, 236 (29.30–1).

96 *Statutes of the Realm*, 5:322, 366, 446–7 (my emphasis). The Corporation Oath omits the final clause ("to endeavour . . . State").

97 For Milton's Arianism, see, among others, Empson, *Milton's God*, 12, 16–17, 244; Bauman, *Milton's Arianism*; Rumrich, *Milton Unbound*, 40–8. For doubts about it in the context of the Exaltation/Coronation scene in *Paradise Lost* 5, see Fallon, *Divided Empire*, 43–4, 48–53.

98 Milton, *De Doctrina*, *CM*, 15:287. My explication of the swearing couplet will parallel William B. Hunter's analysis of the line "This day I have begot" (*Paradise Lost* 5.603), but with reservations about his views on Milton's Arianism and the timing of the Son's Exaltation. See Hunter, "The War in Heaven."

99 Cf. Hutchinson, *Order and Disorder*, 15.230–40, 199, which in the word "resigning" (230) may recall the Exaltation scene in *Paradise Lost*, where God appears to resign but does not really.
100 Milton, *De Doctrina*, *CM*, 14:183; 15:285, 311, 313, 319–22, 331–5.
101 Ibid., 15:13.
102 Ibid., 15:7–9, 11.
103 Ibid., 15:13.
104 Ibid., 14:249. See also 14:277–83, 287–9, 291–5 (esp. 293–5).
105 See the other citations in Milton, *De Doctrina*, *CM*, 14:249–51.
106 Ibid., 14:293–5.
107 Cf. Wittreich, *Why Milton Matters*, 80, 123 on Milton's presenting flickers of heresy.
108 Genesis 22:16; Exodus 33:1; Numbers 14:23; 32:11; Deuteronomy 1:35; 10:11; 31:20–1, 23; 34:4; Joshua 1:6; Judges 2:1; 1 Samuel 3:14; Psalm 89:3; 95:11; 110:4; 119:106; Isaiah 14:24; 45:23; 54:9; 62:8; Jeremiah 5:7; 11:5; 44:26; 49:13; 51:14; Ezekiel 21:23; Amos 4:2; 6:8; 8:7.
109 Waltke and O'Connor, *An Introduction to Biblical Hebrew Syntax*, 488; Conklin, *Oath Formulas in Biblical Hebrew*, 3, 19–21, 53–4. Waltke and O'Connor refer to it as the "instantaneous perfective tense" (488).
110 It is possible that the rule applied to other performative ritual-acts or speech-acts, so that the anointing and begetting described in lines 603–5 of God's speech ("This day I have begot," "him have anointed"), especially the anointing, describe present actions being performed by God's speech rather than past actions, earlier in the "day," however long it may be.
111 In Hebrew the verb "to swear" is always in the passive voice: "to be sworn," "to be sevened." On this point see Trapp, *Commentary . . . upon the Four Evangelists*, 152 (on Matthew 5:33); Ainsworth, *Annotations upon the Five bookes of Moses*, 82–3 (on Genesis 21:31); Anthony Burgess, *An Expository Comment*, 659 (on 2 Corinthians 1:23). So technically, in saying "*nishbati ki* _____," the speaker asserts, "I have been sworn that ____," "I have been sevened that ____."
112 "*B-i nishbati*" is literally "I have been sworn, by myself" – i.e., by referring to myself as the guarantor of my oath. God's self-oath is thus doubly odd because he is not sworn by anybody outside himself, and the usual passive meaning of the verb is rendered useless.
113 Ashmole and Sandford, *Ceremonies*, 16; Walker, *Account*, 100; Ogilby, *Entertainment*, 178.
114 Moshe Weinfeld, "The Covenant of Grant," 184–203, esp. 190–4, and "Covenant Making in Anatolia in Mesopotamia," 136. For texts of such

oath-treaties, see Parpola and Watanabe, *Neo-Assyrian Treaties*, 28–58, 76–7 (cf. 31, 42–3, 64 for hints of rival brothers); *Hittite Diplomatic Texts*, 104–17; Fitzmyer, "Aramaic Inscriptions," 179–87, 208–11.

115 For Israel's transition from theocratic aristocracy to monarchy, see Josephus, *Jewish Antiquities* (6.36–42, 60–1, 83–94), in *Josephus V*, 184–7, 196–7, 208–15. For medieval and early modern debates about it, see, for example, Nelson, *The Hebrew Republic*, 26–37.

116 Milton, *CM*, 17:391; 5:14; 7:109. Solomon is similarly cast as accountable to God and the people by *De Doctrina*'s references to David's presentation of him (Solomon) to the people in 1 Chronicles 28:5–9: "And of all my sons (for the Lord has given me many sons) he has chosen Solomon my son to sit upon the throne of the kingdom of the Lord over Israel. He said to me, 'It is Solomon your son who shall build my home and my courts, for I have chosen him to be my son, and I will be his father. I will establish his kingdom for ever if he continues resolute in keeping my commandments and my ordinances, as he is today." His tenure in office is conditional upon good behaviour and thus a pattern for all whose virtuous lives qualify them for "adoption" as God's "sons." See Milton, *CM*, 14:13; 16:51.

117 Cf. Davies, *Images of Kingship*, 137. By "Trinitarian hymns," I mean the Nicene Creed, sung as part of the coronation, and the "Veni Creator Spiritus," both of which feature Trinitarian lines: respectively, "One God in Persons Three" and "Jesus Christ, the only begotten Son of God . . . begotten, not made, being of one substance with the Father." See Ogilby, *Entertainment*, 176, 184.

118 Cromwell, *Cromwell's Letters and Speeches*, 3:386, 400–1.

119 Cf. the Narrator's comment about Satan's "preventing all reply" in the Council in Hell (2.467).

120 Cf. Davies, *Images of Kingship*, 155. At the time, there appears to be no activity involving regalia such as crown, orb, sceptre, ceremonial swords, although after the fact Abdiel mentions the Son's being "endued / With regal sceptre" at 5.815–16; cf. 3.339. Again, my point is that the coronation as initially described by Raphael at 5.582–615 conspicuously lacks these objects.

121 Davies, *Images of Kingship*, 143, 145.

122 *The New Oxford Study Bible*, 880.

123 Cf. John Dryden's account of Charles II's coronation in "To His Sacred Majesty, A Panegyric on his Coronation," ll. 59–64, where the coronation oath is not mentioned and where something resembling the people's acclamation only arrives after the anointing. See Dryden, *John Dryden: Selected Poems*, 21. In *Paradise Lost*, even if one claims that the angels are allowed a voice later in Book 5, when they sing and dance their approval

of the Son's Exaltation (5.618–27), we do not hear its exact words, as the Narrator lets us do in Book 3, when the angels again praise the Son (3.345–417, esp. 372–415). Nor are their singing and dancing part of the coronation ceremony proper, which ends with God's speech at 5.615. The example of the English coronation ritual, with its ancillary but separate same-day ceremonies of the pre-coronation procession to Westminster Abbey and post-coronation banquet in Westminster Hall, would suggest to Restoration readers of *Paradise Lost* that the angels' later singing, dancing, and feasting (5.618–641) are separate from the Exaltation/ Coronation rite itself.

124 Cf. Norbrook, *Writing the English Republic*, 480; as well as Lejosne, "Milton, Satan, Salmasius, Abdiel," 106, 116.

125 Condren, *Argument and Authority*, 149–52; William Walker, "*Paradise Lost* and the Forms of Government," 270–99, esp. 283, 286, 288–90; Rahe, "Classical Republicanism of John Milton," 243–75, esp. 251–2, 256–7, 268. The most succinct objection to the argument against Milton's anti-monarchism appears in Worden, "English Republicanism," 469. See also Henry Parker, *The Trve Portraitvre of the Kings of England*, 9–10 (misnumbered 11).

126 Milton, *Readie and Easie Way*, *YP*, 7:444–5. Cf. Harrington, *Oceana*, 241.

127 It is telling that God and the Son are never described as wearing a literal crown in *Paradise Lost*. Cf. Davies, *Images of Kingship*, 129, 154. The closest the Son comes is to be crowned with "radiance . . . Of majesty divine, sapience, and love / Immense" (7.194–6). By contrast, almost everything and everyone else in the Creation is crowned in some way, literal or metaphorical. See *Paradise Lost*, 3.319–20, 352; 4.132–7, 143, 146, 224, 727–8; 5.166–9, 636, 839; 7.386; 9.117. Significantly, the only rulers who seem to wear crowns are Satan and Death, who sport "The likeness of a kingly crown," "a golden tiar" or "coronet" (3.625–6, 640; 2.672–3; cf. 2.542–4). Fittingly, the Christ of *Paradise Regained* refuses all crowns, literal and metaphorical: Milton, *Paradise Regained*, 2.457–65, 4.212–14, in *Complete Shorter Poems*, 462, 492. In Milton's world the equivalents of citizens have crowns.

## 6 *Paradise Lost* II: Of Apples, Oaths, and Women

1 Winstanley, *Englands Spirit Unfoulded*, in *The Complete Works*, 2:162–3, 166.

2 Mede, *Diatribae*, 401 (my emphasis); S.W., *The Constant Man's Character*, 66. Cf. *Memorandums of the Conferences*, 16. For the date of Mede's discourse on Acts 5:3–5, from which this quotation comes, see Mede, *Works*, **4r, c1v, which places it in the years 1624–8.

3 In this chapter I follow recent work on early modern women (see, e.g., n. 19 below) in using the term "subject" in the modern sense as a person formed by and thus subject to the norms of a particular society; the related term "political subject" thus emphasizes a person's interest in, knowledge of, and relative autonomy in conceiving of and participating in politics. This is different from the early modern sense of "subject" as someone under the control of a ruler – part of the royalist rather than the republican conception of people in a polity. "Citizen" will thus be used in the classical republican sense revived in the early modern period: an active participant in political affairs, broadly conceived. For the divergences and convergences between "subject" and "citizen" in the early modern English lexicon, see Condren, *The Language of Politics*, 91–114 – updated in his *Argument and Authority*, 17, 63–5, 104, 155.

4 Cf. chapter 5, n. 88 above, as well as Harrington, *Oceana*, 78, 84, 90, 96, 148; Sidney, *Court Maxims*, 133; Plescia, *The Oath and Perjury*, 15–24; Sommerstein and Bayliss, *Oaths and State*, 9–32; Judith Fletcher, "Women and Oaths," in Sommerstein et al., *Oaths and Swearing*, 156–79; Cressy, "The Protestation Protested," 279; and Crawford, "Women and Citizenship," 60, 70. See also Wiesner, "The Holy Roman Empire," 319–20, on women, oaths, and citizenship in early modern German towns.

5 I thank Megan Matchinske for help on this point.

6 Benson, *A Second Testimony*, 4; Ames, *Marrow*, 291.

7 This may explain why, in contrast to Homeric and Virgilian epic (with its postlapsarian subject matter), *Paradise Lost* has comparatively few oaths. Milton self-consciously departs from Homer and Virgil by depicting a time before the Fall.

8 Ovid, *Heroides*, Epistles 20–1, in *Heroides and Amores*, 274–311. For Ovid's brief allusions to the tale in *De Arte Amandi* and *Remedia Amoris*, see *Loves Schoole*, 25, and *Ouidius Naso his Remedie of Love*, D3r, E3r. The earliest extant version of the myth appears in Callimachus's *Aetia*, 50–61 (Fragments 67–75). Cf. the similar story of Ctesylla in Ovid, *Metamorphoses*, 1:368–9 (7:368–70), and Antoninus Liberalis, *Metamorphoses*, 47–8 – both of which draw on Nikander's lost *Heteroeumena*. In Antoninus Liberalis's account, Ctesylla's oath-inscribed apple sets in motion a chain of events leading to both exile and death in childbirth.

9 Spenser, *The Faerie Queene*, 222 (2.7.55.1–3), part of a veritable primer on classical apple stories in stanzas 54–5. See also Burton, *The Anatomy of Melancholy*, 3.239–40. The *Heroides* was a standard schooltext at St Paul's in Milton's time. See, for example, DuRocher, *Milton and Ovid*, 39; Harding, *Milton and the Renaissance Ovid*, 29, 40–1.

10 Grotius, *Of the Law of Warre and Peace*, Part II, ch. 27, 222; Pufendorf, *Of the Law of Nature and Nations*, Book 4, ch. 2, 270.

11 In this oft-cited work, Sanderson curiously offered this story as an example of an invalid claim not to have sworn an oath, even though the requisite words have been spoken – "curiously," for Cydippe has merely mouthed words without intending to perform what they describe, without even knowing what they describe until it is too late. See Sanderson, *De Juramento*, 224–5. Grotius, however, disagreed with this line of argument. The chapter from *De Jure Belli* entitled "In an Oath is required a deliberate minde" notes that "if any one, not conceiving that he swears, utter swearing words, as is related of *Cydippe*, that may be said, which *Ovid* ascribeth to her, taken out of Euripides, *I have not sworn; because my mind went not with my tongue*." See Grotius, *Of the Law of Warre and Peace*, 222. This is the same line from Euripides that Austin uses to make the oath take the fall for the promise's shortcomings in *How To Do Things With Words*, 9–10.

12 See, for example, Samuel Butler, "Upon an Hypocritical Nonconformist, A Pindaric Ode," in *Genuine Remains*, 1:132. "Swallowing an oath" was a common idiom for taking a mandatory oath under duress or with great reservations. See my epigraph from John Selden about oaths as bitter pills.

13 *The Grand Case*, 13–14. Cf. the natural philosopher Robert Boyle's treatise on profane oaths, *A Free Discourse*, 103–4, which stressed that like Adam's eating an apple, profane swearing seems trifling but has drastic consequences.

14 Leech, *Ioannis Leochaei Epigrammatum*, 21. Thanks to Bob Cape for helping with the translation.

15 Cavendish, *CCXI Sociable Letters*, 27–8. Besides the citations of this passage mentioned in notes 17–18 below, see Gallagher, "Embracing the Absolute," 138; Mendelson, *The Mental World*, 23.

16 Hilda L. Smith, *Reason's Disciples*, 79, has described this move as a mere capitulation to a masculinist ideology that justifies its oppression and suppression of women by claiming that they domineer men and thus need to be controlled.

17 Mendelson and Crawford, *Women in Early Modern England*, 49–58, 348, 396–9, 416–17; Crawford, "Women and Citizenship in Britain," 48–50, 65–82 (especially the notion of "subterranean citizenship"). See also Hirst, *The Representative of the People?* 18–19, on which Mendelson and Crawford's discussion of the possibility of women voting is based; as well as Schwoerer, "Women's Public Political Voice," 56–74; Capp, *When Gossips Meet*, 267–319 (ch. 7: "Women as Citizens"); and n. 18 below.

18 Crawford, "'The Poorest She,'" 205–6, and "Women and Citizenship in Britain," 60, 70; Cressy, "The Protestation Protested," 251, 265, 278–9, and *England on Edge*, 243.
19 See, for example, Wiseman, *Conspiracy and Virtue*, 59, 78–80, 91–2, 94, 231–3; Smith and Suzuki, introduction to *Women's Political Writings*, ed. Smith, Suzuki, and Susan Wiseman, 1:xiii–xiv.
20 Knoppers, *Politicizing Domesticity*, 94–164; Suzuki, *Subordinate Subjects*, 162–85; Wiseman, *Conspiracy and Virtue*, 27; Zook, *Protestantism, Politics, and Women*, 8.
21 Chidley, *A New-yeares-gift*, 16–17; Cressy, "Protestation Protested," 265.
22 Milton, *An Apology against a Pamphlet*, *YP*, 1:926.
23 Cf. Suzuki, *Subordinate Subjects*, 5.
24 Ibid., 2, 14–15, 25; Wiseman, *Conspiracy and Virtue*.
25 Cavendish, *Bell in Campo*, in *The Convent of Pleasure*, 121–5 (Part I, Act III, scene xi); cf. 120, 126.
26 In making this claim, I extend a line of argument laid out in McColley, *Milton's Eve*, esp. 142, 149, and Bennett, "Mary Astell, Lucy Hutchinson, John Milton, and Feminist Liberation Theology," 140–5, 166. Cf. William Shullenberger's discussion of the Lady of *A Maske at Ludlow Castle* as what I would consider a republican citizen: see his *Lady in the Labyrinth*, 69, 78–9, 272, 20, 28–9, 40–1.
27 "The 'Caedmonian' *Paradise Lost*," in *The Celestial Cycle*, 30–1, 41; cf. 25, 28.
28 Ibid., 26–7, 36–7.
29 Luther, *Commentary*, 177, 181–2; *Select Works of Martin Luther*, 3:105–7 (a commentary on Psalm 15); *Dr. Martin Luther's Small Catechism*, 38–41; Calvin, *Institution of Christian Religion*, 2:53r–5r (2.8.22–7); Calvin, *A Harmonie*, 178–9 (on Matthew 5:33–7).
30 Calvin, *Institution*, 2.4v (2.1.4), 2.53v (2.8.23), 3.158v (3.6.3); Calvin, *Sermons of Master Iohn Caluin,*, 312 (Sermon 61 on Job 15:30–5), 782 (Sermon 152 on Job 39:8–21); Calvin, *Sermons of M. Iohn Caluine*, 194r–v (Sermon 26 on Galatians 4:8–11).
31 Calvin, *Sermons . . . vpon . . . Iob*, 782 (my emphasis).
32 Without mentioning oaths, Wiseman observes that "Eve's disobedience to God made her an exemplary figure for the drama of obedience and disobedience in a society in which, in theory at least, obedience was an ideal"; however, she goes on to speak of Eve as "an unequal political subject" – a claim somewhat at odds with my argument here. See her "Eve, *Paradise Lost*, and Female Interpretation," 535, 545.
33 Marlowe, *Dr. Faustus* (A-Text), 2.1.93–111, 5.2.26, in *Doctor Faustus and Other Plays*, 153–4, 180; Preedy, *Marlowe's Literary Scepticism*, 34, 160–1, 173–87.

34 Lawson, *Magna Charta Ecclesiae Universalis*, 116. Cf. Lawson, *Theopolitica*, 153, and Watson, *A Body of Practical Divinity*, 411.
35 Bunyan, *Grace Abounding*, 43–4.
36 Bunyan, *Pilgrim's Progress*, 68.
37 Hume, *Annotations*, 106.
38 Milton, *The Tenure of Kings and Magistrates*, in *Milton: Political Writings*, 18–19.
39 Hume, *Annotations*, 106. Cf. n. 2 above on fealty, as well as Butler, *Hudibras*, Part 3, "The Ladies Answer to the Knight," 239–44; Lawson, *Theo-Politica*, 56.
40 Ogilby, *Entertainment*, 176, 173, 181–3. Cf. Davies, *Images of Kingship*, 137.
41 *The Ceremonies*, 19; Balfour, *The Historical Works*, 4:399; Wordsworth, *Manner of the Coronation of Charles I*, 103–4; Prynne, *Signal Loyalty*, 2:314.
42 Maddicott, "The Oath of Marlborough," 294, 298, 305.
43 Ogilby, *Entertainment*, 182–3; Ashmole and Sandford, *Ceremonies*, 22–3; Walker, *Account*, 106–8, 113.
44 Davies, *Images of Kingship*, 144, 131; Blount, *Nomo-Lexikon*, s.v. "Feudum" under "Fee"; Fabian Philipps, *Tenenda Non Tollenda*, 117–21.
45 Charles II, *A Proclamation, Declaring His Majesties Pleasure Touching His Royal Coronation*, 1.
46 Ogilby, *Entertainment*, 181, 188; Ashmole and Sandford, *Ceremonies*, 29; Walker, *Account*, 104, 126. See also the nobles named in Speed, *The Theatre of the Empire*, 591–3, a passage cited by Milton's commonplace book in connection with a sword in the coronation ritual (*YP*, 1:447); Holinshed, *Chronicles*, 3:468, 510, 802; Camden, *Britain*, 472–3; Edward Phillips, *The New World*, 77a.
47 Hume, *Annotations*, 235; cf. 106.
48 For the naming ceremony as coronation, see Radzinowicz, "The Politics of *Paradise Lost*," 212.
49 Cf. Friesenhahn, *Der Politische Eid*, 15.
50 Jones, *Conscience and Allegiance*, 272–3.
51 Ibid., 275, 278, 282–3.
52 Ibid., 279, 280. Bryan Hampton Adams, "'New Laws thou see'st impos'd,'" 141–58, reads Book 5 in light of the Clarendon Code, but without mentioning oaths.
53 Hume, *Annotations*, 102.
54 Evans, *Oaths of Allegiance*, esp. 9–11, 15, 19–21, 25, 31–3, 35, 43, 45, 48–9, 52–3, 56, 63.
55 *JHC*, 8:134 (24 August 1660), 205, 207 (12 December 1660).

56 Philo, *Allegorical Interpretation of Genesis II, III*, in *Philo*, 1:341. Cf. the ambiguity of Milton's own remarks on the issue twenty years earlier in *Tetrachordon*: *YP*, 2:590.

57 James Grantham Turner, *One Flesh*, 297–8. Milton thus magnifies Augustine's point in *The City of God* (bk 14.11, 13), that Adam was completely undeceived about his own Fall: he knew that it was not a venial sin and that he would lose Paradise and immortality. See Augustine, *The City of God*, 4:330–3, 336–7.

58 See, for example, von Maltzahn, *Milton's History of Britain*; the essays collected in *Milton and Republicanism*, ed. Armitage, Himy, and Skinner; Norbrook, *Writing the English Republic*, 433–92; Scodel, *Excess and the Mean*, 260–1, 269–70; Knoppers, *Politicizing Domesticity*, 9–10, 13, 141–55.

59 Skinner, *Liberty before Liberalism*; Martin van Gelderen and Skinner, eds., *Republicanism*; Nigel Smith, *Literature & Revolution*; Scott, *Commonwealth Principles*; Nelson, *The Greek Tradition* and *The Hebrew Republic*.

60 The main exceptions are Norbrook, *Writing the English Republic*, 20–1, 115–18, 482–90, and Knoppers, *Politicizing Domesticity*, 141–55. Knoppers makes a case similar to mine but concentrates more on Eve's domestic, housewifely profile in Eden. By contrast I focus on the more obviously political dimensions of Eve's actions. The essays by Christine Fauré, Catherine Larrère, and Judith Vega in van Gelderen and Skinner's *Republicanism*, 2:125–74, and by Vega, Annabel Brett, Lucien Jaume, and Michele Riot Sarcey, in *States and Citizens*, ed. Skinner and Stråth, 97–144, 191–207, mostly focus on women and continental republicanism.

61 Machiavelli, *Discourses on Livy*, 202, 52–3, 131, 242, 272–3, 306; Sidney, *Discourses*, 159. Cf. Nedham, *Excellencie of a Free-State*, 174–5; Neville, *Newes from the New Exchange, or the Commonvvwealth of Ladies* (30 January 1650), 2 (which parodies both the Engagement and women). However, see the somewhat more positive comments on women in Machiavelli's *Discourses* by Fauré, "Rights or Virtues," 2:131.

62 Cf. Knoppers, *Politicizing Domesticity*, 10, 141–55, who discusses Eve as citizen and fellow republican labourer with Adam, but does not mention oaths or Plato.

63 Philo, *On the Account of the World's Creation Given by Moses*, in *Philo*, 1:112–13.

64 E.g., Milton, *First Defence*, *CM*, 7:11, 29, 39, 391, 393, 493, 557, esp. chapter 12, where Milton compares himself explicitly to Cicero (p. 253 in Gruzelier's translation); *Second Defence*, *CM*, 8:177, 217, 223, 231, 235, 239. Cf. Milton, *Reason of Church Government*, *CM*, 3:236; *Doctrine and Discipline*

*of Divorce*, *CM*, 3:342; and esp. *Areopagitica*, *YP*, 2:485: the title page's rather free translation of a Greek epigraph from Euripides's *Suppliants* – "This is true Liberty when free born men / Having to advise the public may speak free . . . / What can be juster in a State then this?" "Free born men" is Milton's rendering of the Greek *tis* (someone or anyone), and "freeman" was a virtual synonym of "citizen" in the language of common law in early modern England. Milton's "public" translates *polei*, the polis or city-state. On Milton and citizenship, see Lewalski, "Milton on Liberty"; and Achinstein, *Milton and the Revolutionary Reader*, as well as her exhibit at the Bodleian for the 400th anniversary of Milton's birth in 2008, entitled *Citizen Milton* (www.cems.ox.ac.uk/citizenmilton/). On Milton and Ciceronian citizenship, see Dzelzainis, "Milton and Ciceronian Rhetoric," 203–26, esp. 212 (Milton as Cicero in *Areopagitica*).

65 See Milton, *A Defence of the People of England*, trans. Claire Gruzelier, in *Milton: Political Writings*, 52, 64, 103, 106–67, 109, 117, 121, 131–2, 136, 146, 156, 187, 194, 222 (citizens/*cives* vs. subjects/*subditi*), 224, 230, 246, 250–1 – which translate *civis* as "citizen." In a couple of places Gruzelier passes up the opportunity to render *cives* as "citizens," preferring instead the term "countrymen" (156, 252).

66 See *YP*, 6:386–7; *CM*, 15:191. In translating the second passage, I have emended Carey's "subjects" to "citizens."

67 My translation modifies that of the Oxford editors: Milton, *De Doctrina Christiana*, in *Oxford Milton*, 8:1.419 (my emphases). It renders "laesae maiestatis" as "high treason," while Hale and Cullington render it as "injuring human sovereignty." For reasons explained below, it also translates "fundum aut civitatem" as "lands and citizenship."

68 See Lewis and Short's entry for *civitas*, where the first meaning given is "the condition or privileges of a (Roman) citizen, citizenship" and only the second is "the citizens united in a community, the body-politic, the state": *A Latin Dictionary*. See also Sherwin White, *The Roman Citizenship*; J.A. Crook, *Law and Life of Rome*, 255–62; Champion, "Imperial Ideologies."

69 Carey: "his own estate and civil rights"; Oxford editors: "his estate or else his citizenship." See *CM*, 15:191; *YP*, 6:388; *Oxford Milton*, 8:1.419.

70 See William Smith, *A Dictionary of Greek and Roman Antiquities*, s.v. "Fundus" and "Foederatae Civitates, Foederati Socii"; *Harpers Dictionary of Classical Antiquities*, ed. Harry Thurston Peck, s.v. "Foederatae Civitates, Foederati Socii"; William Smith, *A Dictionary of Greek and Roman Geography*, s.v. "Gallia Cisalpina." See also Sherwin White, *Roman Citizenship*, 60–1, 130, 188, and 134–220.

71 Harrington, *Oceana*, 11–13, 16, 20, 113, 197, 208–9, 230.
72 Pruitt, *Gender and the Power of Relationship*, 128.
73 E.g., McColley, *Milton's Eve*, 140–86; Turner, *One Flesh*, 281.
74 E.g., Froula, "When Eve Reads Milton," 328–89, 335; Nyquist, "The Genesis of Gendered Subjectivity," 119–22; Levao, "'Among Unequals What Society,'" 82.
75 Gilbert, "Milton's Bogey," 188, 195, 204; Froula, "When Eve Reads Milton," 328–9, 335; Nyquist, "Genesis of Gendered Subjectivity," 99–102, 117–23; Magro, "Milton's Sexualized Woman," 98; and to a limited extent Halley, "Female Autonomy," 243, 246, who argues that while Eve has a subjectivity, even a liberal individualist subjectivity, it subserves homosocial relations between men.
76 Lewalski, "Milton on Women – Yet Once More," 3, 5–9, 11; Mollenkott, "Milton and Women's Liberation," 100; Webber, "The Politics of Poetry," 12; McColley, *Milton's Eve*, 90, 129, 141–2, 145, 151, 154, 218; Wittreich, *Feminist Milton*, x, 3–4, 12–14, 22, 29–30, 96–7, 101, 117–18; Woods, "How Free Are Milton's Women?" 18, 27; Levao, "'Among Unequals What Society,'" 82; Wilding, "'Thir Sex Not Equal Seem'd,'" 183–4; Pruitt, *Gender and the Power of Relationship*, 111, 128, 134–5. McChrystal, "Redeeming Eve," 491, 493, 495, 497–8, 501–5, 506–8, thinks it varies, and Ng, *Literature and the Politics of Family*, 156, 160, that it grows. James Grantham Turner, "The Aesthetics of Divorce," 51, repeats his argument in *One Flesh* (281–7) that *Paradise Lost* pits an "ecstatic-egalitarian" model of gender relations against a "patriarchal-masculinist" one. In the same volume, Gina Hausknecht comments that Milton's discussion of gender in the divorce tracts "allows for a rational Eve in *Paradise Lost*": see "The Gender of Civic Virtue," 32. See also the very nuanced anti-misogynistic reading of Herman, *Destabilizing Milton*, 127–54, esp. 135. One shoal to avoid is tying Milton's ideas in his early prose, and for that matter *De Doctrina*, too closely to *Paradise Lost*.
77 Gilbert, "Milton's Bogey," 195; Nyquist, "Genesis of Gendered Subjectivity," 99–102, 117–23; Magro, "Milton's Sexualized Woman," 98, 100, 104; Kuzner, "Habermas Goes to Hell," 117–20; Shannon Miller, *Engendering the Fall*, 68, 70–1, 74; Norbrook, *Writing the English Republic*, 483, 488–9; Knoppers, *Politicizing Domesticity*, 11, 141, 145–6. For the original formulation of the idea of the public sphere, see Habermas, *The Structural Transformation of the Public Sphere*.
78 *Pace* William Walker, "Resemblance and Reference," 193: "there is no political society or nation in Eden but only a household." On Eden's

household as state, see, e.g., Ng, *Literature and the Politics of Family*, 149, as well as Knoppers, *Politicizing Domesticity*, 10–13, 116, 141–55, 162, 164.

79 See, e.g., McKeon, *Secret History*, 11–15.

80 Milton, *First Defence*, *YP*, 7:395.

81 In an important chapter on the topic, Michael McKeon tracks the transformation in early modern England of the concept of state as household to the concept of household as state. See McKeon, *Secret History*, 110–61.

82 Milton, *The Doctrine and Discpline of Divorce* (hereafter *DDD*), *YP*, 2:229 (my emphasis); cf. *Tetrachordon*, *YP*, 2:624–5, 666.

83 Milton, *Tetrachordon*, *YP*, 2:578, 579, 582, 624, 640; *DDD*, *YP*, 2:240, 276.

84 Milton, *DDD*, *YP*, 2:229.

85 Milton, *The Tenure of Kings and Magistrates*, in *The Complete Poetry and Essential Prose*, 1024–55.

86 Milton, *DDD*, *YP*, 2:247, 353.

87 Ibid., 274; *Tetrachordon*, *YP*, 2:631.

88 Milton, *DDD*, *YP*, 2:286; *Tetrachordon*, *YP*, 2:625, 632.

89 Cf. Lewalski, "Milton on Women," 6–8. *Samson Agonistes*, of course, is a different story, with a more clearcut yet not absolute division between private and public. See, for example, Guillory. "Dalila's House," 108–10. The same point can be made about *Paradise Regained*, and for the same reason: they both treat postlapsarian events. In Milton's mind the Fall created the main split between public and private. Cf. Knoppers, *Politicizing Domesticity*, 116, though she sees the split as preceding the Fall (148–55, esp. 148, 152).

90 Cf. Webber, "Politics of Poetry," 12.

91 Compare *DDD*, *YP*, 2:324–6, 336, 344, 346–7, 355; *Tetrachordon*, *YP*, 2:589 ("inferiour sexe"), 604, 620–1, 626, 672 with *Paradise Lost*, 4.288–311, 490, 635–9; 5:503–30; 6:908–9; 8.48–50, 383–4, 537–46, 573–5; 9:819–25; 10:145–56. Indeed, the hierarchy diminishes somewhat even over the course of the successive divorce tracts. Compare the passages from the divorce tracts above to *Tetrachordon*, *YP*, 2:589–92, 612, 624–6, 628, 630, 645, 661, 670, 688–9, 691; *Colasterion*, *YP*, 2:748. Some of the passages in *Tetrachordon* still support more gender hierarchy than *DDD*, but less than in *Paradise Lost*, and thus appear in both notes.

92 A point emphasized by Knoppers, *Politicizing Domesticity*, 147–8.

93 Knoppers, *Politicizing Domesticity*, 147–53.

94 On the second line of inquiry, see McKeon, *Secret History*, 334.

95 Harrington, *The Rota*, 5.

96 See, for example, Gregerson, *The Reformation of the Subject*, 148–97, esp. 151–63, 192–7.
97 Ovid, *Metamorphoses*, 3.344–510; Spenser, *Faerie Queene*, 3.2.22–46ff.; Plato, *Republic*, 7.514–19ff. Fowler's note gestures at all three: *Paradise Lost*, 4.460–71n.
98 For Ovid's indebtedness to Plato's Allegory of the Cave, see the echoes/ images of it in *Metamorphoses*, 3.416–17, 432–4, 439, 463, 502–5, in *Metamorphoses*, 1:152–9.
99 Plato, *Republic*, 7.516a-b, in *The Republic*, trans. Paul Shorey, 2:124–7 (my emphasis). All subsequent references will be to Stephanus numbers.
100 Plato, *Republic*, 7.520a–b.
101 Plato, *Republic*, 5.451c–67c (esp. 5.453a–c, 454e–56e), 471d; 7.539d–40d. Cf. Plato, *Laws*, 7.805a–d (cf. 1.639b, 643e; 3.693d–8b; 6.752c–3d, 756c–e, 764c–d, 781a–d, 785b; 7.794a–c, 802e, 804d–6c, 813e–14c; 8.829a–30b, 834c–d, 841c–e; 9.875c–d, 882c; 11.917a, 932b, 937a–b; 12.942a–c, 943b–d, 945e–7e, 955a–b, 964b; *Timaeus*, 17c–19e, 23b–c, 24a–e, 25d–e, 26c–e; *Critias*, 110a–d, 111e–12d. See Plato, *Laws*, trans. R.G. Bury, and *Plato VII: Timaeus, Critias, Cleitophon, Menexenus, Epistles* trans. R.G. Bury. All subsequent references will be to Stephanus numbers. On Plato and women, see, e.g., Vlastos, "Was Plato a Feminist?" 276+; Bobonich, *Plato's Utopia Recast*, 374–450; Samaras, "Family and the Question of Women," 173, 96.

In Plato's *Critias*, the island of Atlantis contains an oath-stele on the Acropolis at the centre of its capital city, an oath-stele that Milton's Tree of Knowledge may resemble. Moreover, the *Critias*'s ancient Athens features a very large acropolis (not unlike Milton's Eden) on which there are gardens (*kēpoi*) in which men and women citizens train for war. See *Critias*, 111e–12d, 113c–e, 116c, 119c–e.
102 For the early modern revival of classical republican citizenship, see, among others, Pocock, *Machiavellian Moment*, 67–89 and "The Ideal of Citizenship," 29–52 (esp. 43); Skinner, "The Idea of Negative Liberty"; Peltonen, *Classical Humanism*, 54–118. See also Lupton, *Citizen-Saints*.
103 Withington, *The Politics of Commonwealth*, 10, 66–7, 75, 78, 93, and "Andrew Marvell's Citizenship," 104–5.
104 *The Putney Debates* (1647), 1239.
105 Plato, *Laws*, 7.806d–7a (cf. 846d–e); Aristotle, *Politics*, 184 (3.5.1277b); Harrington, *Oceana*, 136, 138, and *Rota*, 5.
106 Lewalski, "Milton on Women," 11–12; Norbrook, *Writing the English Republic*, 115, 484.
107 Harrington, *Politicaster*, 13–18, and *The Art of Lawgiving*, 2, 4, 8 ("brethren"); Sidney, *Discourses*, 15, 26, 32, 38, 41.

108 Harrington, *Oceana*, 93; Cavendish, *Bell in Campo*, Part I, 2.9, in *The Convent of Pleasure*, 120.
109 Cf. Ng, *Literature and the Politics of Family*, 165: "By letting Eve articulate the desire for political renewal and change, Milton emphasizes the importance of the politically disenfranchised."
110 Numbers 30:2–15; Ascham, *A Discourse*, 51, and *Of the Confusions*, 87. Cf. the *Babylonian Talmud*'s tract on vows, Nedarim, 3a, 4b, in *The Babylonian Talmud*, trans. Neusner, 10:5, 9. Tony Cartledge, *Vows in the Hebrew Bible*, 25, treats the passage in Numbers as about oaths rather than vows.
111 Milton, *De Doctrina Christiana*, *YP*, 6:681: "No one can make a special vow unless he is his own master rather than in someone else's power, as sons *and daughters* are in their father's power, *wives* in that of their husbands[,] and servants, male *or female*, in that of their master, Num. vi. and xxx. 13" (my emphasis). In comparison to his source for this section of *De Doctrina*, Wolleb's *Compendium*, Milton goes out of his way to specify female underlings: daughters, wives, female servants. See Wolleb, *Compendium*, 263–4. For Milton's remarks on oaths in *De Doctrina*, see 684–90.
112 But the language of rights as such is not prominent in *Paradise Lost*. See Patterson, "Why is there no Rights Talk in Milton's Poetry?" 202–4.
113 Milton, *The Readie and Easie Way to a Free Commonwealth*, *YP*, 7:442.
114 Hobby, "A Woman's Best Setting Out Is Silence," 193, remarks that "the women activists of the Commonwealth and Restoration period appear not to have engaged in debates about suffrage, but instead used their activities to demonstrate women's right to an active part in the political world."
115 Cf. Achinstein, *Milton and the Revolutionary Reader*.
116 Milton, *Readie and Easie Way*, *YP*, 7:411, 429, 432.
117 Blake, *Milton a Poem* (Copy C), in *Milton a Poem*, 138, Plates 12–13 (quotation on Plate 12).
118 Ibid., 23. This line of argument may help explain the notorious engine in Milton's *Lycidas*, ll. 130–1, whose two hands may well be the two oaths of entry to the clergy that Milton found objectionable in 1637 and to which he would not "subscribe slave," as he later put it: the Oath of Canonical Obedience and the Oath of Supremacy.
119 For the oath as fashionable, easily changed clothing, see Wither, *Divine Poems*, 23. Cf. the Ancient Near Eastern idea of the oath as garment: Parpola and Watanabe, *Neo-Assyrian Treaties and Loyalty Oaths*, 11, 72; Kitz, "An Oath, Its Curse, and Anointing Ritual," 315–20.
120 Worden, *Literature and Politics*, 238.
121 Wither, *Speculum Speculativum*, 115.

122 Cf. Addison, *Spectator* 357, 222–3 ("It was the Excess of Love for *Eve*, that ruin'd *Adam*, and his Posterity"); Waldock, *Paradise Lost and Its Critics*, 46–56, 60; Peter, *A Critique of Paradise Lost*, 130–3 ("a necessary and courageous sacrifice" – 131); Empson, *Milton's God*, 182–9 – all discussed in Leonard, *Faithful Labourers*, 2:601, 603, 617, 623–4, 628, 633–4. See also Quint, *Inside Paradise Lost*, 153, 188–9.

123 Milton, *De Doctrina*, in *Oxford Milton*, 8:2.1009.

**Appendix**

1 See the *OED*'s section on "book house" in the entry on "book."

2 Marvell, *P&L*, 2:342, 391.

3 There was also a Bill to Explain (or Amplify the Force of) the 1673 Test, which began in the Lords and might have altered or added to the 1673 Test: *JHL*, 12:661 (17 April 1675), 676 (4 May 1675), 679 (5 May 1675); *JHC*, 9:334 (8 May 1675), 340 (18 May 1675); Grey, *Debates*, 3:166–7 (18 May 1675).

4 *Statutes of the Realm*, 5:894–6 ("An Act for the more effectuall preserving the Kings Person and Government by disableing Papists from sitting in *either House of Parlyament*"); *Book of Oaths* (1689), 240–1. Versions of this measure appeared in several different bills in 1675 (and perhaps earlier): 1) as the Bill for Preventing Catholics from Sitting in Parliament (*JHC*, 9:318 [16 April 1675], 337 [14 May 1675], 340 [17 May 1675], 341 [18 May 1675], 344 [21 May 1675]; Grey, *Debates*, 3:178–80 [21 May 1675]); 2) as part of the Bill for Suppressing the Growth of Popery, or for the Speedier Conviction of Papists (*JHC*, 9:317–18 [16–17 April 1675], 320–1 [21 April 1675], 340 [17 May 1675], 342 [19 May 1675], 346 [27 May 1675]; Grey, *Debates*, 3:15–18 [21 April 1675], 174–5 [19 May 1675], 186 [27 May 1675]).

5 The Bill for Suppressing the Growth of Popery, or for the Speedier Conviction of Papists: *P&L*, 2:146–7, 158–9, 342, 181, 186, 193, 195, 203, 216–17, 222, 224–6; *JHC*, 9:317–18 (16–17 April 1675), 320–1 (21 April 1675), 340 (17 May 1675), 342 (19 May 1675), 346 (27 May 1675); Grey, *Debates*, 3:15–18 (21 April 1675), 174–5 (19 May 1675), 186 (27 May 1675).

6 A "Test for the Members that they had not been bribed": *P&L*, 2:242 (18 June 1678); *JHC*, 9:500–1 (18 June 1678); Grey, *Debates*, 6:103–5 (18 June 1678); it failed to go to committee, on a vote of 100 to 86.

7 Marvell, *AGP*, 281–7, 313–19; *P&L*, 2:338.

8 *P&L*, 2:341–3 (ca. 24 July 1675).

9 *The Works of Andrew Marvell, Esq.*, ed. Thomas Cooke, (1726), vol. 2, sect. 2 ("Carmina Miscellanea"), 47.

10 *P&L*, 2:342, 391.

11 In a personal communication, Nicholas von Maltzahn, who is preparing an edition of Marvell's letters for Yale University Press, agreed with my conjecture about "Both-Houses" and hazarded the idea of Cooke's mistranscription's resulting from the phrase's appearing at the end of a line in the manuscript.
12 *JHC*, 9:318 (16 April 1675); *Statutes of the Realm*, 5:894–6 (my emphasis).
13 Ibid., 341.
14 Ibid.
15 *P&L*, 2:356 (17 November 1677), which Pierre Legouis took to be ironic (2:396). Cf. 2:230 (30 April 1678).

# Bibliography


Achinstein, Sharon. *Citizen Milton* (www.cems.ox.ac.uk/citizenmilton/).

– *Literature and Dissent in Milton's England*. Cambridge: Cambridge University Press, 2003.

– "Milton and King Charles." In *The Royal Image: Representations of Charles I*, edited by Thomas N. Corns, 141–57. Cambridge: Cambridge University Press, 1999.

– *Milton and the Revolutionary Reader*. New Haven and London: Yale University Press, 1994.

– "Milton Catches the Conscience of the King: *Eikonoklastes* and the Engagement Controversy." *Milton Studies* 23 (1993): 143–63.

– "*Samson Agonistes* and the Drama of Dissent." *Milton Studies* 33 (1996): 133–58.

*Acts and Ordinances of the Interregnum, 1642–1660*. Edited by C.H. Firth and R.S. Rait. London, 1911.

Adams, Bryan Hampton. "'New Laws thou see'st impos'd': Milton's Dissenting Angels and the Clarendon Code, 1661–5." In *Paradise Lost: A Poem Written in Ten Books: Essays on the 1667 First Edition*, edited by Michael Lieb and John T. Shawcross, 141–58. Pittsburgh: Duquesne University Press, 2007.

Adams, Michael. *In Praise of Profanity*. Oxford: Oxford University Press, 2016.

– "Peter Chamberlen's Case of Conscience." *Huntington Library Quarterly* 53.4 (1990): 281–309.

Addison, Joseph. *Spectator* 357 (19 April 1712).

Adis, Henry. *A Fanatick's Testimony against Swearing*. London, 1660.

Agamben, Giorgio. *Homo Sacer*. Translated by Daniel Heller-Roazen. Stanford: Stanford University Press, 1998.

– *The Sacrament of Language: An Archaeology of the Oath*. Translated by Adam Kotsko. Stanford: Stanford University Press, 2011.

Ainsworth, Henry. *Annotations on the Five Bookes of Moses, the Booke of the Psalmes, and the Song of Songs*. London, 1627.

Allan, Keith. *Natural Language Semantics*. Oxford: Blackwell, 2001.

Allan, Keith, and Kate Burridge. *Euphemism & Dysphemism*. New York and Oxford: Oxford University Press, 1991.

– *Forbidden Words: Taboo and the Censoring of Language*. Cambridge: Cambridge University Press, 2006.

Ames, William. *Conscience with the Power and Cases Thereof*. Cambridge, 1639.

– *The Marrow of Sacred Divinity*. London, 1642.

*The Anatomy of Dr. Gauden's Idolized Non-sence and Blasphemy*. London, 1660.

Andrewes, Lancelot. Appendix. In Richard Cosin. *An Apologie for Svndrie Proceedings by Iurisdiction Ecclesiasticall*, 242–55. London, 1593.

– *XCVI. Sermons*. London, 1629.

Antoninus Liberalis. *Metamorphoses*. Translated by Francis Celoria. London and New York: Routledge, 1992.

Ariosto, Ludovico. *Orlando Fvrioso in English Heroical Verse*. Translated by John Harington. London, 1591.

Aristophanes. *Aristophanes III*. Translated by Benjamin Bickley Rogers. London: Heinemann; New York, Putnam, 1931.

Aristotle. *Politics*. Translated by H. Rackham. Cambridge, MA, and London: Harvard University Press, 1998.

Ascham, Anthony. *The Bounds & Bonds of Publique Obedience*. London, 1649.

– *A Combate between Two Seconds*. London, 1649.

– *A Discourse: Wherein Is Examined, What Is Particularly Lawfull during the Cnfusions and Revolutions of Government*. London, 1649.

– *Genesis Kai Telos Exousias* [*Γενεσις και Τελος Εξουσιας*]: *The Original and End of Civil Power*. London, 1649.

– *Of the Confusions and Revolutions of Gover[n]ments*. 2nd ed. London, 1649.

– *A Reply to a Paper of Dr. Sandersons*. London, 1650.

Ashmole, Elias, and Francis Sandford, eds. *The Entire Ceremonies of the Coronations of His Majesty King Charles II. and of her Majesty Queen Mary, Consort to James II*. London, 1761.

Assheton, William. *Toleration Disapprov'd and Condemn'd*. 2nd ed. Oxford, 1670.

Aucher, John. *Arguments and Reasons to Prove the Inconvenience & Vnlawfulness of Taking the New Engagement*. London, 1650.

Augustine. *The City of God*. Translated by G.E. McCracken et al. 7 vols. Cambridge, MA: Harvard University Press; London: Heinemann, 1963–81.

Austin, J.L. *How To Do Things with Words*. Edited by J.O. Urmson and Marina Sbisa. 2nd ed. Cambridge, MA: Harvard University Press, 1975.

B., T. *The Engagement Vindicated*. London, 1649/50.

*The Babylonian Talmud*. Edited and translated by Jacob Neusner. 22 vols. Peabody, MA: Hendrickson, 2011.

*The Babylonian Talmud: Nazir*. Edited and translated by by B.D. Klien. London: Soncino Press, 1936.

*The Babylonian Talmud: Sotah*. Edited and translated by A. Cohen. London: Soncino Press, 1936.

Bach, Kent, and Robert M. Harnish. *Linguistic Communication and Speech Acts*. Cambridge, MA, and London: MIT Press, 1979.

Bal, Mieke. *Death and Dissymmetry: The Politics of Coherence in the Book of Judges*. Chicago and London: University of Chicago Press, 1988.

Balfour, James. *The Historical Works of Sir James Balfour*. Vol. 4. London, 1825.

Bancroft, Thomas. *Time's Out of Tune*. London, 1658.

Barber, Sarah. "The Engagement for the Council of State and the Establishment of the Commonwealth Government." *Historical Research* 63.150 (February 1990): 44–57.

– *Regicide and Republicanism*. Edinburgh: Edinburgh University Press, 1998.

Barbour, John. *The Actes and Life of the Most Victorious Conquerour, Robert Bruce*. Edinburgh, 1620.

Barlow, William. *Answer to a Catholike English-man*. London, 1609.

Bartlett, Mike. *King Charles III: A Future History Play*. New York: Theatre Communications Group, 2015.

Basier, Isaac. *The History of the English and Scotch Presbytery*. N.p., 1660.

Bate, Frank. *The Declaration of Indulgence 1672: A Study in the Rise of Organised Dissent*. London: Archibald Constable for Liverpool University Press, 1908.

Battigelli, Anna. *Margaret Cavendish and the Exiles of the Mind*. Lexington: University of Kentucky Press, 1998.

Bauman, Michael. *Milton's Arianism*. Frankfurt am Main, Bern, New York: Peter Lang, 1987.

Baxter, Richard. *An Apology for Nonconformists Ministry*. London, 1681.

– *A Christian Directory, or, A Summ of Practical Theologie and Cases of Conscience*. London, 1673.

– *A Paraphrase on the New Testament*. London, 1685.

– *Reliquiae Baxterianae*. London, 1696.

– *Sacrilegious Desertion of the Holy Ministery Rebuked*. [London], 1672.

Becon, Thomas. *An Inuectyue agenst the Moost Wicked Detestable Vyce of Swearing*. [London], 1543.

Bell, Catherine. *Ritual: Perspectives and Dimensions*. 2nd ed. Oxford: Oxford University Press, 2009.

Bell, Elizabeth. *Theories of Performance*. Los Angeles: Sage, 2008.

Bennett, Joan. "Mary Astell, Lucy Hutchinson, John Milton, and Feminist Liberation Theology." In *Milton in the Age of Fish*, edited by Michael Lieb and Albert C. Labriola, 140–66. Pittsburgh: Duquesne University Press, 2006.

Benson, Gervase. *A Second Testimony Concerning Oaths and Swearing*. London, 1675.

Benveniste, Emile. *Indo-European Language and Society*. Translated by Elizabeth Palmer. Coral Gables, FL: University of Miami Press, 1973.

Bergen, Benjamin K. *What the F: What Swearing Reveals about Our Language, Our Brains, and Ourselves*. New York: Basic Books, 2016.

Bicknoll, Edward. *A Svvoord agaynst Swearyng*. London, 1579.

Binning, Hugh. *An Useful Case of Conscience*. [Edinburgh?], 1693.

Blake, William. *Milton a Poem and the Final Illuminated Works*. Edited by Robert N. Essick and Joseph Viscomi. Princeton: Princeton University Press for the William Blake Trust, 1993.

Blount, Thomas. *Glossographia*. London, 1661.

– *Nomo-Lexikon*. [London], 1671.

Bobonich, Christopher. *Plato's Utopia Recast*. Oxford: Clarendon Press, 2002.

*The Book of Oaths*. London, 1649.

*The Book of Oaths*. London, 1689.

Bond, Richard P. *English Burlesque Poetry 1700–1750*. Cambridge, MA: Harvard University Press, 1932.

Bowles, Edward. *The Dutie and Danger of Swearing*. York, 1645.

Boyle, Robert. *A Free Discourse against Customary Swearing*. London, 1695.

Boyle, Roger. *The History of Henry the Fifth*. In *The Broadview Anthology of Restoration and Early Eighteenth-Century Drama*, edited by J. Douglas Canfield and Maja-Lisa von Sneidern, 3–37. Peterborough, Ontario: Broadview Press, 2001.

Brabourn, Theophilus. *Of the Lawfulness of the Oath of Allegiance to the King, and Of the Other Oath to His Svpremacy*. London, 1661.

Braddick, Michael. *State Formation in Early Modern England c. 1550–1700*. Cambridge: Cambridge University Press, 2000.

Bramhall, John. *A Fair Warning for England to Take Heed of the Presbyterian Government of Scotland*. London, 1661.

Braverman, Richard. *Plots and Counterplots*. Cambridge: Cambridge University Press, 1993.

*A Brief Resolution of That Grand Case of Conscience*. London, 1650.

Bristow, Richard. *A Reply to Fulke*. London, 1580.

Brooks, Cleanth. "Criticism and Literary History: Marvell's Horatian Ode." *Sewanee Review* 55.2 (April–June 1947): 199–222.

Brown, John. *An Apologeticall Relation of the Particular Sufferings of the Faithfull Ministers & Professours of the Church of Scotland, Since August, 1660*. [Edinburgh?], 1665.
Brown, Francis, Samuel R. Driver, and Charles A. Briggs. *A Hebrew and English Lexikon of the Old Testament*. Oxford: Clarendon Press, 1936.
Browne, Thomas. *Pseudodoxia Epidemica*. London, 1646.
Bryson, Michael. *The Tyranny of Heaven: Milton's Rejection of God as King*. Newark: University of Delaware Press, 2004.
Bunyan, John. *Grace Abounding*. London, 1666.
– *The Life and Death of Mr. Badman and The Holy War*. Edited by John Brown. Cambridge: Cambridge University Press, 1905.
– *Pilgrim's Progress*. London, 1678.
– *Pilgrim's Progress*. Edited by Cynthia Wall. New York and London: Norton, 2009.
Burges, Cornelius. *The First Sermon, Preached to the Honourable House of Commons*. London, 1641.
Burgess, Anthony. *An Expository Comment . . . upon the Whole First Chapter to the Second Epistle of St. Paul to the Corinthians*. London, 1661.
Burgess, Glenn. "Usurpation, Obligation and Obedience in the Thought of the Engagement Controversy." *Historical Journal* 29.3 (September 1986): 515–36.
Burkert, Walter. *Creation of the Sacred: Tracks of Biology in Early Religions*. Cambridge, MA, and London: Harvard University Press, 1996.
Burnet, Gilbert. *An Exposition of the Thirty-Nine Articles of the Church of England*. London, 1700.
Burroughs, Jeremiah. *Moses His Self-Denyall*. London, 1641.
Burton, Robert. *The Anatomy of Melancholy*. Edited by Holbrook Jackson and William H. Gass. New York: New York Review Books, 2001.
Bush, Douglas. "Marvell's Horatian Ode." *Sewanee Review* 60.3 (July-September 1952): 362–76.
Butler, Judith. *Undoing Gender*. New York and London: Routledge, 2004.
Butler, Samuel. *Characters*. Edited by Charles W. Daves. Cleveland and London: Case Western Reserve University Press, 1970.
– *The Genuine Remains in Verse and Prose of Mr. Samuel Butler*. Edited by Robert Thyer. 2 vols. London, 1759.
– *Hudibras*. Edited by Zachary Grey. 2 vols. Cambridge, 1744.
– *Hudibras*. Edited by Treadway Russel Nash. 3 vols. London, 1793.
– *Hudibras*. Edited by John Wilders. Oxford: Clarendon Press, 1967.
– *Posthumous Works*. 3 vols. 4th ed. London, 1732.
– *Prose Observations*. Edited by Hugh De Quehen. Oxford: Clarendon Press, 1979.

– *Satires and Miscellaneous Poetry and Prose*. Edited by René Lamar. Cambridge: Cambridge University Press, 1928.

– *The Transproser Rehears'd*. London, 1673.

[Butler, Samuel?]. *A Proposall Humbly Offered for the Farming of Liberty of Conscience*. [London,] 1662/3.

"The 'Caedmonian' *Paradise Lost*." In *The Celestial Cycle: The Theme of Paradise Lost in World Literature with Translations of the Major Analogues*. Translated by Watson Kirkconnell, 19–43. New York: Gordian Press, 1967.

Calamy, Edmund. *Gods Free Mercy to England*. London, 1642.

– *The Great Danger of Covenant-Refusing and Covenant-Breaking*. London, 1646.

Callimachus. *Aetia*. Translated by C.A. Trypanis. Cambridge, MA: Harvard University Press; London: Heinemann, 1958.

Calvin, John. *A Harmonie vpon the Three Euangelists, Matthew, Mark and Luke . . .* 2 vols. London, 1584.

– *Institution of Christian Religion*. Translated by Thomas Norton. London, 1561.

– *Sermons of M. Iohn Caluine vpon the Epistle of Saincte Paule to the Galathians*. Translated by Arthur Golding. London, 1574.

– *Sermons of Master Iohn Caluin, vpon the Booke of Iob*. Translated by Arthur Golding. London, 1574.

Camden, William. *Britain*. Translated by Philemon Holland. London, 1637.

Campbell, Gordon, and Thomas N. Corns. *John Milton: Life, Work, and Thought*. Oxford: Oxford University Press, 2010.

Campbell, Gordon, et al. *Milton and the Manuscript of De Doctrina Christiana*. Oxford: Oxford University Press, 2007.

Canfield, J. Douglas. *Word as Bond in English Literature from the Middle Ages to the Restoration*. Philadelphia: University of Pennsylvania Press, 1989.

Cant, Andrew. *A Sermon Preached at a General Meeting in the Gray-Friar-Church of Edinburgh, Upon the 13. Day of June 1638*. Edinburgh, 1720.

Capp, Bernard. *When Gossips Meet*. Oxford: Oxford University Press, 2003.

Carastro, Marcello. "Fabriquer du Lien en Grèce Ancienne: Serments, Sacrifices, Ligatures." *Mètis* ns 10 (2012): 77–105.

Carre, Thomas [= Miles Pinkney?]. *A Treatise of Subjection to the Powers*. London, 1651.

Cartledge, Paul. *After Thermopylae: The Oath of Plataea and the End of the Graeco-Persian Wars*. Oxford: Oxford University Press, 2013.

Cartledge, Tony. *Vows in the Hebrew Bible and the Ancient Near East*. Sheffield: Sheffield Academic Press, 1992.

Caryl, Joseph. *The Nature, Solemnity, Grounds, Property, and Benefits of a Sacred Covenant*. London, 1643.

Case, Thomas. *The Quarrell of the Covenant*. London, 1644.

– *Sermon III*. In *A Collection of Several Remarkable and Valuable Sermons, Speeches, and Exhortations at Renewing and Subscribing the National Covenant of Scotland: and at Entering into and Subscribing the Solemn League and Covenant*, 325–78. Glasgow, 1799.

Castrop, Helmut. *Die Varronische Satire in England 1660–1690: Studien zu Butler, Marvell und Dryden*. Heidelberg: Carl Winter Universitätsverlag, 1983.

Caton, William. *An Epistle to King Charles*. London, 1660.

Cavendish, Margaret. *CCXI Sociable Letters*. London, 1664.

– *The Convent of Pleasure and Other Plays*. Edited by Anne Shaver. Baltimore and London: Johns Hopkins University Press, 1999.

– *Sociable Letters*. Edited by James Fitzmaurice. Peterborough, Ontario: Broadview Press, 2004.

*The Celestial Cycle: The Theme of Paradise Lost in World Literature with Translations of the Major Analogues*. Edited by Watson Kirkconnell. New York: Gordian Press, 1967.

*The Ceremonies . . . at the Coronation of King James the First and . . . the Coronation of King Charles the First in Scotland*. London, 1685.

Champion, Craig B. "Imperial Ideologies, Citizenship Myths, and Legal Disputes in Classical Athens and Republican Rome." In *A Companion to Greek and Roman Political Thought*, edited by Ryan K. Balot, 85–100. Malden, MA, and Oxford: Wiley-Blackwell, 2013.

Chapman, Hester. *Great Villiers: A Study of George Villiers, Second Duke of Buckingham, 1628–1687*. London: Secker & Warburg, 1949.

Charles I and John Gauden. *Ειχων Βασιλιχη* [*Eikon Basilike*]. London, 1649.

Charles II. *A Proclamation against Vicious, Debauch'd, & Profane Persons*. London, 1660.

– *A Proclamation, Declaring His Majesties Pleasure Touching His Royal Coronation*. London, 1661.

– *A Proclamation for Publishing a Former Proclamation of the 30th of May last (Entituled A Proclamation against Vicious, Debauch'd, & Profane Persons)*. London, 1660.

– *A Proclamation for the Observation of the Lords-Day, and for Renewing a Former Proclamation against Vicious, Debauched, & Profane Persons*. London, 1663.

Chernaik, Warren L. *The Poet's Time: Politics and Religion in the Work of Andrew Marvell*. Cambridge: Cambridge University Press, 1983.

– "Was Marvell a Republican?" *The Seventeenth Century* 20.1 (2005): 77–96.

Chidley, Katherine. *A New-yeares-gift, or, A Brief Exhortation to Mr. Thomas Edwards*. London, 1645.

Church of England. *Articles*. [London], 1571.

– *The Book of Common-Prayer*. London, 1662.

Churchill, Randolph S. *The Story of the Coronation*. London: Derek Verschoyle, 1953.

Cicero. *De Officiis*. Edited by Walter Miller. Cambridge, MA, and London: Harvard University Press, 2005.

Clarke, Samuel. *The Saints Nosegay*. London, 1642.

*The Cloud Opened, or, The English Heroe*. London, 1670.

Collier, Jeremy. *A Short View of the Immorality and Profaneness of the English Stage*. London, 1698.

Collins, Jeffrey. *The Allegiance of Thomas Hobbes*. Oxford: Oxford University Press, 2005.

Collins, John. *Farewell Sermon*. In *An Exact Collection of Farewel Sermons Preached by the Late London-Minister*, 362–88. London, 1662.

Colvill, John. *The Palinod of Iohn Coluill*. [Edinburgh], 1600.

*A Common-Place-Book out of The Rehearsal Transpros'd*. London, 1673.

Condren, Conal. *Argument and Authority in Early Modern England: The Presupposition of Oaths and Offices*. Cambridge: Cambridge University Press, 2006.

– *The Language of Politics in Seventeenth-Century England*. Houndmills: Macmillan; New York: St Martin's Press, 1994.

– "Marvell's 'Horation Ode on Cromwell's Return from Ireland' and the Context of the Engagement Controversy." In *Renaissance Poetry and Drama in Context*, edited by Andrew Lynch and Anne M. Scott, 257–67. Newcastle upon Tyne: Cambridge Scholars, 2008.

Conklin, Blane. *Oath Formulas in Biblical Hebrew*. Winona Lake, IN: Eisenbrauns, 2011.

Connell, Philip. "Marvell, Milton, and the Protectoral Church Settlement." *Review of English Studies*, ns 62.256 (2011): 562–93.

*The Constitutional Documents of the Puritan Revolution, 1625–1660*. Edited by S.R. Gardiner. 3rd rev. ed. Oxford: Clarendon Press, 1968.

Coolidge, John S. "Marvell and Horace." *Modern Philology* 63.2 (November 1965): 111–20.

Cooper, Thomas. *Thesaurus Linguae Latinae & Britannicae*. 2nd ed. London, 1578.

Cooper, William. *Farewell Sermon*. In *A Compleat Collection of Farewel Sermons*, Zzz3r–Bbbb4v. London, 1663.

Cope, Esther. *Handmaid of the Holy Spirit: Dame Eleanor Davies*. Ann Arbor: University of Michigan Press, 1992.

Corbet, John. *A Discourse of the Religion of England*. London, 1667.

– *The Epistle Congratulatorie of Lysimachus Nicanor of the Societie of Jesu, to the Covenanters in Scotland*. London, 1640.

Corns, Thomas. "Milton and the Characteristics of a Free Commonwealth." In *Milton and Republicanism*, edited by David Armitage, Armand Himy, and Quentin Skinner, 25–42. Cambridge: Cambridge University Press, 1995.
– *Regaining Paradise Lost*. London and New York: Pearson Longman, 2003.
Cosin, Richard. *An Apologie for Svndrie Proceedings by Iurisdiction Ecclesiasticall*. London, 1593.
Cousins, A.D. "The Idea of a 'Restoration' and the Verse Satires of Butler and Marvell." *Southern Review* 14 (1981): 131–42.
*The Covenanters Plea against Absolvers*. London, 1661.
Coverdale, Miles. *A Christen Exhortacion vnto Customable Swearers*. [London], 1543.
Coward, Barry. *The Stuart Age*. 2nd ed. London and New York: Longman, 1994.
Cowley, Abraham. *Poems*. London, 1663.
Crawford, Patricia. "'The Poorest She': Women and Citizenship in Early Modern England." In *The Putney Debates of 1647: The Army, the Levellers, and the English State*, edited by Michael Mendle, 197–218. New York: Cambridge University Press, 2001.
– "Women and Citizenship in Britain 1500–1800." In *Women as Australian Citizens*, edited by Crawford and Philippa Maddern, 48–82. Carlton: Melbourne University Press, 2001.
Crawley, A.E. "Oath." *Encyclopedia of Religion and Ethics*. Vol. 9, 430–4. New York: Charles Scribner's Sons, 1933.
Cressener, Robert. *Anti-Baal-Berith Justified*. London, 1662.
Cressy, David. *England on Edge*. Oxford: Oxford University Press, 2006.
– "The Protestation Protested, 1641 and 1642." *Historical Journal* 45.2 (June 2002): 251–69.
Crofton, Zachary. *Analepsis*. London, 1660.
– *Analepsis Anelephthe*. London, 1660.
– *Berith Anti-Baal*. London, 1660.
– *Defence against the Dread of Death*. [London], 1665.
Cromwell, Oliver. *Oliver Cromwell's Letters and Speeches*. Edited by Thomas Carlyle. 3rd ed. 4 vols. London: Chapman and Hall, 1850.
Crook, J.A. *Law and Life of Rome, 90 B.C.–A.D. 212*. Ithaca and New York: Cornell University Press, 1967.
Crook, John. *The Case of Swearing (At All) Discussed*. London, 1660.
– *Sixteen Reasons*. London, 1661.
– *Twenty Cases of Conscience*. London, 1667.
Crouch, John. *The Man in the Moon* 37 (2–9 January 1650) and 48 (13–20 March 1650).

Crowne, John. *City Politiques*. London, 1682.

Curley, Edwin. "Hobbes and the Cause of Religious Toleration." In *The Cambridge Companion to Hobbes's Leviathan*, edited by Patricia Sprinborg, 309–34. Cambridge: Cambridge University Press, 2007.

D., J. *A Discourse Concerning the Solemne League and Covenant*. London, 1661.

Danet, Pierre. *A Complete Dictionary of the Greek and Roman Antiquities*. London, 1700.

Daniel, Clay. "Royal Samson." *Milton Studies* 46 (2007): 123–46.

Davies, Stevie. *Images of Kingship in Paradise Lost*. Columbia, MO: University of Missouri Press, 1983.

De Beer, E.S. "The Later Life of Samuel Butler." *Review of English Studies* 4.14 (April 1928): 159–66.

De Krey, Gary. *London and the Restoration, 1659–1683*. Cambridge: Cambridge University Press, 2005.

Denne, Henry. *An Epistle Recommended to All the Prisons*. London, 1660.

Dering, Edward. *The Parliamentary Diary of Sir Edward Dering, 1670–1673*. Edited by Basil Duke Henning. New Haven, CT: Yale University Press, 1940.

Derrida, Jacques. *Acts of Religion*. Edited by Gil Anidjar. New York: Routledge, 2001.

– *Adieu to Emmanuel Levinas*. Translated by Pascale-Anne Brault and Michael Nass. Stanford, CA: Stanford University Press, 1999.

– *A Derrida Reader*. Edited by Peggy Kamuf. New York: Columbia University Press, 1991.

– *Negotiations*. Translated by E. Rottenberg. Stanford, CA: Stanford University Press, 2002.

– *Politics of Friendship*. Translated by George Collins. London and New York: Verso, 1997.

– "Signature Event Context." In *Limited Inc.*, edited by Gerald Graff and translated by Samuel Weber and Jeffrey Mehlman, 1–23. Evanston, IL: Northwestern University Press, 1988.

– *Sovereignties in Question: The Poetics of Paul Celan*. Edited by Thomas Dutoit and Outi Pasanen. New York: Fordham University Press, 2005.

– *Without Alibi*. Edited and translated by Peggy Kamuf. Stanford, CA: Stanford University Press, 2002.

Diodati, Giovanni. *Pious Annotations upon the Holy Bible*. London, 1643.

DiSalvo, Jackie. "Intestine Thorn: Samson's Struggle with the Woman Within." In *Milton and the Idea of Woman*, edited by Julia M. Walker, 211–29. Urbana and Chicago: University of Illinois Press, 1987.

Dixon, William Macneile. *English Epic and Heroic Poetry*. London: Dent, 1912.

*The Doctrine and Discipline of the Kirke of Scotland*. Edinburgh, 1641.

Donagan, Barbara. "Varieties of Royalism." In *Royalists and Royalism during the English Civil Wars*, edited by Jason McElligott and David L. Smith, 66–88. Cambridge: Cambridge University Press, 2007.

Donne, John. *The Oxford Authors: John Donne*. Edited by John Carey. New York and Oxford: Oxford University Press, 1992.

– *Pseudo-Martyr*. Edited by Anthony Raspa. Montreal and Kingston: McGill University Press, 1993.

Doody, Margaret. *The Daring Muse*. Cambridge: Cambridge University Press, 1985.

Douglas, Eleanor Davies. *A Prayer or Petition for Peace. November 22. 1644*. London, 1649.

– *Samsons Fall*. London, 1643.

– *Samsons Legacie*. London, 1643.

Downame, John. *Fovre Treatises*. London, 1608.

Downame, John, et al. *Annotations upon the Old and New Testament*. London, 1645.

– *Annotations upon the Old and New Testament*. London, 1657.

Drew, John. *The Northern Subscribers Plea, Vindicated*. London, 1651.

Dryden, John. *John Dryden: Selected Poems*. Edited by Steven N. Zwicker and David Bywaters. London: Penguin, 2001.

Du Moulin, Lewis. *The Power of the Christian Magistrate in Sacred Things*. London, 1650.

Duncan Jones, E.E. "The Erect Sword in Marvell's *Horatian Ode*." *Etudes Anglaises* 15.2 (April 1962): 172–4.

DuRocher, Richard. *Milton and Ovid*. Ithaca, NY and London: Cornell University Press, 1985.

Dury, John. *A Case of Conscience Resolved*. London, 1649.

– *Considerations Concerning the Engagement*. London, 1649.

– *A Disingag'd Survey of the Engagement*. London, 1650.

– *Just Reproposals*. London, 1650.

– *Objections against the Taking of the Engagement Answered*. London, 1650.

– *A Second Parcel of Objections against the Engagement Answered*. London, 1650.

– *Two Treatises Concerning . . . the Engagement*. London, 1650.

– *The Unchanged, Constant and Single-hearted Peace-Maker*. London, 1650.

Dzelzainis, Martin. "Milton and Ciceronian Rhetoric." In *English Renaissance Prose: History, Language, Politics*, edited by Neil Rhodes, 203–26. Tempe, AZ: Medieval and Renaissance Texts and Studies, 1997.

– "Milton and the Protectorate in 1658." In *Milton and Republicanism*, edited by David Armitage, Armand Himy, and Quentin Skinner, 181–205. Cambridge: Cambridge University Press, 1995.

– "Milton's Classical Republicanism." In *Milton and Republicanism*, edited by David Armitage, Armand Himy, and Quentin Skinner, 3–24. Cambridge: Cambridge University Press, 1995.

*Eikon Alethine [ΕΙΚΩΝ ΑΛΗΘΙΝΗ ]*. London, 1649.

*Eikon Hē Pistē [ΕΙΚΩΝ Η ΠΙΣΤΕ]*. London, 1649.

Empson, William. "A Defense of Delilah." *Sewanee Review* 68.2 (April–June 1960): 247–55.

– *Milton's God*. London: Chatto & Windus, 1961.

*England Uniting to Her Sovereign; or, Advancing of the King: A Solemne League and Covenant*. London, 1660.

Engler, Balz. "*Hudibras* and the Problem of Satirical Distance." *English Studies* 60 (1979): 436–43.

*The English-man's Allegiance*. [London], 1691.

Esterhammer, Angela. *Creating States: Studies in the Performative Language of John Milton and William Blake*. Toronto, Buffalo, and London: University of Toronto Press, 1994.

*Etudes Epistémè: Revue de Littérature et de Civilisation (XVIe –XVIIe Siècles)* 24 (2013).

Evans, Charles. *Oaths of Allegiance in Colonial New England*. N.p.: American Antiquarian Society, 1921.

Evelyn, John. *The Diary of John Evelyn*. Edited by E.S. De Beer. 6 vols. Oxford: Clarendon Press, 1955.

Everett, Barbara. "The Shooting of the Bears: Poetry and Politics in Andrew Marvell." In *Andrew Marvell: Essays on the Tercentenary of his Death*, edited by R.L. Brett, 62–103. Oxford: Oxford University Press, 1979.

F., D. *Reason and Judgement, or, Special Remarques of the Life of the Renowned Dr. Sanderson*. London, 1663.

Fallon, Robert Thomas. *Divided Empire: Milton's Political Imagery*. University Park: Pennsylvania State University Press, 1995.

Farley-Hills, David. *The Benevolence of Laughter*. London: Macmillan, 1974.

Fauré, Christine. "Rights or Virtues: Women and the Republic." In *Republicanism*. 2 vols, edited by Martin Van Gelderen and Quentin Skinner, 2:125–38. Cambridge: Cambridge University Press, 2002.

Featley, Daniel. *The League Illegal*. London, 1660.

– *Virtumnus Romanus*. London, 1642.

Felman, Shoshana. *The Scandal of the Speaking Body*. Stanford, CA: Stanford University Press, 2002.

Ferguson, Robert. *A Representation of the Threatning Dangers Impending over Protestants in Great Brittain*. London, 1687.

Fezas, Jean. "Le Serment, Lien Social et Lien Politique." In *Le Serment*. 2 vols, edited by Raymond Verdier, 1:223–35. Paris: Èditions du Centre National de la Recherche Scientifique, 1991.

Fish, Stanley. *Is There A Text in This Class?* Cambridge, MA, and London: Harvard University Press, 1980.

Fisher, Samuel. *One Antidote More, against that Provoking Sin of Swearing*. London, 1660.

Fitzmyer, Joseph A. "The Aramaic Inscriptions of Sefire I and II." *Journal of the American Oriental Society* 81.3 (August–September 1961): 178–222.

Fletcher, Judith. *Performing Oaths in Classical Greek Drama*. Cambridge: Cambridge University Press, 2012.

Fletcher, R[obert]. *Mercurius Heliconicus*. London, 1651.

– *Radius Heliconicus*. London, 1650.

*The Form and Order of the Coronation of Charles the Second*. Aberdeen, 1651.

Fox, George. *Our Covenant with God*. London, 1660.

Foxley, Rachel. "Oliver Cromwell on Religion and Resistance." In *England's Wars of Religion Revisited*, edited by Charles W.A. Prior and Glenn Burgess, 209–30. Farnham and Burlington: Ashgate, 2011.

Frazer, James George. *The Golden Bough*. New York: Collier, 1963.

Friesenhahn, Ernst. *Der Politische Eid*. Bonn: Verlag Ludwig Röhrscheid, 1927.

Froula, Christine. "When Eve Reads Milton." *Critical Inquiry* 10.2 (December 1983): 321–47.

Frye, Roland Mushat. *Milton's Imagery and the Visual Arts: Iconographic Tradition in the Epic Poems*. Princeton: Princeton University Press, 1978.

Fullwood, Francis. *The Doctrine of Schism*. London, 1672.

– *The Grand Case of the Present Ministry*. London, 1663.

Gallagher, Catherine. "Embracing the Absolute: Margaret Cavendish and the Politics of the Female Subject in Seventeenth-Century England." In *Early Women Writers: 1600–1720*, edited by Anita Pacheco, 133–45. London and New York: Longman, 1998.

Garganigo, Alex. "God's Swearing by Himself: Milton's Troubling Coronation Oath." In *With Wandering Steps: Generative Ambiguity in Milton's Poetics*, edited by Mary G. Fenton and Louis Schwartz, 3–34. Pittsburgh, PA: Duquesne University Press, 2016.

– "Mourning the Headless Body Politic: The Regicide Elegies and Marvell's 'Horatian Ode.'" *Exemplaria* 15.2 (Fall 2003): 509–50.

– "Samson's Cords: Imposing Oaths in *Samson Agonistes*," *Milton Studies* 50 (2009): 125–49.

Gauden, John. *Analysis*. London, 1660.

– *Anti-Baal Berith*. London, 1661.

– *Certain Doubts and Scruples of Conscience about Taking the Solemn League and Covenant*. London, 1660.
– *A Discourse Concering Publick Oaths*. London, 1662.
– *A Pillar of Gratitude*. London, 1661.
Gaunt, Peter. *Oliver Cromwell*. Oxford: Blackwell, 1996.
Gee, Edward. *An Exercitation Concerning Usurped Powers*. London, 1649.
– *A Plea for Non-Scribers*. 2 vols. London, 1650.
– *A Vindication of the Oath of Allegiance*. London, 1650.
Gibson, Abraham. *The Lands Mourning for Vain Swearing*. London, 1613.
Gibson, Dan J., Jr. "Samuel Butler." In *Seventeenth Century Studies*, series 1, edited by Robert Shafer, 279–335. Princeton, NJ: Princeton University Press, 1933.
Gibson, William. *Religion and the Enlightenment 1600–1800: Conflict and the Rise of Civic Humanism in Taunton*. Oxford and Bern: Peter Lang, 2007.
Gilbert, Sandra. "Milton's Bogey." In Gilbert and Susan Gubar, *The Madwoman in the Attic*, 188–204. New Haven, CT: Yale University Press, 1979.
Gillespie, George. *An Assertion of the Government of the Church of Scotland*. Edinburgh, 1641.
Girard, René. *The Scapegoat*. Baltimore, MD, and London: Johns Hopkins University Press, 1986.
– *Violence and the Sacred*. Baltimore, MD, and London: Johns Hopkins University Press, 1977.
Goodwin, John. *Englands Apology for Its Late Change*. London, 1651.
Gorton, Samuel. *Saltmarsh Returned*. London 1655.
*The Government of the Commonwealth . . . As It Was Publickly Declared at Westminster, the 16. Day of December, 1653*. London, 1654.
*The Grand Case of Conscience Concerning the Engagement Stated and Resolved*. London, 1650.
Gray, Jonathan. *Oaths and the English Reformation*. Cambridge: Cambridge University Press, 2012.
Greaves, Richard. *Enemies under His Feet: Radicals and Nonconformists in Britain, 1664–1677*. Stanford, CA: Stanford University Press, 1990.
Gregerson, Linda. *The Reformation of the Subject*. Cambridge: Cambridge University Press, 1995.
Gregg, Pauline. *Free-Born John: A Biography of John Lilburne*. London: Harrap, 1961.
Grey, Anchitell, ed. *Debates of the House of Commons*. 10 vols. London, 1763.
Grey, Enoch. *Vox Coeli*. London, 1649.
Grey, Zachary. *Critical, Historical, and Explanatory Notes upon Hudibras*. London, 1752.

Grotius, Hugo. *Of the Law of Warre and Peace*. London, 1655.
Grymeston, Elizabeth. *Miscellanea*. In *Women Writing in Renaissance England*, edited by Randall Martin, 100–16. London and New York: Longman, 1997.
Guillory, John. "Dalila's House: *Samson Agonistes* and the Sexual Division of Labor." In *Rewriting the Renaissance*, edited by Margaret W. Ferguson, Maureen Quilligan, and Nancy J. Vickers, 106–22. Chicago and London: University of Chicago Press, 1986.
Guthrie, John. *A Sermon . . . upon Breach of Covenant*. London, 1663.
Haak, Theodore. *The Dutch Annotations upon the Whole Bible*. London, 1657.
Habermas, Jürgen. "Dialogue: Jürgen Habermas and Charles Taylor." In *The Power of Religion in the Public Sphere*, edited by Eduardo Mendieta and Jonathan VanAntwerpen, 60–9. New York: Columbia University Press, 2011.
– "'The Political': The Rational Meaning of a Questionable Inheritance of Political Theology." In *The Power of Religion in the Public Sphere*, edited by Eduardo Mendieta and Jonathan VanAntwerpen, 15–33. New York: Columbia University Press, 2011.
– *The Structural Transformation of the Public Sphere*. Translated by Thomas Burger and Frederick Lawrence. Cambridge, MA: MIT Press, 1989.
Hadfield, Andrew. *Lying in Early Modern English Culture: From the Oath of Supremacy to the Oath of Allegiance*. Oxford: Oxford University Press, 2017.
Hall, Henry. *Digitus Testium*. London, 1651.
Hall, Joseph. *Cases of Conscience Practically Resolved*. London, 1654.
– *Resolutions and Decisions of Divers Practicall Cases of Conscience*. London, 1649.
Hall, Thomas. *Samarias Downfall*. London, 1660.
Halley, Janet. "Female Autonomy in Milton's Sexual Poetics." In *Milton and the Idea of Woman*, edited by Julia M. Walker, 230–46. Urbana and Chicago: University of Illinois Press, 1987.
Hamilton, Donna B. *Shakespeare and the Politics of Protestant England*. Lexington: University Press of Kentucky, 1992.
Hammond, Samuel. *Gods Judgements upon Drunkards, Swearers, and Sabbath-Breakers*. London, 1659.
Harding, Davis P. *Milton and the Renaissance Ovid*. N.p.: Folcroft Library Editions, 1977.
*Harpers Dictionary of Classical Antiquitie*. Edited by Harry Thurston Peck. New York: Harpers, 1898.
Harrington, James. *The Art of Lawgiving*. London, 1659.
– *Oceana*. Edited by J.G.A. Pocock. Cambridge: Cambridge University Press, 1992.
– *Politicaster*. London, 1659.
– *The Rota*. London, 1660.
Harris, Tim. *Restoration: Charles II and His Kingdoms*. London: Penguin, 2005.

Hausknecht, Gina. "The Gender of Civic Virtue." In *Milton and Gender*, edited by Catherine Gimelli Martin, 19–33. Cambridge: Cambridge University Press, 2004.

Hawes, Stephen. *The Co[n]uercyon of Swerers*. [London], 1509.

Heath, James. *The Glories and Magnificent Triumphs of The Blessed Restitution of His Sacred Majesty K. Charles II*. London, 1662.

[Herle, Charles.] *The Exercitation Answered*. London, 1650.

Herman, Peter. *Destabilizing Milton: "Paradise Lost" and the Poetics of Incertitude*. New York: Palgrave Macmillan, 2005.

Herodotus. *The Histories*. Translated by Aubrey de Selincourt and A.R. Burn. Harmondsworth: Penguin, 1985.

Heyrick, Richard. *Queen Esthers Resolves . . . a Sermon*. London, 1646.

– *A Sermon . . . on . . . the Coronation-Day of . . . Charles II*. London, 1661.

– *Three Sermons*. London, 1640.

Hickeringill, Edmund. *Gregory, Father-Greybeard, with His Vizor Off*. London, 1673.

Hill, Christopher. *God's Englishman*. New York: Harper & Row, 1972

– *Society and Puritanism in Pre-Revolutionary England*. New York: St Martin's Press, 1997.

Hilliam, David. *Crown, Orb & Sceptre: The True Stories of English Coronations*. Phoenix Mill: Sutton, 2002.

Hirst, Derek. "The Privy Council and the Problems of Enforcement in the 1620s." *Journal of British Studies* 18.1 (Autumn 1978): 46–66.

– *The Representative of the People? Voters and Voting in England under the Early Stuarts*. Cambridge: Cambridge University Press, 1975.

Hirst, Derek, and Steven N. Zwicker. *Andrew Marvell: Orphan of the Hurricane*. Oxford: Oxford University Press, 2012.

*Hittite Diplomatic Texts*. Translated by Gary Beckman and ed. Harry A. Hofner, Jr. Atlanta: Scholars Press, 1996.

Hoak, Dale. "The Case of Edward VI, Mary I, and Elizabeth I, and the Transformation of the Tudor Monarchy." In *Westminster Abbey Reformed*, edited by C.S. Knighton and Richard Mortimer, 115–50. Aldershot: Ashgate, 2003.

Hobbes, Thomas. *De Cive*. Paris, 1642.

– *De Corpore Politico. Or The Elements of Law*. London, 1650.

– *The Elements of Law Natural and Politic*. Edited by J.C.A. Gaskin. Oxford and New York: Oxford University Press, 1994.

– *The English Works of Thomas Hobbes*. Edited by William Molesworth. Vol. 6. London, 1890.

– *Humane Nature*. London, 1650.

– *Leviathan*. Edited by C.B. Macpherson. Harmondsworth: Penguin, 1984.
– *Leviathan*. Edited by Richard Tuck. Cambridge: Cambridge University Press, 1991.
– *Philosophicall Rudiments Concerning Government and Society Or, A Dissertation Conerning Man in his Severall Habitudes and Respects, as the Member of a Society, first Secular, and then Sacred*. Translated by Charles Cotton. London, 1651.
Hobby, Elaine. "A Woman's Best Setting Out Is Silence: The Writings of Hannah Wolley." In *Culture and Society in the Stuart Restoration*, edited by Gerald MacLean, 179–200. Cambridge: Cambridge University Press, 1996.
Holinshed, Raphael. *Chronicles*. Vol. 3. London, 1587.
*The Holy Bible . . . Authorized King James Version*. 2 vols. New York and Scarborough: n.d.
Hookes, Ellis. *The Spirit of Christ . . . against Swearing*. London, 1661.
Horace. *The Odes and Epodes*. Translated by C.E. Bennett. Cambridge, MA: Harvard University Press; London: Heinemann, 1988.
Houston, R.A. *Scottish Literacy and Scottish Identity*. Cambridge: Cambridge University Press, 1985.
Howard, Robert. *The Committee*. In *The Broadview Anthology of Restoration & Early Eighteenth-Century Drama*, edited by J. Douglas Canfield and Maja-Lisa von Sneidern, 473–525. Peterborough: Broadview Press, 2001.
Hoyt, Robert S. "The Coronation Oath of 1308." *English Historical Review* 71.280 (July 1956): 353–83.
Hubberthorn, Richard. *Antichristianism Reproved*. London, 1660.
Hubberthorn, Richard, and George Fox the Younger. *Something against Swearing and Concerning the Oath of Allegiance and Svpremacy*. London, 1660.
*Hudibras. The Second Part* (1663). Edited by George Wasserman. Delmar, NY: Scholars' Facsimiles & Reprints, 1993.
Hughes, Geoffrey. *An Encyclopedia of Swearing*. Armonk, NY, and London: M.E. Sharpe, 2006.
– *Swearing: A Social History*. London: Penguin, 1991.
Hume, Alexander. *A Treatise of the Felicitie of the Life to Come*. Edinburgh, 1594.
Hume, David. *The History of the Houses of Douglas and Angus*. Edinburgh and London, 1648.
Hume, Patrick. *Annotations on Milton's Paradise Lost*. London, 1695.
Humfrey, John. *A Case of Conscience*. London, 1669.
– *Comprehension Promoted* (1663). London, 1704.
– *A Proposition for the Safety & Happiness of King and Kingdom*. London, 1667.
Hunt, Alice. *The Drama of Coronation: Medieval Ceremony in Early Modern England*. Cambridge: Cambridge University Press, 2008.

Hunter, William B. "The War in Heaven: The Exaltation of the Son." In *Bright Essence: Studies in Milton's Theology*, edited by Hunter, C.A. Patrides, and J.H. Adamson, 115–30. Salt Lake City: University of Utah Press, 1973.

Hutchinson, Lucy. *Memoirs of the Life of Colonel Hutchinson*. London: George Bell and Sons, 1907.

– *Order and Disorder*. Edited by David Norbrook. Oxford: Blackwell, 2001.

Hyman, Harold. *To Try Men's Souls: Loyalty Tests in American History*. Berkeley and Los Angeles: University of California Press, 1960.

Ibrahim, M. Zakyi. "Oaths in the Qur'an: Bint al-Shati's Literary Contribution." *Islamic Studies* 48.4 (Winter 2009): 475–98.

*Indulgence Not to Be Refused. Comprehension Humbly Desired*. London, 1672.

Ireland, Thomas. *The Oath of Allegeance Defended*. London, 1610.

Ives, Jeremiah. *The Great Case of Conscience Opened . . . about the Lawfulness or Unlawfulness of Swearing*. London, 1660.

Jack, Ian. *Augustan Satire*. Oxford: Clarendon Press, 1957.

Jackson, Arthur. *Annotations upon the Remaining Historicall Part of the Old Testament*. Cambridge, 1646.

Jacomb, Thomas. *Forenoon Sermon*. In *An Exact Collection of Farewel Sermons Preached by the Late London-Ministers*, 71–83. London, 1662.

James I. *Triplici Nodo, Triplex Cuneus or An Apologie for the Oath of Allegiance*. London, 1607.

Jane, Joseph. *ΕΙΚΩΝ ΑΚΛΑΣΤΟΣ* [*Eikon Aklastos*]. London, 1651.

Jay, Timothy. *Cursing in America*. Philadelphia and Amsterdam: John Benjamins, 1992.

– *Why We Curse: A Neuro-Psycho-Social Theory of Speech*. Philadelphia and Amsterdam: John Benjamins, 2000.

[Jenkin, David?]. Preface. *The Judgment of Richard Baxter Concerning Ceremonies and Conformity*. London, 1667.

Johnson, Samuel. *A Dictionary of the English Language*. 2nd ed. 2 vols. London, 1755–6.

– *The Lives of the Most Eminent English Poets*. Vol. 1. Edited by Roger Lonsdale. Oxford: Clarendon Press; Oxford and New York: Oxford University Press, 2006.

– *Prefaces, Biographical and Critical, to the Works of the English Poets*. 10 vols. London, 1779.

Johnston, Archibald. *Diary of Sir Archibald Johnston of Wariston 1632–1639*. Edited by George Morison Paul. Edinburgh: Edinburgh University Press, 1911.

– "The Unconquerable!" In *Lays of Edina and Aulk Reekie Musings*, 88–90. Edinburgh: Archibald Muir and James Mushet, 1864.

Jones, D.M. *Conscience and Allegiance in Seventeenth-Century England: The Political Significance of Oaths and Engagements*. Rochester, NY: University of Rochester Press, 1999.

Jones, Edward. "The Loyalty and Subsidy Returns of 1641 and 1642: What They Can Tell Us about the Milton Family." In *Milton's Legacy*, edited by Kristin A. Pruitt and Charles W. Durham, 234–47. Selinsgrove, PA: Susquehanna University Press, 2005.

Jordan, Thomas. *A Cure for the Tongue-Evill, or, A Receipt against Vain Oaths*. London, 1662.

Josephus, Flavius. *Josephus V*. Translated by H. St. J. Thackeray and Ralph Marcus. Cambridge: Harvard University Press; London: Heinemann, 1958.

*Journal of the House of Commons*. 12 vols. London, 1802–3.

*Journal of the House of Lords*. 64 vols. London, 1767–1833.

Joyce, James. *Ulysses*. Edited by Hans Walter Gabler with Wolfhard Steppe and Claus Melchior. New York: Vintage, 1986.

JVCO. *Amsterdam: Toleration, or No Toleration*. London, 1663.

Kahn, Victoria. *Wayward Contracts: The Crisis of Political Obligation in England, 1640–1674*. Princeton, NJ, and Oxford: Princeton University Press, 2004.

Kantorowicz, Ernst. *The King's Two Bodies*. Princeton: Princeton University Press, 1957.

Katz, Jerrold I. *Propositional Structure and Illocutionary Force*. Cambridge, MA: Harvard University Press, 1980.

Keay, Anna. *The Magnificent Monarch: Charles II and the Ceremonies of Power*. London: Continuum, 2008.

Kelliher, Hilton. *Andrew Marvell: Poet & Politician*. London: British Library, 1978.

Kenyon, J.P., ed. *The Stuart Constitution*. 2nd ed. Cambridge: Cambridge University Press, 1986.

Ker, William. *The Sober Conformists Answer to a Rigid Conformists Reasons*. [London?], 1689.

Kerrigan, John. *Shakespeare's Binding Language*. Oxford: Oxford University Press, 2016.

Kerrigan, William. *Shakespeare's Promises*. Baltimore, MD: Johns Hopkins University Press, 1999.

Kitts, Margo. *Sanctified Violence in Homeric Society: Oath-Making Rituals in the Iliad*. Cambridge: Cambridge University Press, 2005.

Kitz, Anne Marie. "An Oath, Its Curse, and Anointing Ritual." *Journal of the American Oriental Society* 124.2 (April–June 2004): 315–21.

Knights, Mark. *Representation and Misrepresentation in Later Stuart Britain*. Oxford: Oxford University Press, 2005.

Knolles, Richard. *The Generall Historie of the Turkes*. London, 1603.

Knoppers, Laura Lunger. "'League with You I Seek': Milton's Concept of Covenant." PhD diss., Harvard University, 1986.

– *Politicizing Domesticity from Henrietta Maria to Milton's Eve*. Cambridge: Cambridge University Press, 2011.

Komorowski, Michael. "Public Verse and Property: Marvell's Horatian Ode and the Ownership of Politics." *ELH* 79.2 (Summer 2012): 316–34.

Krouse, F. Michael. *Milton's Samson and the Christian Tradition*. Princeton: Princeton University Press, 1949.

Kuzner, James. "Habermas Goes to Hell: Pleasure, Public Reason, and the Republicanism of *Paradise Lost*." *Criticism* 51.1 (Winter 2009): 105–45.

Lacey, Douglas R. *Dissent and Parliamentary Politics, 1661–1689*. New Brunswick, NJ: Rutgers University Press, 1969.

Landmann, Michael. "Die Aufteilung der Chöre im Carmen Saeculare." In *Aparchai* 4 (*Gedenkschrift für Georg Rohde*), 173–9. Tübingen: Max Niemeyer Verlag, 1961.

Landy, Marcia. "Character Portrayal in *Samson Agonistes*." *Texas Studies in Language and Literature* 7.3 (Autumn 1965): 239–53.

Lares, Jameela. *Milton and the Preaching Arts*. Pittsburgh, PA: Duquesne University Press, 2001.

Lawson, George. *Magna Charta Ecclesiae Universalis*. London, 1686.

– *Theo-Politica*. London, 1659.

Leech, John. *Ioannis Leochaei Epigrammatum Libri Quatuor*. London, 1623.

Legouis, Pierre. *André Marvell: Poète, Puritain, Patriote, 1621–1678*. Paris: Henri Didier; London: Oxford University Press, 1928.

– *Andrew Marvell: Poet Puritan Patriot*. Oxford: Clarendon Press, 1965.

Lehmann, Manfred R. "Biblical Oaths." *Zeitschrift für die Alttestamentliche Wissenschaft* 81 (1969): 74–92.

Leigh, Edward. *Critica Sacra*. 4th ed. London, 1664.

Lejosne, Roger. "Milton, Satan, Salmasius, Abdiel." In *Milton and Republicanism*, edited by David Armitage, Armand Himy, and Quentin Skinner, 106–16. Cambridge: Cambridge University Press, 1995.

Leonard, John. *Faithful Labourers: A Reception History of Paradise Lost, 1667–1970*. 2 vols. Oxford: Oxford University Press, 2013.

*A Letter from a Person of Quality to His Friend in the Country*. [London], 1675.

*A Letter to a Member of This Present Parliament, for Liberty of Conscience*. London, 1668.

Levao, Ronald. "'Among Unequals What Society': *Paradise Lost* and the Forms of Intimacy." *Modern Language Quarterly* 61.1 (March 2000): 79–107.

Lewalski, Barbara K. *The Life of John Milton*. Revised ed. Oxford: Blackwell, 2000.

– "Milton on Liberty, Servility, and the Paradise Within." In *Milton, Rights and Liberties*, edited by Christophe Tournu and Neil Forsyth, 31–53. Bern and Berlin: Peter Lang, 2007.
– "Milton on Women – Yet Once More." *Milton Studies* 6 (1974): 3–20.
Lewis, Charlton T., and Charles Short. *A Latin Dictionary*. Oxford: Clarendon Press, 1879.
*Liber Regalis*. London, 1871.
Lieb, Michael. *Theological Milton: Deity, Discourse and Heresy in the Miltonic Canon*. Pittsburgh, PA: Duquesne University Press, 2006.
Lightbody, George. *Against the Apple of the Left Eye of Antichrist*. [Amsterdam?], 1638.
Lightfoot, John. *Works*. London, 1684.
Lilburne, John. *An Answer to Nine Arguments*. London, 1645.
– *The Engagement Vindicated & Explained*. London, 1650.
– *Ionahs Cry out of the Belly*. London, 1647.
– *The Prisoner's Plea for a Habeas Corpus*. London, 1648.
– *Rash Oaths Unwarrantable*. London, 1647.
– *The Resolved Man's Resolution*. London, 1647.
– *An Unhappy Game at Scotch and English*. London, 1646.
*Lilly Lash't with His Own Rod*. [London], 1660.
Lilly, William. *History of His Life and Times*. London, 1715.
– *The Starry Messenger*. London, 1645.
Llanvaedonon, William. *A Brief Exposition upon the Second Psalme*. London, 1655.
Lloyd, David. *Modern Policy Compleated*. London, 1660.
– *Never Faile*. London, 1663.
Locke, John. *Locke: Political Essays*. Edited by Mark Goldie. Cambridge: Cambridge University Press, 1997.
*A Logical Demonstration of the Lawfulness of Subscribing the Engagement*. London, 1650.
Loscocco, Paula. "'Not Less Renown'd than Jael': Heroic Chastity in *Samson Agonistes*." *Milton Studies* 40 (2001): 181–200.
Lovett, Frank. "Milton's Case for a Free Commonwealth." *American Journal of Political Science* 49.3 (July 2005): 466–78.
Loxley, James. *Performativity*. London and New York: Routledge, 2007.
Ludlow, Edmund. *A Voyce from the Watch Tower, Part Five: 1660–1662*. Edited by A.B. Worden. London: Royal Historical Society, 1978.
Lupton, Julia Reinhard. *Citizen-Saints: Shakespeare and Political Theology*. Chicago and London: University of Chicago Press, 2005.
Luther, Martin. *Commentary on the Sermon on the Mount*. Translated by Charles A. Hays. Philadelphia. PA: Lutheran Publication Society, 1892.

– *Dr. Martin Luther's Small Catechism*. New York: J.E. Stohlmann, 1888.
– *Select Works of Martin Luther*. Translated by Henry Cole. Vol. 3. London: W. Simpkin and R. Marshall, 1826.
Lye [Leigh], Thomas. *Second Sermon*. In *A Compleat Collection of Farewel Sermons*, Z2v–Bb2v. London, 1663.
M., T. *The History of Independency. The Fourth and Last Part*. London, 1660.
Machiavelli, Niccolo. *Discourses on Livy*. Translated by Harvey C. Mansfield and Nathan Tarcov. Chicago and London: University of Chicago Press, 1996.
Maddicott, J.R. "The Oath of Marlborough, 1209: Fear, Government and Popular Allegiance in the Reign of King John." *English Historical Review* 126.519 (2011): 281–318.
Madway, Lorraine. "'The Most Conspicuous Solemnity': The Coronation of Charles II." In *The Stuart Courts*, edited by Eveline Cruickshanks, 141–57. Stroud, UK: The History Press, 2009.
Magro, Maria. "Milton's Sexualized Woman and the Creation of a Gendered Public Sphere." *Milton Quarterly* 35.2 (2001): 98–112.
Maimonides, Moses. *The Code of Maimonides, Book Six: The Book of Asseverations*. Translated by B.D. Klien. New Haven and London: Yale University Press, 1962.
*The Manner of the Solemnity of the Coronation of His Most Sacred Majesty King Charles*. London, 1661.
Marlowe, Christopher. *Doctor Faustus and Other Plays*. Edited by David Bevington and Eric Rasmussen. Oxford: Oxford University Press, 2008.
Marshall, Ashley. "The Aims of Butler's Satire in *Hudibras*." *Modern Philology* 105.4 (May 2008): 637–55.
– *The Practice of Satire in England, 1658–1770*. Baltimore, MD: Johns Hopkins University Press, 2013.
Marshall, Stephen. *A Sermon Preached before the Honourable House of Commons . . . November 17. 1640*. London, 1641.
– *A Tvvo-Edged Svvord out of the Mouth of Babes*. London, 1646.
Martinez, David G. "Achilleus' Vow of Abstinence." *Metis* ns 10 (2012): 37–49.
Marvell, Andrew. *Complete Poetry*. Edited by George deF. Lord. New York: Modern Library, 1968.
– *The Poems of Andrew Marvell*. Edited by Nigel Smith. Rev ed. London and New York: Longman, 2007.
– *The Poems and Letters of Andrew Marvell*. Edited by H.M. Margoliouth, Pierre Legouis, and E.E. Duncan-Jones. 3rd ed. 2 vols. Oxford: Clarendon Press, 1971.
– *The Prose Works of Andrew Marvell*. Edited by Martin Dzelzainis et al. 2 vols. New Haven, CT, and London: Yale University Press, 2003.

– *The Rehearsal Transpros'd and The Rehearsal Transpros'd The Second Part*. Edited by D.I.B. Smith. Oxford: Clarendon Press, 1971.
– *The Works of Andrew Marvell, Esq*. Edited by Thomas Cooke. 2 vols. London, 1726.
Masson, David. *The Life of John Milton: Narrated in Connexion with the Political, Ecclesiastical, and Literary History of His Time*. 6 vols. Revised ed. New York, 1946.
Matchinske, Megan. *Women Writing History in Early Modern England*. Cambridge: Cambridge University Press, 2009.
Mazzeo, Joseph A. "Cromwell as Davidic King." In *Reason and the Imagination: Studies in the History of Ideas, 1600–1800*, edited by Mazzeo, 19–55. New York and London: Columbia University Press, 1962.
– "Cromwell as Machiavellian Prince in Marvell's 'An Horatian Ode.'" *Journal of the History of Ideas* 21.1 (January–March 1960): 1–17.
McAlindon, Tom. "Swearing and Forswearing in Shakespeare's Histories: The Playwright as Contra-Machiavel." *Review of English Studies* ns 51, no. 202 (May 2000): 208–29.
McChrystal, Deirdre. "Redeeming Eve." *English Literary Renaissance* 23 (1993): 491–508.
McColley, Diane. *Milton's Eve*. Urbana, Chicago, London: University of Illinois Press, 1983.
McCrea, Adriana. "Reason's Muse: Andrew Marvell, R. Fletcher, and the Politics of Poetry in the Engagement Debate." *Albion* 23.4 (Winter 1991): 655–80.
McDowell, Nicholas. "Marvell among the Cromwellians." In *The Oxford Handbook of Literature and the English Revolution*, edited by Laura Knoppers, 481–97. Oxford: Oxford University Press, 2012.
– *Poetry and Allegiance in the English Civil Wars: Marvell and the Cause of Wit*. Oxford: Oxford University Press, 2008.
McEnery, Tony. *Swearing in English*. London and New York: Routledge, 2006.
McKeon, Michael. *The Secret History of Domesticity*. Baltimore, MD: Johns Hopkins University Press, 2005.
Mede, Joseph. *Diatribae*. London, 1642.
– *Works*. 3rd ed. London, 1672.
*Memorandums of the Conferences Held between the Brethren [who] Scrupled at the Engagement; and Others who Were Satisfied with It*. London, 1650.
Mendelson, Sara. *The Mental World of Stuart Women*. Amherst: University of Massachusetts Press, 1987.
Mendelson, Sara, and Patricia Crawford. *Women in Early Modern England*. Oxford: Clarendon Press, 1998.

*Mètis* (*Dossier: Serments et Paroles Efficaces*) ns 10 (2012).

*Midrash Rabbah*. Translated and edited by H. Freedman. 10 vols. London and Bournemouth: Soncino Press, 1951.

Miege, Guy. *A New Dictionary English and French*. London, 1677.

Miller, J. Hillis. *Speech Acts in Literature*. Stanford, CA: Stanford University Press, 2001.

Miller, Shannon. *Engendering the Fall: John Milton and Seventeenth-Century Women Writers*. Philadelphia: University of Pennsylvania Press, 2008.

*Milton and Republicanism*. Edited by David Armitage, Armand Himy, and Quentin Skinner. Cambridge: Cambridge University Press, 1995.

Milton, John. *The Complete Poetry and Essential Prose of John Milton*. Edited by William Kerrigan, John Rumrich, and Stephen M. Fallon. New York: Modern Library, 2007.

– *Complete Prose Works of John Milton*. Edited by Don M. Wolfe et al. 8 vols. New Haven, CT, and London: Yale University Press, 1953–82.

– *The Complete Works of John Milton*. Vol. 8. Edited by John K. Hale and J. Donald Cullington. Oxford: Oxford University Press, 2008.

– *ΕΙΚΟΝΟΚΛΑΣΤΗΣ* [*Eikonoklastes*]. London, 1650.

– *John Milton: Complete Shorter Poems*. Edited by John Carey. 2nd ed. Harlow: Longman, 1997.

– *John Milton: The Complete Poems*. Edited by John Leonard. London: Penguin, 1998.

– *Milton: Political Writings*. Edited by Martin Dzelzainis. Cambridge: Cambridge University Press, 1991.

– *The Oxford Authors: John Milton*. Edited by Stephen Orgel and Jonathan Goldberg. Oxford and New York, 1991.

– *Paradise Lost*. Edited by Alastair Fowler. 2nd ed. London and New York: Longman, 1998.

– *The Riverside Milton*. Edited by Roy Flannagan. Boston and New York: Houghton Mifflin, 1998.

– *The Works of John Milton*. Edited by Frank Allen Patteron. 18 vols. New York: Columbia University Press, 1931–8.

Miner, Earl. *The Restoration Mode from Milton to Dryden*. Princeton: Princeton University Press, 1974.

Mocket, Richard. *God and the King: or, A Dialogue Shewing that Our Soueraigne Lord the King . . . Doth Rightly Claim Whatsoever Is Required by the Oath of Allegiance*. York, 1663.

Mohr, Melissa. *Holy Sh*t: A Brief History of Swearing*. Oxford: Oxford University Press, 2013.

Mollenkott, Virginia R. "Milton and Women's Liberation: A Note on Teaching Method." *Milton Quarterly* 7 (1973): 99–103.

Montagu, Ashley. *The Anatomy of Swearing*. London: Rapp & Whiting, 1967.
Montaño, John Patrick. *Courting the Moderates*. Newark: Delaware Press; London: Associated University Presses, 2002.
Moore, Peter R. "The Irony of Marvell's Horatian Ode." *English Studies* 1 (2003): 33–56.
Moulton, Charles Wells, ed. *The Library of Literary Criticism of English and American Authors*. 8 vols. New York: Henry Malkan, 1910.
Mueller, Janel. "The Figure and the Ground: Samson as a Hero of London Nonconformity, 1662–1667." In *Milton and the Terms of Liberty*, edited by Graham Parry and Joad Raymond, 137–62. Cambridge: D.S. Brewer, 2002.
Nedham, Marchamont. *The Case of the Common-Wealth of England, Stated*. 1st ed. London, 1650.
– *The Case of the Common-Wealth of England Stated*. 2nd ed. London, 1650.
– *The Case of the Kingdom Stated*. London, 1647.
– *The Excellencie of a Free-State*. 2nd ed. London, 1656.
– *Independencie No Schisme*. London, 1646.
– *Mercurius Politicus* 4 (27 June–4 July 1650), 12 (22–9 August 1650), 87 (29 January–5 February 1652), 369 (25 June–2 July 1657), 432 (2–9 September 1658).
Nelson, Eric. *The Greek Tradition in Republican Thought*. Cambridge: Cambridge University Press, 2004.
– *The Hebrew Republic: Jewish Sources and the Transformation of European Political Thought*. Cambridge: Cambridge University Press, 2011.
Nenner, Howard. "Loyalty and the Law: The Meaning of Trust and the Right of Resistance in Seventeenth-Century England." *Journal of British Studies* 48.4 (2009): 859–70.
Ness, Christopher. *A Chrystal Mirour*. London, 1679.
– *A Compleat History and Mystery of the Old and New Testament*. London, 1696.
Neville, Henry. *Newes from the New Exchange, or the Commonvvwealth of Ladies*. London, 1650.
– *Plato Redivivus*. London, 1681.
Nevo, Ruth. *The Dial of Virtue*. Princeton, NJ: Princeton University Press, 1963.
*The New Oxford Study Bible . . . Revised Standard Version*. Edited by Herbert G. May and Bruce M. Metzger. Oxford and New York: Oxford University Press, 1977.
*A New Protestant Litany*. London, 1689.
Ng, Su Fang. *Literature and the Politics of Family in Seventeenth-Century England*. Cambridge: Cambridge University Press, 2007.
Norbrook, David. *Writing the English Republic*. Cambridge: Cambridge University Press, 1998.

North, Dudley. *A Forest of Varieties*. London, 1645.

[Norton, John]. *An Humble Apology for Non-Conformists*. [London], 1669.

Nussbaum, Felicity. *The Brink of All We Hate*. Lexington: University of Kentucky Press, 1984.

Nuttall, Geoffrey F. "The First Nonconformists." In *From Uniformity to Unity 1662–1962*, edited by Geoffrey F. Nuttall and Owen Chadwick, 149–87. London: SPCK, 1962.

– Nuttall, *Richard Baxter*. Stanford: Stanford University Press, 1965.

Nyquist, Mary. "The Genesis of Gendered Subjectivity in the Divorce Tracts and in *Paradise Lost*." In *Re-membering Milton*, edited by Nyquist and Margaret W. Ferguson, 99–127. New York and London: Methuen, 1987.

Ogilby, John. *The Entertainment of His Most Excellent Majestie Charles II, in His Passage through the City of London to His Coronation . . . A Brief Narrative of His Majestie's Solemn Coronation*. London, 1662.

Ohmann, Richard. "'Instrumental Style': Notes on the Theory of Speech as Action." In *Current Trends in Stylistics*, edited by Braj B. Kachru and Herbert F.W. Stahlke, 115–41. Edmonton, Alberta, and Carbondale, IL: Linguistic Research, 1972.

– "Speech, Action, and Style." In *Literary Style: A Symposium*, edited by Seymour Chatman, 241–54. London and New York: Oxford University Press, 1971.

*The Old Protestant His Consciencious Queries about the New Engagement*. London, [1650].

O'Neill, John. *George Villiers, Second Duke of Buckingham*. Boston: Twayne, 1984.

Osborne, Francis. *A Perswasive to a Mutuall Compliance under the Present Government*. Oxford, 1651/2.

Ovid. *Heroides and Amores*. Translated by Grant Showerman and G.P. Goold. Cambridge, MA: Harvard University Press; London: Heinemann, 1986.

– *Loves Schoole: Publii Ovidii Nasonis De Arte Amandi, or, The Art of Loue*. London, 1625.

– *Metamorphoses*. Translated by Frank Justus Miller. 2 vols. Cambridge, MA: Harvard University Press; London: Heinemann, 1984.

– *Ouidius Naso his Remedie of Love*. London, 1600.

Owen, John. *A Discourse Concerning Evangelical Love, Church-Peace and Unity*. London, 1672.

– *An Expostulatory Letter to the Author of the Late Slanderous Libel against Dr. O.* London, 1671.

– *Indulgence and Toleration Considered*. London, 1667.

– *A Peace-Offering*. London, 1667.

– *Truth and Innocence Vindicated*. London, 1669.

*A Pack of Old Puritans. Maintaining the Unlawfulness & Inexpediency of Subscribing the New Engagement*. London, 1650.
Parker, Blanford. *The Triumph of Augustan Poetics*. Cambridge: Cambridge University Press, 1998.
Parker, Henry. *Scotlands Holy War*. London, 1650/1.
– *The Trve Portraitvre of the Kings of England*. London, 1650.
Parker, Samuel. *A Defence and Continuation of the Ecclesiastical Politie*. London, 1671.
– *A Discourse of Ecclesiastical Politie*. London, 1670.
– *A Preface* to *Bishop Bramhall's Vindication of Himself and the Episcopal Clergy*. London, 1672.
– *Reasons for Abrogating the Test Imposed upon All Members of Parliament. Anno 1678*. London, 1688.
– *A Reproof to the Rehearsal Transprosed*. London, 1673.
– *Tentamina Physico-Theologica De Deo*. Oxford, 1665.
Parkin, Jon. "Liberty Transpros'd: Andrew Marvell and Samuel Parker." In *Marvell and Liberty*, edited by Warren Chernaik and Martin Dzelzainis, 269–89. Houndmills: Macmillan; New York: St Martin's Press, 1999.
– *Taming the Leviathan*. Cambridge: Cambridge University Press, 2007.
Parpola, Simo, and Kazuko Watanabe. *Neo-Assyrian Treaties and Loyalty Oaths*. Helsinki: Helsinki University Press, 1988.
Patrick, Simon. *An Appendix to the Third Part of the Friendly Debate*. London, 1670.
– *A Continuation of the Friendly Debate*. London, 1669.
– *A Friendly Debate betwixt . . . A Conformist [and] A Non-Conformist*. [London], 1668.
– *A Further Continuation and Defence, or, A Third Part of the Friendly Debate*. London, 1670.
Patterson, Annabel. *Marvell and the Civic Crown*. Princeton, NJ: Princeton University Press, 1978.
– *Marvell: The Writer in Public Life*. Harlow: Longman, 2000.
– "Why is there no Rights Talk in Milton's Poetry?" In *Milton, Rights, and Liberties*, edited by Christoph Tournu and Neil Forsyth, 197–209. Berlin: Peter Lang, 2007.
Peck, Linda Levy. "Kingship, Counsel, and Law in Early Stuart Britain." In *The Varieties of British Political Thought, 1500–1800*, edited by J.G.A. Pocock, 80–117. Cambridge: Cambridge University Press, 1993.
Peltonen, Markku. *Classical Humanism and Republicanism in English Political Thought 1570–1640*. Cambridge: Cambridge University Press, 1995.
Pepys, Samuel. *The Diary of Samuel Pepys*. Edited by Robert Latham and William Matthews. 11 vols. Berkeley and Los Angeles: University of California Press; London: HarperCollins, 2000.

Perkins, William. *The Whole Treatise of the Cases of Conscience*. Edited by T. Pickering. 2nd ed. Cambridge, 1606.

Perrinchief, Richard. *A Discourse of Toleration*. London, 1668.

– *Indulgence Not Justified*. London, 1668.

Peter, John. *A Critique of Paradise Lost*. New York: Columbia University Press; London: Longmans, 1960.

Petrey, Sandy. *Speech Acts and Literary Theory*. New York and London: Routledge, 1990.

Phil-Alethio. *A Brief Resolution of the Present Case of the Subjects of Scotland in Order to Episcopal Government*. [London], 1661.

Philipps, Fabian. *Ligeancia Lugens, or, Loyaltie Lamenting*. London, 1661.

– *Tenenda Non Tollenda*. London, 1660.

Phillips, Edward. *The New World of English Words, or, A General Dictionary*. London, 1658.

Philo of Alexandria. *Philo*. Edited by F.H. Colson, et al. 10 vols. Cambridge, MA: Harvard University Press; London: Heinemann: 1929–53.

Pittis, Thomas. *A Private Conference . . . Wherein Is Discoursed the Obligation of Oaths*. London, 1670.

Plato. *Laws*. Translated by R.G. Bury. Cambridge, MA, and London: Harvard University Press, 2001.

– *Plato VII: Timaeus, Critias, Cleitophon, Menexenus, Epistles*. Translated by R.G. Bury. London: Heinemann; New York: Putnam, 1929.

– *The Republic*. Translated by Paul Shorey. 2 vols. Cambridge, MA, and London: Harvard University Press, 2006.

Plescia, Joseph. *The Oath and Perjury in Ancient Greece*. Tallahassee: Florida State University Press, 1970.

Plutarch. *Life of Lysander*. *Lives*. Vol. 4. Translated by Bernadotte Perrin. Cambridge, MA, and London: Harvard University Press, 2006.

– *Moralia*. 15 vols. Cambridge, MA, and London: Harvard University Press, 1931–61.

Pocock, J.G.A. *The Ancient Constituion and Feudal Law*. 2nd ed. Cambridge: Cambridge University Press, 1987.

– "The Ideal of Citizenship since Classical Times." In *Theorizing Citizenship*, edited by Ronald Beiner, 29–52. Albany: State University of New York Press, 1995.

– *The Machiavellian Moment*. Princeton, NJ: Princeton University Press, 1975.

Powell, Walter. *A Summons for Swearers*. London, 1645.

Preedy, Chloe Kathleen. *Marlowe's Literary Scepticism*. London: Bloomsbury, 2012.

Prestwich, John. *Respublica: Or a Display of the Honours, Ceremonies & Ensigns of the Common-Wealth, under the Protectorship of Oliver Cromwell*. London, 1787.

Pruitt, Kristin. *Gender and the Power of Relationship: "United as Once Individual Soul" in Paradise Lost*. Pittsburgh, PA: Duquesne University Press, 2003.

Prynne, William. *A Brief Apologie for All Non-Scribers*. London, 1650.

– *Concordia Discors*. London, 1659.

– *The Signal Loyalty and Devotion of Gods True Saints and Pious Christians (as also of Idolatrous Pagans) towards Their Kings*. 2 vols. London, 1660.

– *The Soveraigne Povver of Parliaments and Kingdoms*. 2nd ed. London, 1643.

– *A Summary Collection of the Principal Fundamental Rights, Liberties, Proprieties of all English Freemen*. London, 1656.

– *The Time-Serving Proteus*. London, 1650.

Pufendorf, Samuel. *Of the Law of Nature and Nations*. 2nd ed. Oxford, 1710.

Putnam, Michael C.J. *Horace's Carmen Saeculare: Ritual Magic and the Poet's Art*. New Haven, CT, and London: Yale University Press, 2000.

*The Putney Debates* (1647). In *The Broadview Anthology of Seventeenth-Century Verse & Prose*, edited by Alan Rudrum, Joseph Black, and Holly Faith Nelson, 1238–60. Peterborough, Ontario: Broadview Press, 2000.

Pynchon, William. *The Covenant of Nature*. London, 1662.

Quarles, Francis. *The Historie of Samson*. In *The Complete Works in Prose and Verse of Francis Quarles*, edited by Alexander Grosart, 2:133–68. New York: AMS Press, 1967.

Quint, David. *Inside Paradise Lost*. Princeton, NJ: Princeton University Press, 2014.

Quintana, Ricardo. "Samuel Butler: A Restoration Figure in a Modern Light." *English Literary History* 18.1 (March 1951): 7–31.

Radzinowicz, Mary Ann. "The Politics of *Paradise Lost*." In *Politics of Discourse: The Literature and History of Seventeenth-Century England*, edited by Kevin Sharpe and Steven N. Zwicker, 204–29. Berkeley, Los Angeles, London: University of California Press, 1987.

Rahe, Paul. "The Classical Republicanism of John Milton." *The History of Political Thought* 25.2 (Summer 2004): 243–75.

Rappaport, Roy. *Ritual and Religion in the Making of Humanity*. Cambridge: Cambridge University Press, 1999.

Raylor, Timothy. *Cavaliers, Clubs, and Literary Culture*. Newark: University of Delaware Press; London and Toronto: Associated University Presses, 1994.

Raymond, Joad. "Marchamont Nedham." In *The Oxford Handbook of Literature and the English Revolution*, edited by Laura Knoppers, 375–94. Oxford: Oxford University Press, 2012.

Reddy, William. *The Navigation of Feeling: A Framework for the History of Emotions*. Cambridge: Cambridge University Press, 2001.

Reeves, John. *Considerations on the Coronation Oath*. London, 1801.

*The Register of the Privy Council of Scotland*. Edited by John Hill Burton. Vol. 1. Edinburgh, 1877.

*A Remonstrance of the Lords and Commons Now Assembled in Parliament*. London, 1642.

*A Remonstrance or Declaration of the Lords and Commons Now Assembled in Parliament, 26. of May. 1642 . . . Whereunto is Added the Nineteen Propositions*. London, 1642.

Revard, Stella. "Dalila as Euripidean Heroine." *Papers on Language and Literature* 23.3 (Summer 1987): 291–302.

Reynolds, Edward. *The Humble Proposals of Sundry Learned and Pious Divines*. London, 1649.

Richards, Edward A. *Hudibras in the Burlesque Tradition*. New York: Columbia University Press, 1937.

Richards, Judith. "Literary History and the Historian: Towards Reconstructing Marvell's Meaning in 'An Horatian Ode.'" *Literature and History* 7.1 (Spring 1981): 25–47.

Richardson, John, Richard Ussher, and Thomas Gataker. *Choice Observations upon the Old Testament*. London, 1655.

Robbins, Caroline. "A Note on General Naturalization under the Stuarts and a Speech in the House of Commons on the Subject in 1664." *Journal of Modern History* 34.2 (June 1962): 168–77.

– "The Oxford Session of the Long Parliament of Charles II, 9–31 October 1665." *Bulletin of the Institute of Historical Research* 21.64 (1948): 214–24.

– "Selden's Pills: State Oaths in England, 1558–1714." *Huntington Library Quarterly* 35, no. 4 (August 1972): 303–21.

Rocket, John. *The Christian Subject*. London, 1651.

*A Rod for the Fools Back: or, An Answer to a Scurrilous Libel, called The Changeling*. London, 1663.

Rogers, John. *Sagrir*. London, 1654.

Rogers, Richard. *A Commentary vpon the VVhole Booke of Iudges*. London, 1615.

Rolls, Samuel. *Londons Resurrection*. London, 1668.

– *A Sober Answer to the Friendly Debate*. London, 1669.

Rous, Francis. *The Lavvfulnes of Obeying the Present Government*. 1st ed. London, 1649.

– *The Lavvfulnes of Obeying the Present Government*. 2nd ed. London, 1649.

Rowland, John. *A Reply to the Answer of Anonymus to Doctor Gauden's Analysis of the Sense of the Covenant*. London, 1660.

Rumrich, John. *Milton Unbound*. Cambridge: Cambridge University Press, 1996.

Rushworth, John. *Historical Collections*. London, 1659.

Rutherford, Samuel. *Joshua Redivivus, or, Mr. Rutherfoord's Letters.* [Edinburgh?], 1664.

Ryves, Bruno. *Mercurius Rusticus*. London, 1646.

*Salmasius His Dissection and Confutation of the Diabolical Rebel Milton*. London, 1660.

Samaras, Thanassis. "Family and the Question of Women in the *Laws*." In *Plato's Laws: A Critical Guide*, edited by Christopher Bobonich, 173–96. Cambridge: Cambridge University Press, 2010.

[Sancroft, William?]. *Modern Policies*. 4th ed. London, 1653.

Sanderson, Robert. *De Juramento*. London, 1655.

– *Eight Cases of Conscience*. London, 1674.

Sanderson, Robert, et al. *Reasons of the Present Judgement of the University of Oxford, Concerning the Solemne League and Covenant*. London, 1660.

Saunders, Richard. *Plenary Possession Makes a Lawfull Power*. London, 1651.

Schalkwyk, David. "Shakespeare's Speech." *Journal of Medieval and Early Modern Studies* 40.2 (2010): 374–400.

Schechner, Richard. *Between Theater & Anthropology*. Philadelphia: University of Pennsylvania Press, 1985.

– *Performance Studies: An Introduction*. 3rd ed. New York and London: Routledge, 2013.

Schmitt, Carl. *The Concept of the Political*. Chicago and London: University of Chicago Press, 2007.

– *Constitutional Theory*. Durham, NC, and London: Duke University Press, 2006.

– *Political Theology*. Chicago and London: University of Chicago Press, 2006.

Schochet, Gordon. "Between Lambeth and Leviathan: Samuel Parker on the Church of England and Political Order." In *Political Discourse in Early Modern Britain*, edited by Nicholas Phillipson and Quentin Skinner, 189–208. Cambridge: Cambridge University Press, 1993.

Schramm, Percy. *A History of the English Coronation*. Translated by L.G.W. Legg. Oxford: Clarendon Press, 1937.

Schwoerer, Lois. "Women's Public Political Voice." In *Women Writers and the Early Modern British Political Tradition*, edited by Hilda L. Smith, 56–74. Cambridge and New York: Cambridge University Press, 1998.

Scodel, Joshua. *Excess and the Mean in Early Modern English Literature.* Princeton, NJ: Princeton University Press, 2002.

Scot, Reginald. *Scot's Discovery of VVitchcraft*. [London], 1651.

*The Scotch Covenant Condemned*. London, 1660.

*The Scotch Riddle Unfolded*. London, 1666.

Scott, Jonathan. *Commonwealth Principles*. Cambridge: Cambridge University Press, 2004.

Searle, John R. *Expression and Meaning: Studies in the Theory of Speech Acts*. Cambridge: Cambridge University Press, 1979.

– *Intentionality: An Essay in the Philosophy of Mind*. Cambridge: Cambridge University Press, 1983.

– *Speech Acts: An Essay in the Philosophy of Language*. Cambridge: Cambridge University Press, 1969.

Searle, John R., and Daniel Vanderveken. *Foundations of Illocutionary Logic*. Cambridge: Cambridge University Press, 1985.

Seaward, Paul. "Gilbert Sheldon, the London Vestries, and the Defence of the Church." In *The Politics of Religion in Restoration England*, edited by Tim Harris, Paul Seaward, and Mark Goldie, 49–73. Oxford: Blackwell, 1990.

*A Second Letter to a Member of this Present Parliament, against Comprehension*. London, 1668.

Seidel, Michael. *Satiric Inheritance*. Princeton, NJ: Princeton University Press, 1979.

Selden, John. *Table Talk*. 2nd ed. London, 1696.

Selden, Raman. *English Verse Satire 1590–1675*. London: Allen & Unwin, 1978.

Sempill, Robert. *The Kingis Complaint*. Edinburgh, 1567.

– *The Sempill Ballates*. Edinburgh: Thomas George Stevenson, 1872.

– *The Testament and Tragedie of . . . King Henry Stewart*. Edinburgh, 1567.

Sergeant, John. *Reflexions upon the Oathes of Supremacy and Allegiance*. London, 1661.

Settle, Elkanah. *Absalom Senior, or, Achitophel Transpros'd*. London, 1682.

*Severall Proceedings in Parliament* 14 (28 December 1649–4 January 1650).

*Severall Proceedings of State Affaires* (15–22 December 1653). London, 1653.

Shakespeare, William. *The Norton Shakespeare*. Edited by Stephen Greenblatt et al. 2nd ed. New York and London: Norton, 2008.

Shapiro, Barbara. "Oaths, Credibility and the Legal Process in Early Modern England." *Law and Humanities* 6.2 (2012): 145–78.

Sharpe, Kevin. *Rebranding Rule: The Restoration and Revolution Monarchy, 1660–1714*. New Haven, NJ, and London: Yale University Press, 2013.

Sherwin White, A.N. *The Roman Citizenship*. 2nd ed. Oxford: Clarendon Press, 1973.

Sherwood, Roy. *The Court of Oliver Cromwell*. Cambridge: Willingham Press, 1989.

– *Oliver Cromwell: King in All But Name 1653–1658*. Phoenix Mill, UK: Sutton, 1997.

Shils, Edward, and Michael Young. "The Meaning of the Coronation." *Sociological Review* ns 1.2 (December 1953): 63–81.

Shirley, Frances. *Swearing & Perjury in Shakespeare's Plays*. London and Boston: Allen & Unwin, 1979.

Shullenberger, William. *Lady in the Labyrinth: Milton's Comus as Initiation*. Madison and Teaneck, NJ: Fairleigh Dickinson University Press, 2008.
Sibbes, Richard. *The Bruised Reede and Smoaking Flax*. London, 1630.
– *A Learned Commentary ... upon the First Chapter of the Second Epistle of S. Paul to the Corinthians*. London, 1655.
Sidney, Algernon. *Court Maxims*. Edited by Hans W. Blom, Eco Haitsma Mulier, and Ronald Janse. Cambridge: Cambridge University Press, 1996.
– *Discourses Concerning Government*. London, 1698.
– *The Very Copy of a Paper Delivered to the Sheriffs upon the Scaffold on Tower-Hill, on Friday Decemb. 7, 1683 by Algernon Sidney, Esq., before his Execution*. London, 1683.
Silving, Helen. "The Oath." *Yale Law Journal* 68.7 (June 1959): 1329–90, and 68.8 (July 1959): 1527–77.
Skinner, Quentin. "Conquest and Consent: Thomas Hobbes and the Engagement Controversy." In *The Interregnum: The Quest for Settlement 1646–1660*, edited by G.E. Aylmer, 80–95. London: Macmillan, 1972.
– "Conventions and the Understanding of Speech-Acts." *Philological Quarterly* 20.79 (April 1970): 118–38.
– "Hermeneutics and the Role of History." *New Literary History* 7.1 (Autumn 1975): 209–32.
– "History and Ideology in the English Revolution." *Historical Journal* 8.2 (1965): 162–71.
– "The Idea of Negative Liberty: Machiavellian and Modern Perspectives." In *Visions of Politics*, 2:196–212. Cambridge: Cambridge University Press, 2002.
– "The Ideological Context of Hobbes's Political Thought." *Historical Journal* 9.3 (1966): 295–315.
– *Liberty before Liberalism*. Cambridge: Cambridge University Press, 1998.
– *Meaning and Context: Quentin Skinner and His Critics*. Edited by James Tully. Princeton: Princeton University Press, 1988.
– "On Performing and Explaining Linguistic Actions." *Philological Quarterly* 21.82 (January 1971): 1–21.
Skinner, Quentin, and Bo Stråth., eds. *States and Citizens*. Cambridge: Cambridge University Press, 2003.
Slights, Camille W. *The Casuistical Tradition in Shakespeare, Donne, Herbert, and Milton*. Princeton: Princeton University Press, 1981.
Slights, William W.E. "'Swear By Thy Gracious Self': Self-Referential Oaths in Shakespeare." *English Studies in Canada* 13.2 (June 1987): 147–60.
Smallwood, Alan. *A Sermon Preached at Carlisle*. York, 1664.
Smith, David L. "Oliver Cromwell, the First Protectorate, and Religious Reform." *Parliamentary History* 19.1 (March 2000): 38–48.

Smith, George. *The Three Kingdomes Healing-Plaister. Or the Solemn Covenant . . . Explained*. London, 1643.

Smith, Hilda L. *Reason's Disciples: Seventeenth-Century English Feminists*. Urbana, Chicago, London: University of Illinois Press, 1982.

Smith, Hilda L., Mihoko Suzuki, and Susan Wiseman, eds. *Women's Political Writings, 1610–1725*. 3 vols. London: Pickering & Chatto, 2007.

Smith, Nigel. *Andrew Marvell: The Chameleon*. Princeton, NJ: Princeton University Press, 2010.

– *Literature and Revolution in England, 1640–1660*. New Haven, CT, and London: Yale University Press, 1994.

Smith, William. *A Dictionary of Greek and Roman Antiquities*. London: John Murray, 1843.

– *A Dictionary of Greek and Roman Geography*. London: Walton and Maberly and John Murray, 1854.

Snider, Alvin. "By Equivocation Swear: *Hudibras* and the Politics of Interpretation." *The Seventeenth Century* 5.2 (1990): 157–72.

– *Origin and Authority in Seventeenth-Century England: Bacon, Milton, Butler*. Toronto, Buffalo, London: University of Toronto Press, 1994.

*A Solemn League and Covenant for Reformation and Defence of Religion, the Honour and Happinesse of the King, and the Peace and Safety of the Three Kingdoms of England, Scotland, and Ireland*. [London, 1643].

Sommerstein, Alan, and Andrew J. Bayliss. *Oath and State in Ancient Greece*. Berlin and Boston: De Gruyter, 2013.

Sommerstein, Alan, and Judith Fletcher., eds. *Horkos: The Oath in Greek Society*. Bristol: Phoenix Press, 2007.

Sommerstein, Alan, Isabelle C. Torrance, et al. *Oaths and Swearing in Ancient Greece*. Berlin and Boston: De Gruyter, 2014.

Sommerville, Johann P. "Hobbes and Independency." *Rivista di Storia della Filosofia* 59 (2004): 155–73.

– "The 'New Art of Lying': Equivocation, Mental Reservation, and Casuistry." In *Conscience and Casuistry in Early Modern Europe*, edited by Edmund Leites, 159–84. Cambridge: Cambridge University Press, 1988.

– "Papalist Political Thought and the Controversy over the Jacobean Oath of Allegiance." In *Catholics and the "Protestant Nation": Religious Politics and Identity in Early Modern England*, edited by Ethan Shagan, 162–84. Manchester: Manchester University Press, 2005.

– *Politics and Ideology in England 1603–1640*. London and New York: Longman, 1986.

Speed, John. *The Theatre of the Empire of Great Britaine*. London, 1612.

Spenser, Edmund. *The Faerie Queene*. Edited by A.C. Hamilton, Hiroshi Yamashita, and Toshiyuki Suzuki. Harlow: Longman, 2001.
– *The Yale Edition of the Shorter Poems of Edmund Spenser*. Edited by William A. Oram, et al. New Haven, CT, and London: Yale University Press, 1989.
*The Spiritual Bee*. Oxford, 1662.
Spottiswoode, John. *The History of the Church of Scotland*. London, 1655.
Spurr, John. "The Church of England, Comprehension and the Toleration Act of 1689." *English Historical Review* 104.413 (October 1989): 927–46.
– *England in the 1670s*. Oxford: Blackwell, 2000.
– "Perjury, Profanity and Politics." *The Seventeenth Century* 8.1 (1993): 29–50.
– "A Profane History of Early Modern Oaths." *Transactions of the Royal Historical Society* 11 (2001): 37–63.
– "'The Strongest Bond of Conscience': Oaths and the Limits of Tolerance in Early Modern England." In *Contexts of Conscience in Europe*, 1500–1700, edited by Harald E. Braun and Edward Vallance, 151–65. New York: St Martin's Press, 2004.
– "'Virtue, Religion and Government': the Anglican Uses of Providence." In *The Politics of Religion in Restoration England*, edited by Tim Harris, Paul Seaward, and Mark Goldie, 29–47. Oxford: Basil Blackwell, 1990.
*Statutes of the Realm*. Edited by John Raithby. 11 vols. London, 1819.
Staves, Susan. *Players' Scepters: Fictions of Authority in the Restoration*. Lincoln, NB, and London: University of Nebraska Press, 1979.
Stevenson, David. "The National Covenant: A List of Known Copies." *Records of the Scottish Church History Society* 23.2 (1988): 255–99.
– *The Scottish Revolution 1637–1644*. Edinburgh: John Donald, 2003.
– "The Solemn League and Covenant: A List of Signed Copies." *Records of the Scottish Church Historical Society* 25.1 (1993): 154–87.
[Stileman, John.] *A Discourse of the Nature and Obligation of Oaths*. London, 1662.
Strine, C.A. *Sworn Enemies: The Divine Oath, the Book of Ezekiel, and the Polemics of Exile*. Berlin and Boston: De Gruyter, 2013.
Strode, William. *A Sermon Concerning Swearing*. Oxford, 1644.
– *A Sermon Preached at a Visitation Held at Lin in Norfolk*. London, 1660.
Strong, Roy. *Coronation from the 8th to the 21st Century*. London and NY: Harper Perennial, 2005.
Sturgion, John. *A Plea for Tolleration*. London, 1661.
Suarez, Francisco. *Opera Omnia*. Vol. 14. Paris: Ludovicum Vives, 1859.
Sutherland, James. *English Literature of the Late Seventeenth Century*. Oxford: Clarendon Press, 1969.
Sutherland, W.O.S. *The Art of the Satirist*. Austin: University of Texas Press, 1965.

Suzuki, Mihoko. *Subordinate Subjects: Gender, the Political Nation, and Literary Form in England, 1588–1688*. Aldershot and Burlington: Ashgate, 2003.

Swadlin, Thomas. *A Letter of an Independent to an Honoured Friend in London*. London, 1647.

Swatland, Andrew. *The House of Lords in the Reign of Charles II*. Cambridge: Cambridge University Press, 1996.

*Swearing and Lying*. In *Poems on Affairs of State*. Vol 1. Edited by George deForest Lord, 307–11. New Haven and London: Yale University Press, 1963.

Swift, Jonathan. *On The Testimony of Conscience*. In *Works*, 8:231. Dublin and Glasgow, 1752.

Syfret, R.H. "Marvell's 'Horatian Ode.'" *Review of English Studies* ns 12.46 (May 1961): 160–72.

Sykes, Norman. *From Sheldon to Secker: Aspects of English Church History 1660–1768*. Cambridge: Cambridge University Press, 1959.

Sypniewski, Holly M., and Anne MacMaster. "Double Motivation and the Ambiguity of 'Ungodly Deeds': Euripides' *Medea* and Milton's *Samson Agonistes*." *Milton Quarterly* 44.3 (2010): 145–67.

Tabor, John. *Seasonable Thoughts in Sad Times*. London, 1667.

Taylor, Charles. "Dialogue: Jürgen Habermas and Charles Taylor." In *The Power of Religion in the Public Sphere*, edited by Eduardo Mendieta and Jonathan VanAntwerpen, 60–9. New York: Columbia University Press, 2011.

– *A Secular Age*. Cambridge, MA: Belknap Press, 2007.

– "Western Secularity." In *Rethinking Secularism*, edited by Craig Calhoun, Mark Juergensmeyer, and Jonathan VanAntwerpen, 31–53. Oxford and New York: Oxford University Press, 2011.

– "Why We Need a Radical Redefinition of Secularism." In *The Power of Religion in the Public Sphere*, edited by Eduardo Mendieta and Jonathan VanAntwerpen, 34–59. New York: Columbia University Press, 2011.

Taylor, Francis. *The Danger of Vowes Neglected*. London, 1646.

Taylor, Jeremy. *Ductor Dubitantium, or, The Rule of Conscience*. 2 vols. London, 1660.

Testart, Alain. "Le Lien et Le Liant." In *Le Serment*, edited by Raymond Verdier, 2:245–55. Paris: Èditions du Centre National de la Recherche Scientifique, 1991.

Thomas, Roger. "Comprehension and Indulgence." In *From Uniformity to Unity 1662–1962*, edited by Geoffrey F. Nuttall and Owen Chadwick, 189–253. London: SPCK, 1962.

Thorndike, Herbert. *The Theological Works of Herbert Thorndike*. 6 vols. Oxford: J.H. Parker, 1844–56.

Tickell, John. *A Serious Enquiry about the New Oath Enjoyned on Non-Conformists*. Oxford, 1665.

Timorcus, Theophilus [Richard Vines, Richard Baxter, Thomas Gataker?]. *The Covenanters Plea against Absolvers*. London, 1661.

Togashi, Go. "Milton and the Presbyterian Opposition, 1649–1650: The Engagement Controversy and *The Tenure of Kings and Magistrates*, Second Edition (1649)." *Milton Quarterly* 39.2 (2005): 59–81.

*The Toleration Intolerable*. London, 1670.

Tombes, John. *Sephersheba*. London, 1662.

– *A Serious Consideration of the Oath of the Kings Supremacy*. London, 1660.

– *A Supplement to the Serious Consideration of the Oaths of the Kings Supremacy*. London, 1661.

Tomkins, Thomas. *The Inconveniencies of Toleration*. London, 1667.

– *Short Strictures. London, 1661.*

Trapp, John. *Annotations upon the Old and New Testament*. London, 1662.

– *A Commentary . . . upon the Books of Ezra, Nehemiah, Esther, Job and Psalms*. London, 1657.

– *A Commentary . . . upon the Four Evangelists and the Acts of the Apostles*. London, 1647.

– *A Commentary . . . upon . . . Proverbs . . . Ecclesiastes, the Song of Songs, Isaiah, Jeremiah, Lamentations, Ezekiel & Daniel*. 2 vols. London, 1660.

– *A Commentary . . . upon the XII Minor Prophets*. London, 1654.

*The Trial of Charles I: A Documentary History*. Edited by David Lagomarsino and Charles T. Wood. Hanover, NH, and London: University Press of New England, 1989.

Tuck, Richard. "The Civil Religion of Thomas Hobbes." In *Political Discourse in Early Modern Britain*, edited by Nicholas Phillipson and Quentin Skinner, 120–38. Cambridge: Cambridge University Press, 1993.

Turner, Francis Charles. *James II*. London: Eyre & Spottiswoode, 1950.

Turner, James Grantham. "The Aesthetics of Divorce: 'Masculinism,' Idolatry, and Poetic Authority in *Paradise Lost*." In *Milton and Gender*, edited by Catherine Gimelli Martin, 34–52. Cambridge: Cambridge University Press, 2004.

– *One Flesh: Paradisal Marriage and Sexual Relations in the Age of Milton*. Oxford: Clarendon Press, 1987.

Turner, Victor. *Dramas, Fields, and Metaphors*. Ithaca, NY, and London: Cornell University Press, 1974.

Tutino, Stefania. *Empire of Souls: Robert Bellarmine and the Christian Commonwealth*. Oxford: Oxford University Press, 2010.

– *Law and Conscience: Catholicism in Early Modern England, 1570–1625*. Aldershot and Burlington: Ashgate, 2007.

– *Shadows of Doubt: Language and Truth in Post-Reformation Catholic Culture*. Oxford: Oxford University Press, 2014.

– *Thomas White and the Blackloists: Between Politics and Theology during the English Civil War*. Aldershot and Burlington: Ashgate, 2008.

*Two Speeches*. Amsterdam, 1675.

Tylor, Edward. "Oaths." *Encyclopedia Britannica*. Vol.19, 939–40. Cambridge and New York: Cambridge University Press, 1911.

Ulreich, John C., Jr. "'Incident to All Our Sex': The Tragedy of Dalila." In *Milton and the Idea of Woman*, edited by Julia M. Walker, 185–210. Urbana and Chicago: University of Illinois Press, 1988.

Ussher, James. *A Sermon Preached before the Commo[n]s House of Parliament, in Saint Margarets Church at Westminster, the 18. of February. 1620*. London, 1624.

Vallance, Edward. *Revolutionary England and the National Covenant: State Oaths, Protestantism and the Political Nation, 1553–1682*. Woodbridge, Suffolk: Boydell, 2005.

Van Gennep, Arnold. *The Rites of Passage*. New York: Routledge, 2004.

Vane, Henry. *The Tryal of Sir Henry Vane . . . also his Speech and Prayer, &c. on the Scaffold*. London, 1662.

Veldkamp, Jan. *Samuel Butler: The Author of Hudibras*. N.p.: Foxcroft Library Editions, 1977.

Vernon, George. *Letter to a Friend Concerning Dr. John Owens Principles and Practices*. London, 1670.

Vicars, John. *Dagon Demolished*. London, 1660.

Vlastos, Gregory. "Was Plato a Feminist?" *Times Literary Supplement* (17 March 1989): 276+.

Von Maltzahn, Nicholas. *An Andrew Marvell Chronology*. Houndmills and New York: Palgrave Macmillan, 2005.

– "The First Reception of Paradise Lost (1667)." *Review of English Studies* ns 47.188 (October 1996): 479–99.

– "Marvell and the Lord Wharton." *The Seventeenth Century* 18.2 (2003): 252–65.

– "Milton, Marvell and Toleration." In *Milton and Toleration*, edited by Sharon Achinstein and Elizabeth Sauer, 86–104. Oxford: Oxford University Press, 2007.

– *Milton's History of Britain: Republican Historiography in the English Revolution*. Oxford: Oxford University Press, 1992.

– "Samuel Butler's Milton." *Studies in Philology* 92.4 (Fall 1995): 482–95.

Vondel, Joost van den. *Samson, Of Heilige Wraeck*. In *That Invincible Samson: The Theme of Samson Agonistes in World Literature with Translations of the Major Analogues*. Translated by Watson Kirkconnell, 77–142. Toronto: University of Toronto Press, 1964.

*The Vow and Covenant Appointed by the Lords and Commons Assembled in Parliament*. London, 1643.

*Vox Veritatis*. London, 1650.

W., N. *A Discourse Concerning the Engagement*. London, 1649/50.

W., S. *The Constant Man's Character*. London, 1650.

W[armestry], T. *The Oaths of Allegiance and Supremacy*. London, 1660.

Waldock, A.J.A. *Paradise Lost and Its Critics*. Cambridge: Cambridge University Press, 1947.

Walker, Clement. *The High Court of Justice. Or Cromwells New Slaughter-house in England . . . Being the III.Part of the Historie of Independencie*. [London], 1651.

Walker, Edward. *A Circumstantial Account of the Preparations for the Coronation of His Majesty King Charles the Second*. London, 1820.

Walker, William. "*Paradise Lost* and the Forms of Government." *The History of Political Thought* 22.2 (Summer 2001): 270–99.

– "Resemblance and Reference in Recent Criticism on *Paradise Lost*." *Milton Quarterly* 40.3 (2006): 189–206.

Wallace, John. *Destiny His Choice: The Loyalism of Andrew Marvell*. Cambridge: Cambridge University Press, 1968.

– "The Engagement Controversy 1649–1652: An Annotated List of Pamphlets." *Bulletin of the New York Public Library* 68 (1964): 390–405.

Walsh, Peter. *The Advocate of Conscience*. [London], 1672.

– *Some Few Questions concerning the Oath of Allegiance*. London, 1661.

Waltke, Bruce K., and M. O'Connor. *An Introduction to Biblical Hebrew Syntax*. Winona Lake, IN: Eisenbrauns, 1990.

Walwyn, William. *A Word in Season*. London, 1646.

Ward, Nathaniel. *Discolliminium. Or, A Most Obedient Reply to a Late Book Called, Bounds & Bonds*. London, 1650.

– *The Grand Case of Conscience Stated, about Submission to the New and Present Power*. London, 1649.

– *A Religious Demurrer Concerning Submission to the Present Power*. London, 1649.

Ward, Samuel. *Iethro's Iustice of Peace*. London, 1618.

Warren, Albertus. *The Royalist Reform'd*. London, 1649.

Wasserman, George. *Samuel "Hudibras" Butler*. Updated ed. Boston: Twayne, 1989

– "'That Paultry Story': *The Spurious Hudibras: The Second Part*." *Philological Quarterly* 72 (1992): 459–77.

Watson, Thomas. *A Body of Practical Divinity*. London, 1692.

– *Sermon against Popery*. In *A Compleat Collection of Farewel Sermons*, Hhhh1r–Iiii1r. London, 1663.

Webber, Joan. "The Politics of Poetry: Feminism and *Paradise Lost*." *Milton Studies* 14 (1980): 3–24.

Webster, Jeremy. *Performing Libertinism in Charles II's Court*. New York: Palgrave Macmillan, 2005.

Weinfeld, Moshe. "Covenant Making in Anatolia in Mesopotamia," *Journal of the Ancient Near Eastern Society* 22 (1993): 135–9.

– "The Covenant of Grant in the Old Testament and in the Ancient Near East." *Journal of the American Oriental Society* 90.2 (April–June 1970): 184–203.

Westermarck, Edward. *The Origin and Development of the Moral Ideas*. 2 vols. London: Macmillan, 1908.

Wharton, George. *A Vindication of Mercurius Elencticus. (alias) Wharton. From the False Aspersions of the Scandalous, Abusive, and Blasphemous Pen of William Lilly*. [London], 1648.

*A Whip for the Devil, or, The Roman Conjuror*. London, 1683.

White, Christopher. *Of Oathes*. London, 1627.

Whitehead, George. *A Brief Account of Some of the Late and Present Sufferings of the People Called Quakers*. London, 1680.

Whiteman, Anne. "The Restoration of the Church of England." In *From Uniformity to Unity 1662–1962*, edited by Geoffrey F. Nuttall and Owen Chadwick, 19–88. London: SPCK, 1962.

Wickham Legg, J., ed. *The Coronation Order of James I*. London, F.E. Robinson, 1902.

Wickham Legg, Leopold G., ed. *English Coronation Records*. Westminster: Archibald Constable, 1901.

Wiesner, Merry. "The Holy Roman Empire: Women and Politics beyond Liberalism, Individual Rights, and Revolutionary Theory." In *Women Writers and the Early Modern British Political Tradition*, edited by Hilda L. Smith, 305–23. Cambridge: Cambridge University Press, 1998.

Wilcher, Robert. *The Writing of Royalism 1628–1660*. Cambridge: Cambridge University Press, 2001.

Wild, Robert. *The Loyal Nonconformist*. In *Poems on Affairs of State*. Vol. 1. Edited by George deForest Lord, 302–6. New Haven and London: Yale University Press, 1963.

Wilding, Michael. *Dragons Teeth: Literature in the English Revolution*. Oxford: Clarendon Press, 1987.

– "'Thir Sex Not Equal Seem'd': Equality in *Paradise Lost*." In *Of Poetry and Politics: New Essays on Milton and His World*, edited by P.G. Stanwood, 171–85. Tempe, AZ: Medieval and Renaissance Texts and Studies, 1997.

Wilkins, John. *An Essay towards a Real Character, and a Philosophical Language*. London, 1668.

Wilmot, John. *The Complete Poems of John Wilmot, Earl of Rochester.* Edited by David M. Vieth. New Haven, CT, and London: Yale University Press, 1968.
Wilson, John. *The Cheats*. London, 1663.
Winship, Michael P. "Algernon Sidney's Calvinist Republicanism." *Journal of British Studies* 49.4 (October 2010): 753–73.
Winstanley, Gerrard. *The Complete Works of Gerrard Winstanley*. Edited by Thomas N. Corns, Ann Hughes, and David Loewenstein. 2 vols. Oxford: Oxford University Press, 2009.
Winter, John. *Observations upon . . . the Oath of Supremacy*. London, 1662.
Wiseman, Susan. *Conspiracy and Virtue: Women, Writing, and Politics in Seventeenth-Century England*. Oxford: Oxford University Press, 2006.
– "Eve, *Paradise Lost*, and Female Interpretation." In *The Oxford Handbook of Milton*, edited by Nicholas McDowell and Nigel Smith, 534–46. Oxford: Oxford University Press, 2009.
Wither, George. *The British Appeals*. London, 1651.
– *Divine Poems*. London, 1688.
– *Respublica Anglicana*. London, 1650.
– *Speculum Speculativum*. London, 1660.
Withington, Phil. "Andrew Marvell's Citizenship." In *The Cambridge Companion to Andrew Marvell*, edited by Derek Hirst and Steven N. Zwicker, 102–21. Cambridge: Cambridge University Press, 2011.
– *The Politics of Commonwealth: Citizens and Freemen in Early Modern England*. Cambridge: Cambridge University Press, 2005.
Wittreich, Joseph. *Feminist Milton*. Ithaca, NY, and London: Cornell University Press, 1987.
– *Interpreting Samson Agonistes*. Princeton, NJ: Princeton University Press, 1986.
– *Shifting Contexts: Reinterpreting Samson Agonistes*. Pittsburgh, PA: Duquesne University Press, 2002.
– *Why Milton Matters*. New York: Palgrave Macmillan, 2006.
Wolleb, Johannes. *The Abridgment of Christian Divinitie*. 3rd ed. London, 1660.
– *Compendium Theologiae Christianae*. Oxford, 1657.
Wolseley, Charles. *Liberty of Conscience . . . Asserted & Vindicated*. London, 1668.
Womock, Laurence. *The Solemn League and Covenant Arraigned and Condemned*. London, 1661.
Woods, Susanne. "How Free Are Milton's Women?" In *Milton and the Idea of Woman*, edited by Julia M. Walker, 15–31. Urbana and Chicago: University of Illinois Press, 1987.
Woodward, Ezekias. *The Solemne League and Covenant of Three Kingdomes, Cleared*. London, 1643.

Woolrych, Austin. *Britain in Revolution*. Oxford: Oxford University Press, 2002.

Worden, Blair. "Andrew Marvell, Oliver Cromwell, and the Horatian Ode." In *Politics of Discourse: The Literature and History of Seventeenth-Century England*, edited by Kevin Sharpe and Steven N. Zwicker, 147–80. Berkeley, Los Angeles, London: University of California Press, 1987.

– *The English Civil Wars 1640–1660*. London: Phoenix, 2009.

– "English Republicanism." In *The Cambridge History of Political Thought 1450–1700*, edited by J.H. Burns and Mark Goldie, 443–75. Cambridge: Cambridge University Press, 1991.

– *God's Instruments*. Oxford: Oxford University Press, 2012.

– *Literature and Politics in Cromwellian England*. Oxford: Oxford University Press, 2007.

– "Milton's Republicanism and the Tyranny of Heaven." In *Machiavelli and Republicanism*, edited by Gisela Bock, Quentin Skinner, and Maurizio Viroli, 225–45. Cambridge: Cambridge University Press, 1990.

– "The Question of Secularism." In *A Nation Transformed: England after the Restoration*, edited by Alan Houston and Steve Pincus, 20–40. Cambridge: Cambridge University Press, 2001.

– "Republicanism, Regicide and Republic: The English Experience." In *Republicanism*, edited by Martin van Gelderen and Quentin Skinner, 1: 307–27. Cambridge: Cambridge University Press, 2002.

– *The Rump Parliament*. Cambridge: Cambridge University Press, 1974.

Wordsworth, Christopher. *The Manner of the Coronation of Charles I*. London, 1892.

Wortham, Christopher. "Marvell's Cromwell Poems: An Accidental Triptych." In *The Political Identity of Andrew Marvell*, edited by Conal Condren and A.D. Cousins, 16–52. Aldershot: Scolar Press, 1990.

Yadav, Alok. "Fractured Meanings: 'Hudibras' and the Historicity of the Literary Text." *English Literary History* 62.3 (Fall 1995): 529–49.

Yates, John. *A Modell of Divinitie*. London, 1622.

Zagorin, Perez. *A History of Political Thought in the English Revolution*. New York: Humanities Press, 1977.

Zehnder, Markus. "Building on Stone? Deuteronomy and Esarhaddon's Loyalty Oaths (Part 2): Some Additional Observations." *Bulletin for Biblical Research* 19.4 (2009): 511–35.

Ziegler, Yael. *Promises to Keep: The Oath in Biblical Narrative*. Leiden: Brill, 2008.

Zizek, Slavoj, Eric L. Santner, and Kenneth Reinhard. *The Neighbor*. Chicago and London: University of Chicago Press, 2005.

Zook, Melinda. *Protestantism, Politics, and Women in Britain, 1660–1714*. New York: Palgrave Macmillan, 2013.

Zwicker, Steven N. "Passions and Occasions: Milton, Marvell, and the Politics of Reading c. 1649." In *Form and Reform in Renaissance England*, edited by Amy Boesky and Mary Thomas Crane, 288–305. Newark: University of Delaware Press; London: Associated University Presses, 2000.

# Index

(Boldface indicates the main discussion of a topic)

www.ingramcontent.com/pod-product-compliance
Lightning Source LLC
LaVergne TN
LVHW041114090826
844660LV00062B/938/J

* 9 7 8 1 4 8 7 5 0 0 9 8 6 *